The Economics of Economists

The profession of academic economics has been widely criticized for being excessively dependent on technical models based on unrealistic assumptions about rationality and individual behavior, and yet it remains a sparsely studied area. This volume presents a series of background readings on the profession by leading scholars in the history of economic thought and economic methodology. Adopting a fresh critique, the contributors investigate the individual incentives prevalent in academic economics, describing economists as rational actors who react to their intellectual environment and the incentives for economic research. Timely topics are addressed, including the financial crisis and the consequences for the discipline, as well as more traditional themes such as pluralism in research, academic organizations, teaching methodology, gender issues, and professional ethics. This collection will appeal to scholars working on topics related to economic methodology and the teaching of economics.

ALESSANDRO LANTERI is Assistant Professor of Management in the Olayan School of Business at the American University of Beirut. His research rests at the borders between economics, ethics, and psychology and has appeared in the *European Journal of the History of Economic Thought, Philosophical Quarterly, Philosophical Studies,* and the *Journal of Business Ethics.*

JACK VROMEN is Professor of Theoretical Philosophy and Dean of the Faculty of Philosophy at Erasmus University Rotterdam. He is also Academic Director of EIPE (Erasmus Institute for Philosophy and Economics). His research focuses on theoretical and meta-theoretical issues in economics and evolution. Recently, he has also developed research interests in neuro-economics, in social mechanisms, and in the popularizing "Economics Made Fun" genre.

The Economics of Economists

Institutional Setting, Individual Incentives, and Future Prospects

Edited by

Alessandro Lanteri and
Jack Vromen

CAMBRIDGE
UNIVERSITY PRESS

CAMBRIDGE
UNIVERSITY PRESS

University Printing House, Cambridge CB2 8BS, United Kingdom

Cambridge University Press is part of the University of Cambridge.

It furthers the University's mission by disseminating knowledge in the pursuit of education, learning and research at the highest international levels of excellence.

www.cambridge.org
Information on this title: www.cambridge.org/9781107015708

© Cambridge University Press 2014

First published 2014

Printed in the United Kingdom by Clays, St Ives plc

A catalog record for this publication is available from the British Library

Library of Congress Cataloguing in Publication data
The economics of economists : institutional setting, individual incentives and future prospects / edited by Alessandro Lanteri and Jack Vromen.
　　pages cm
ISBN 978-1-107-01570-8 (Hardback)
1. Economics–Research.　2. Economics–Study and teaching (Higher)
I. Lanteri, Alessandro.　II. Vromen, Jack J., 1958–
H62.E3256 2014
330–dc23　2014007623

ISBN 978-1-107-01570-8 Hardback

We dedicate this volume to our friend, colleague, and mentor, the late Mark Blaug.

Alessandro and Jack

Contents

Figures

Tables

Contributors

ALBERTO BACCINI Professor of Economics, Faculty of Law, Department of Political Economy, University of Siena, Italy

LUCIO BARABESI Full Professor of Statistics, Faculty of Economics, University of Siena, Italy

DAVID COLANDER Christian A. Johnson Distinguished Professor of Economics, Department of Economics, Middlebury College, Middlebury, Vermont, USA

HANS FOLLMER Professor Emeritus of Mathematics, Humboldt-Universität zu Berlin. Andrew D. White Professor-at-Large, Cornell University, Ithaca, New York, USA

MARION FOURCADE Associate Professor of Sociology, UC Berkeley Sociology Department, UC Berkeley, California, USA

ROBERT FRANK Henrietta Johnson Louis Professor of Management and Professor of Economics, Samuel Curtis Johnson Graduate School of Management, Cornell University, Ithaca, New York, USA

BRUNO S. FREY Professor of Economics, Department of Economics, University of Zürich, Switzerland

DONNA GINTHER Professor of Economics, Economics Department, and Director of the Centre for Science, Technology & Economic Policy at the Institute for Policy & Social Research, University of Kansas, USA

MICHAEL GOLDBERG Todd H. Crockett Professor of Economics, Peter T. Paul College of Business and Economics, University of New Hampshire, USA

ARMIN HAAS Senior Researcher, Potsdam Institute for Climate Impact Research, Potsdam, Germany

WADE HANDS Distinguished Professor of Economics, Department of Economics, University of Puget Sound, Tacoma, Washington, USA

KATARINA JUSELIUS Professor, Department of Economics, University of Copenhagen, Denmark

SHULAMIT KAHN Associate Professor, Boston University School of Management, Boston University, USA

ALAN KIRMAN Professor Emeritus of Economics, Université Aix-Marseille III, France, and Ecole des Hautes Etudes en Sciences Sociales, Paris, France

ARJO KLAMER Professor of the Economics of Art and Culture, Department of History and Arts, Erasmus University Rotterdam, Netherlands

ALESSANDRO LANTERI Assistant Professor of Management, Olayan School of Business, American University of Beirut, Lebanon

THOMAS LUX Professor of Monetary Economics and International Finance, Department of Economics, University of Kiel, Germany

DEIRDRE MCCLOSKEY UIC Distinguished Professor of Economics and of History, College of Arts and Science, University of Illinois at Chicago, USA

MARGIT OSTERLOH Professor of Business Administration and Management of Technology and Innovation, Department of Business Administration, University of Zürich, Switzerland. Full Professor of Management Science at Warwick Business School, University of Warwick, UK

SALVATORE RIZZELLO Professor of Economics and Director of the Department of Law and Political Science, Università degli Studi del Piemonte Orientale "Amedeo Avogadro", Italy

JOHN SIEGFRIED Professor Emeritus of Economics, Department of Economics, Vanderbilt University, Nashville, Tennessee, USA

BRIGITTE SLOTH Professor at the Department of Business and Economics, University of Southern Denmark, Odense, Denmark

WENDY STOCK Department Head and Professor, Department of Agricultural Economics and Economics, Montana State University, USA

JACK VROMEN: Professor of Theoretical Philosophy and Dean of the Faculty of Philosophy, Erasmus University Rotterdam, Netherlands

Introduction

Alessandro Lanteri and Jack Vromen

For most people, the most important economic activity is the one they are engaged in. For lawyers and accountants it is corporate consulting, for volunteers and activists it is the third sector, for nurses and doctors it is healthcare, for politicians and public officers it is the public sector. So, for economics scholars, the most important economic activity is their own trade: academic economics. This is precisely what this volume is about.

The economics of economics

Given the importance of academic economics for economists, it's not surprising that the topic has been studied and debated for quite some time now. Already in the 1970s, economists were employing the tools of economic analysis to investigate their own discipline (e.g. Siegfried 1971; Berg 1971; Hansen and Weisbrod 1972; Lovell 1973; Stigler and Friedland 1975, 1979). However, these early investigations, and those of the following two decades, are best regarded as case studies in the broader field of the economics of science (Stephan 1996; Mirowski and Sent 2002; Diamond 2008), whereas the full awareness of the existence of a distinct subject that could legitimately be called the economics of economics is a fairly recent business, dating from around the end of the 1990s (Colander 1989; Hands 1994; Maki 1999).

Partly because its history is brief and partly because it is two-headed (see below), the economics of economics does not have – as of yet – a coherent theoretical framework or even a consensus over a body of knowledge. At this stage, the field is best defined by its object (academic economics), rather than its methods. Some of the strands that have emerged in the economic investigations of academic economics have been the following:[1]

---

[1] A full review of the field would be beyond the scope of this introduction. The reader may refer to Medema and Samuels (1996) and Coupé (2004) as starting points. The works

1

(i) applied studies in other subfields of economics (e.g. economics of education and labor economics);[2]
(ii) studies based on the application of specific methods (e.g. the experiments on the ethics of economists);[3]
(iii) comparative studies on economics as an academic discipline (e.g. the ranking of economists, economic journals, and economic departments, and assessments of the discipline at large);[4]
(iv) studies derived from the economics of science (e.g. the content and the production of economics knowledge);[5]
(v) studies derived from the sociology of scientific knowledge and the philosophy and methodology of economics (e.g. institutional analysis of the economics discipline).[6]

Consequently, the early years of the economics of economics have been characterized (if we are excused for this simplistic taxonomy) by progress along parallel lines. The one promoted by, as it were, full-blown economists (roughly the bullet points (i) through (iv) above) and the other by methodologists, philosophers of science, and sociologists. The former tended to be more descriptive about the state of the discipline, while the latter has been more normative, and critical at that.[7] It is time, we believe, to bring these two strands together.

The main reason to do so is that economics is bound to undergo some changes, to which methodologists can positively contribute. The recent (or current, by most accounts) financial crisis has put extra pressure on the profession. This time, not just from outside the Departments of Economics, but even from outside academia. For example, the July 18, 2009 issue of *The Economist* featured a cover portraying a book of "Modern Economics Theory" melting like an ice-cream, accompanied by the discouraging title "where it went wrong – and how the crisis is changing it".

---

cited in the following footnotes do not hope to cover entire fields or subfields of research, but more modestly to testify to their scope and variety.
[2] E.g. Carson and Navarro (1988), Diamond (1986), Siegfried (1971), Stock and Siegfried (2001).
[3] E.g. Frank et al. (1993), Frey and Meier (2003).
[4] E.g. Amir and Knauff (2008), Bowen (1953), Grijalva and Nowell (2008), Kalaitzidakis et al. (2003), Krueger et al. (1991), Siegfried et al. (1991).
[5] E.g. Ellison (2002), Oster and Hamermesh (1998).
[6] E.g. Hodgson (2007), Hodgson and Rothman (1999), Maki (1999).
[7] That the criticism came from outside the profession has certainly diminished its impact. The indifference of economists to the recommendations of methodologists was an early theme in the economic methodology literature (Caldwell 1990; Hands 1990). In recent years, it should be noted, also this strand of research has become more positive.

Economics without crisis

When we first began working on this volume, in the early months of 2008, the financial crisis had not yet played out to the extent that we were later to witness. Though that event induced us to make some changes, this is not a volume about the financial crisis. Some excellent pieces of research have been published on the topic already (e.g. Lawson 2009, Schneider and Kirchgaessner 2009), so there would be little need for another one.

Neither is this volume about the crisis in academic economics. For one, we are not so sure that academic economics is in a crisis. (Or, at any rate, that it is in an any worse crisis than it has been for the past half-century.) We concede that this time the complaints about the state of economics also come from the insiders and the public, and not just from the ranks of the methodologists, but more and more vociferous complaints attest to a heightened perception of what could be taken as signs of a crisis, not to its increased severity.

While – as methodologists – we cannot but welcome this stirring debate on the state of academic economics, we ought to make clear from the outset that we do not regard this as an opportunity for (further) economics bashing. The profession of academic economics has been long and widely criticized. However, it has been studied only sparsely. In this volume, we take up the challenge to understand before any criticism.

We agree that economics has a rich conceptual apparatus that is fit for studying many social phenomena (and especially so when it borrows freely from the tools of the heterodoxy and of the other social sciences), including of course the conduct of economic scholars and the organization of academic economics. The starting assumption of this volume, therefore, is that economists are just intelligent people, who try to navigate (and succeed in) their professional and social environment. In words more familiar to the profession, economists are rational actors who react to incentives.

The economics of economists

In Part I, the volume proceeds to identify these incentives, by means of exploring the environment within which academic economics takes place. Part II uncovers the incentives individual scholars face in their professional lives. That it does not pursue outright economics bashing, however, should not suggest that this volume is an apologetic account of the profession. Many of the chapters take very critical stances on several issues. Part III, moreover, directly addresses many challenges to the profession and discusses possible solutions. The themes addressed in the volume are so broad that they naturally cross individual chapters. There are, therefore, many ways to read this volume. The most natural would be to follow the order of the chapters, which have been arranged within each section roughly from the most general to the most specific. Let us also suggest one alternative.

The first chapter, by Arjo Klamer, introduces the culture of academic economics, the economists' way of being, the broad and loosely defined set of the conventions and values that make academic economists different from any other group. The notion of culture evokes a social and shared dimension. Although typically overlooked, the social dimension is central to understanding any scientific community. Chapter 4, by Alberto Baccini and Lucio Barabesi, tackles the issue with the tools of network analysis, and explores the connections between the editorial boards of economic journals. When an editor sits on more than one board, she constitutes a link between the two journals. The ensemble of these connections forms the overall social network of economic journals, analyzing which they uncover some fascinating patterns in the functioning of the profession.

The indices commonly used to evaluate scientific quality – crucially, the number of citations received by one's publications in peer-reviewed journals and the Impact Factor of those journals – reflect the relational and communal dimensions inherent in academia, too. Such indices are used to establish the performance of individual researchers and the quality of entire departments, on whose basis entire rankings are compiled. In Chapter 3, Bruno Frey and Margit Osterloh discuss the advantages and the disadvantages of these rankings. They point to the major issue that scholars will change their behavior to respond to the incentives created by the rankings, which might trump the benefits of the rankings themselves. They also propose alternative, and superior, options.

The growing reliance on standardized indices of academic performance reflects one of the major developments in economics over the twentieth century: its globalization. As Marion Fourcade explains in Chapter 2, the profession has evolved to become increasingly homogenous across several countries, following the same (and typically US-based) professional standards. Yet, in Chapter 5 David Colander regrets this may not be for the better. As European economists chase after the Americans, they sacrifice their traditional strengths and renounce their chance to develop into "a true global economics power."

Increasingly, therefore, we can expect also the training of economists to converge toward an international standard that defines the skills and knowledge which ought to be passed on to graduate students. Such standards have been a hot issue in economics at least since the late 1980s, when the American Economics Association established the Commission on Graduate Education in Economics (COGEE) in reaction to the interviews with graduate students conducted by two of the contributors of this volume (Colander and Klamer 1987). The major finding of the COGEE was a reported isolation of the profession from real-world economic problems (Krueger et al. 1991), perpetrated by means of teaching an array of theoretical notions and mathematical techniques to economists in the making. The COGEE does not seem to have had any consequence on the profession (Colander 1998). At long last, even graduate education in economics may have to change.

Although we would welcome several changes in the training of economists, this volume does not endorse any specific change. Economists are traditionally averse to reforms of their Ph.D. programs, but Chapter 6, by Wendy Stock and John Siegfried, offers further reasons to consider updating graduate education in economics: there is a mismatch between the skills graduate students acquire and those that, as economists, they require to succeed in their profession. After following a cohort of Ph.D. students over a ten-year period, Stock and Siegfried report that they consistently identify as a weakness of their graduate economics programs the little emphasis put on application of theory to real-world problems, and on understanding economic institutions and history.

The almost exclusive focus on abstract economic models, moreover, is alleged to be one of the main culprits of the financial crisis, as Colander et al. argue in Chapter 13. On the one hand, therefore, graduate schools could serve better the new economists they train by expanding their focus. On the other, they would also serve the larger interest of producing relevant and useful knowledge. Such change would also require economists to introduce changes both in attitude and methodologies. Along these lines, Deirdre McCloskey, in Chapter 8, proposes a full overview of the (few) virtues and the (many and of varying severity) sins of economics. Among these, two "mortal sins" stand out: the devotion to qualitative existence theorems based on implausible assumptions and to testing statistical significance (instead of substantive significance). Though they often prove of limited practical consequence, economists employ (only) both of them to draw conclusions about real-world economic phenomena.

In Chapter 9, Robert Frank suggests one possible solution to the seeming irrelevance of economics classes for an understanding of real-world economic phenomena, though his solution is aimed at undergraduates rather than at graduate students. He proposes to teach students only a small number of basic concepts (e.g. cost–benefit analysis) and then stimulate them to employ such concepts to understand some phenomenon in the world that surrounds them. Finally, students should try and describe such economic understanding in narrative form. Such technique, called the "Economic Naturalist" has several merits. It might, however, induce narrow-mindedness in students instead of stimulating their intellectual curiosity, as Jack Vromen argues in Chapter 10. Like "ordinary people," students are not free from confirmation biases. Once they are hooked on thinking as an economist, they might be disinclined to think of alternative hypotheses and to give them a fair chance. Telling the students that after having mustered the typical economic way of making sense of phenomena there is still the need for critical empirical testing might come too late.

Moreover, by helping students "think like economists" it might foster selfish conduct. Indeed, another sensitive item in McCloskey's inventory of economists' sins, and one of the main topics in economics of economics, is an alleged tendency to selfish conduct. In Chapter 7, Wade Hands brings this topic to quite an extreme realization. Having one's name attached to a scientific finding (e.g. Nash equilibrium, Say's law, Phillips curve...) is one of the greatest academic rewards. It is thus puzzling that priority fights, as the squabbles about the attribution of important findings are called, are non-existent in economics. Yet, priority fights in science are usually conducted not by the authors in the pursuit of selfish goals, but by their colleagues and out of moral indignation for the mistaken attribution. Hands traces this puzzle down to the lack of such moral indignation among economists – who do not stand to earn anything from the correct attribution of a finding to some colleague. Alessandro Lanteri and Salvatore Rizzello, in Chapter 12, argue that the self-interested behavior of economists can be described not as an individual inclination of economists, who are selfish individuals who self-select in the dismal science, as it is often suggested in the experimental literature on economists' conduct. Instead, it might be an adjustment to the stereotype of the economist. They support such a conclusion with a novel experiment, in which students of Occupational Therapy are triggered to defect more than students of Economics.

Yet another point raised by McCloskey, though one not pursued in this volume is that some of the sins of economics are distinctively masculine, and that men are overrepresented in the discipline. However, Donna Ginther and Shulamit Kahn show in Chapter 11 that there is no difference between men and women in the likelihood of getting tenure or becoming full professors. More specifically, the difference is in the consequences of choosing to have a family, which induces women, but not men, to abandon their academic career. So, the observed gender differences can be explained by such choices.

References

Amir, R. and Knauff, M. 2008. "Ranking Economics Departments Worldwide on the Basis of PhD Placement," *Review of Economics and Statistics*, 90(1): 185–190.

Berg, S. V. 1971. "Increasing the Efficiency of the Economics Journal Market," *Journal of Economic Literature*, 9(3): 798–813.

Bowen, H. R. 1953. "Graduate Education in Economics," *American Economic Review*, 43(4).

Caldwell, B. 1990. "Does Methodology Matter? How Should it be Practiced?" *Finnish Economic Papers*, 3(1): 64–71.

Carson, R. and Navarro, P. 1988. "A Seller's (& Buyer's) Guide to the Job Market for Beginning Academic Economists," *Journal of Economic Perspectives*, 2: 137–148.

Colander, D. 1989. "Research on the Economics Profession," *Journal of Economic Perspectives*, 3(4): 137–148.

1998. "The Sounds of Silence: The Profession's Response to the COGEE Report," *American Journal of Agricultural Economics*, 80(3): 600–607.

Colander, D. and Klamer, A. 1987. "The Making of an Economist," *Journal of Economic Perspectives*, 1(2): 95–111.

Coupé, T. 2004. "What Do We Know about Ourselves? On the Economics of Economics," *Kyklos*, 57(2): 197–216.

Diamond, A. 1986. "What is a Citation Worth?" *The Journal of Human Resources* 21: 200–215.

2008. "Science, Economics of," in S. N. Durlauf and L. E. Blume (eds.), *The New Palgrave Dictionary of Economics*, 2nd Edition, London: Palgrave Macmillan.

Frank, R., Gilovich, T., and Regan, D. 1993. "Does Studying Economics Inhibit Cooperation?" *Journal of Economic Perspectives*, 7: 159–171.

Frey, B. and Meier, S. 2003. "Are Political Economists Selfish and Indoctrinated? Evidence from a Natural Experiment," *Economic Inquiry*, 41(3): 448–462.

Glenn, E. 2002. "The Slowdown of the Economics Publishing Process," *Journal of Political Economy*, 110(5): 947–993.

Grijalva, T. and Nowell, C. 2008. "A Guide to Graduate Study in Economics: Ranking Economics Departments by Fields of Expertise," *Southern Economic Journal*, 74(4): 971–996.

Hands, W. 1990. "Thirteen Theses on Progress in Economic Methodology," *Finnish Economic Papers*, 3(1): 72–76.

1994. "The Sociology of Scientific Knowledge and Economics: Some Thoughts on the Possibilites," pp. 75–106 in R. Backhouse (ed.), *New Developments in Economic Methodology*, London: Routledge.

Hansen, W. L. and Weisbrod, B. A. W. 1972. "Toward a General Theory of Awards or Do Economists Need a Hall of Fame?" *Journal of Political Economy*, 80(2): 422–431.

Hodgson, G. 2007. "Evolutionary and Institutional Economics as the New Mainstream?" *Evolutionary and Institutional Economics Review*, 4(1): 7–25.

Hodgson, G. and Rothman, H. 1999. "The Editors and Authors of Economics Journals: A Case of Institutional Oligopoly?" *The Economic Journal*, 109: F165–F186.

Kalaitzidakis, P., Mamuneas, T., and Stengos, T. 2003. "Rankings of Academic Journals and Institutions in Economics," *Journal of the European Economic Association*, 1: 1346–1366.

Krueger, A. O., Arrow, K. J., Blanchard, O. J., Blinder, A. S., Goldin, C., Leamer, E. E., Lucas, R., Panzar, J., Penner, R. G., Schultz, T. P., Stiglitz, J. E., and Summers, L. H. 1991. "Report of the Commission on Graduate Education in Economics," *Journal of Economic Literature*, 29(3): 1035–1053.

Laband, D. and Piette, M. 1994, "Favoritism versus Search for Good Papers: Empirical Evidence Regarding the Behavior of Journal Editors," *Journal of Political Economy*, 102(1): 194–203.

Lawson, T. 2009. "The Current Economic Crisis: Its Nature and the Course of Academic Economics," *Cambridge Journal of Economics*, 33: 759–777.

Lovell, M. C. 1973. "The Production of Economic Literature: An Interpretation," *Journal of Economic Literature*, 11(1): 27–55.

Maki, U. 1999. "Science as a Free Market: A Reflexivity Test in an Economics of Economics," *Perspectives on Science*, 7(4): 486–509.

Medema, S. and Samuels, W. (eds.) 1996. *Foundations of Research in Economics: How Do Economists Do Economics?* Aldershot: Edward Elgar Publishing.

Mirowski, P. and Sent, E. M. (eds.) 2002. *Science Bought and Sold: Essays in the Economics of Science*, University of Chicago Press.

Oster, S. and Hamermesh, D. 1998. "Aging and Productivity Among Economists," *The Review of Economics and Statistics*, 80(1): 154–156.

Schneider, F. and Kirchgaessner, G. 2009. "Financial and World Economic Crisis: What Did Economists Contribute?" *Public Choice*, 140: 319–327.

Siegfried, J. 1971. "Rate of Return to the Ph.D. in Economics," *Industrial and Labor Relations Review*, 24(3): 420–431.

Siegfried, J., Bartlett, R., Hansen, L., Kelley, A., McCloskey, D., and Tietenberg, T. 1991. "The Status and Prospects of the Economics Major," *The Journal of Economic Education*, 22(3): 197–224.

Stephan, P. E. 1996. "The Economics of Science," *Journal of Economic Literature*, 34(3): 1199–1235.

Stigler, G. J. and Friedland, C. 1975. "The Citation Practices of Doctorates in Economics," *Journal of Political Economy*, 83(3): 477–507.

1979. "The Pattern of Citation Practices in Economics," *History of Political Economy*, 11(1): 1–20.

Stock, W. and Siegfried, J. 2001. "So You Want to Earn a Ph.D. in Economics: How Much Do You Think You'll Make?" *Economic Inquiry*, 39(2): 320–335.

Part I

The institutional setting of academic economics

1 The culture of academic economics

Arjo Klamer

Students who aspire to become economists, may think that all they need to do is learn the techniques, do the exams, and get on with it. How naïve students can be. In this chapter I reveal to them what it takes to become an academic economist, that is, an economist at a university. For, so I would warn them, it makes a world of difference whether they want to work inside or outside academia. How so, they will find out shortly.

The inside view that I am about to provide of the world of scientific economists may also be clarifying for those who are looking at it from the outside. Just like visiting a foreign country, the outsider is likely to be puzzled, if not dumbfounded when finding out what academic economists actually do each day. We say that we are busy so what are we doing when we teach only a few hours a week? When they visit us in our university departments they may catch us chatting a great deal, if they catch us at all as most of the time we are absent, working at home or attending a conference at some resort. And when they prod us with urgent economic questions ("where is the dollar heading?" and "what should governments do to get out of the crisis?") they may scratch their head because of the evasiveness and the variety of the answers they get – if we bother to give the answers as we may be too preoccupied with our research.

The confusion will be compounded when outsiders wander into the lobby of the hotel that houses a large economics conference. Much ado about nothing, they must think when they eavesdrop on our chatter about colleagues, papers we are working on, baseball or soccer (depending of whether the conference is in the US or Europe), and some university politics. When they take the courage to walk into our "sessions" they must feel like people from Mars coming to Earth. Is this what the making of science is all about? Most sessions take place in rather small rooms with only a few people in attendance. Interaction is scarce: economists

Based on Chapter 3 of *Speaking of Economics: How to Get in the Conversation* (2007).

appear most at ease in the monologue. The ballrooms are for the stars. They draw the crowds. They interact even less. The question lingers: what do all these economists do to make sense of the economy? The language they use is obscure; the talks rarely address issues that laypeople would be interested in. Who is making sense of what? Why would anyone be interested in studying in order to be part of such a weird world? And why would governments spend any tax money on such frivolous activities?

In *Speaking of Economics: How to Get in the Conversation* (2007), I address the misguided expectations that non-economists, and in particular the non-academics have of the science of economics. (I hasten to add that quite a few academic economists seem to be similarly misguided in their perception of their own science.) When people expect definite results as the natural sciences appear to produce, reliable predictions ("the next crisis will occur in the next six months," and "the interest rate will increase by 3% over the next year"), and a disciplined search for the truth about the economy, they are to be seriously disappointed. They will also be disappointed when they expect to find economists engaged in serious, open, and intellectually challenging discussions in search of the definite truth. And they will be bothered by the at times meaningless and frivolous activities that the serious scientists that economists presumably are, engage in.

What I would like to suggest to these outsiders, as well as students approaching our discipline, is that such disappointments and frustrations are due to an outdated perception of what a science like economics looks and feels like. It is not a world that merely consists of odorless formulas and dispassionate scientists seeking results that are useful for the outside world. Economics is not such a tough science. In *Speaking of Economics*, I show that the world of academic economists looks less strange, rather mundane and human actually, if you think about it as a conversation, or rather a bunch of conversations. Realize that these academic economists are participating in a particular conversation, just like soccer fans or musicians are, and you will understand all the chatter that fills the world of academic economists. You will recognize that economics is a practice, something people do for a living. And, of course, they will do all the things people do when they engage with each other. It is like the game of soccer. It is not just the game, with its rules and techniques, that playing is all about. The game of soccer also involves talk, lots of it. Soccer players do not only play with each other, they also socialize with each other; and if they are any good they will find themselves in the centre of attention of a whole world that is about soccer. In order to become such a soccer player you need to learn more than the rules and the techniques; you have to learn to be a soccer player and that means learning what it takes to be part of the world of soccer. For students of economics it is not that different.

The conversation of economists, therefore, represents a culture, a way of being.

In all the literature about economics as a science the culture of academic economic conversation has received hardly any attention thus far. That is strange as newcomers to the discipline and outsiders run up against the particular conventions, the values that constitute the culture of academic economists. To see the culture of (academic) economists is to recognize those conventions, the things that economists do, the values that make them different from any other group. I advance the notion of culture, therefore, to make more sense for those who seek to be part of the world of economists as well as for those who are looking in.

There is also another, more critical reason to highlight the culture of economics. Having a keen sense of what constitutes the appropriate culture of academics in general and of academic economics in particular, we can be more alert to forces that undermine the fabric of that culture. We may for example become aware of the possible undermining influence of the economic way of thinking. For instance, if it turns out that cooperative interaction is a critical component of academic culture, then the pricing of contributions may seriously upset a critical balance.

Introducing the notion of culture

When the term culture pops up, the question is inevitably what it means. Culture is typically one of those terms that confuses as we cannot grasp it, hold onto it, or nail it down. I mean by culture what we mean when we experience American life, or Italian life, as an outsider. Americans may think nothing special when they spontaneously invite a newcomer to their house or when they forget the name of a very good friend; for foreigners that is typical American. And when Italians gather in the late afternoon in one of their wonderful squares to chat and argue with everything they have got, they do what they are used to doing but to non-Italians they seem very Italian doing so. Italian culture, therefore, is what makes an Italian different from, say, an American or Dutchman.

So what does it take to be Italian? More than a declaration, or a passport; more than respecting Italian customs and frequenting its squares. You can learn to speak with your hands, be perfectly fluent in Italian, and prefer Italian food over any other, but if you are not Italian, you will be found out. And you will be forever aware of your own foreignness. To be Italian you need to be so Italian that you are not aware of being Italian unless it is pointed out to you. That is culture.

Culture is for humans what water is for fish: we become aware of it only when it does not surround us. Culture sits so comfortably in us that we do not feel it. Likewise, the academic economist needs to grow into and assimilate the academic economist's culture so much so that she is unaware of it.

The academically inclined will want to know in more precise terms what I mean by "culture." Economists, especially, are wary, since "culture" is not part of their conversation (yet). It has no mention in economic handbooks, no entry in the exhaustive *Palgrave Dictionary of Economics* (Durlauf and Blume 2008), nor does it appear in the *Handbook of Economic Methodology* (Davis, Wade Hands, and Maki 1998). Clifford Geertz, an anthropologist, calls culture "deep play" (Geertz 1973). When Balinese men engage in cockfights – a famous case of his – they play out a distinct variety of customs, values, emotions, stories, and sentiments without necessarily being conscious of them. Onlookers can learn the elements of play, but it is too deep for them to be players without elements of artifice. Pursuing Geertz's resolve I dare to propose the following definition: Culture denotes beliefs, customs, values, emotions, stories, and sentiments that every member of a group (e.g. Balinese men, Italians, academic economists) has in common and, crucially, by which they distinguish themselves as a group. The distinction is a great matter: Italians are quite unlike non-Italians and academic economists are quite unlike sociologists, businessmen, and non-academic economists.

Distinctive for the world of academic economists is their conversation, the way they communicate, the terms they use, but also the values that they express in their everyday interactions in their academic world. Academic economists keep the company of other academic economists and in their interactions they perform the deep play of academic economics without being found out. Being in the economic conversation is like being in a world or, as sociologists like to say, operating in a field. "Worlds" and "fields" are fine concepts to make sense of academic economics as a cultural practice, but I prefer "conversation" because of the linguistic performance that being in a world or field entails. The culture of economics becomes evident in its conversation. An outsider will be lost in its unexpected deep play, and no one prepares anyone for it because no one is much aware of it.

The first acquaintance with the culture appears to be easy. Good teachers of introductory economics do their best to make the subject interesting. They initiate the students by teaching them concepts, playing with the four lines that they call the market (students who buy that game make a big stride in the direction of the inner sanctum of academic economists), and to make it all attractive they refer to actual economic

events and attempt to show how abstract economic concepts apply to the
real economy. But that is only the introduction. Students who have
finished an introductory course have not yet a clue about what being an
academic economist is about. They do not even get it after they have
achieved a bachelor in economics. Infectious exposure to the culture of
economics comes with working toward a Ph.D., where life plans are often
rethought and learning the tacit rules of the conversation is a must.
Amidst it come the shocks and waves of a new culture.

How shocking the experience can be, David Colander and I revealed in
a series of interviews with graduate students (Klamer and Colander
1987). Their frustrations were evident in our conversations. Some
acknowledged that they already had given up plans to become policy
advisors because that was not the thing to do. Others had given up their
reading in other subjects, like psychology, philosophy, and the like
because that, too, was not the thing to do. General intellectual curiosity
was not appreciated in their new surroundings. To some the experience
was downright painful. As one first-year Harvard student so vividly told it:

It seems to me that the first year is going to shape the rest of our professional
career as economists to a great extent. I find it really disturbing. We are being
socialized into something, but nobody in the faculty seems to know what that is,
except they were socialized themselves five years ago. It's like being brainwashed.
You may have heard stories of brainwashing during the Korean War. You are
deprived of sleep, you are subjected to extreme stress, bombarded with
contradictory convictions – you end up accepting anything. You end up in the
middle of the semester completely malleable. You write down whatever you can
and try to understand it. If you get your head above water, you survive. But you
don't know where you are – all the intellectual landmarks have been leveled.

Granted, this student was unusually aware of what was going on, and
unusually eloquent in expressing it. His fellow students seemed to identify with his observations, though. They laughed in approval at the image
of brainwashing.

The experience of graduate school is not so much about "science as
knowledge" as it is about "science as practice."[1] Studying results, findings, and methods consumes the time, but the essence of the experience
is reading, listening, talking, writing, socializing, visiting professors,
attending seminars, showing off skills and knowledge, demonstrating
the proper intentions, and so on. It is the practice of science, not the
knowledge of it, that makes economists and reshapes their worldview.
They stealthily move into conversation with like-minded people and out
of the conversations of so many others, such as sociologists, business

---

[1] The distinction is from Pickering (1992).

economists, psychologists, natural scientists, engineers, historians, and all others they may have once cared about. At a point unknown to themselves, they have adapted and are cloaked in the culture of economics, in its nervous system.

In representing the world we intervene, as philosopher Ian Hacking argued in one of his books (Hacking 1983). Economics professors intervene by asking for a great deal of study and they expect, simultaneously, total attention to the acclimatization of their "habitus"[2] and to the shedding of all others'. This is not necessarily wrong – I do the same by wanting others to adjust to the values of "economics is a conversation." But the intervention is not neutral, dispassionate, objective, that is, it does not express any of the values that people tend to attribute to the practice of science. Being aware of the intervention is good, though, so I would suggest. It stimulates students and other onlookers to think of science as a practice, and to think of the practice of science as culture.

Academic dogs

To see the academic community of economics as a separate culture it helps to step away from it. Only by looking from the outside do we see its strange, different, and unexpected characteristics. When the press learned about the outcomes of the survey that Colander and I had conducted among graduate students, they gave it wide notice. How could these budding economists not care about the real world, as the answers suggested? Were they out of their minds? Journalists saw it as a grand occasion for economics bashing. The implication was obvious: if economics is not about the real world, economists are not of much use.

Insiders, however, read it quite differently. To them, the students had understood what counts in the conversation and what it takes to sustain that all-important conversation. Practical concerns, like the latest move of the Federal Reserve, or globalization, are distractions for which there is not much time and energy left, at least not at the beginning of a career. The academic conversation does not prepare for practical jobs, for policy advising, for changing the world, or for journalism. Especially at the better schools economics graduate students gradually discover that they have trained to become Academic Professionals, that is, economists who have made it their profession to operate in academia.

A Professional Academic is strangely unlike others who have undergone tough academic training, such as doctors or lawyers, in that doctors and

---

[2] From sociologist Pierre Bourdieu, who speaks of the habitus of academic life, meaning what we are disposed to do in the setting of academia.

lawyers are trained to perform for people outside their own spheres. The Professional Academic is trained to entertain, impress, and intimidate other Professional Academics. Their goals are to teach in the best economics departments, publish in the best journals, and speak at the most important conferences. Extra-curricular activities like the writing of textbooks, consulting, policy advising, and speaking for general audiences jeopardize his or her academic standing. The focus of the community is inward.

At the time of the survey I had a young, rather ill-behaved cocker spaniel. I opted for obedience school on his behalf. The experience was analogous to the inward-focused, exclusive academic community. The first surprise was that Fittipaldi, my dog, that is, had to do undergraduate training (he was put in a class for beginners only; apparently, there existed something like Graduate Obedience.) In these classes, I was struck by the number of exercises that did not serve the simple objectives of the real world – having him heel, come at my command, not bite people.

When I noted the goings-on of the graduate training, it dawned on me that we were being prepared for just that, higher learning, which, in turn, was to prepare us for performances at dog shows. Fittipaldi was being trained to become a Professional Academic Dog; that is, a dog that entertains, impresses, and intimidates owners and dogs of the academic dog world. Having no such ambitions, we abandoned the conversation of dog shows.

About half of the graduate students do not quit. They undergo the initiation, master the rhetoric, and go on to be academics, questioning little along the way. As they read academic journals, they observe that the accolades go to theoretical and technical articles. As they note how their professors, often a few years out of graduate school themselves, perform in the classroom, in seminars, and in personal exchanges, they emulate. They listen to the jokes and join in the gossip. And most become Professional Academic Dogs ... er, Professional Academics.

Academic versus non-academic culture

Part of becoming an academic economist is becoming an academic. Academic economists share a culture that is different from economists at banks, government institutions, and think tanks. The manner of life is different – life at a university is not life at the offices of product-oriented or bureaucratic organizations. It shows in the discomfort that people experience when they move over from one to the other.

Some differences between academic and non-academic economists manifest on the surface. Wandering through a university building (noisy, poster-filled, helter-skelter, cluttered, and usually unoccupied offices) is not like wandering through a bank or government office (quieter, more formal, organized, office-occupied). Academics are looser with their schedules. Faculty work at home most of the time. Many are off at conferences. Vacations are taken informally. In thirty-five years of university teaching, I have not checked with anyone about going on vacation. Could a banker or government employee ever do the same?

Academic freedom has its price. The younger faculty may have trouble with the loneliness of their academic existence. It is one reason that some turn back from an academic career, preferring lively teamwork to solitary plodding. An academic is like a self-made entrepreneur. Lunching and talking with colleagues goes on, but the actual work is usually hard to share in process. A colleague of mine is advanced in the mathematics of network analysis. No one around understands what he is doing, including me. Now and then he communicates with a couple of like-minded people abroad but most of the time he works alone.

Underneath the surface are the values, attitudes, and dispositions that comprise the academic life. Habitus is more than mere habit; in Bourdieu's terms, it is more like the interiorization of the exterior. Only when an outsider is in the house do academics, who know how to behave without thinking about it, become aware of the rules. When a mathematical invention in a game-theoretic setting is the issue, someone in the know does not bring up the importance of emotions. No one cites the newspaper, no matter how relevant. The response to habitus violations is usually awkward silence.

Academics do find outsiders out. At a Washington, DC university where I taught for a few years, political economists ("policy entrepreneurs" Paul Krugman calls them) came by occasionally to give seminars. Their culture is about political clout, citation in newspapers, and recognition by the general population. The blending of this culture with that of the university seminar room proved to be quite ugly. After a polite presentation come seemingly innocent questions leading to what academics are good at: problematization and scathing and purely recreational criticism. "The statistical methods you used are not quite appropriate." "[An academic economist], probably not known to you, has shown the opposite of what you are arguing here." "Your thesis is blown down by rational expectations." The poor fellow! The argument that worked so well with important politicians evaporates in the presence of obscure academicians. The awkward realization sets in that he does not know the data, has not kept up with the literature, and has no idea what his fellow economists are talking about.

The treatment is reciprocated when academics present their work in a political environment. There no one cares about the technical intricacies of the analysis and everyone demands to know about its practical relevance. "What does this do for us? What bearing does it have on the interest rate, unemployment, justice, global peace?" Honest academics, and those who think of their academic reputation, will refuse to say more. And they will long for the academic community to whom their performance is entertaining and impressive.

And how about consultants? They, too, have a hard time in the corridors of academia, receiving almost insulting criticism for being superficial and all that. We economists are after all seeking the truth, whereas consultants want to make money. And indeed, they make a great deal of money, much much more than academic economists do when they are doing some consulting. Bouwmeester (2010) investigated the situation, and found consultants simply more responsive to the questions that were asked. When academic economists try to act as consultants, they usually get even sloppier and more unreliable than the consultants that they are so ready to condemn. The conclusion has to be that academic economists are best at their own game. Policy advising and consulting are other games.

Non-academics do not have a clue about the academic game. "Only a few hours of teaching each week, and you are complaining about being too busy?" Even many academics do not have a clue. A source of confusion is the group whose applause they want to seek and to whom they want to be accountable. Many mistakenly believe that they do the work to impress their local environment: the dean or the colleagues in their department or, if the university is small, the entire faculty. But the opinion of those who are circumstantially nearby does not necessarily have relevance to the caliber of work. Yes, the university pays the salary and yes, senior colleagues decide on tenure, and yes, praise feels warm, but the significant community is often elsewhere. Diana Crane's notion of the "invisible college" (Crane 1972) is so pertinent because it suggests a world with no walls, scattered as it is over the globe. Collins (1998) more fashionably terms it a "network." Whatever its name, the community that shares a particular area of expertise counts more than the community that shares the immediacies of hallways and cafeterias. The community at large, whose members drift in and out, decides the academic's fate by deciding whether or not to publish work, cite work, and thereby constitute the relevant conversation. Tenure, salary, and what local colleagues think are based, in large part, on how the academic performs in that conversation.

This preoccupation with whom to please makes for risk-balancing behavior. Duties at the home institution are important, but efforts to fulfill them may be at the expense of activities in the academic community.

Teaching and serving on university committees may take so much time that there is none left to write papers and be published. On the other hand, time-consuming research may cause the neglect of duties at the university – students complain, colleagues resent bearing the brunt of home duties for those forever away at conferences. In general, it is better to risk the latter. Affronting students and eschewing dutiful behavior is less of a matter to an academic than being overlooked by the academic community.

The academic commons

Being in a community, sharing values and dispositions, implies that the individual academic has a great deal in common with fellow academics. This is particularly manifest with academic economists, who share a distinct conversation. Their oral and written products are a contribution to the common conversation. Academic etiquette requires awarding authorship to contributions by means of citation, but the contribution is a common possession, accessible to anyone. No matter how selfish, narcissistic, and autistic an individual academic can be, he has to recognize the communal nature of the discourse in which he partakes.

The practice shows in the language. The papers academics write are "contributions" and they are "pleased" to "share" their latest findings with seminar audiences. And, in fact, most are "eager" to share. The commonness of the conversation induces the values of collegiality and reciprocity. I vividly recall my first attempt to get published. The editors requested that I resubmit the paper after having incorporated the comments of referees, and I panicked when they asked for some technical additions I did not know about. I timidly approached Jim Grant, our in-house econometrician. His response was "Sure, no problem!" He sacrificed a solid day to read the paper and an entire afternoon to help make the revisions with me. I knew enough of the academic code to know that the most I could do in return was thank him kindly and acknowledge him in a footnote. Monetary compensation was out of the question. Suggestion of it would have been an insult. *Thinking* of it would have been a sign of bad faith. His assistance was a gift, not necessarily to me, his colleague, but to the academic conversation. After this, I knew what to do when a colleague asked for my help.

The gift is the means by which individuals support what they have in common with others.[3] Academics give all the time. And they reciprocate. I got plenty of help and have given plenty of help, some of which, I like to

---

[3] I found the first reference to this phenomenon in Hagstrom (1965).

think, was significant. I have also worked closely with colleagues who, so I noticed later, unwittingly appropriated some of my ideas as their own. I am sure that a great deal of what I am writing here I owe to them, too, without being aware of it. It is all a contribution to the common good. Ideas are gifts, too.

The giving goes further. I have spent a good deal of time organizing conferences, convening seminars, preparing commentaries, advising Ph.D. candidates, and refereeing papers for journals. Only when reviewing books for publishers do I receive some nominal payment, usually in the form of books. Many colleagues give a great deal more. The community spirit that so many display is remarkable and moving. Editing journals, for example, is hard work and often a thankless job. An endless stream of papers crosses editors' desks. They send them to referees and subsequently have to beg for the comments that never seem to meet deadlines. They deal with the desperation of those facing the "publish or perish" dilemma. They receive five to ten times more papers than they can publish, and thus are always breaking some poor fellow's heart. Enemies are easily accumulated. Yet it is a gift to the community, with the meager returns of reputation and small change. The same applies to academics serving on boards of associations, or worse, organizers of the major associations' conferences.

Fame and reputation demand a toll and, as a result, gift-giving some-times has to be deferred. The well-known are inundated with requests to present papers at seminars, give lectures to students, write references for tenure cases, and so on. A stack of papers and letters arrive daily with the kind request for a response. Most of them become quite efficient in responding: "Thanks for your paper. It looks interesting. You seem to have an important point. As soon as I have time, I will give it a serious look." But they can be caught in their routines. A colleague was chatting with a visitor about a paper he had brought to him. The discussion went on for some time and he expressed interest in his ideas. As the visitor was leaving, my colleague was startled when he asked him if he wanted another copy of his paper. With some embarrassment, he realized that while talking he had mindlessly thrown the paper in the waste bin, as was his custom with papers given to him.

Being an academic implies the continuous enriching and sustaining of the community and conversation, the academic commons. Economists who see gift-giving as a market exchange miss the point. The reputation effect is a reward of sorts but is in no way proportional to the work. The real recompense is the thrill of being part of and contributing to the common accumulation of knowledge. Randall Collins, a sociologist, points to the emotional energy that academics experience from time to time. The excitement comes, Collins suggests, when the academic senses that she has hit upon something greater than she, something that may significantly contribute to the common conversation. Thus, being part of an academic conversation calls for sacrifices but the return is the emotional energy that gives a sense of meaning and purpose to what academics are doing.

The ambiguity of academic values

The academic habitus implies an academic attitude and the enactment of implicit academic norms. Novices interiorize the vaguer rules by practicing. Some norms I dare make explicit here: take the relevant literature seriously, be systematic in the analysis, cite generously, do not refer to non-academic literature, adhere to the academic mode of writing, be impersonal, keep the anecdotal to a minimum, be excessive with footnote references, be brief, do not be too inventive (stay within the bounds of the conversation!), defer to the relevant authorities, be a willing referee, be a good colleague, and recognize the circumstances under which certain rules can be broken (as I do in this "contribution").

Underlying such norms are scientific values such as the values of truth, objectivity, seriousness, intellectual honesty, collegiality. Some values are contradictory. Scientists are supposed to be disinterested, objective, and emotionally flat. Yet they have (and rightly so) interest in their own careers and fervently defend their research against criticism. University politics invites emotional argument. Scientific careers require avid self-promotion; each academic needs and wants to be heard. Like everyone else, scientists have passionate political views. How objective can scientists be when their causes inextricably mingle with issues outside the academic community? Emotions are part of eliciting, sharing, and sometimes vehemently arguing about important ideas. Scientists could not do their work without them. Without passion, good science would not come about, as Michael Polanyi (1962) more poignantly points out.

Open-mindedness, too, is cherished in the academic disposition. Academics maintain that they are open to criticism and that they eschew the dogmatic. The practice? Criticism is sneered at or ignored. Dogmatism and fortress-holding abound. The dogmatic disposition thwarts creativity, another value preached in academics. Judging how open a scientific conversation is to creativity is a risky matter. A little imagination is all right but leaping too far from acknowledged platforms means leaping right out of the conversation. Creative contributions are cumbersome. To address them is to admit they might be right, and that could mean their previous work is wrong. The price for admitting to have been wrong is high; the times that that happens, are remarkably scarce. Thus, in the conversation, taking little steps to new ideas is the better approach.

In principle, academic economists are egalitarian and democratic. In reality, academic economists are power mongers. They compete for good positions, funding, spots in journals, and places at conferences. They discriminate in favor of like-minded colleagues and obstruct the entry of dissenters. The suggestion of egalitarianism and democracy is as polite a pretense as the suggestion of objectivity and disinterest. A keen sense of who is worthy lends itself to the quick and relentless judgment of who gets the spotlight. The scientific community is really an aristocracy, ruled by those perceived to be the very best.

So what?

This is what: the disagreements, disputes, common history, i.e., conversations that distinguish "us" as academic economists – and that are things "they" cannot function without – justify speaking of a "culture." People who talk continuously in terms of rational, self-interested, individual behavior, and imagine the world as one complex mechanical system will, of course, differ in "deep play" from those preoccupied with social power, human culture, or physical phenomena.

The application of "culture" to academia makes practical sense. It helps to account for differences and to guide the outsider amidst certain curious practices. It makes clearer how much is required to be in the economic conversation and that it involves a change of heart, or even soul. It takes years of training and practice to negotiate the strange contradictions of the academic culture but, once there, one can seriously proclaim objectivity while enthusiastically hustling for status – and not be troubled by the conflict.

To sense and recognize the culture in which academic economists operate is to be cautious with interventions in the system. Proposals to measure contributions in terms of money, for example, may upset the delicate process of gift giving that supports the academic community. The mutual support system with the free refereeing, the sacrifices made in editing journals and organizing conferences brings about the fabric of collegiality, of a commons that seems so crucial for the spirit of research. The introduction of the logic of exchange, no matter how naturally such logic comes to economists, may tear the fabric apart. Similarly, when management techniques are applied in an attempt to control the seemingly arbitrary way in which academic economists operate, they risk alienating academic economists as they see conflicts arise with the mixture of values that their culture fosters. The culture of academic economics requires trust, trust that amidst all the bickering, the chatting, the ego drives, the best research will float to the surface. When things go wrong, as they seemed to do during the so-called crisis, academic economists will go to work to restore the damage themselves. Interventions from the outside may only make things worse.

Still not convinced that academic culture is different? Then give David Lodge's novels a try. His stories lend the academic experience a genuineness that a scholarly account could never reproduce. *Small World* (1984, not to be read at conference breaks) is the story of Moris Zapp, a well-known English professor (with remarkable resemblance to the real-life Stanley Fish) who is continually traipsing from one academic conference to another. It is a hilarious account of the absurdities of what goes on at them and may motivate one to reconsider academic ambitions. *Changing Places* (1975) is a satirical work on the differences between American and British academic institutions. *Nice Work* (1989) juxtaposes an academic with a businessman; only love enables the two characters to overcome cultural prejudices. Whether in realism or parody, the books say, "An academic is different."

References

Bouwmeester, O. 2010. *Economic Advice and Rhetoric: Why do Consultants Perform Better than Academic Advisers?* Cheltenham: Elgar

Collins, R. 1998. *The Sociology and Professionalization of Economics: British and American Economic Essays*, vol. II, London: Routledge.

Crane, D. 1972. *Invisible Colleges: Diffusion of Knowledge in Scientific Communities*, University of Chicago Press.

David, J. B., Wade Hands, D., and Maki, U. 1998. *The Handbook of Economic Methodology*, Northampton: Edward Elgar Publishing Inc.

Durlauf, S. and Blume, L. 2008. *The New Palgrave Dictionary of Economics*, London: Palgrave Macmillan.

Geertz, C. 1973. *The Interpretation of Cultures: Selected Essays*, New York: Basic Books.

Hacking, I. 1983. *Representing and Intervening: Introductory Topics in the Philosophy of Natural Science*, Cambridge University Press.

Hagstrom, W. O. 1965. *The Scientific Community*, New York: Basic Books.

Klamer, A. 2007. *Speaking of Economics*, London: Routledge.

Klamer, A. and Colander, D. C. 1987. "The Making of an Economist," *Journal of Economic Perspectives*, 1(2): 95–111.

Lodge, D. 1975. *Changing Places: A Tale of Two Campuses*, London: Secker and Warburg.

1984. *Small World: An Academic Romance*, London: Secker and Warburg.

1989. *Nice Work*, London: Penguin Books.

Polanyi, M. 1962. *Personal Knowledge: Towards a Post-Critical Philosophy*, University of Chicago Press.

2 The construction of a global profession: the transnationalization of economics

Marion Fourcade

This article relies on an analysis of the institutionalization of economics worldwide during the twentieth century to argue that the logic of professional development in this particular field has come to be increasingly defined in global terms. Connections to (mainly) US-based standards of work and professional practice are routinely used in the local competition whereby different professional segments and groups seek to assert their authority on particular jurisdictions (scientific, corporate, or political). In this process of professional construction (or reconstruction), economies are being transformed through complex transnational mechanisms which, ultimately, feed back into the identity and jurisdictional claims of the economics profession itself, both in the "core" and in the "periphery."

In one of the most famous passages of the Communist Manifesto, Karl Marx and Friedrich Engels described the logic of modern capitalism in the following terms:

The bourgeoisie cannot exist without constantly revolutionizing the instruments of production, and thereby the relations of production, and with them the whole relations in society... All fixed, fast-frozen relations, with their train of ancient and venerable prejudices and opinions are swept away, all new-formed ones become antiquated before they can ossify. All that is solid melts into air, all that is holy is profaned, and man is at last compelled to face with sober senses, his real conditions of life, and his relations with his kind. The need of a constantly expanding market for its products chases the bourgeoisie over the whole surface of the globe. It must nestle everywhere, settle everywhere, establish connections everywhere. (Marx and Engels [1848] 1998, p. 54)

The inexorable search for profit prompts capitalism both to alter its technological base constantly *and* to globalize its activities. Its extraordinary transformative power, then, is both directed at itself and at the world.

This is a reprint of: Marion Fourcade (2006) "The Construction of a Global Profession: The Transnationalization of Economics." *American Journal of Sociology*, 112(1): 145–194.

Like many living organisms, capitalism develops through a process of metamorphosis. It grows and expands only by destroying its old shells, leaving behind the chrysalides of antiquated structures, technologies, and ideas.

Marx's passage was written to describe economic modernity, yet its main insights apply remarkably more broadly. Since the late 1970s, not only economies but also technologies of government have *both revolutionized and internationalized.* Industrial planning, public investment in national industries, and import controls have been replaced by a new set of policy tools – privatization, trade opening, tax cuts, and capital account liberalization. Once formulated, these new model policies were reproduced far and wide, often carried by transnational technocrats trained in the latest received economic wisdom. There have certainly been numerous variations in the extent and manner in which these changes took place and were implemented, yet the broadly promarket outlook of the new policy consensus was unmistakable (Fourcade-Gourinchas and Babb 2002).

Of course the story does not end there. Although still remarkably influential, the neoliberal creed itself has come to breed its own critique and negation, and came under sharp attack in the late 1990s as Russia, East Asia, and Argentina underwent spectacular economic crises, and third-world countries and movements became more outspoken in their opposition. Things, in short, are no more fast frozen today than they were before: new economic knowledge and tools are being devised; in some cases, old instruments (e.g. capital controls) are being refurbished, promoted by a new breed of nonaligned transnational experts and political activists (Stiglitz 2002).

The strength of Marx's picture is that it brings to light the dual character of the capitalist developmental logic – the intensification of exploitation through both technological upheaval (the vertical or temporal dimension) *and* worldwide expansion (the horizontal or geographical dimension). Just like the capitalist production process, economic ideas and technologies are never fixed – they work continuously at their own revolution. And just like capitalism, they strive for international diffusion.

Professionals – private consultants, public technocrats, and scientific experts, many of whom are trained economists – constitute the main vehicles of these transformations.

The fact that we rarely connect these two phenomena suggests that the fundamental role of economics as an agent of globalization is not very well understood by sociologists. Partly this is because we tend to see processes of global expansion as fairly homogeneous and unidirectional exports from the "core," or the "world society," to the "periphery." But we are not very well equipped to see these processes as dynamically reshaping the nature of the economic knowledge diffused and the jurisdictional control of the economics profession, both in the core and the periphery.

The present article seeks to respond to this analytical challenge by showing *how its very internationalism feeds into the intellectual and professional dynamics of economics*. More generally, it stresses the necessity for sociologists to look at globalization as a critical factor in the transformation of professions and professional dynamics in the modern era.

The next section proposes a generic typology of the mechanisms that may prompt the globalization of professions. I then draw on neoinstitutional theory, field theory, and the theory of professions to propose that we analyze processes of international diffusion in a dialectic and dynamic framework that takes into account changes in the object of diffusion itself. I suggest that economics offers a particularly fruitful way to illustrate this phenomenon, and I analyze the transnational mechanisms at work in this case in considerable empirical detail. In the final section, I discuss the consequences of these transnational processes for the construction and development of the science and profession of economics itself.

Global professions

Professionalization is traditionally understood as a local, geographically bound process. Typically, we consider that the nation-state sets the boundaries of the ecologies within which professions emerge, structure themselves, and interact with each other. The main reason is that professions' rights of entry are typically regulated locally, either at the national or the state level (as is partly the case with law). As a result, the sociology of professions has been a particularly fertile ground for developing crossnational and comparative arguments (Rueschemeyer 1973; Sarfatti-Larson 1979; Abbott 1988; Burrage and Torstendahl 1990; Torstendahl and Burrage 1990; Krause 1996; Savelsberg and King 2005). For instance, the literature draws a sharp contrast between the state-regulated professions of continental Europe and the privately regulated professions of the Anglo-Saxon world, even though finer distinctions have often been made within these categories.

The link between nation and profession holds in reverse as well: professionalization is often seen as one of the processes whereby nation building takes place historically. This is especially clear in the case of certain professions, such as the civil service or the military, that directly participate in the institutionalization of public authority (Silberman 1993; Skowronek 2002). Abbott (2005) even suggests that the argument applies more broadly – states, he argues, constructed and defined themselves partly in relation to the very effort made by the emerging professions to establish their own space.

Because of the "nationalist" disposition of the professions literature, the field is just now beginning to analyze what happens when a profession extends its influence beyond its national boundaries. The process may at first not seem so remarkable: by and large, how professions internationalize looks *analytically* similar to how they nationalized; that is, it is determined primarily by markets and politics (Sarfatti-Larson 1979). Yet how markets and politics interact at the international level to influence professional dynamics is a quite complex matter. No international state exists, and international markets are still far from being integrated at a level comparable to national markets. For the most part, national boundaries and regulations continue to limit the extent to which economic activities (including professional ones) can be transplanted from one country to another. With these limitations in mind, I identify below three mechanisms through which professionals may expand their activities beyond their country of origin.

The professional "common market"

A first possible mechanism is the establishment of what we may call "professional free trade" through the transnationalization of the political regulations and controls applying to professions. Certainly, some professional segments function as free enterprises at the international level.

Typically, being an elite member of many artistic professions allows, even demands, the transgression of national boundaries. A famous musician or opera singer will perform around the globe, and a celebrated architect may leave his or her mark on urban landscapes anywhere. Internationalism, in this case, is both a consequence and a sign of status – and beyond status, of artistic genius or exceptional skill.

Still, for those professions – or professionals – whose work remains bounded by national regulations, the opening of borders may signify a quite dramatic jurisdictional change. The main example here is the European Union, which has grown into a truly transnational administrative institution with far-reaching regulatory powers over a unified regional market. Not surprisingly, today, professions in the European Union are going transnational as a result of (1) the free movement of workers and professionals (institutionalized in the Schengen treaty, which took practical effect in 1995), and (2) the transnationalization of political and economic regulations, particularly the fact that the European Commission now oversees the licensing systems of over 100 professions. Both developments have accelerated the federation of local (i.e., national) organizations into transnational professional bodies and a homogenization of training requirements across countries, particularly noticeable in the legal field (Todd and Neale 1992, p. 35; Evetts 1998; Evetts and Dingwall 2002). The Europeanization of regulatory power also means that less established occupational groups will now use Europe rather than national states to further their professionalizing claims, thereby defining themselves as transnational enterprises from the very beginning (Roach Anleu 1992).

This suggests that Europeanized professions are becoming important players in the process of construction of Europe as a supranational political entity – just like national professions, in an earlier era, participated in the construction of national political institutions (Evetts and Dingwall 2002).

International jurisdictions

Where the reach of transnational regulatory authorities is more limited, however, the internationalization process will look more decentralized and competitive. A second way professions may go transnational is when jurisdictions emerge directly at the international level – that is, when the object of jurisdictional control is by nature international. This process will typically involve a competition among different national professional styles, as in, for instance, the case of international commercial arbitration, which has oscillated between the continental European model of the *lex mercatoria* and the American litigation model (Dezalay and Garth 1996). Or it may entail a more creative bricolage of resources of various origins, particularly where a professional field is created de novo at the international level, as in international criminal law (Hagan and Levi 2004).

Since the legal profession as a whole is still very much regulated at the national level – by licensing and training systems, legal codes, and practices – the development of international jurisdictions, particularly in the "new" areas where legal knowledge is unsettled, takes place amidst competitive struggles over which legal tradition(s) will prevail.[1] The outcome of such struggles in turn feeds back into the national fields, ushering local dynamics of transformation and change (Dezalay and Garth 1996).

---

[1] Of course part of the process of "Europeanization" involves some of the same mechanisms, as, for instance, a distinct body of "European law" emerges, partly autonomously and partly as a result of the harmonization of local regulations.

Creative destruction

The reconstruction of an existing jurisdiction through the diffusion of a particular set of norms and practices constitutes a third mechanism of internationalization, and it may be the most complex to understand and analyze. The international circulation of capital, whether public (aid) or private (foreign direct investment) is obviously a major vehicle for the internationalization of professional expertise: Western companies investing abroad, like governments or international financial institutions lending money, carry with them scores of lawyers and consultants, who then find themselves in a powerful position to penetrate the local markets, and in the process to impose their own definition of reality – their norms, concepts, language, tools, and so on – to eventually engage in a profound reconstruction of the local economic setting. This explains why the diffusion metaphor is often insufficient to describe the process of professional transnationalization: market penetration involves not only territorial expansion, but also forces a deep *transformation* of the local way to do business itself, which may reinforce the foreign professionals' advantage.

For instance, if economic laws in East Asia, under International Monetary Fund (IMF) influence (or some other international economic influence, such as large foreign corporations), are being transformed in a way that is consistent with US antitrust or bankruptcy law, American legal firms will obviously have the upper hand in the legal competition that opposes them to European firms for the capture of these local markets, and American law schools will become the natural place where lawyers from the region will look for training (Carruthers and Halliday 2006; Kelemen and Sibbitt 2004). In the example cited above, the American legal profession will have gained its local influence not by competing directly with entrenched local professional elites, but by engaging in what Schumpeter (1975, pp. 82–85), drawing on Marx, called "creative destruction," that is, by "revolutionizing the structure from within" and engineering a reconstruction (and in some cases a construction) of the local law itself, which may ultimately force a (superficial or thorough) reconstruction of the local legal profession along its own professional model (Dezalay and Garth, forthcoming).[2]

---

[2] A good example is the recent and dramatic rise of the presence of US law firms in foreign countries. In 1985, 80 US law firms had offices overseas that employed 803 lawyers altogether. In 1999, the number of firms had grown to 245, and they employed 4,319 lawyers (Kelemen and Sibbitt 2004, p. 114). Some US or British firms, such as Baker and McKenzie, Clifford and Chance, or Freshfields, have a *majority* of their staff in overseas offices (Sassen 2001, p. 34).

The case of economics

Intuitively, such creative destruction processes should be particularly exacerbated in the case of those professional entities, which lack both firm political control and clear jurisdictional boundaries, such as economics or consulting. What separates economists or consultants from doctors is indeed the (apparently) more fluid and "contestable" nature of their jurisdiction: while one cannot be a lawyer without passing a bar exam, or a doctor without a board certification, one can become a consultant or claim oneself as an "economist" without advanced training or licensing.[3] As Freidson (1986, p. 71) has shown, however, institutional contexts typically make sure that such discrepancies are the exception rather than the norm: universities, for instance, normally will not hire "economists" without Ph.D.s. Government agencies will act in a similar manner for high-level jobs. Formal organization and a posteriori recognition (in the form of positions reserved to credentialed economists) thus provide the basis for the formulation of a number of exclusive jurisdictional claims, such as the extensive formalization of economics positions within public administration and business.[4] Institutional, not occupational, licensing is the real source of professional power.[5] Moreover, there is little question that as a result of these mechanisms, economists regard themselves, and are regarded by others, as a well-bounded community – a feature Sarfatti-Larson (1979, pp. 220–32) long ago identified as a hallmark of professional ideology.

Nonetheless, some consequences of weaker occupational control may be considered: first, economics will be more vulnerable to competitive challenges from other professions, which try to penetrate its jurisdictional space (Abbott 1988, p. 109). Second, as a highly "heteronomous" field, economics will be subject to external social and political pressure (Lebaron 2000a). Finally (and this has not been, to my knowledge, emphasized in the literature), we should also expect economics to be especially amenable to international expansion: not hampered by the barrier of national regulations and licensing systems, it should be allowed to operate more freely across national borders. Such transnational expansion will not necessarily occur in a uniform manner, however. By and

---

[3] I borrow the term "contestable" from the industrial economics literature. According to Baumol, Panzer, and Willig (1986) a market is *contestable* when barriers to entry (such as special licenses, patents, copyrights, high fixed costs, and marketing barriers) are low, and it is *perfectly contestable* when such barriers are nonexistent.

[4] See, for instance, the existence of institutional quasi-monopolies such as the Council of Economic Advisers in the United States, the Sachverständigenrat in Germany, or the Conseil d'Analyse Économique in France.

[5] I am very grateful to an *AJS* reviewer for reminding me of this distinction.

large it has been very asymmetrical, in economics as well as in other weakly bound professions, such as consulting. The latter, for instance, is dominated by a handful of American companies with subsidiaries all over the globe (Djelic 2004). Likewise, economists who have received their doctorates from US or British institutions populate the world of economic advising, the main international economic institutions, as well as the leading economics departments and upper-level technocratic positions of many countries, particularly in the developing world. The *internationally* permeable nature of professional boundaries gives credentials acquired in the United States, and to a lesser extent in Europe, access to a geographically unspecific jurisdiction: they are not bound to the country or region that issued them but have virtually universal value. (By contrast, a US medical degree does not [yet] give its bearer the right to practice medicine in Italy.) In theory, of course, this is true of *every* advanced economics degree, no matter its geographical origin. A Brazilian doctorate *could* suffice to make someone an economist in the United States. Yet in practice, such cases are more the exception than the rule. A specific segment of the economics profession, generally US or UK educated, thus establishes its international power on the very basis of the contestability of national economics markets. In doing so, however, it makes the latter less contestable – that is, it creates new *implicit* barriers of entry and new stratification principles: everything is happening as if American graduate and professional schools (and to lesser extent European ones) were functioning as elite licensing institutions for much of the rest of the world.

This inherently *professional* transformation is of enormous *practical* consequence. The end result of this process is indeed a form of institutional and intellectual convergence between the economics professions in peripheral countries and those at the center, as foreigners and foreign-trained professionals increasingly penetrate local institutions, and as these institutions try to emulate dominant foreign models.

While neoinstitutional theorists (see especially Strang and Meyer 1994) have extensively studied the broad dynamics of diffusion processes, we still know little about the practical mechanisms that drive these transformations over the long run. In particular, the necessary revolutionary element (the "creative destruction") in the process is often overlooked in favor of the empirical fact of diffusion. It is indeed one thing to point to transnational institutions, communities, and actors and to show that they generate distinctive outcomes (e.g. the diffusion of norms about human rights or economic policies). It is quite another to show how their very existence relates to broader patterns of social and economic transformation. The next section proposes to build on insights from neoinstitutional theory, field analysis, and the sociology of professions to make sense of the internationalization of professional development dynamics in economics. I then analyze these dynamics in considerable empirical detail. Finally, the last section describes the substantive reconstructions undergone by the economics profession as it diffuses and institutionalizes widely, and suggests that transnationalism is, in fact, a key mechanism by which economists establish jurisdictional control.

Beyond diffusion: thinking about the globalization of economics

We may begin with the observation that, as a professional practice, economics diffused in a way consistent with neoinstitutional theory. The theory suggests that relatively stable forms (e.g. specialized training curricula, certification procedures, professional organizations, specific work locations) institutionalize sequentially throughout the globe. Many such forms emerged in Western Europe or the United States in the late nineteenth century or early twentieth century and were progressively reproduced, with a number of variants that more or less followed colonial, neocolonial, or, more recently, international-institutional linkages, in Latin America, Eastern Europe, Asia, and, lastly, Africa.

Figure 2.1, for instance, clearly identifies this type of pattern in the case of professional associations of economists. As expected, professional associations of economists were initially established in core countries during the nineteenth century. After World War II, such organizational patterns spread progressively to the periphery and closely followed the emergence of new nation-states. How should we, then, interpret the worldwide institutionalization of economics?

According to neoinstitutional theory, the key mechanism underlying diffusion processes is "isomorphism" – that is, the idea that distinct organizations come to structure themselves in very similar ways. DiMaggio and Powell (1983) identified three fundamental rationales for isomorphic diffusion – competitive pressure (competitive isomorphism), the compliance with external constraints (coercive isomorphism), or the normative agreement with an expert-legitimated order (normative isomorphism). Professions are part of the third category: they are among the "rationalized others" (Meyer 1994) that produce such legitimate worldviews, "modern myths" (Meyer and Rowan 1977, p. 344) that generate a large amount of highly rationalized formal structure and constitute, therefore, one of the main carriers of "normative isomorphism" (DiMaggio and Powell 1983, p. 152).

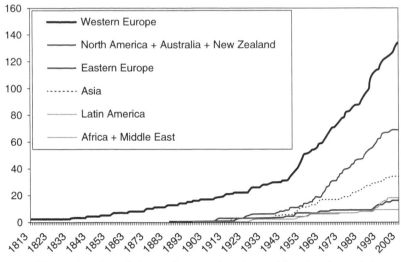

Figure 2.1 Associations of economists, by world region (cumulative findings, internationals associations not included).
Source: World Guide to Scientific Associations and Learned Societies, Saur 2002, 1997 and 1983 eds.; additional data from "Economics Associations and Learned Societies," on EDIRC (Economics Departments, Institutes and Research Centers in the World), 1995–2006, Christian Zimmermann, http://edirc.repec.org/assocs.html. Thanks to Daniel Buch for his help in collecting the data.

It might be worth restating here the theoretical boundaries of the concept of isomorphism as defined by its initial sponsors. Indeed, the term has become so successful as an empirical tool that it serves as a nearuniversal metaphor for any process of widespread institutionalization. Yet it is easy to forget that the theory was designed to apply chiefly to the *formal* traits of organizational structures. Consequently, Meyer and Rowan (1977, 1978) represent diffusion largely as a process of "decoupling" where some external features are adopted ceremoniously but contents remain largely determined by local processes and institutions.

There is certainly substantial empirical evidence that outcomes of isomorphic processes are often quite disconnected from the formal models that initiated them in the first place (see, e.g. Ferguson [1994] on development policies). Yet by emphasizing the separation between form and content, the concept still obscures a key theoretical point: namely, that the very fact of diffusion participates in the construction of the diffused form itself – in other words, that "diffusability" constitutes one of the defining elements in processes of institutional or organizational change, not simply the other way around. For the case of professions, this idea suggests that the sheer "reproducibility" of certain knowledge or organizational forms is part of what constructs them as legitimate or desirable.

Understanding which forms diffuse and which do not – pinning down the substantive conditions that support "diffusability" – therefore, remains a question of considerable theoretical importance, which I address in the next section.

A second constraint of the isomorphism metaphor (which also follows from its focus on form rather than content) is that it treats processes of diffusion primarily as the result of scripting (Meyer and Rowan 1977). Neoinstitutionalist theory regards the object of diffusion as rather invariable and concentrates on the moment of its "adoption." As some scholars have suggested (e.g. Abbott 1995, p. 876), this produces a discontinuous, rather than process-oriented, view of the very changes the theory seeks to understand.[6] By isolating a "diffusing element" of interest (an organizational practice, a technical standard, a formal right), the concept of isomorphism thus overshadows the fact that diffusion is a multifaceted process, involving ideas, actors, and organizations *coevolving in the very process of diffusion*. Hence the example of bankruptcy law mentioned earlier suggests that the diffusion of a particular legal tool to East Asia cannot happen without triggering a whole set of institutional changes in the very structure of the legal profession itself. Similarly, when the practice of economics diffuses worldwide, it relies on certain organizational arrangements, worldviews, social relations, and policy tools, all of which diffuse at the same time and are being tested – and contested – simultaneously. It is thus the transformation of this entire ecology, beyond that of its constitutive elements, which has to be accounted for.

Furthermore, the dynamics of diffusion are very unsettled and constantly changing. Which knowledges, which forms of expertise will disseminate is driven in great part by intraprofessional struggles and by what Bourdieu calls *field dynamics*: economists, for instance, use international arenas to settle disciplinary and ideological conflicts, and to assert their control over a particular geographical, intellectual, or practical turf *from other economists* with whom they are competing. As suggested earlier, the main reason why economics is particularly susceptible to such struggles has to do with the contestability of its professional market and the heteronomous nature of its intellectual and material jurisdiction.

---

[6] As others have suggested (e.g. Fligstein 2001), the emphasis on scripting also makes a proper theory of action unnecessary, if not contradictory.

Finally, as pointed out by Abbott (1988, 2005), it may be relevant to analyze transformations in one particular professional ecology in relation to concomitant changes in other professional ecologies competing with it, or in other institutional ecologies, which are linked to it – that is, to focus not only on intraprofessional but also interprofessional conflicts. Although Abbott himself does not draw implications of his theory for the study of "international" professional enterprises, his focus on the interactions between the work of professionals, its knowledge or discursive base, and the jurisdictional domain they claim control upon lends itself naturally to such an extension. In this perspective, the internationalization of jurisdictions may become one of the means whereby interprofessional competition is carried out. This process will, for instance, be reflected in the successful displacement, by economists with international capital (i.e., international credentials and experience), of locally bound lawyers and engineers from the state jurisdiction – a typical pattern in Latin America (Markoff and Montecinos 1993; Babb 2001; Dezalay and Garth 2002).

In other words, we ought to move from studying the *globalization* of the particular professional domain of economics to considering the *global logic* of its professional development as such – that is, to include in our study the interactions between economists and their jurisdictions, both local and global. Understanding the problem from the point of view of such a "global" logic does not mean, however, that "isomorphic" considerations should be abandoned. The approach outlined here, by contrast, aims to build isomorphic processes directly into a broader dynamic and ecological framework, which analyzes transnationalism as a fundamental element in the dialectical relationship between economics and the economy. In other words, we have to move beyond the concept of diffusion to show how economics (like capitalism) *constantly constructs and reconstructs itself* in the course of expanding its influence worldwide.

The remainder of this article is devoted to an in-depth empirical analysis of the mechanisms that sustain the transnationalization of economics. This strategy allows me to explore the complex global dynamics between the diffusion of knowledge, the diffusion of professional practices, the transformation of jurisdictions, and the changing occupational/social identity of economic professionals.

In the next section I argue that three factors have been critical to the institutionalization of economics on a global scale: (1) the establishment of a broadly universalistic rhetoric within economic science, (2) the transformation of economic knowledge into a technology of political and bureaucratic power, and (3) the existence of transnational linkages dominated by the United States. The first point emphasizes the fact that the substantive nature of economic knowledge is not neutral vis-a-vis the process of internationalization. The neoclassical paradigm, evolved mainly in the West, was constructed historically as an abstract representation of the economy, which is not vested in specific local or historical experiences. Under this scientific form, then, economic knowledge appeared inherently transferable and "transformative," both politically and institutionally, thereby authorizing easy replication and diffusion independently from the national context. The second point suggests that the worldwide rise of economics as a professional practice relied on a profound and global transformation of the role of the state, whose ability to *act on the economy* came to be defined as a legitimate expression of national sovereignty. The third point documents the mechanisms of construction of these communities of experts that are entrusted with the authority to "act" upon the economy in many countries around the world. I show that these communities, particularly in the developing world, have had to rely extensively on outside sources of legitimation, both virtually through the uniformizing culture of the neoclassical paradigm, and materially through countless formal and informal linkages with international organizations and foreign scholarly and professional communities.

In the final section, I analyze the symbolic and material rewards that economics derives from its transnationalism. I suggest that their global linkages give economic professionals the authority to reconstruct societies according to the principles of the dominant economic ideology. However, the effects of these transformations are not only local, but also feed back into the professionalization and social definition of economists worldwide, sustaining a process of intellectual and professional "creative destruction" and thereby the continued economic vitality of the field. Economics, then, works on itself in part by continuously capturing and reinterpreting international arenas in order to formulate new intellectual and professional claims.

Before I move on to the more empirical part of the discussion, however, a few words of caution are warranted. First, my intention is neither to argue that the globalization of economics is a uniquely modern phenomenon nor to deny the validity of the considerable literature that documents the historical importance of cross-national intellectual transfers in economics (as well as in other sciences and disciplines).[7] After

---

[7] See Wuthnow (1987, chap. 7) on science. On economics, see, for instance, Tribe (1988) on the influence of Smithianism in Germany, Herbst (1965) on the influence of historicism in the United States, or Turner (1989) on the postwar dialogues between Cambridge (UK) and Cambridge (Mass.).

all, local traditions are always complex cultural constructions involving positive and negative positioning toward, and appropriation of, foreign elements and references (Molnar 2004). The intensity and nature of these transnational processes vary historically, however, and my contention is that the current period is worthy of a specific treatment. As I show below, the twentieth century has witnessed the progressive legitimization of economics to provide not simply discourses about the world we live in but also systematic strategies, designs, and sophisticated tools that transform and even engineer or "perform" this world (Callon 1998; MacKenzie and Millo 2003; Ferraro, Pfeffer, and Sutton 2005). This dialectical relationship between economics and the economy, which is so characteristic of our modernity, means that we cannot treat the globalization of the economics profession independently from the economic transformations it produces and responds to.[8]

Second, my focus on the global dimensions of professionalization in economics should not override considerations about the persistent diversity of national experiences. To a large extent, all countries have followed their unique route to fill the emerging niches for economic expertise in science, policy, or business. In older polities (e.g. France, Germany, Japan), distinctive economics traditions got entrenched quite early in the educational and administrative systems, and continue to display original features stemming from their conditions of emergence and maintained, in some cases, by the relatively closed nature of their civil service and higher education systems (Fourcade, forthcoming).

The universalism of economic knowledge

Economic knowledge has sought to formulate itself in general terms from the very beginning. In seventeenth- and eighteenth-century French and British writings, such a quest was often represented by the search for "natural laws." Certain policy principles (e.g. free trade) were then defended on the grounds that trying to bypass them would upset the natural order. During the nineteenth century, these universalistic aspirations became more explicitly cast in the discourse of science. Historians

---

[8] The literature on this question is vast (see mainly Hall 1989; Campbell 1998, 2002). Studies tend to agree that "knowledge regimes" (in this case, the terms of the debate set by academic economics) play an important role in "regulating what sorts of arguments and evidence can be heard" (Breslau 1997, p. 894), but they tend to be suspicious of the specific argument that the presence of economists as top-level technocrats and politicians makes a large difference in economic policy. This is especially true of Western countries, which have witnessed dramatic changes in their policy regimes since the 1970s without any significant influx of economists in government (Fourcade-Gourinchas and Babb 2002).

have repeatedly shown how scientific expansion profoundly affected intellectual developments in Victorian England and progressively replaced the authority of the "men of letters" by that of the "scientific experts." Between the 1850s and the 1900s, most knowledge enterprises in search for legitimacy (e.g. the emerging disciplinary fields of sociology, economics, and even education, history, and theology) formulated claims to full scientific status (Heyck 1982, p. 121; Soffer 1978).

British economic writers cultivated the analogy with the natural sciences (physics in particular) in a very self-conscious manner (Mirowski 1994). Many were trained in mathematics, and indeed were often mathematicians turned economists (Weintraub 2002). The domination of a scientific imagery in economics established itself further during the twentieth century, especially in the Anglo-Saxon countries and in France among public engineers, leading to the strengthening of the neoclassical approach and the corresponding weakening of historical and institutional influences coming out of the German tradition. By the end of World War II, the latter had lost much of their original appeal among younger cohorts of economists (Yonay 1998). The methodology of the field was set in a positivist framework, which Friedman codified in a tremendously influential essay (Friedman 1953). The use of mathematics, both as applied technique (econometrics) and as theoretical medium (models), became legitimate practice – the accepted way to "do science" (Reder 1999; Mirowski 2002). Bibliometric analyses of academic publications in economics have, for instance, shown the rapid increase, between 1970 and 1990, of the relative impact of journals focused on mathematical and statistical techniques (Laband and Piette 1994).

This disciplinary evolution of economics is not without important organizational consequences. A specific language is a fundamental element in the establishment of a coherent jurisdictional monopoly. Bourdieu argues that rational, formalist language fulfills a specific purpose by granting a "symbolic effectiveness" to whoever commands it (Bourdieu 1987, 1993). In a similar vein, Abbott suggests that professions use abstract knowledge (mainly in the sense of positive formalism) in order to strengthen their jurisdiction: abstraction authorizes the creative redefinition of the professional domain, makes the seizing of new problems and new tasks possible, and thereby enables survival in the competitive system of professions (Abbott 1988, pp. 8, 102–4).

We can regard international expansion as a key aspect of jurisdictional strengthening and point to the rhetorical qualities of abstract knowledge in authorizing such a process. As many authors have noticed, the purity of form produced by economics' "rhetoric of quantification" is in part the source of its rhetorical appeal (McCloskey 1985). First, mathematical formalism acts as an effective agent of disciplinary homogenization, and not simply because any mathematical language is, in essence, a universalistic device. By providing a medium of communication that overcomes linguistic barriers, it served historically (and still does) as a powerful element for the integration of foreign scholars and for the construction of an international community of practitioners.[9] Today, Williamson remarks, "an economist's nationality (does) not contribute significantly to explaining the techniques that he or she uses and the beliefs that he or she holds" (Williamson 1996, p. 365; also see Reay [2004] on the uniformity of beliefs within American economics).

Second, the intellectual and methodological universalism of neoclassical economics means that, both as an academic corpus and as a source for policy design, it is more amenable to diffusion. Academic economics relies on abstract, universal reasoning in terms of "representative agents" and "representative economy," with an essentially metaphorical connection to real-life situations. Economic problems are detached from their local (historical and geographical) context, and are generally understood to be instances of some universal phenomena. The prosperity of the "mic-macmetrics" (microeconomics, macroeconomics, econometrics) regime at the core of American graduate programs, and the concomitant weakening of area studies, economic history, and the history of economic thought since the 1960s, as well as the disappearance of foreign language requirements, epitomize the ideal of a "monoeconomics," tool-centered knowledge relatively insensitive to historical and geographical variations (Hirschman 1981; Hodgson 1996; though the recent wave of neoinstitutional scholarship tends to make this point more relative). The collapse of specificity oriented paradigms (most notably development economics), attests to the widespread conviction among mainstream economics practitioners that countries do not fundamentally differ from one another, and allows for a similar treatment of the rich and the poor, the agricultural and the industrial, the open and the closed economies, and so on.[10] It is, for instance, quite remarkable that economists routinely locate their claims to expertise in certain technical areas, like

---

[9] For example, many European emigrants (and, among them, many mathematically inclined members of the Austrian school) entered the American academia during the interwar period and World War II (see Krohn 1993; Dezalay and Garth 1998). These studies, however, rightly point out that the mathematization of economics during the interwar period is as much the result of the integration of these European-born foreigners as it is the cause of their easy incorporation.

[10] "Are the Poor Different?" *The Economist*, April 27, 1996.

monetary or fiscal policy, and much more rarely in particular geographical contexts, like individual countries or regions, which are preferably left to the less "scientific" enterprises of sociologists or political scientists. Third, the production of theories in which social units appear comparable (Meyer 1994; Strang and Meyer 1994), or of organizational designs and policies that hold "universal" validity, has a neutralizing effect that helps rationalize a post-hoc consensus among economists and makes it appear as the outcome of the cumulative progress of science – hence legitimating isomorphic diffusion as a positive, rather than normative phenomenon and concealing its hegemonic origins (Bourdieu and Wacquant 1998).

The worldwide institutionalization of economics

Admittedly, the universalism of economic knowledge and the relative consensus it produces on basic economic policy prescriptions (e.g. the virtues of competition, the mobility of goods and factors of production, the flexibility of prices, free trade, the emphasis on efficiency as opposed to equity, the emphasis on market mechanisms as opposed to public management, etc.) both constitute powerful arguments for its practical implementation. Yet why modern nation-states have become so preoccupied with the production of economic knowledge and receptive to the arguments of economists is not, at first, completely obvious. In this section, I argue that economics institutionalized worldwide because it was closely tied to the emergence and consolidation of the nation-state. In that sense, the international "diffusion" of economics is partly a by-product of the "diffusion" of the nation-state project itself – and more specifically the rise of the university and public bureaucracy as central components of a sovereign polity.

The rise of economics

Scholars have long recognized that the international diffusion, from the end of the nineteenth century, of universities and public bureaucracies as core elements of the nation served as a powerful vehicle for the expansion of the social sciences in general, and of economics in particular (Wagner, Weiss, et al. 1991; Wagner, Wittrock, et al. 1991). First, as secular substitutes for religion, social scientific subjects were increasingly seen as a central element in the broader societal purpose of higher education: to "construct" the nation by providing a moral education to the masses and a technocratic training to the elite. Second, economic knowledge was an integral part of the construction of national bureaucratic capabilities in the twentieth century.

Continental European countries such as Sweden and Germany were first to institutionalize the study of political economy within universities in the eighteenth century. As higher education systems expanded and consolidated during the second half of the nineteenth century, the study of economics established its place across the rest of Europe, as well as in North America and Japan. Some Latin American nations created economics faculties during the interwar period: for instance, in Chile, the Catholic University opened a School of Economics and Business Administration in 1924, "largely devoted to training in accounting and commerce" (Montecinos and Markoff 2000, p. 114). Mexico established an "economics section" at the national university (Universidad Nacional Autónoma de México, or UNAM) in 1929, whose purpose was chiefly to train experts for the state bureaucracy (Babb 2001). The majority of the world, however, had to wait until after World War II to follow suit, with Africa being the most delayed (often until the 1970s–1980s).

Table 2.1 reports the expansion of economics faculties worldwide during the second half of the twentieth century. Two points are worth commenting upon. First is the obvious prevalence of economics in educational and research systems worldwide.[11] Today virtually every country in the world organizes higher education in the discipline, and has often instituted compulsory economics courses in lower grade levels as well. By 1959, about 49% of the world's universities included faculties of economics; by 1971, however, this percentage reached almost 61% (it has slightly declined since then, to 57% in 1991). Additional data from Frank and Gabler (2006) shows that economics also grew as a relative proportion of university faculty, from 1.7% of world university faculty in 1915–35 to nearly 4% in 1976–95, again reaching a plateau toward the mid 1970s.[12] A second important point is the distinctiveness of the

---

[11] The trends in academic research are similar to those in higher education; for instance, the number of specialized economic reviews worldwide increased five times between 1959 and 1993, from about 500 to over 2,500 (source: UNESCO, *International Bibliography of Economics*, [1955] 2005, vols. 1–52).

[12] Frank and Gabler's data show that although the social sciences generally increased their share of university faculty worldwide, from about 10% in 1915–35 to 30% in 1976–95, the paths of the different disciplines can be quite varied, from rapid growth in sociology (but of course sociology was barely institutionalized before World War II), solid growth in economics and political science, to the flatter profiles of psychology and the "boom-and-bust" pattern in anthropology, which mirrors the rise and fall of colonial empires.

Table 2.1 *Universities and Economics Faculties Worldwide, 1959–1991*

	1959			1971			1991		
	NCW	CW	Total	NCW	CW	Total	NCW	CW	Total
Universities, total ...	391	87	478	877	244	1,121	1,762	435	2,197
Economics faculties, total ...	177	59	236	466	214	680	959	297	1,256
% economics ...	45.2	67.8	49.3	53.1	87.7	60.6	54.4	68.2	57.1

Note: CW=commonwealth; NCW=noncommonwealth. The United States was excluded because of sheer size. Japan was excluded on the basis of the complexity of the information recorded in the *International Handbook of Universities*, which made it difficult to adjudicate between different institutional forms (universities, specialized vocational schools, research institutes). In most cases, I counted as "economics faculties" all faculties including "economics" in their title (e.g. "faculty of law and economics" or "faculty of commerce and economics"). I also recorded as "economics faculties" certain faculties with different titles (e.g. "faculty of social sciences") that nonetheless offered specialized graduate degrees in economics. Data exist for the most recent period (e.g. 2001); however, the changing logic of inclusion in the *International Handbook of Universities* and the broadening of the definition of "university" to include all specialized schools risks making the coding inconsistent with earlier periods. (The *Commonwealth* database, on the other hand, has remained quite consistent.)
Source: International Handbook of Universities (1959, 1971, 1991) and *Commonwealth Universities Yearbook* (1959, 1971, 1991).

commonwealth countries, which have inherited the greater emphasis of their colonial power on the core status of economics as a discipline. Finally, a closer look at the data suggests that everywhere economics has undergone a process of academic autonomization (from either the "social sciences," law, or commerce) in addition to growth. Therefore, beyond the empirical fact of the worldwide institutionalization of economics in practically every nation's higher education system, we also need to account for the field's *growing centrality* in it – until the 1970s at least.

I argue below that *economics has become more central to the nation* (as evidenced by its growing place in the university curriculum) *because the nation itself has become more economic*: over the course of the twentieth century, acting upon the economy became an increasingly legitimate practice, carried out by ever more specialized experts. Indeed, the worldwide expansion of economics relied first and foremost on the idea, institutionalized broadly in the postwar period, that economic development and growth can be engineered, or that poorly performing economies can be fixed. In this process of institutionalization of an intellectual object called "the economy" (Polanyi 1944; Hirschman 1977), the latter was socially constructed so that "experts" could claim analytical and tutelary power over it.

The ongoing reconstruction of national societies as economies

In a certain sense, "individual economies" would not "exist" without the regulation, intervention, and representation operated by economic science, acting on behalf of the nation-state (Callon 1998; Mitchell 1998). The concept of "economy" – understood as the "totality of relations of production, distribution and consumption of goods and services within a given country or region" (Mitchell 1998, p. 84; also see Breslau 2003), is itself very recent: it emerged sometime between the Great Depression and World War II, in the wake of the national accounts and econometric revolutions, on the one hand, and the emergence of new discourses about government, on the other. It is only since then that nations have come to "imagine" themselves as "economic communities," to paraphrase Anderson's (1983) felicitous formula.

As they organized around the political model of a sovereign state (Meyer et al. 1997), new countries sought to reconstruct their societies as "legitimate" economies, turning their territories into distinct and self-contained economic spaces by creating separate economic instruments (currencies, tariffs, exchange controls, a fiscal system, etc.) and institutions (central banks, stock exchanges, ministries of economics and finance, development and planning agencies, etc.). These designs, in turn, helped construct the idea that the national economy is a "real thing" that should be acted upon.

Figure 2.2 reports the timing of founding of the world's central banks. The movement of establishing a central, nationwide banking institution started in Europe between the seventeenth and the nineteenth centuries. Many of these institutions then established issue monopoly during the second half of the nineteenth century. The United States founded the Federal Reserve Board in 1913. In 1920 the League of Nations unanimously passed the resolution that "in countries where there is no central bank of issue, one should be established" (Helleiner 2003, p. 146). British and US policy makers, who held considerable power over these institutions, actively promoted the central bank with monopoly note issue as a desirable and necessary component of a modern nation-state. These officials strongly believed that by insulating monetary management from government control, central banks would become a

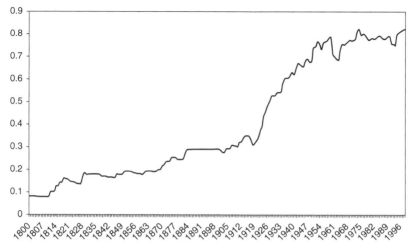

Figure 2.2 Central banks of the world (density), 1880–1998.
Source: Data on central banks compiled from Alan J. Day, ed., 1986,
*Government Economic Agencies of the World: An International Directory
of Govermental Organizations Concerned with Economic Development
and Planning;* completed with information from individual world
central banks (accessed through the directory Central Banks of the
World, New York University School of Law, www.law.nyu.edu/
centralbankscenter/banks/index.html, accessed on 3/13/2006).
Data on independent nation-states graciously provided by Evan
Schofer (see Schofer 2003).

fundamental pillar of stability in the gold standard system (Helleiner
2003, p. 148). The main Latin American and Eastern European central
banks were created during the 1920s, with tacit US support.[13] In other
countries, the founding of central banks followed quite closely the timing
of decolonization, usually taking place within five to ten years of
independence.

Why nations come to see such institutional designs as desirable is
not necessarily a simple matter. Certainly technological requirements
to produce a viable economic space in a complex environment play
their part, yet the definition of what constitutes "appropriate" economic
behavior, and what the "right" economic institutions and policies are for
implementing it, are also very much the result of a process of normative

---

[13] Edwin Kemmerer, a professor at Princeton University, thus helped establish central
banks in Chile (1925), Columbia (1923), Ecuador (1927), Bolivia (1928–29), Peru
(1923), and Guatemala (1929; Helleiner 2003, p. 147).

construction dominated by powerful actors and countries, as is clear from the above example. From an external point of view, the setting up of certain economic infrastructures and the reliance on specialized economic expertise to manage them come to be seen by local elites as a vital step to acquire – or maintain – a place in the worldwide community of national economic actors and to look like responsible states, legitimate trading partners, sound international borrowers, or attractive locations for foreign direct investment (Schneider 1998; Polillo and Guillén 2005; Brune, Garrett, and Kogut 2004). From an internal point of view, these institutions serve to establish and reinforce national political sovereignty (Helleiner 2003).

The reconstruction of states around economics

The ongoing reconstruction of economies is thus inextricably linked to the ongoing reconstruction and rationalization of states as economic actors. As national states started to assume increasingly complex tasks in macroeconomic management and social reform after World War II, "acting" upon the economy was redefined as a normal and desirable expression of state power. And as politics was redefined as the pursuit of growth, economic specialists secured an area of legitimacy by linking their expert capabilities to various "public goods": fiscal capacity, full employment, development, industrialization, and monetary stability, among others. In many cases (e.g. in continental Europe, Latin America, and Japan), public authorities sponsored directly the foundation or expansion of economics training programs as part of their processes of bureaucratic consolidation. Large contingents of economic specialists entered the world's public bureaucracies in the 1960s and 1970s, a rising class of technocrats with sophisticated technical skills. The worldwide institutionalization of the economics jurisdiction, then, was first and foremost carried out in the universities and public bureaucracies of emerging or consolidating nation-states.

In short, it was set in motion by processes of *national* construction. Ironically, of course, the rise of economic technocracies would ultimately undermine one of the very institutions they originated from – the national state itself. With the return of economic liberalism, national economic institutions have been progressively emptied of their politically transformative meaning and redefined as objects for efficient management rather than as means toward the realization of loftier ideals. The decline and universal disparagement of interventionist schemes like national planning on the one hand (Scott 1998; Easterly 2002), and the growing assertiveness of the neoliberal technology of government (Eyal 2000) – which rejects both national boundaries and public management as sources of economic inefficiency – on the other, have made this transformation more complete.[14]

The advent of grave economic crises and subsequent paradigmatic changes in policy have pushed these transformations of the state structure further, by making the claimed ability to identify problems and anomalies in the economy and, consequently, the ability to govern the reform or transition processes that necessarily ensue from these diagnoses a critical *political*, not simply bureaucratic, asset. Thus the reconstruction of the world economies along freer market lines was accompanied by the increased political prominence of economic management institutions (such as central banks, ministries of finance) and their leaders. As Markoff and Montecinos (1993) demonstrated in a landmark article, economic experts themselves have gained access to political leadership in their countries' party and cabinet systems, where they often disturbed the traditional supremacy of lawyers (also see Dezalay and Garth 2002). In 1993, *The Economist* noted that "finance ministers in nine of twelve large third-world or former communist countries have an economic degree, and all but one of the central-bank governors are economists."[15]

Centeno has shown that the proportion of Mexican cabinet members with a degree in economics in this country rose from less than 10% to about 50% between the 1950s and the early 1980s (Centeno 1994, p. 121). Several of the contenders in recent Chilean presidential elections were trained Ph.D. economists (Montecinos 1998), as were Argentina's finance minister and presidential candidate Domingo Cavallo (a Harvard economics graduate and certainly Latin America's highest-profile economic consultant throughout the 1990s) and former Mexican president Ernesto Zedillo (1994–2000). In Central and Eastern Europe (e.g. Hungary, the Czech Republic, Poland, and Russia, to a lesser extent) "reform economists" also rose to political prominence, undertaking programs of transition to the market economy.[16] In 1992, the Czech Republic underwent a monetarist turn under the guidance of Vaclav Klaus, whose first government included seven trained economists

---

[14] This shift is particularly obvious in the redefinition of the purpose of economic development from an older, "political economy" model where economic expertise is embedded in broad, often transformative goals, toward a more "managerial" model (Santiso 2002) particularly noticeable in the peripheral states after the 1980s debt crisis. This "governmentalization" of the state (Foucault 1979) is, however, no less transformative of people's lives.

[15] "Economists (Should) Rule, OK." *The Economist*, April 14, 1993.

[16] Although connections with foreign works and academic communities were conspicuous in their case too, Kovács (1992, 1994) shows that the critique of the central planning system they forged was largely based on their own experience with it and on their pragmatic attempts at reforming it.

in key positions (Eyal 2000).[17] A recent study of 160 countries worldwide showed that in 1998, 79 of them had at least one government leader with an economics degree (including 16 countries, mainly Middle Eastern and Latin American, with at least one leader with *a Western economics Ph.D.* [Shayo 2002, p. 27]).[18] Similarly, a survey of the world's central bankers in the 1990s reports that a third of them have been educated in the United States, and one-fifth in the United Kingdom (Lebaron 2000b, p. 106).

This economicization of the technocracy on the one hand, and of the political elite on the other (particularly noticeable in middle-income countries) are two dimensions of the institutionalization of economic knowledge within the state in the twentieth century. The significance of these transformations goes beyond the fact that economists worldwide have captured important jurisdictions within the state. More important, they suggest that *the state itself has been redefined as a key professional terrain for economists.* In short, it has been reconstructed and governmentalized so as to legitimize the claims of economists. Economics has become central to the nation, then, because the nation has become more economic. I discuss in the section below the channels through which these reconstructions have taken place, emphasizing especially the role of international linkages.

Global social structures: transnational flows, international institutions, and hybridization

If economics institutionalized globally for reasons that had much to do with the global institutionalization and economicization of the nation state itself as a legitimate political form, the shape and content of the professions that were being created still owe a lot to processes of international emulation and transfer, and to transnational socialization and policy networks. After the universalism of economic knowledge and the worldwide institutionalization of economics as expert and scientific practice, then, transnational connectedness constitutes a third dimension underlying the process of global professionalization in economics. I discuss below some of the global social structures (Knorr-Cetina and Bruegger 2002) that sustain these communities.

---

[17] With a few exceptions, however, most of these Eastern European economists were educated at home, although some of them (e.g. the Czech monetarists) had spent time studying abroad.

[18] In the study, "government leader" was defined as "the president or head of state; the prime minister; the vice-president or vice-premier; and the ministers of finance, economy, budget, treasury" (whenever they exist; Shayo 2002, p. 27).

International influences in the rise of economics

Emerging economics programs in peripheral countries were often set up in imitation of some Western archetype. Germany, England, and France each provided strong, alternative models for organizing economics as an academic domain – as they did for the entire university system (Karady 1998).[19] Colonial European powers exported educational designs to their core colonies during the first half of the twentieth century. In Egypt, the institutionalization of economics borrowed both from the French model (with the organization of economics as a subordinate subject in the law faculties) and from the British (with the establishment of economics courses in faculties of commerce [Messiha 1954]). In India, the Oxford program of PPE (politics, philosophy, and economics) was adopted extensively (Ambirajan 1996, p. 82). In Indonesia during the colonial period, economics as well as the other social sciences were part of the law curriculum – a pattern consonant with continental European influences. Other countries, including many independent nations, borrowed more idiosyncratically, often for ideological or strategic reasons. Thus in Thaïland, the early curricula in economics also took some inspiration from the European system, and were designed in a bureaucratic fashion, that is, primarily to "serve the state and the government" (Kohkongka 1985). Latin American nations imitated the French extensively, while German influence was prominent in the design of Japanese institutions of economics education. Finally, Eastern Europe and Russia/the Soviet Union provided another model altogether, dominated by specialized institutes and academies connected to the state administration.

After World War II, international exchanges and influences became more and more centered on the Anglo-Saxon pole, and within it, the United States, which from then on provided the main model for the organization of economics education and expertise, even among other first world countries. Part of the United States' influence on the new institutions of academic and bureaucratic economics in the nonsocialist world was a matter of sheer hegemony. Scientifically, the center of academic economics had decisively moved to the United States during the war and immediate after-war period. Politically, the country had been extraordinarily influential in designing the post-war international economic order of "embedded liberalism" (Ruggie 1982; Ikenberry 1992). The post-1945 context, then, placed the United States in an unparalleled position to export its own ideologies, meanings, and representations, not

---

[19] The German model of research organization, for instance, exerted a powerful influence on the American social sciences (and especially economics) at the end of the nineteenth century (Haskell 1977; Herbst 1965).

by outright force, but rather through the "structural" channels of its own domination in international politics, science, economic relations, and popular culture.

One of the channels of international hegemony in the post-war era came from a large-scale and purposive use of philanthropy. Postgraduate economics programs were set up in collaboration with international foundations, which sponsored prolonged visits from foreign professors and researchers, most of them from the United States. For peripheral countries, such educational linkages often constituted a means to raise their own local institutions' profiles by associating them with the international community of researchers, which controlled reputations. For organizations and governments in rich countries, motivations may have been diverse, but in the context of the Cold War they were often straightforwardly political. The American economic aid programs of the 1950s and 1960s, for instance, were unambiguously aimed at preventing countries from joining the communist camp, as well as at helping to open up new markets. From that perspective, disseminating a liberal worldview by sending out Western economists to work in foreign countries and professionalizing the study of economics there seemed like a matter of national interest. This position was particularly well articulated by American state organizations and private foundations. As Berman argues, "Foundation personnel felt that the socialization of key Third-World nationals into the norms of Western social science could play a determining role in helping to ensure that those individuals would follow development paths that, minimally, were not antagonistic to the interests of the United States" (Berman 1983, p. 83; see Guilhot 2005 for an update on the role of American foundations).

Core countries, and the United States in particular, thus contributed directly to the consolidation of economics scientific communities at the periphery, and the diffusion of a model of professional legitimacy rooted in the academic system (Lourciro 1998, p. 43). During the early post-war decades, at a time when local training in economics was either poor or barely existent, international institutions and American foundations organized economic curricula for government officials and other important actors from the developing world. The United Nations' Economic Commission for Latin America, set up in 1948 and famous for its "historical structuralist" theories of development and for its support of import substitution industrialization, had a major influence in educating public sector technocrats in the region during the 1960s (Haddad 1981). In 1954 the World Bank established its Economic Development Institute, which provided ready-made teaching and training materials in the areas of macroeconomics and development policy.

Beginning in the 1950s and 1960s, the intellectual and institutional framework of the social sciences worldwide started undergoing rapid expansion and transformation. Foreign experts were actively involved in the construction of powerful university, research, and policy bases for economics in peripheral countries. Joan Robinson, the renowned Cambridge economist, once bitterly remarked that what she called the "bastard" Keynesian doctrine "evolved in the United States, invaded the economics faculties of the world, floating on the wings of the almighty dollar" (quoted in Turner 1989, p. 112). Whether the picture is as gloomy as she painted it remains a matter for discussion, yet it is unquestionable that the financial involvement of American organizations was considerable. The Ford Foundation, for instance, which established its Economic Development and Administration Program in 1953, became "the largest financial supporter of social science research in Latin America" (Berman 1983, pp. 79–80; also see Loureiro 1996 and Dezalay and Garth 2002 on the role of the Ford Foundation in Brazilian economics).[20] It was remarkably active in Asia as well, where its grants helped create important research organizations in India, Pakistan, and Indonesia.[21] In Africa, the foundations also supported universities and social sciences research institutes, especially in locally powerful states (see, e.g. the West African Institute of Social and Economic Research in Nigeria or the Uganda-based East African Institute for Social Research).

The transnational socialization of economists

Direct financial involvement by American organizations thus played an important role in shaping the design of economic policy and research institutions at the periphery. Yet the vehicles of professional socialization are transnational in other ways. In part this is the result of the extremely hierarchical structure of economics as a scientific enterprise. The top American economics departments represent the vast majority of the authoritative work produced by the discipline, and they exercise a considerable amount of hierarchical control over the rest of the field (Whitley 1983, 1984; Han 2003). As suggested earlier individual researchers in these institutions exhibit a large degree of consensus about the procedures that are necessary to achieve "science" in economics. Certainly there are bitter controversies about ways to model

[20] A precedent for all these ventures existed in the involvement of foundations, particularly the Rockefeller Foundation, in financing *European* social science during the interwar period (see Arnove 1980; Fisher 1993).

[21] The Pakistan Institute of Development Economics was thus modeled after the Brookings Institution in the United States and the National Institute of Economic and Social Research (NIESR) in Britain (see Rosen 1985; Berman 1983, pp. 83–84).

economic behavior – about fundamental hypotheses, and about the goals of economic policies. Yet mathematical models, by and large, are widely perceived as a rhetorical necessity, as *the* natural scientific medium (McCloskey 1985). Students in core departments are generally taught standardized rules for exercising their skills and judging the abilities of others to "do" economics (Klamer and Colander 1990), so that the boundaries of what constitutes "serious" work in economics are fairly explicit and clearly enforced.

In contrast to other fields of expertise or scholarship, and especially other social sciences, one of the distinctive traits of the practice of economics worldwide is its *globalized* (as opposed to purely *global*) character. The existence of a "Nobel" prize in economics, and of distinguished international awards, such as a fellowship of the Econometric Society, suggests the image of a field where international consensus on excellence is routinely and easily achieved.[22] (Of course, the construction of such an image is perhaps one of the most important functions of these awards.) Individual economic specialists tend to define themselves in relation to a transnational, Western-dominated status hierarchy, which commands implicit, yet powerful, influence upon their immediate professional environment. The internationalization of reputation and evaluation mechanisms has led the authority of individuals with foreign (and especially American) credentials to rise inexorably.[23]

International student flows

International education networks, which encourage elite students from foreign countries to train abroad, have always existed. Generations of students from the Far East were educated in Japan or China. The Central and Eastern European countries used to send students to the USSR. Thanks to their colonial past, British, French, and German universities have traditionally trained large numbers of foreign individuals. The last 20 years, however, have witnessed a general reinforcement of American and British influence in the education of foreign nationals, particularly noticeable in economics. The United States' share of the world foreign student population has hovered around one-third between the 1960s

---

[22] In spite of its name, the economics "Nobel Prize" is in fact awarded annually by the Royal Bank of Sweden. See also Lebaron (2002).

[23] As is well known, scientific publications can be hierarchically ranked worldwide based on citation counts. The Social Science Citation Index, which constitutes the most complete database for this purpose, indexes only about 120 (most cited) economic journals worldwide. These are overwhelmingly Western (if not American), and (with a few exceptions) they are also representative of the neoclassical orthodoxy. English is by far the dominant language, even among foreign publications included in the SSCI.

and the 1990s (Research Institute for Higher Education 1989, p. 289; UNESCO). In 2000, nearly 26% of all graduate students in the United States had temporary student visas, yet the figure for economics was 54%: more foreign students today get a Ph.D. in economics in American universities than do native-born students, with the largest contingents coming from Asia (South and East), Western Europe, and Latin America (National Science Foundation 2000; also see Aslanbeigui and Montecinos 1998).[24] In England, the proportion of foreign students in 1991 reached 47%, up from 39% a decade earlier (National Science Foundation 2000). Again, the figures for economics are much more dramatic. A recent Economic and Social Research Council report stated that barely 10% of the students enrolled in Ph.D. programs in top-rated UK economics departments are British citizens (Machin and Oswald 1999).

By contrast, the share of the world foreign student population going to France and Germany has steadily declined in the last two decades.[25] The proportion of foreign students in French universities, for instance, has dropped from 13.6% in 1985 to 8.6% in 1996. In addition, the low tuition policy in French and German higher education tends to attract students from poorer world regions. In 1996–97, slightly over 50% of foreign students in France, but 63.4% of foreign students in economics, came from African countries.[26]

The importance of foreign graduates (and, especially, given their sheer weight in the foreign student population, of US graduates) on the intellectual makeup of national fields of economic knowledge cannot be underestimated. In the post-war period, returning graduates with doctorates from American institutions constituted an essential channel for the profound transformation, and internationalization, of the national educational and research systems in economics, as well as of the main institutions for economic policy. In particular, they often played a critical role in the establishment of economic research and policy organizations in peripheral countries, imitating Western models perceived as successful (e.g. the Brookings Institution was widely copied). From the 1960s on in many third-world countries, newly created development planning agencies and key economic administrations were typically staffed with native economic experts who had graduated from top American universities. Loureiro's (1998, p. 49) work on Brazil shows that among the 70% of

---

[24] In "science, engineering and health" fields (National Science Foundation 2002).

[25] From 12% to 11% for France between the 1960s and the 1990s, and 10% to 4.5% for Germany over the same period (UNESCO).

[26] The percentage of foreign doctoral students in Germany has also slightly declined from about 8% in 1980 to about 6.5% in 1993 (National Science Foundation 2000).

officials from the Central Bank who did postgraduate work over the 1965–95 period, 54% studied in the United States. The case of the "Chicago Boys" in Chile is perhaps one of the most extreme examples of such transfers, although it is by no means an isolated one.[27] More generally, Ivy League-educated economics graduates have shaped much of the economic policy of Latin American countries since the 1980s debt crisis (*Business Week* 1992; Markoff and Montecinos 1993). In Indonesia, the economic technocrats who ran the country under Suharto's rule were known as the "Berkeley mafia" (Dezalay and Garth, forthcoming).

The relative status and institutional success of the US-trained economists within national fields, however, is not uniform within or across nations. Certainly, in many countries, especially developing ones, an American degree often constitutes an entry point into positions of intellectual or political power – a phenomenon that is reflected by the higher concentrations of people who received their doctoral degrees in the United States in the "core" institutions of the higher education system and in important public administrations, such as central banks and ministries of finance. In the late twentieth century, divisions between a "nationally oriented" crowd – which is more frequently locally trained (or foreign, but non-American), of the political economy style, more nationalist, and more interventionist – and an "internationally oriented" crowd – which is US-trained, more scientistic in its methodological approach, universalistic, and often promarket – were sometimes quite acute.[28] These divisions were all the more intense, in fact, since they were often embedded in differences in social background (foreign degrees are typically an elite career path) and, as we saw, in local conflicts over the distribution of scientific and political authority. Writing in 1996, Loureiro stated that over 80% of the professors at the two main economics departments in Rio de Janeiro (Brazil) had a North American doctorate, as opposed to about 7% at the largest department in São Paulo and even smaller percentages in more provincial universities (Loureiro 1996, p. 192). Similar patterns could be found in other parts of the world.

---

[27] Between 1957 and 1970, about 100 Chilean students from the Universita Catolica were educated at the economics department of the University of Chicago, partly sponsored by the American government. Upon their return, not only did they have a profound impact on economic discourse in their country, revolutionizing the curriculum at their home institution and dramatically altering the terms of the public debate on economic issues through their incessant media activism, but they also came to occupy key positions in the state administration after Pinochet's coup in 1973 and lead the country toward neoliberal reform and an "economic miracle," which was for a time celebrated as a model (Montecinos 1988; Valdes 1995).

[28] See Babb (2001) for a superb account of such competition in the Mexican case.

A 1985 report on the teaching of economics in Asia stated that 30 out of 38 faculty members of the University of the Philippines School of Economics had received their Ph.D. from an American university, although such patterns were less true of other universities (Tan 1985). Wade (1990, p. 220) argues that the central division in the Taiwanese economics field opposes people trained in the United States (who constitute the core of academia and the main public administrations) to those educated in East Asia (who tend to be employed in journalism, business, or other governmental agencies). A study on South Korea mentions that more than half the members of the Korean Economic Society holding a Ph.D. were trained in the United States, and that disproportionate numbers of these are found in Seoul (Choi 1996).

More developed countries, like France, Germany, or even England, are not exempt from these divisions either. Yet in these cases, a partly insular academic labor market, a closed civil service, strong autochthonous intellectual traditions, and less exposure to international policy pressures have sometimes worked *against,* rather than in favor of the incorporation of US-trained economists in core administrative and educational institutions. Still, even when they operate "negatively," international connections constitute a fundamental mechanism of field structuration.

The US roots of regionalization in economic science
We can gain further intuition into the historical and geographical variability of the relationship between international connections and national field structuration by analyzing transformations in the *levels* of organization in the field of economics worldwide. Figure 2.3 is based on the same associational data as Figure 2.1, this time coded by the geographical focus of the organization (national, regional, or international), and by the generalist or specialized character of its orientation. The figure shows an interesting pattern of institutionalization. Consistent with the model presented in the preceding sections, the graph confirms that the development of economics was initially centered on the national community (e.g. the Economic Society of South Africa) and reflects the embeddedness of economics in the institutional apparatus of the nation-state. As these national fields grew in size, they became more specialized (which is indicated by the "national-specialized" category in the graph, e.g. the French Association of Economic Historians). After World War II, associational founding patterns also became more international in scope and purpose, although international associations often remained based in the United States and continued to be dominated – numerically and hierarchically – by scholars established there.

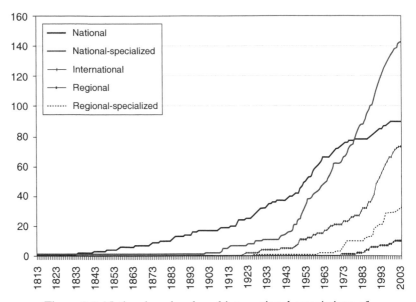

Figure 2.3 National, regional, and international associations of economists (cumulative foundings).
Source: Same as Fig. 2.1.

Since the late 1970s, however, a third phase is unfolding, with the clear emergence of a regional pattern of organization. Like the international associations of the earlier era, regional associations host disproportionate numbers of members educated in the core (most prominently in America) but who have returned to their home countries. We may mention the history of the construction of a truly "European" economics profession as an illustration of this phenomenon. The Europeanization of the economics profession was the result of the combined effects of the construction of Europe and of the transatlantic connections of the most internationalized segments of the national economics professions in European countries.

Up until the mid 1980s, economists socialized in American scientific norms entertained bilateral relationships with the United States, rather than among themselves. Several persons I interviewed in the mid 1990s even recounted that "internationally oriented" economists then met much more often in the United States than in their home region or even country.[29] Starting in the early 1980s, however, integration into "European" institutions (the European Economic Review, the European

---

[29] Source: interviews with French and British economists, summers of 1995 (France) and 1997 (Great Britain).

Economic Association, and the Center for Economic Policy Research) came to be seen by these scholars as a strategy to overcome their relative isolation within their national fields.[30] The construction of the European Community, which relied heavily on these networks to satisfy its demands for expertise, gave further impetus to these institutions.[31]

Regional associations (e.g. the European Economic Association) and the regional chapters of international associations (e.g. the Latin American meetings of the Econometric Society) thus constitute "intermediary bodies" that are both solidly tied to the American research community and play a critical role in the socialization of peripheral economics communities into the research, professional norms, and intellectual frameworks produced in US academia (see, e.g. Williamson [1996] on the role of the regional chapter of the Econometric Society in Latin America). Nonetheless, once started, these regional institutions follow a logic of their own. There is some indication, for instance, that the movement of regionalization is becoming self-sustaining, particularly in the case of Europe, where higher education is increasingly organized on a regional basis, thus bypassing the United States as an obligatory training ground.

Internationalization, then, leads regionalization (rather than the other way around). This point is important theoretically. It further establishes that diffusion is not a one-step phenomenon, but takes place as a gradual, multilayered process of professional stratification and concomitant reconstruction.

International institutions

Not only scholarly communities, but also economic policy networks (sometimes closely linked to the former) are directly constructed at the international level. With the globalization of economies, the audiences and constituencies of policy actors are increasingly located outside of the country, among multinational corporations, international financial markets, and multilateral economic organizations. Probably the most visible vehicle of the transnational socialization of elites at the periphery, in fact, is their embeddedness in this broad international society of economic actors.

---

[30] US authors even contribute a significant share of publications in European journals (above 30% in the *European Economic Review* and the *Economic Journal* [see Elliott, Greenaway, and Sapsford 1998]).

[31] By making funding contingent on cross-national collaborations, EC (now EU) research policies have been an important vector of cross-national integration – initially benefiting the US- or UK-trained mainstream just described, but growing to incorporate a much broader range of approaches to economics (such as those represented in the European Association for Evolutionary Political Economy).

International organizations have been shown to spread worldwide "regimes" – about development, science, environment, or education, for example (Chabbott 1996; Finnemore 1993; Meyer et al. 1991; Meyer et al. 1997; Nadelmann 1990). "Epistemic communities" located in the international sphere are powerful producers and disseminators of norms about economic policy, which foster international homogeneity among comparable national institutions (Adler and Haas 1992). These may include scientists and technical assistants in governmental and nongovernmental organizations, as well as individuals in multinational firms and banks, or journalists in economic newspapers and magazines diffused internationally (e.g. the *Wall Street Journal* and the *Financial Times*).

Such institutions and networks routinely participate in the diffusion of economics worldwide and in the international reconstruction of the economics profession around the neoclassical paradigm. First, linkages to an international sphere dominated by Western organizations, and deeply rooted in mainstream economics, have contributed to legitimizing particular approaches to development, which typically emphasize internal deficiencies (e.g. quality of labor, property rights allocation [Mitchell 2005], size of public sector), rather than external economic relations (e.g. dependency), as sources of underdevelopment. Hence there was widespread implementation, starting in the 1950s, of policies based on manpower planning and, later, human capital theories (Berman 1983). Second, these institutions have encouraged forms of social-scientific research geared toward solving well-defined problems of public policy. Certainly, earlier generations of economists, especially in the developing world, often saw their role as not only managing the national economy, but also as involving broader societal reform, sometimes even the transformation of international economic relations (Hirschman 1981). These views, however, were never able to secure a stronghold in US academia or in international financial organizations – and were often dismissed as mere "ideology" conflicting with more desirable standards of professionalism. Instead international institutions have promoted a technocratic view of development problems, which sees the economist as a "social engineer" (McCloskey 1997) and the scientific apparatus of economics as a device to solve narrowly defined problems of policy advice, and consequently encourage the construction of technical elites with strong quantitative skills. (Today this outlook is evolving, however, partly under pressure from below to address structural relations between the first and third worlds.)

Naturally, the most conspicuous dimension of the international organizations' influence remains the direct action on economic policy through the provision of expert advice. Foreign economic expertise is in fact an old business that emerged around 1900, often as an outgrowth of colonial administration or neocolonial relations (Cooper and Packard 1998).[32] During the interwar period it came to be increasingly understood as the activity of independent technicians acting on the basis of their expertise and responding to explicit requests by sovereign nation-states (Rosenberg and Rosenberg 1994). "International money doctors" from the United States and Western Europe began traveling the world providing advice to the governments of peripheral countries. For instance, Edwin Kemmerer, a professor of economics at Princeton University, is often described as the "one-man IMF" of his time (Seidel 1972; Drake 1994; Rosenberg 1999). International bodies such as the League of Nations also undertook important economic consulting activities, notably in Central Europe (De Marchi 1991).

After World War II, nationalist elites in the developing world were eager to lead their country on the path to industrialization and development. This position partly stimulated a flourish of new "development" knowledge within academia (Cooper and Packard 1998), which was further supported by a proactivist expert consensus institutionalized in international organizations.[33] International economic consulting grew into a considerably large industry, dominated by advisers from Organisation for Economic Co-operation and Development (OECD) countries (Currie 1981, p. 245). It became a very diverse field, involving governmental and nongovernmental sources, private and nonprofit. Most prominent of all, the IMF has the ability to exercise direct control on the economic policies of its member states through its use of multilateral economic surveillance (in the form of obligatory consultations) and its ability to make lending conditional (Pauly 1997; Babb 2003).[34]

The sheer volume of economic expertise available in international organizations is remarkable, and it overshadows any other economic institution worldwide. Economists recruited from core US and UK economics departments have traditionally staffed positions (including

---

[32] In some cases, one can look further back in time. Hence, the French liberal economist Jean de Courcelle-Seneuil famously advised Chilean governments in the 1850s and 1870s to adopt a set of laissez-faire reforms that would not be unlike what the Chicago Boys would advocate over a century later (Glaser 2003).

[33] This consensus has often been referred to as "embedded liberalism" (Ruggie 1982; Ikenberry 1992; also see Arndt 1987; Helleiner 2003).

[34] It used to be that world powers ensured economic compliance by military means. A famous example of this enforcement strategy occurred when Venezuela failed to repay its debt in 1902. At the time, British and German vessels blockaded the country's ports (Singh 1999).

those "reserved" for foreigners) at the World Bank, the regional United Nations agencies and development banks, the World Trade Organization, and, most prominently, the IMF, where they numbered 1,227 in 2001 (International Monetary Fund 2002).[35] Less than 40% of the fund's economists came from developing countries – a percentage that masks strong variations between grade levels: higher in lower grades, lower in higher grades (Evans and Finnemore 2001). Furthermore, economists recruited through the prestigious Economist program in 1999 graduated *exclusively* from North European or North American universities, with a disproportionate share (50% in 1999) going to US graduates (Evans and Finnemore 2001). The normative effect of these patterns of recruitment is further deepened by the fact that economists are the professional group most typically involved in field missions and direct consulting (Polak 1996). It is therefore particularly vital for countries' representatives and negotiators to share the economic culture and language of their counterparts in international organizations. Both to external and internal audiences (particularly business audiences), foreign or foreign-trained expertise will then appear not only much "safer" than its counterpart grown at home, but also the only way to ensure communication and legitimacy in a situation of asymmetrical power. Thus a witness of the 1950s missions in Chile commented: "The bringing of these foreign experts is not because we do not have true capabilities in financial matters but rather because those experts are backed by an international reputation that makes their proposals less controvertible" (Valdes 1995, p. 107).[36]

This long discussion of the global social structures in economics suggests two main conclusions: First, at the microlevel, economics has partly become a profession of transnational hybrids – a "creolized" profession, to apply Ulf Hannerz's (1987) terminology. Second, at the macrolevel, it is characterized by a set of properly "global" dynamics, whereby professional communities *everywhere* are being reshaped by the international circulation of actors, scientific models, professional practices, and policies. This is the last point of my argument, which I now turn to.

---

[35] Baldwin (1986) reports that while only 25% of the World Bank professionals are trained economists, the same group represents 50% of the bank's vice presidents and one-third of its division chiefs (1982 figures). In contrast to the IMF, which was conceived, designed, and staffed by economists from its beginnings (Polak 1996), the rise of economists at the bank came somewhat later (in the 1960s).

[36] Likewise, there is substantial evidence that countries that owe the IMF money (and are thus constrained by IMF conditionality in their policy options) receive a "credibility bonus" from foreign investors (Brune et al. 2004).

Global competition and the legitimacy of the economics profession

How, then, are the dynamics of professional development affected by transnational networks? Through which mechanisms do these international connections transform the nature of economic knowledge and the jurisdiction of the economics profession? I argue below that global linkages affect the professional construction (and reconstruction) of economics because they shape the competition for intellectual and jurisdictional space. In other words, many of the competitive mechanisms that drive professional development in economics are taking place at the global level. This happens mainly through three channels: (1) through the mobilization of international resources in the process of intellectual competition within economic science – both in the core and in the periphery, (2) through the internationalization of the process of creative destruction of jurisdictions, and (3) through the use of international arenas to expand economics' jurisdictional control away from other professions.

The globalization of intellectual and jurisdictional battles

We have seen how foreign credentials allow economists from developing countries to gain access to positions of power within their national political and academic fields. Yet the dynamics set in motion by the transnational socialization of economists are, in fact, much more powerful. The professional empowerment of transnational economists (itself linked to the international reconstruction of economies) serves to reinforce considerably the world that contributed to produce them – namely, top economics departments, most of which are located in the United States – and the international organizations and foundations that supported their coming of age.[37] Hence the Chicago Boys' experiment in Chile, and the country's ultimate democratic transition, gave monetarist ideas considerable publicity and helped enhance the position of the University of Chicago's Department of Economics within the American academic field (Becker 1997; Dezalay and Garth 2002). In an interview conducted in 1999, Arnold Harberger, a professor at the University of Chicago for

---

[37] One should not forget that in an earlier time, it was German universities whose international prestige was enhanced by the foreign students they educated. Upon their return, these American young turks contested mainstream American economics and founded the American Economic Association on a resolutely progressive platform (Yonay 1998).

38 years, thus commented evocatively: "I think *my* number of ministers is now crossing 25, and I know *my* number of central bank presidents has already crossed a dozen. Right now the central bank presidents of Chile, Argentina and Israel were *my students*, and the immediate former central bank presidents in Argentina, Chile and Costa Rica were also *my students*" (*The Region* 1999, emphasis added).

Eastern and Central Europe provides another striking example. Bockman and Eyal (2002), for instance, have shown that in their effort to craft a space for promarket ideas, libertarians in the United States and Western Europe during the 1960s used their connections to Eastern European reform economists to turn the critique of socialist planning into a weapon against Western Keynesianism. The Russian transition to capitalism was the site of a fierce competition between American and European (including East European) advisers sponsored by their respective governments (or the European Union), as well as a number of free-lancers (some of whom financed themselves), who sought to use the Russian scene as a platform for self-promotion (Murrel 1995; Wedel 1998; Ivanova and Wyplosz 2003).

Internationalization thus appears to be one of the key mechanisms by which different segments of the (mainly) dominant economics profession seek to assert their authority on an economic jurisdiction. The ability to transnationalize knowledge through educational or policy influence is a fundamental source of intellectual legitimacy and material power: it also leads to financial resources, social capital, and jurisdictional control.

Dezalay and Garth (2002) describe this logic of field development with the terms "internationalization of palace wars." In their account, the competitive struggles within Western economics ("palace wars," a concept adapted from Bourdieu, 1993) are being internationalized – that is, fought through third parties in distant places worldwide. International connections, then, enter the process of field structuration both ways: on the one hand, connections *to* the United States (especially) constitute a form of symbolic capital, which domestic actors in other countries manipulate in their own attempt to establish legitimacy within their local field. On the other hand, the international connections *of* Western economists and economic institutions feed back into the competitive processes in the core itself. The transnationalization of American economics, then, is profoundly dual, fostering a complex (and of course highly asymmetrical) dialectic of export–import. This also implies that transnationalization is not a power-neutral mechanism, but instead entails very strategic elements on both sides – I shall soon return to this point.

The creative destruction of economic jurisdictions

The second global dynamic in the professionalization process has to do with the relationship between internationalization and the reconstruction of the jurisdictional basis of the economics profession. In advocating and implementing the reconstruction of the world economies (usually according to the current wisdom in mainstream economics), economic experts worldwide participate in the ongoing reconstruction, transformation, and expansion of their own jurisdictional domain.

The "creative destruction" of jurisdictions is one of the mechanisms whereby competing segments of a profession and new generations of practitioners can gain power and legitimacy within their field. Yet a characteristic of economics as a profession is that the creative destruction of jurisdictions is largely an *endogenous* process, rather than a result of external forces. Economics generates its own jurisdictions not only through the development of new analytical and practical tools, but also through its participation in the ongoing economic reconstruction of societies. It is as if the development of medicine relied on constantly generating new pathologies (rather than on the development of new treatments and techniques for existing pathologies).[38]

One consequence of this is that many of the competitive processes that drive professional development in economics originate in competitive struggles *within the profession itself* to gain authority on this process of reconstruction, rather than at the level of the *system* of professions (which I examine next). An example will illustrate this point. When state-led development was the received wisdom, in the 1960s, the economists' professional jurisdiction typically included national planning (Robertson 1984), demand management, industrial policy, or macroeconomic model building. The worldwide move to freer markets – itself partly triggered by new economic ideas and policy technologies – has left vacant some of these traditional occupations. Certain institutions and groups have found their knowledge becoming increasingly obsolete (e.g. structuralist economists within the Economic Commission for Latin America and specialists of central planning in Eastern Europe and Russia [Sikkink 1998]). Newer actors, on the other hand, have seen their prestige and authority within the national fields grow. I suggested earlier that transnational hybrids have benefited most clearly from these transformations, as have, interestingly, the mainly privately funded institutions of higher education, which

---

[38] Of course a case can be made that a similar logic does, indeed, apply to medicine, psychiatry, and like fields. (Foucault made this argument about the mutual constitution of knowledge and its object long ago.)

often harbor them (e.g. Mexico's Technological Institute, or ITAM [Babb 2001], Fundação Getulio Vargas in Brazil [Loureiro 1998], Institute Di Tella in Argentina [Neiburg and Plotkin 2004], and Central European University in Eastern Europe [Guilhot 2004; Ivanova and Wyplosz 2003]).[39] In Russia the competition for the control of the economic transition process at the beginning of the 1990s saw the birth of a group of small economic research institutes, populated by a new generation of reform economists well versed in the knowledge of neoclassical economics (Chmatko 2002).

The economic reforms of the 1980s and 1990s (e.g. privatization of state assets, deregulation of financial markets, elimination of foreign exchange and capital controls, revival of antitrust policies) have also opened up new spaces of professional expertise and control, especially toward the private sector. Economic knowledge becomes relevant not only to governments, but also to trade organizations, financial institutions, and business corporations. Although these processes of "privatization of economic knowledge" are not in themselves inherently international, they have first benefited Western corporations and the Western economics profession, which have found new outlets abroad for an expertise sometimes difficult to market at home, where competition is more intense and economic reform programs have either been already implemented or, in some cases, are not implemented because of domestic political pressures. *The Economist*, for instance, reported, "As privatization has spread across the world, so British economists have found that expertise gained at home (during the Thatcher years) is highly marketable. Also, because antitrust cases now turn on economic as well as legal arguments, companies are paying big fees to economists as well as lawyers" (*The Economist*, May 9, 1998; also see Wedel 1998, p. 51).

As the example above suggests, and in striking parallel with Marx's quote at the outset of this article, competition and the search for profit (whether this profit is monetary or symbolic) in economics can give rise either to the transformation of work (through the creation of new jurisdictions) or to the expansion of the geographical scale of economic activities (through the export of economic ideas and tools), and often to both. In fact, the creative transformation of jurisdictions and the process of internationalization are intimately connected through market competition. This should not come as a surprise: professions are, after

---

[39] Babb (2001) has examined the process by which the ITAM and other private institutions have gained more influence within the Mexican government at the expense of the public university (UNAM), which used to enjoy a near monopoly on bureaucratic recruitment. Central European University was founded in 1991 by George Soros.

all, capitalist enterprises (Sarfatti-Larson 1979). The ongoing reconstruction of economies worldwide is thus symbiotically related to the
ongoing transformation of the intellectual and professional jurisdictions
of economists. It is a constantly evolving process, driven by competition,
and it is highly unbalanced and stratified internationally because core
countries and institutions typically control, to use Marxist terms, the
means of mental and material production.[40]

Global dynamics within the system of professions

The third underlying force in the global dynamics of the economics
profession comes from other professions. Abbott's account of the professionalization process rested on the capture of jurisdictions from other
professional competitors: "Professions constitute an interdependent
system. A move by one inevitably affects the others" (Abbott 1988,
p. 87). Through the creative destruction of jurisdictions, the internationalization of economics involves not only the reconstruction of the economics profession itself, but also that of the entire ecological milieu this
profession interacts with, each segment of which also follows its own
logic of international diffusion. For instance, the combined processes of
the universalization of the "rule of law" on the one hand, and of the
general "economicization" of legal arguments on the other, creates a de
facto jurisdictional opening for economists in legal arenas worldwide
(Dezalay and Garth 2002). From this point of view, the globalization
of economics might thus be driven by the globalization of law itself.
Conversely, the emergence of new forms of economic control, based
on regulation rather than administrative guidance profoundly transforms
the exercise of legal expertise, as exemplified by the quote from *The
Economist* above. In this new environment economics becomes part of
new professional terrains like law, finance, and consulting, all of which
entered the business of economic advice massively in the 1980s. The
international diffusion of economic reforms such as privatization, antitrust legislation, or financial liberalization thus feeds back into the
professionalization process of economics (but also of law, the financial
services industry, etc.) both in the core and the periphery (see Kelemen
and Sibbitt 2004). For instance, a large proportion of the assistance for
economic restructuring to the former Soviet countries in the early 1990s

---

[40] There are some important exceptions, however: see, for instance, Import Substitution
Industrialization, which originated in the work of Raul Prebish at ECLA or, more
recently, Peruvian economist De Soto's (2000) influential pamphlet on asset
management as a key resource for economic development.

was contracted out to large Western accounting firms, in particular the (then) "Big Six" (Wedel 1998). In their process of expansion, these organizations have relied heavily on transnational hybrids. International linkages and the increased organization of the economy along market lines – a process partly set in motion by the *intellectual* reconstruction of neoclassical economics around the free market – thus also drive the "privatization" of economics as a professional enterprise and its reconstruction as a corporate activity in its own right.

A global case of professionalization?

Taken together, the patterns described in this article exemplify a logic of professional development, which is produced (and reproduced) at the global level through the dialectical relationship between economics and the economy (Callon 1998). The functioning of economies gets "academicized" into scientific models, largely produced in core countries and in reference to the prevailing model view of the economy there. These models in turn help legitimize or formulate reforms, both at home but especially abroad (Blinder 1999). In the process of constant recreation of what an economy is supposed to look like, new jurisdictions open up for economists, not only because of the creation of new areas of expertise (e.g. deregulation, privatization), but also because economists are able to convert their professional credibility into other forms of "capital" (economic, political). Scientific representations, policy paradigms, and international linkages all enter the competitive processes whereby different segments and groups in the various national economics professions seek to assert their authority on particular jurisdictions (professional, scientific, or political), ultimately transforming the world they claim control upon, and their own professional "identity" in the process.

A neoinstitutional interpretation of this process would certainly account for its formal aspects – the "global diffusion" of economics through the institutionalization of specialized economics curricula, government organizations, professional associations, and so on. To a large extent it also helps us understand the mechanisms (mimetic, coercive, and normative) that encourage the establishment of such transnational linkages as international student flows or recruitment patterns in international organizations. Neoinstitutional theory, however, does not acknowledge that the diffusion of professional models and institutions supposes a constant reconstruction on *both* sides of the diffusion process, a transformation that goes well above and beyond what institutionalist scholars often call the "mediating" effect of local institutions (Guillén 1994). What happens in the case of economics is a form of "global professionalization," rooted in the dialectical interaction between the real world (the economy) and the profession (economics), which claims tutelary power over it. In fact, I have gone as far as to suggest that globalization constitutes, in fact, a fundamental element in the professionalization of economics: for "peripheral" elites, transnational linkages to the mainstream economics profession are a necessity (sometimes eagerly accepted), a function of their double (scientific and political) marginality. They may also be an essential strategic vehicle for the transmission of local claims and grievances. For instance, when Joseph Stiglitz – an economics Nobel Prize winner and former World Bank chief economist – loudly condemns IMF policies in East Asia, the relevant countries are de facto encouraged to leverage his reputation in the battle that opposes them to international financial institutions. Conversely for Stiglitz, the *enfant terrible* of American economics, the stake is both reputational (to reinforce his own position within the US field) and intellectual/political (to establish the viability of alternative policies). Global jurisdictions, then, constitute an essential source of legitimacy and resources for "core" economists, too. Since the more peripheral places of the world economy are more vulnerable to the professional influence of economists (both local and foreign), they, in fact, constitute a fundamental space where individual experts and organizations fight key intellectual and jurisdictional battles through the ongoing economic reconstruction of societies – a process that is not, and never will be, settled.

References

Abbott, Andrew 1988. *The System of Professions: An Essay on the Division of Expert Labor*. University of Chicago Press.

  1995. "Things of Boundaries." *Social Research* 62 (4): 857–882.

  2005. "Linked Ecologies: States and Universities as Environments for Professions." *Sociological Theory* 23 (3): 245–274.

Adler, Emanuel and Haas, Peter 1992. "Epistemic Communities, World Order, and the Creation of a Reflective Research Program." *International Organization* 46 (1): 367–390.

Ambirajan, S. 1996. "The Professionalization of Economics in India," pp. 80–96 in *The Post-1945 Internationalization of Economics*, edited by A. W. Bob Coats. Durham, N.C.: Duke University Press.

Anderson, Benedict 1983. *Imagined Communities: Reflections on the Origins and Spread of Nationalism*. London: Verson.

Arndt, H. W. 1987. *Economic Development: History of an Idea*. University of Chicago Press.

Arnove, Robert F. (ed.) 1980. *Philanthropy and Cultural Imperialism: The Foundations at Home and Abroad*. Boston: G. K. Hall.

Aslanbeigui, Nahid and Montecinos, Veronica 1998. "Foreign Students in U.S. Doctoral Programs." *Journal of Economic Perspectives* 12 (3): 171–82.

Babb, Sarah L. 2001. *Managing Mexico: Mexican Economics from Nationalism to Neoliberalism*. Princeton University Press.

2003. "The IMF in Sociological Perspective: A Tale of Organizational Slippage." *Studies in Comparative International Development* 38 (2): 3–28.

Baldwin, George 1986. "Economics and Economists in the World Bank," pp. 67–90 in *Economists in International Agencies*, edited by A. W. Bob Coats. New York: Praeger.

Baumol, William J., Panzer, J. and Willig, R. D. 1986. *Contestable Markets and the Theory of Industrial Structure*. New York: Harcourt Brace.

Becker, Gary 1997. "Latin America Owes a Lot to Its 'Chicago Boys.'" *BusinessWeek*, June 9.

Berman, Edward H. 1983. *The Influence of the Carnegie, Ford, and Rockefeller Foundations on American Foreign Policy: The Ideology of Philanthropy*. Albany: State University of New York Press.

Blinder, Alan 1999. "Life Imitates Art: How the Economy Came to Resemble the Model." Adam Smith Award Address at the meeting of the National Association of Business Economists, San Francisco, September.

Bockman, Johana and Eyal, Gil 2002. "Eastern Europe as a Laboratory for Economic Knowledge: The Transnational Roots of Neoliberalism." *American Journal of Sociology* 108 (2): 310–352.

Bourdieu, Pierre 1987. "The Force of Law: Toward a Sociology of the Judicial Field." *Hastings Law Journal* 38 (5): 805–53.

1993. *Language and Symbolic Power*. Cambridge, Mass.: Harvard University Press.

Bourdieu, Pierre and Wacquant, Loïc 1998. "Sur les ruses de la raison impérialiste." *Actes de la Recherche en Sciences Sociales* 121–22: 110–19.

Breslau, Daniel 1997. "The Political Power of Research Methods: Knowledge Regimes in U.S. Labor-Market Policy." *Theory and Society* 26 (6): 869–902.

2003. "Economics Invents the Economy: Mathematics, Statistics, and Models in the Work of Irving Fisher and Wesley Mitchell." *Theory and Society* 32 (3): 379–411.

Brune, Nancy, Garrett, Geoffrey and Kogut, Bruce 2004. "The International Monetary Fund and the Global Spread of Privatization." *IMP Staff Papers* 51 (2): 192–219.

Burrage, Michael and Torstendahl, Rolf 1990. *Professions in Theory and History: Rethinking the Study of the Professions*. London: Sage.

Business Week 1992. "The Latin Revolution Has Ivy League Roots." June 15.

Callon, Michel 1998. "The Embeddedness of Economic Markets in Economics," pp. 1–57 in *The Laws of the Markets*, edited by M. Callon. Oxford: Blackwell.

Campbell, John 1998. "Institutional Analysis and the Role of Ideas in Political Economy." *Theory and Society* 27: 377–409.

2002. "Ideas, Politics and Public Policies." *Annual Review of Sociology* 28: 21–38.

Carruthers, Bruce G. and Halliday, Terence C. 2006. "Institutionalizing Creative Destruction: Predictable and Transparent Bankruptcy Law in the

Wake of the East Asian Financial Crisis." In *Neoliberalism and Institutional Reform in East Asia*, edited by Meredith Woo-Cumings. UNRISD.

Centeno, Miguel Angel 1994. *Democracy within Reason: Technocratic Revolution in Mexico*. College Station: Pennsylvania State University Press.

Chabbott, Colette 1996. "Constructing Educational Development: International Development Organizations and the World Conference on Education for All". Ph.D. dissertation. Stanford University, Department of Sociology.

Chmatko, Natalia 2002. "Les économistes russes entre l'orthodoxie marxiste et le radicalisme libéral." *Genèses* 47: 123–139.

Choi, Young Back 1996. "The Americanization of Economics in Korea," pp. 97–122 in *The Post-1945 Internationalization of Economics*, edited by A. W. Bob Coats. Durham, N.C.: Duke University Press.

Cooper, Frederick and Packard, Randall 1998. "Introd. to *International Development and the Social Sciences*," edited by F. Cooper and R. Packard. Berkeley and Los Angeles: University of California Press.

Currie, Lauchlin 1981. *The Role of Economic Advisers in Developing Countries: Contributions in Economics and Economic History*. Westport, Conn.: Greenwood.

De Marchi, Neil 1991. "The League of Nations Economists and the Ideal of Peaceful Change in the Decade of the Thirties," pp. 143–178 in *Economics and National Security: A History of Their Interaction*, edited by C. Goodwin. Durham, N.C.: Duke University Press.

De Soto, Hernando 2000. *The Mystery of Capital: Why Capitalism Triumphs in the West and Fails Everywhere Else*. New York: Basic Books.

Dezalay, Yves and Bryant, Garth 1996. *Dealing in Virtue: International Commercial Arbitration and the Construction of a Transnational Legal Order*. University of Chicago Press.

  1998. "Le 'Washington Consensus': Contribution à une sociologie de l'hégémonie du libéralisme." *Actes de la Recherche en Sciences Sociales* 121–22: 3–22.

  2002. *The Internationalization of Palace Wars: Lawyers, Economists and the Transformation of Latin-American States*. University of Chicago Press.

  2008. "*Revamping Legal Virtue: Legal Strategies, True Believers and Profiteers in the Market for Global Hegemony*." Manuscript.

  Forthcoming. "Les usages nationaux d'une science 'globale': La diffusion de nouveaux paradigmes économiques comme stratégie hégémonique et enjeu domestique dans les champs nationaux de reproduction dans élites d'Etat." *Sociologie du travail*.

DiMaggio, Paul and Powell, Walter 1983. "The Iron Cage Revisited: Institutional Isomorphism and Collective Rationality in Organizational Fields." *American Sociological Review* 48 (2): 147–160.

Djelic, Marie-Laure 2004. "L'arbre banian de la mondialisation." *Actes de la Recherche en Sciences Sociales* 151–52: 107–113.

Drake, Paul W. 1994. *Money Doctors, Foreign Debts, and Economic Reforms in Latin America from the 1890s to the Present*. Wilmington: Jaguar Books.

Easterly, William 2002. *The Elusive Quest for Growth: Economists' Adventures and Misadventures in the Tropics*. Cambridge, Mass.: MIT Press.

Elliott, Caroline, Greenaway, David and Sapsford, David 1998. "Who's Publishing Who? The National Composition of Contributors to Some Core U.S. and European Journals." *European Economic Review* 42 (1): 201–6.

Evans, Peter and Finnemore, Martha 2001. "Organizational Reform and the Expansion of the South's Voice at the Fund." Paper presented at the meeting of the G-24 Technical Group, Washington, D.C., April.

Evetts, Julia 1998. "Professionalism beyond the Nation-State: International Systems of Professional Regulation in Europe." *International Journal of Sociology and Social Policy* 18: 47–64.

Evetts, Julia and Dingwall, Robert 2002. "Professional Occupations in the United Kingdom and Europe: Legitimation and Governmentality." *International Review of Sociology* 12 (2): 159–171.

Eyal, Gil 2000. "Anti-Politics and the Spirit of Capitalism: Dissidents, Monetarists and the Czech Transition to Capitalism." *Theory and Society* 29: 49–92.

Ferguson, James 1994. *"The Anti-Politics Machine: Development, Depoliticization, and Bureaucratic Power in Lesotho."* University of Minnesota Press.

Ferraro, Fabrizio, Pfeffer, Jeffrey, and Sutton, Robert 2005. "Economics Language and Assumptions: How Theories Can Become Self-Fulfilling." *Academy of Management Review* 30 (1): 8–24.

Finnemore, Martha 1993. "International Organizations as Teachers of Norms: The United Nations Educational, Scientific and Cultural Organization and Science Policy." *International Organization* 47 (4): 565–598.

Fisher, Donald 1993. *Fundamental Development of the Social Sciences: Rockefeller Philanthropy and the United States Social Science Research Council.* Ann Arbor: University of Michigan Press.

Fligstein, Neil 2001. "Social Skill and the Theory of Fields." *Sociological Theory* 19 (2): 105–125.

Foucault, Michel 1979. "On Governmentality." *Ideology and Consciousness* 6: 5–21.

Fourcade, Marion. Forthcoming. *Economists and Societies.* Princeton University Press.

Fourcade-Gourinchas, Marion and Babb, Sarah 2002. "The Rebirth of the Liberal Creed: Paths to Neoliberalism in Four Countries." *American Journal of Sociology* 108 (3): 533–579.

Frank, David and Gabler, Jay 2006. "Reconstructing the University: Worldwide Changes in Academic Emphases over the Twentieth Century." Stanford, Calif.: University Press.

Freidson, Eliot 1986. *Professional Powers: A Study in the Institutionalization of Formal Knowledge.* University of Chicago Press.

Friedman, Milton 1953. "The Methodology of Positive Economics," pp. 3–46 in *Essays in Positive Economics*, edited by M. Friedman. University of Chicago Press.

Glaser, Elizabeth 2003. "Chile's Monetarist Doctors, 1850–1988," pp. 166–89 in *Money Doctors: The Experience of International Financial Advising, 1850–2000*, edited by M. Flandreau. New York: Routledge.

Guilhot, Nicolas 2004. "Une vocation philanthropique: George Soros, les sciences sociales et la régulation du marché mondial." *Actes de la Recherche en Sciences Sociales* 151–152: 36–48.

2005. *The Democracy Makers: Human Rights and the Politics of Global Order.* New York: Columbia University Press.

Guillén, Mauro 1994. *Models of Management: Work, Authority, and Organization in a Comparative Perspective.* University of Chicago Press.

Haddad, Paulo Roberto 1981. "Brazil: Economists in a Bureaucratic-Authoritarian System," pp. 319–342 in *Economists in Government: An International Comparative Study,* edited by A. W. Bob Coats. Durham, N.C.: Duke University Press.

Hagan, John and Levi, Ron 2004. "Social Skill, the Milosevic Indictment, and the Rebirth of International Criminal Justice." *European Journal of Criminology* 1 (4): 445–475.

Hall, Peter (ed.) 1989. *The Political Power of Economic Ideas: Keynesianism across Nations.* Princeton University Press.

Han, Shin-Kap. 2003. "Tribal Regimes in Academia: A Comparative Analysis of Market Structure across Disciplines." *Social Networks* 25: 251–280.

Hannerz, Ulf 1987. "The World in Creolization." *Africa* 57: 546–559.

Haskell, Thomas 1977. *The Emergence of Professional Social Science: The American Social Science Association and the Nineteenth Century Crisis of Authority.* Baltimore: Johns Hopkins University Press.

Helleiner, Eric 2003. *The Making of National Money: Territorial Currencies in Historical Perspective.* Ithaca, N.Y.: Cornell University Press.

Herbst, Jürgen 1965. *The German Historical School in American Scholarship: A Study in the Transfer of Culture.* Ithaca, N.Y.: Cornell University Press.

Heyck, T. W. 1982. *The Transformation of Intellectual Life in Victorian England.* New York: St. Martin's.

Hirschman, Albert O. 1977. *The Passions and the Interests.* Princeton University Press.

1981. *Essays in Trespassing: Economics to Politics and Beyond.* Cambridge University Press.

Hodgson, Geoffrey M. 1996. "Varieties of Capitalism and Varieties of Economic Theory." *Review of International Political Economy* 3 (3): 380–433.

Ikenberry, John 1992. "A World Restored: Expert Consensus and the Anglo-American Post-War Settlement." *International Organization* 46 (1): 289–321.

International Monetary Fund 2002. *Diversity Annual Report 2001.* www.imf.org/external/np/div/2002/ar02.pdf.

Ivanova, Nadezhda and Wyplosz, Charles 2003. "Who Lost Russia in 1998?" pp. 105–137 in *Money Doctors: The Experience of International Financial Advising, 1850–2000,* edited by M. Flandreau. New York: Routledge.

Karady, Victor 1998. "La République des lettres des temps modernes: L'internationalisation des marchés universitaires occidentaux avant la Grande Guerre." *Actes de la Recherche en Sciences Sociales* 121–22: 92–103.

Kelemen, R. Daniel and Sibbitt, Eric C. 2004. "The Globalization of American Law." *International Organization* 58 (1): 103–136.

Klamer, Arjo and Colander, David 1990. *The Making of an Economist*. Boulder, Colo.: Westview.

Knorr-Cetina, Karin and Bruegger, Urs 2002. "Global Microstructures: The Virtual Societies of the Financial Markets." *American Journal of Sociology* 107 (4): 905–950.

Kohkongka, Unchalee 1985. *In Economics in Asia: Status Report on Teaching and Research in Nine Countries*. Bangkok: UNESCO, Regional Office for Education in Asia and the Pacific.

Kovács, János Mátyá 1992. "Engineers of the Transition (Interventionist Temptations in Eastern European Economic Thought)." *Acta Oeconomica* 44: 37–52.

(ed.) 1994. *Transition to Capitalism? The Communist Legacy in Eastern Europe*. New Brunswick, N.J.: Transaction.

Krause, Elliott 1996. *Death of the Guilds: Professions, States and Advanced Capitalism, 1930 to the Present*. New Haven, Conn.: Yale University Press.

Krohn, Claus-Dieter 1993. *Intellectuals in Exile: Refugee Scholars and the New School for Social Research*. Amherst: University of Massachusetts Press.

Laband, David N. and Piette, Michael J. 1994. "The Relative Impact of Economic Journals: 1970–1990." *Journal of Economic Literature* 32 (2): 640–666.

Lebaron, Frédéric 2000a. *La croyance économique: Les économistes entre science et politique*. Paris: Seuil.

2000b. "The Space of Economic Neutrality: Types of Legitimacy and Trajectories of Central Bank Managers." *International Journal of Contemporary Sociology* 37 (2): 207–228.

2002. "Le Nobel d'économie." *Actes de la Recherche en Sciences Sociales* 141–42: 62–65.

Loureiro, Maria Rita 1996. "The Professional and Political Impacts of the Internationalization of Economics in Brazil," pp. 184–209 in *The Post-1945 Internationalization of Economics*, edited by A. W. Bob Coats. Durham, N.C.: Duke University Press.

1998. "L'internationalisation des milieux dirigeants au Brésil." *Actes de la Recherche en Sciences Sociales* 121–22: 42–51.

Machin, Stephen and Oswald, Andrew 1999. *Signs of Disintegration: A Report on UK Economics PhDs and ESRC Studentship Demand*. London: Economic and Social Research Council.

MacKenzie, Donald and Millo, Yuval 2003. "Constructing a Market, Performing a Theory: The Historical Sociology of Financial Derivatives Exchange." *American Journal of Sociology* 109 (1): 107–145.

Markoff, John and Montecinos, Veronica 1993. "The Ubiquitous Rise of Economists." *Journal of Public Policy* 13 (1): 37–68.

Marx, Karl and Engels, Freidrich 1848. *The Communist Manifesto*. New York: Penguin.

McCloskey, Deirdre 1997. *The Vices of Economists, The Virtues of the Bourgeoisie*. Amsterdam University Press.

McCloskey, Donald 1985. *The Rhetoric of Economics*. Madison: University of Wisconsin Press.

Messiha, Wahib 1954. *The University Teaching of Social Sciences: Economics*. Paris: UNESCO.

Meyer, John W. 1994. "Rationalized Environments," pp. 28–54 in *Institutional Environments and Organizations: Structural Complexity and Individualism*, edited by John W. Meyer and W. Richard Scott. Thousand Oaks, Calif.: Sage.

Meyer, John W., Boli, John, Thomas, George, and Ramirez, Francisco 1997. "World Society and the Nation-State." *American Journal of Sociology* 103: 144–81.

Meyer, John W., Frank, David, Hironaka, Ann, Schofer, Evan, and Tuma, Nancy Brandon 1997. "The Structuring of a World Environmental Regime." *International Organization* 51(4): 623–651.

Meyer, John W., Kamens, David, Benavot, Aaron, Cha, Yun Kyoung, and Wong, Suk-Ying 1991 "Knowledge for the Masses: World Models and National Curricula, 1920–1986." *American Sociological Review* 56: 85–100.

Meyer, John W. and Rowan, Brian 1977. "Institutionalized Organizations: Formal Structure as Myth and Ceremony." *American Journal of Sociology* 83 (2): 340–363.

1978. "The Structure of Educational Organizations," pp. 78–109 in *Environments and Organizations*, edited by J. Meyer. San Francisco: Jossey-Bass.

Mitchell, Timothy 1998. "Fixing the Economy." *Cultural Studies* 12 (1): 82–101.

2005. "The Work of Economists: How a Discipline Makes Its World." *European Journal of Sociology* 46: 297–320.

Mirowski, Philip 1994. *Natural Images in Economic Thought*. Cambridge University Press.

2002. *Machine Dreams*. Cambridge University Press.

Montecinos, Veronica 1988. "Economics and Power: Chilean Economists in Government, 1958–1985." Ph.D. dissertation. University of Pittsburgh, Department of Sociology.

1998. "Economists in Party Politics: Chilean Democracy in the Era of the Markets," pp. 126–41 in *The Politics of Expertise in Latin America*, edited by M. Centeno and P. Silva. New York: St Martin's.

Montecinos, Veronica and Markoff, John 2000. "From the Power of Economic Ideas to the Power of Economists," pp. 105–50 in *The Other Mirror: Grand Theory through the Lens of Latin America*, edited by Miguel Angel Centeno and Fernando López-Alves. Princeton University Press.

Molnar, Virag 2004. "The Cultural Production of Locality: Reclaiming the 'European City' in Post-Wall Berlin." Manuscript. Princeton University, Department of Sociology.

Murrell, Peter 1995. "The Transition According to Cambridge, Mass." *Journal of Economic Literature* 33 (1): 164–179.

Nadelmann, E. 1990. "Global Prohibition Regimes: The Evolution of Norms in International Society." *International Organization* 44 (4): 479–527.

National Science Foundation 2000. *Graduate Education Reform in Europe, Asia, and the Americas and International Mobility of Scientists and Engineers: Proceedings of an NSF Workshop*. NSF 00–318, project officer Jean M. Johnson, Arlington, Va.

2002. *Graduate Students and Postdoctorates in Science and Engineering: Fall 2000.* NSF 02–314, project officer Joan S. Burrelli, Arlington, Va.

Neiburg, Federico and Plotkin, Mariano 2004. "Internationalisation et développement: Les « Di Tella » et la nouvelle économie en Argentine." *Actes de la Recherche en Sciences Sociales* 151–52: 57–68.

Pauly, Louis W. 1997. *Who Elected the Bankers? Surveillance and Control in the World Economy.* Ithaca, N.Y.: Cornell University Press.

Polak, Jacques 1996. "The Contribution of the International Monetary Fund," pp. 211–224 in *The Post-1945 Internationalization of Economics,* edited by A. W. Bob Coats. Durham, N.C.: Duke University Press.

Polanyi, Karl 1944. *The Great Transformation: The Political and Economic Origins of Our Time.* Boston: Beacon.

Polillo, Simone and Guillén, Mauro 2005. "Globalization Pressures and the State: The Global Spread of Central Bank Independence." *American Journal of Sociology* 110 (6): 1764–1802.

Reay, Michael John 2004. "Economic Experts and Economic Knowledge." Ph.D. dissertation. University of Chicago, Department of Sociology.

Reder, Melvin 1999. *Economics: The Culture of a Controversial Science.* University of Chicago Press.

The Region 1999. "Interview with Arnold Harberger, Dean of the Chicago Economists." March. Published by the Federal Reserve Bank of Minneapolis. (Interview available at http://minneapolisfed.org/pubs/region/99_03/harberger.cfm.)

Research Institute for Higher Education. 1989. *Foreign Students and Internationalization of Higher Education: Proceedings of the OECD/JAPAN Seminar on Higher Education and the Flow of Foreign Students.* Hiroshima University, Research Institute for Higher Education.

Roach-Anleu, Sharyn 1992. "The Professionalization of Social Work? A Case Study of Three Organizational Settings." *Sociology* 26 (1): 23–43.

Robertson, A. F. 1984. *People and the State: An Anthropology of Planned Development.* Cambridge University Press.

Rosen, George 1985. *Western Economists and Eastern Societies: Aspects of Change in South Asia, 1950–1970.* Dehli: Oxford University Press.

Rosenberg, Emily S. 1999. *Financial Missionaries to the World: The Politics and Culture of Dollar Diplomacy, 1900–1930.* Cambridge, Mass.: Harvard University Press.

Rosenberg, Emily S. and Rosenberg, Norman L. 1994. "From Colonialism to Professionalism: The Public-Private Dynamic in United States Foreign Financial Advising, 1898–1929," pp. 59–84 in *Money Doctors, Foreign Debts, and Economic Reforms in Latin America from the 1890s to the Present,* edited by Paul W. Drake. Wilmington: Jaguar Books.

Rueschemeyer, Dietrich 1973. *Lawyers and Their Societies.* University of Chicago Press.

Ruggie, John Gerard 1982. "International Regimes, Transactions and Change: Embedded Liberalism in the Postwar Economic Order." *International Organization* 36: 379–415.

Santiso, Javier 2002. "Du Bon Révolutionnaire au Bon Libéral ? A propos d'un étrange caméléon latino-américain," pp. 225–259 in *A la recherche de la démocratie: Mélanges offerts à Guy Hermet*, edited by Javier Santiso. Paris: Karthala.

Sarfatti-Larson, Magali 1979. *The Rise of Professionalism: A Sociological Analysis*. Berkeley and Los Angeles: University of California Press.

Sassen, Saskia 2001. *The Global City: New York, London, Tokyo*. 2nd edn. Princeton University Press.

Savelsberg, Joachim and King, Ryan D. 2005. "Institutionalizing Collective Memories of Hate: Law and Law Enforcement in Germany and the United States." *American Journal of Sociology* 111 (2): 579–616.

Schneider, Ben Ross 1998. "The Material Bases of Technocracy: Investor Confidence and Neoliberalism in Latin America," pp. 77–95 in *The Politics of Expertise in Latin America*, edited by M. A. Centeno and P. Silva. New York: St. Martin's.

Schofer, Evan 2003. "The Global Institutionalization of Geological Science, 1800 to 1990." *American Sociological Review* 68 (5): 730–759.

2004. "Cross-national Differences in the Diffusion of Western Science." *Social Forces* 83 (1): 215–247.

Schumpeter, Joseph (1942) 1975. *Capitalism, Socialism and Democracy*. New York: Harper.

Scott, James 1998. *Seeing Like a State: How Certain Schemes to Improve the Human Condition Have Failed*. New Haven, Conn.: Yale University Press.

Seidel, Robert N. 1972. "American Reformers Abroad: The Kemmerer Missions in South America, 1923–1931." *Journal of Economic History* 32 (2): 520–545.

Shayo, Moses 2002. "Economists as Political Players: An Exploratory Study." Manuscript. Princeton University, Department of Economics.

Sikkink, Kathryn 1998. "Development Ideas in Latin America: Paradigm Shift and the Economic Commission for Latin America," pp. 228–258 in *International Development and the Social Sciences*, edited by F. Cooper and R. Packard. Berkeley and Los Angeles: University of California Press.

Silberman, Bernard 1993. *Cages of Reason: The Rise of the Rational State in France, Japan, the United States, and Great Britain*. University of Chicago Press.

Singh, Kelvin 1999. "Big Power Pressure on Venezuela during the Presidency of Cipriano Castro." *Review Americana* 29: 125–43.

Skowronek, Stephen (1982) 2002. *Building a New American State: The Expansion of National Administrative Capacities*. Cambridge University Press.

Soffer, Reba 1978. *Ethics and Society in England: The Revolution in the Social Sciences, 1870–1914*. Berkeley: University of California Press.

Stiglitz, Joseph 2002. *Globalization and Its Discontents*. New York: Norton.

Strang, David and Meyer, John 1994. "Institutional Conditions for Diffusion," pp. 103–12 in *Institutional Environments and Organizations: Structural Complexity and Individualism*, edited by John W. Meyer and W. Richard Scott. Thousand Oaks, Calif.: Sage.

Tan, Edith 1985. "Philippines." In *Economics in Asia: Status Report on Teaching and Research in Nine Countries*. Bangkok: UNESCO.

Todd, Frankie and Neale, Pauline 1992. "Professions without Frontiers? The 'European Project' and UK Professional Associations." *International Journal of Sociology and Social Policy* 12 (3): 26–58.

Torstendahl, Rolf and Burrage, Michael 1990. *The Formation of Professions: Knowledge, State and Strategy.* Newbury Park, Calif.: Sage.

Tribe, Keith 1988. *Governing Economy: The Reformation of German Economic Discourse, 1750–1850.* Cambridge University Press.

Turner, Marjorie 1989. *Joan Robinson and the Americans.* Armonk, N.Y.: M. E. Sharpe.

UNESCO. *Statistical Yearbooks, 1960s–1990s.* Available from the International Network Archive at www.princeton.edu/~ina/students/index.html (accessed 4/11/2003).

Valdes, Juan Gabriel 1995. *Pinochet's Economists: The Chicago School of Economics in Chile, A Study in the Transfer of Ideas.* Cambridge University Press.

Wade, Robert 1990. *Governing the Market: Economic Theory and the Role of Government in East Asian Industrialization.* Princeton University Press.

Wagner, Peter, Weiss, C., Wittrock, B., and Wollmann, H., eds. 1991. *Social Sciences and Modern States: National Experiences and Theoretical Crossroads.* Cambridge University Press.

Wagner, Peter, Wittrock, Bjorn, and Whitley, Richard, eds. 1991. *Discourses on Society: The Shaping of the Social Science Disciplines. Vol. XV in Sociology of the Sciences.* Boston: Kluwer Academic Publishers.

Wedel, Janine R. 1998. *Collision and Collusion: The Strange Case of Western Aid to Eastern Europe, 1989–1998.* New York: St Martin's.

Weintraub, Sidney 2002. *How Economics Became a Mathematical Science.* Durham, N.C.: Duke University Press.

Whitley, Richard 1983. "The Structure and Context of Economics as a Scientific Field." *Research in the History of Economic Thought and Methodology* 4: 179–209.

    1984. *The Intellectual and Social Organization of the Sciences.* Oxford: Clarendon.

Williamson, John 1996. "Comments," pp. 364–368 in *The Post-1945 Internationalization of Economics*, edited by A. W. Bob Coats. Durham, N.C.: Duke University Press.

Wuthnow, Robert 1987. *Meaning and Moral Order: Explorations in Cultural Analysis.* Berkeley and Los Angeles: University of California Press.

Yonay, Yuval P. 1998. *The Struggle over the Soul of Economics: Institutionalist and Neoclassical Economists in America between the Wars.* Princeton University Press.

3 Academic rankings between the "republic of science" and "new public management"

Margit Osterloh and Bruno S. Frey

Introduction

Today, academic rankings based on publications and citations dominate research governance in academia. Moreover, they serve as the basis for assessing the performance and impact of scholars, faculties, and universities for three purposes.

First, they are widely used to make decisions on the hiring, tenure, and income of scholars. In many countries, recent reforms have increasingly linked scholars' salaries to the number of publications they have in international journals. Some universities, for example, in Australia, China, and Korea, provide cash bonuses for publications in key journals in order to raise their position in international and national rankings (Fuyuno and Cyranoski 2006; Franzoni et al. 2010). The assumption is that such measures lead to more and better publications in highly ranked journals.

Second, academic rankings supposedly give the public a transparent picture of scholarly activity. A common view of academic rankings is that they make scientific merits visible to politicians, public officials, deans, university administrators, and journalists, people who have no special knowledge of the field (see e.g. Worrell 2009).

Third, academic rankings supposedly make universities more accountable for their use of public money. They might help to allocate resources more efficiently according to indicators that measure past performance in an objective way.

However, in recent times, academic rankings have come under scrutiny. A lively discussion about the quality of academic rankings is taking place (e.g. Butler 2007; Adler and Harzing 2009; Albers 2009). This discussion focuses on the method used to determine academic rankings and the tools available to improve it. That more and better indicators are needed to enhance the quality of rankings is taken as a given (e.g. Starbuck 2009; Lane 2010). Only in a few cases is it asked whether rankings may produce unintended negative side effects, even if the indicators for research quality are perfect (e.g. Espeland and Sauder 2007; Osterloh 2010). Consequently, whether there are viable alternatives to academic rankings as an instrument for academic governance remains open.

In this chapter, we discuss four issues. First, we analyze the theoretical basis of the present research governance, namely, on the one side "new public management" and on the other side the concept of the "republic of science." Second, we discuss advantages and disadvantages of peer reviews and rankings on the background of empirically based findings. Third, we discuss in particular an aspect often disregarded, namely, the behavioral reactions to rankings that may overcompensate their advantages. Fourth, we discuss four suggestions to mitigate the tensions between new public management and the republic of science: Informed peer review, input control, awards, and partially random selection.

Conceptual issues: new public management versus republic of science

The popularity of academic rankings grew with the adoption of the idea of new public management in research governance; namely, the idea that universities, like other public services, such as hospitals, schools, or public transport, should be subjected to a similar governance as for-profit enterprises. "More market" and "strong leadership" have become the key words (Schimank 2005). This is reflected in procedures transferred from private companies such as management by objectives or pay-for-performance for scholars. Overall, the reforms are aimed at the establishment of an "enterprise university" (Clark 1998; Marginson and Considine 2000; Bok 2003; Willmott 2003; Khurana 2007; Donoghue 2008).

At first glance, this view stands in stark contrast to the ideal of self-governance of the scientific community. This ideal was undisputed for a long time. Over three hundred years ago, Gottfried Leibniz, a seventeenth-century philosopher and mathematician, promoted the "republic of letters" – an independent, self-defining network of scholars that transcends national and religious boundaries (Leibniz 1931).[1] Polanyi (1962/2002, p. 479) contends: "The soil of academic science must be exterritorial in order to secure its rule by scientific opinion." His republic of science is based on the self-coordination of independent scientists. Authority "is established between scientists, not above them" (Polanyi p. 471). Authors like Bush (1945), Merton (1973), and Stokes (1997) warn that outside actors are tempted to shape science according to their own value systems and thus jeopardize the mission of science. This view is supported by the

---

[1] For a discussion, see Ultee (1987).

economics of science (Arrow 1962; Nelson 1959, 2004; Dasgupta and David 1994; Stephan 1996). According to this view, in academia, the evaluation by peers has to substitute for the evaluation by the market because of two fundamental characteristics of science: its public nature and high uncertainty that lead to market failures.

The public nature of scientific discoveries has been intensively discussed by Arrow (1962) and Nelson (1959, 2006). The fundamental uncertainty of scientific endeavors exists because success in academia is reflected by success in the market often only after a long delay or sometimes not at all (Bush 1945; Nelson 1959, 2004, 2006). In addition, research often produces serendipity effects; that is, it provides answers to unasked questions (Stephan 1996; Simonton 2004). As it is often not predictable which usefulness a particular research endeavor produces and whether it ever will be marketable, peers instead of the market have to evaluate whether a piece of research represents an advance. Peers have the opportunity to identify possible errors and risks; they can profit themselves from the innovation to push forward their own research, redundancies are avoided, and the new knowledge can quickly be used for new and cheaper technologies. Instead of market prices there is a special "currency" that governs the republic of science – the priority rule (Merton 1973; Dasgupta and David 1994; Stephan 1996; Gittelman and Kogut 2003). This rule attributes success to the person who first makes an invention, and who the scientific community recognizes to be first. The priority rule serves two purposes, hastening discoveries and their disclosure (Dasgupta and David 1994, p. 499): A discovery must be communicated as quickly as possible to the community of peers in order to gain their recognition.

Consequently, the peer review system is taken to be the founding stone of academic research evaluation. Indicators are awards, honorary doctorates, or membership in prestigious academies (Stephan 1996; Frey and Neckermann 2008).[2] Its main form for the majority of scholars consists of publications and citations in professional journals with high impact factors. Such indicators are provided by academic rankings, based on peer-reviewed publications, citations, and the impact factors of journals like Thomson Reuters' *Impact Factor* (JIF) (see Garfield 2006, for a historical review) and the relatively recent h-index (Hirsch 2005).[3]

---

[2] Zuckerman (1992) estimates that by the beginning of the 1990s around 3,000 different scientific awards existed in North America.

[3] Examples of prominent rankings are the ISI Web of Knowledge Journal Citation Report (The Thomson Corporation, 2008b), ISI Web of Knowledge Essential Science Indicators (The Thomson Corporation, 2008a), IDEAS Ranking (IDEAS, 2008),

However, peer reviews as the founding stones of academic governance are faced with serious problems that have recently been discussed (e.g. Armstrong 1997; Wenneras and Wold 1999; Brook 2003; Frey 2003; Bedeian 2004; Starbuck 2005, 2006; Tsang and Frey 2007; Gillies 2005, 2008; Abramo, Angelo, and Caprasecca 2009; Bornmann and Daniel 2009).[4]

- *Low inter-rater reliability.* There is an extensive literature on the low extent to which reviewing reports conform to each other (Miner and MacDonald 1981; Cole 1992; Weller 2001; Miller 2006). The correlation between the judgments of two peers falls between 0.09 and 0.5 (Starbuck 2005). In clinical neuroscience, it was found that the correlations among reviewers' recommendations "was little greater than would be expected by chance alone" (Rothwell and Martyn 2000, p. 1964).[5] Peters and Ceci (1982) conducted a study of peer reviewing that was the subject of much discussion. They resubmitted 12 articles to the top-tier journals that had published them only 18 to 32 months earlier, giving the articles fictitious authors at obscure institutions. Only 3 of 38 editors and reviewers recognized that the articles had already been published. Of the remaining 9 articles, 8 were rejected. It is important that the correlation is higher for papers rejected than for papers accepted (Cichetti 1991). This means that peer reviewers are better able to identify academic low performers; that is, it is easier to identify papers that do not meet minimum quality standards than those that are a result of excellent research (Lindsey 1991; Moed 2007).
- *Low prognostic quality.* The reviewers' rating of manuscript quality has been found to correlate only 0.24 with later citations (Gottfredson 1978). According to Starbuck (2006, pp. 83–84), the correlation of a particular reviewer's evaluation with the actual quality as measured by later citations of the manuscript reviewed is between 0.25 and 0.30. This correlation rarely rises above 0.37, although there is evidence that higher prestige journals publish more high-value articles (Judge, Cable, Colbert, and Rynes 2007). Because of some randomness in

Academic Ranking of World Universities (Shanghai Jiao Tong University, 2007); or Handelsblatt Ranking (Handelsblatt, 2010).

[4] See also the special issue of *Science and Public Policy* (2007) and the Special Theme Section on "The use and misuse of bibliometric indices in evaluating scholarly performance" of *Ethics in Science and Environmental Politics*, June 8, 2008.

[5] According to Fletcher and Fletcher (2003, p. 66) it needs "to have at least six reviewers, all favouring publication or rejection, for their votes to yield a statistical significant conclusion."

editorial selections (Starbuck 2005),[6] one editor even advises rejected authors to "Just Try, Try Again" (Durso 1997).[7]

- *Low consistency over time.* Many rejections of papers in highly ranked journals are documented that later were awarded high prizes, including the Nobel Prize (Gans and Shepherd 1994; Campanario 1996; Horrobin 1996; Lawrence 2003). This means that, in the case of radical innovations or paradigm shifts (Kuhn 1962), peer reviews often fail.
- *Confirmation biases.* Reviewers find methodological shortcomings in 71 percent of papers contradicting the mainstream, compared to only 25 percent of papers supporting the mainstream (Mahoney 1977).

As a consequence, the "republic of science" is based on a shaky ground since the quality of peer evaluations is questionable.

Advantages of academic rankings

Rankings have several advantages compared to qualitative peer reviews that help to explain why they have become so popular in the last years (Abramo et al. 2009).

- Rankings are more objective than qualitative approaches because they are based on more than the three or four evaluations typical for review processes. Through statistical aggregation, individual reviewers' biases may be balanced (Weingart 2005).
- The influence of the old boys' network may be avoided. An instrument is provided to dismantle unfounded claims to fame. Rankings can serve as fruitful, exogenous shocks to some schools and make them care more about the reactions of the public (Khurana 2007, p. 337).
- Rankings are cheaper than pure qualitative reviews, at least in terms of time. They admit updates and rapid intertemporal comparisons.
- Rankings facilitate the comparison between a large numbers of scholars or institutions.
- They give research administrators, politicians, journalists, and students an easy to use device to evaluate the standing of the research. As a consequence, attention for research outcomes and the willingness to spend money might arise.

---

[6] See also the "Social Text"-Affair, which deals with the malfunction of editors: The physicist Alain D. Sokal published an article in a (non-refereed) special issue of the journal *Social Text*, which was written as a parody. The editors did not realize that the bogus article was a hoax (see Sokal 1996).

[7] However, this strategy overburdens reviewers and may lower the quality of reviews. For example, they have neither enough time nor the incentive to check the quality of the data and of the statistical methods employed, as some striking examples in economics demonstrate (Hamermesh 2007).

Disadvantages of academic rankings: technical and methodological problems

In recent times, it became clear that rankings might counterbalance some problems of qualitative peer reviews but that they have disadvantages of their own (Butler 2007; Donovan 2007; Adler, Ewing, and Taylor 2008; Adler and Harzing 2009). Until now, mainly technical and methodological problems were highlighted (van Raan 2005).

Technical problems consist of errors in the citing–cited matching process, leading to a loss of citations to a specific publication. First, it is estimated that this loss amounts on average to 7 percent of the citations. In specific situations, this percentage may even be as high as 30 percent (Moed 2002). Second, there are many errors made in attributing publications and citations to the source, for example, institutes, departments, or universities. In the popular ranking of the Shanghai Jiao Tong University, these errors led to differences of possibly 5 to 10 positions in the European list and about 25 to 50 positions in the world list (Moed 2002). The impact factor of Thomson's ISI Web of Science is accused of having many faults (Monastersky 2005; Taylor, Perakakis, and Trachana, 2008). It is unlikely that the errors are distributed equally. Kotiaho, Tomkin, and Simmons (1999) find that names from unfamiliar languages lead to a geographical bias against non-English speaking countries. Third, it has been shown that small changes in measurement techniques and classifications can have large effects on the position in rankings (Ursprung and Zimmer 2006; Frey and Rost 2010).

Methodological problems of constructing meaningful and consistent indices to measure scientific output have been widely discussed recently (Lawrence 2002, 2003; Frey 2003, 2009; Adler et al. 2008; Adler and Harzing 2009).

First, there are selection problems. Often only journal articles are selected for incorporation in the rankings, although books, proceedings, or blogs contribute considerably to scholarly work. Other difficulties include the low representation of small research fields, non-English papers, regional journals, and journals from other disciplines even if they are highly ranked in their respective disciplines. Hence, collaboration across disciplinary boundaries is not furthered.

Second, citations can have a supportive or rejective meaning or merely a herding effect. The probability of being cited is a function of previous citations according to the "Matthew effect" in science (Merton 1968). Simkin and Roychowdhury (2005) estimate that, according to an analysis of misprints turning up repeatedly in citations, about 70–90 percent of scientific citations are copied from the list of references used in other papers; that is, 70–90 percent of the papers cited have not been read. Consequently, incorrect citations are endemic. They are promoted by the increasing use of meta-analyses, which generally do not distinguish between high and low quality analyses (Todd and Ladle 2008). In addition, citations may reflect fleeting references to fashionable "hot topics."

Third, using the impact factor of a journal as a proxy for the quality of a single article leads to substantial misclassification. It has been found that many top articles are published in non-top journals, and many articles in top journals generate very few citations in management research (Starbuck 2005; Singh, Haddad, and Chow 2007), economics (Laband and Tollison 2003; Oswald 2007), and science (Campbell 2008; Rinia et al. 1998). A study of the "International Mathematical Union" even concludes that the use of impact factors can be "breathtakingly naïve" (Adler et al. 2008, p. 14) because it leads to large error probabilities.

Fourth, there are difficulties comparing citations and impact factors between disciplines and even between subdisciplines (Bornman, Mutz, Neuhaus, and Daniel 2008).

Disadvantages of academic rankings: unintended side effects

Even if over time the methodological and technical problems could be handled, severe problems remain, which are caused by the unintended side effects of rankings on the side of individuals and institutions. First, they consist of the so-called reactive measures (Campbell 1957), caused by the fact that people change their behavior strategically in reaction to being observed or measured, in particular if the measurement is not accepted voluntarily (Espeland and Sauder 2007). Reactivity threatens the validity of measures according to the saying: "When a measure becomes a target, it ceases to be a good measure" (Strathern 1996, p. 4). Second, the unintended consequences consist of the danger of reducing the intrinsically motivated curiosity of researchers. Both problems, which are discussed only by a few authors in the research governance literature, have consequences on the level of individual scholars and institutions.

Level of individual scholars

Reactivity on the level of individual scholars may take the form of *goal displacement* or of counterstrategies to "beat the system." Goal displacement (Perrin, 1998) means that people maximize indicators that are easy to measure and disregard features that are hard to measure. This problem is also discussed as the multiple-tasking effect (Holmstrom and Milgrom 1991; Ethiraj and Levinthal 2009). There is much evidence of this effect in laboratory experiments (Staw and Boettger 1990; Gilliland and Landis 1992; Schweitzer, Ordonez, and Douma 2004; Ordonez, Schweitzer, Galinsky, and Bazerman 2009).[8] For example, Fehr and Schmidt (2004) show that output-dependent financial incentives lead to the neglect of noncontractible tasks.

In academia, examples of goal displacement can be found, for example, as "slicing strategy," by breaking them into as many papers as possible to increase their publication list. Another example of goal displacement is the lowering of standards for Ph.D. candidates when the amount of completed Ph.D.s is used as a measure in rankings.

Empirical field evidence of goal displacement in academia is shown in an Australian study (Butler 2003). The mid 1990s saw a linking of the number of peer-reviewed publications to the funding of universities and individual scholars. The number of publications increased dramatically, but the quality as measured by relative citation rates decreased.[9] A recent study that examined how incentive systems affected submissions and publications to the journal *Science* during the last decade found that submissions per year increased significantly with incentives. However, there was no significant impact of incentives on publications (Franzoni et al. 2010).

Counterstrategies are more difficult to observe than goal displacement. They consist of altering research behavior itself (Moed 2007). Numerous examples can be found in educational evaluation (e.g. Haney 2002; Nichols, Glass, and Berliner 2006; Heilig and Darling-Hammond 2008). The following behaviors are of special relevance in academia.

Scholars distort their results to please, or at least not to oppose, prospective referees. Bedeian (2003) finds evidence that no less than 25 percent of authors revise their manuscripts according to the suggestions of the referee although they know that the change is incorrect. Frey (2003) calls this behavior "academic prostitution."

Authors cite possible reviewers because the latter are prone to judge papers more favorably that approvingly cite their work, and

---

[8] Locke and Latham (2009) in a rejoinder provide counterevidence to Ordonez et al. (2009). They argue that goal setting has no negative effects. However, they disregard that goal setting may well work for simple but not for complex tasks within an organization. For the latter case, see Earley, Connolly, and Ekegren (1989) and Ethiraj and Levinthal (2009).

[9] It could be argued that a remedy to this problem consists of resorting to citation counts. Although this remedy overcomes some of the shortcomings of publication counts, it is subject to the technical and methodological problems mentioned.

these same reviewers tend to reject papers that threaten their previous work (Lawrence 2003, p. 260).[10] Some editors admit freely that they encourage authors to cite their respective journals in order to raise their impact rankings (Garfield 1997; Smith 1997; Monastersky 2005).

To meet the expectations of their peers – many of whom consist of mainstream scholars – authors may be discouraged from conducting and submitting creative and unorthodox research (Horrobin 1996; Prichard and Willmott 1997; Armstrong 1997; Gillies 2008).

The effects of reactivity are enforced if the second kind of unintended consequences takes place, the decrease of *intrinsically motivated curiosity* which generally is acknowledged to be of decisive importance in academic research (Amabile 1996, 1998; Spangenberg et al. 1990; Stephan 1996; Simonton 2004). In both psychology and psychological economics,[11] there exists considerable empirical evidence that there is a crowding-out effect of intrinsic motivation by externally imposed goals linked to incentives that do not give a supportive feedback and are perceived to be controlling.[12] (Hennessey and Amabile 1998; Frey 1992, 1997; Deci, Koestner, and Ryan 1999; Gagné and Deci 2005; Falk and Kosfeld 2006; Ordonez et al. 2009.)[13]

From that point of view, rankings tend to crowd out intrinsically motivated curiosity. First, in contrast to qualitative peer reviews, rankings do not give a supportive feedback as they do not tell scholars how to improve their research. Second, because rankings are mostly imposed from outside, the content of research is in danger of losing importance. It is substituted by the position in the rankings. As a consequence, the dysfunctional reactions of scholars (e.g. goal displacement and counter-strategies) are enforced because they are not constrained by intrinsic preferences. The inducement to "game the system" in an instrumental way may get the upper hand.

---

[10] Such problems of sabotage in tournaments have been extensively discussed in personnel economics; see Lazear and Shaw (2007).

[11] We prefer the expression psychological economics instead of the more common expression behavioral economics for two reasons. First, economists had already examined human behavior before this new field emerged. Second, Simon (1985) points out that the term behavioral is misleading because it may be confounded with the behaviorist approach in psychology.

[12] A third precondition is social relatedness, see Gagne and Deci (2005).

[13] The crowding-out effect sometimes is contested, for example, Eizenberger and Cameron (1996), Gerhart and Rynes (2003), Locke and Latham (2009). However, the empirical evidence for complex tasks and actors intrinsically motivated in the first place is strong (Deci et al., 1999; Weibel, Rost, and Osterloh, 2010). For a survey of the empirical evidence see Frey and Jegen (2001).

Level of institutions

Reactivity on the institutional level takes several forms. First, if rankings are used as a measure to allocate resources and positions, they create a lock-in effect. Even those scholars and academic institutions that are aware of the deficiencies of rankings do well not to oppose them. If they did so, they would not only be accused of being afraid of competition, but also of not contributing to the prestige and resources of their department or university. Therefore, it is a better strategy to follow the rules and to play the game. For example, in several countries, highly cited scientists are hired in order to raise publication and citation records. Such stars are highly paid although they often have little involvement with the respective university (Brook 2003; Stephan 2008).

Second, a negative walling-off effect sets in. Scholars themselves are inclined to apply rankings to evaluate candidates in order to gain more resources for their research group or department. In addition, it is easier to count the publications and citations of colleagues than to evaluate the content of their scholarly contributions. This practice is defended by arguing that specialization in science has increased so much that even within disciplines it is impossible to evaluate the research in neighboring fields (Swanson 2004; van Fleet, McWilliams, and Siegel 2000). However, this practice in turn reinforces specialization and furthers a walling-off effect between disciplines and subdisciplines. By using output indicators instead of communicating on the contents, the knowledge in the various fields becomes increasingly disconnected.

Third, research is in danger of being increasingly homogenized. Research endeavors tend to lose the diversity that is necessary for a creative research environment. This consequence was pointed out for business schools by Gioia and Corley (2002). For economics, Great Britain provides an example: the share of heterodox, not strictly neoclassical, economics sank drastically since the ranking of departments became important. Heterodox journals have become less attractive for researchers due to their smaller impact factor when compared to mainstream journals (Lee 2007; Holcombe 2004). This is due to the fact that all kinds of rankings are by definition one-dimensional. They press the multifacetedness, heterogeneity, and ambiguity of scholarly endeavors into a simple order. Such an order is easy to understand by the public, comparable to football leagues or hit parades. However, in contrast to such endeavors, scholarly work is characterized by controversial disputes, which are essential for scientific progress. Rankings tend to suppress such disputes because they generate dominant views – not by disputes about the contents but by counting numbers (Heintz 2008). This contradicts the idea of research as institutionalized scepticism (Merton 1973). In contrast, peer reviews, though they have many short-comings, produce a great heterogeneity of scientific content and views. This heterogeneity fuels scholarly debates. Moreover, peer reviews discourage scholars with unorthodox views less than rankings. If rejected by the reviewers of one journal, the reviewers of another equivalent journal might accept the article. This may be of special importance during radical innovations or paradigm shifts according to Kuhn (1962).

Fourth, the establishment of new research areas is inhibited. It has been argued that in Great Britain, the Research Assessment Exercise has discouraged research with uncertain outcomes and has encouraged projects with quick payoffs (Hargreaves Heap 2002).

Fifth, it is argued that a positional competition or a rent-seeking game takes place instead of an enhancement of research quality by the increased investment by universities and journals in evaluating research (Ehrenberg 2000). It has been shown that the percentage of "dry holes" (i.e., articles in refereed journals that have never been cited) in economic research during 1974 to 1996 has remained constant (Laband and Tollison 2003), although the resources to improve the screening of papers have risen substantially.

With respect to the motivational aspects of rankings on the institutional level, a negative selection effect is to be expected, in particular, when monetary rewards are linked to the position in rankings. In academia, a special incentive system called "taste for science" exists (Merton 1973; Dasgupta and David 1994; Stephan 1996; Sorenson and Fleming 2004; Roach and Sauermann 2010). It is characterized by a relatively low importance of monetary incentives and a high importance of peer recognition and autonomy. People are attracted to research for which, at the margin, the autonomy to satisfy their curiosity and to gain peer recognition is more important than money. They value the possibility of following their own scientific goals more than financial rewards (Bhagwat et al. 2004). These scholars are prepared to trade-off autonomy against money, as empirically documented by Roach and Sauermann (2010) and Stern (2004): scientists pay to be scientists. The preference for autonomy to choose their own goals is important for innovative research in two ways. It leads to a useful self-selection effect, and autonomy is the most important precondition for intrinsic motivation, which in turn is required for creative research (Amabile et al. 1996; Amabile 1998; R. Mudambi, S. Mudambi, and Navarra 2007).

Suggestions to improve academic governance

We discuss four suggestions to improve academic governance and at the same time to mitigate the tensions between "new public management" and the "republic of science": Informed peer review, input control, awards, and partially random selection.

Informed peer review

A much discussed proposal to mitigate the disadvantages of rankings are informed peer reviews. That is a combination of qualitative peer reviews and rankings (e.g. Butler 2007; Moed 2007). Only peers should use rankings in conjunction with qualitative judgments. Peers should be familiar with the standards of good practice for the analysis, interpretation, and presentation of rankings (van Raan 2005; Bornmann et al. 2008). This includes the exploratory use of different rankings because their results differ markedly (e.g. Adler and Harzing 2009), in particular with respect to the ranking of individuals (Frey and Rost 2010).

This proposal mitigates the problems associated with rankings. However, the use of rankings as a handy instrument for politicians, public officials, administrators, journalists, and other non-experts is considerably reduced. Moreover, the use of different rankings induces high costs not only on the side of the evaluators but also on the side of those being evaluated. Too much energy and time is being consumed in reporting, negotiating, reframing, and presenting performance indicators, all of which distracts from the performance that is desired.

Moreover, it will not mitigate the problem that peers often evaluate path-breaking ideas negatively because they threaten their accumulated knowledge capital (Kuhn 1962).

Input control

Input control refers to insights from managerial control theory (e.g. Ouchi 1977, 1979; Eizenhardt 1985; Schreyögg and Steinmann 1987). According to this approach, three different kinds of controls may be distinguished: output control, process control, and input control. Output control is useful if well-defined unambiguous indicators are available to the evaluator. Such controls are attractive to non-experts. However, as discussed, rankings are far from delivering such unambiguous indicators. *Process control* is useful when outputs are not easy to measure and to attribute, but when the controller has an appropriate knowledge of cause–effect relationships or the transformation process of inputs into outputs. Process control is applicable only for peers who are familiar with the state of the art in the respective research field. If neither output control nor process control works sufficiently well because of the complexity or the ambiguity of the tasks being evaluated, *input control* has to be applied.[14] This kind of control is usually applied when easy-to-measure outputs are not available or processes are not precisely observable. Input control is based on careful selection, socialization, and placement of the candidates. It intends to make sure that individuals have internalized norms and professional standards. Input control takes place inside professional groups, such as life-tenured judges (e.g. Benz and Frey 2007; Posner 2010). Once a candidate has passed the input control that candidate becomes a member of a profession. Autonomy is curtailed only by professional norms that are confirmed by institutionalized rituals.

In the case of research governance, input control means that aspiring scholars should be carefully socialized and selected by peers to prove that they have mastered the state of the art, have preferences according to the "taste for science" (Merton 1973), and are able to direct themselves. Those who have an "entrance ticket" to the republic of science after having passed a rigorous input control can be given much autonomy to foster their creativity and intrinsically motivated curiosity. This includes the provision of basic funds to provide a certain degree of independence after having passed the entrance barriers (Gillies 2008; Horrobin 1996).

Input control is part of the "Principles Governing Research at Harvard," which state, "The primary means for controlling the quality of scholarly activities of this Faculty is through the rigorous academic standards applied in selecting its members."[15] Input control has empirically proven to be successful also in R&D organizations of industrial companies (Abernethy and Brownell 1997). This is in accordance with empirical findings in psychological economics, which show that on average intrinsically motivated people do not shirk when given autonomy (Frey 1992; Gneezy and Rustichini 2000; Fong and Tosi 2007). Instead, they raise their efforts when they perceive that they are trusted (Osterloh and Frey 2000; Falk and Kosfeld 2006; Frost et al. 2010).

Input control has advantages and disadvantages. The advantages first consist of downplaying the unfortunate ranking games while inducing young scholars to learn the professional standards of their discipline

[14] Ouchi (1979) calls this kind of control "clan control."
[15] See "Principles governing research at Harvard," www.fas.harvard.edu/research/greybook/principles.html (last accessed: 3 June 2011).

under the assistance of peers. Second, although input control still requires process and output control in the form of informed peer evaluations, this applies during limited time periods, namely during situations of status passage. Thus, input control draws consequences from the fact that peer control, as well as rankings, are problematic in assessing academic quality. Third, input control is a decentralized form of peer evaluation, for example, when submitting papers or applying for jobs. It supports the heterogeneity of scholarly views central to the scientific communication process. Fourth, input control is a kind of "informed peer review" that is able to use output indicators in an exploratory way.

The disadvantages consist first in the danger that some scholars who have passed the selection might misuse their autonomy, reduce their work effort, and waste their funds. This disadvantage is lowered when the selection process is conducted rigorously. Second, input control is in danger of being submitted to groupthink and cronyism (Janis 1972). This danger can be mitigated by fostering the diversity of scholarly approaches within the relevant peer group. Third, the public as well as university administrators do not have an easy to comprehend picture of scholarly activities, as is the case for output control based on rankings.[16] People outside the scholarly community have to acknowledge that evaluating scholarly activities is a particularly difficult task.

Awards

Awards compensate to a certain extent for the limited visibility of input control to the public. Awards like prizes and titles as well as different kinds of professorships and fellowships (from assistant to distinguished) signal the recognition of peers to non-experts (Frey and Osterloh 2010). They consist of an overall evaluation, which avoids the issue that particular metrics can be manipulated (Frey and Neckermann 2008).

Awards are partly extrinsic motivators. However, as empirical evidence shows, they do not crowd out intrinsic motivation (Neckermann, Cueni, and Frey 2010). They match the motivational factors that conform to the "taste of science." These factors consist in the first place of peer recognition and the granting of autonomy, while pay plays a secondary role (Jimenex-Contreras, de Moya Anegon, and Delgado Lopez-Cozar

---

[16] As a result, university leaders like presidents, vice chancellors, and deans should consist of accomplished scholars. In contrast to pure managers, top scholars have a better understanding of the research process. Goodall (2009) showed that for a panel of 55 research universities, a university's research performance is improved after an accomplished scholar has been hired as president.

2003; Stern 2004; Roach and Sauermann 2010). They motivate well even for those who do not actually win such an award.[17]

Partially random selection

The fourth proposal to mitigate the problems of rankings and peer reviews is the most radical one. Nevertheless, the use of random procedures to reach desired social outcomes has a long history (Buchstein 2009; Buchstein and Jörke 2007).[18] In classical Athens and the Venetian Republic, many of the political positions were chosen by lot among the citizens. Random selection plays a role in the selection of juries in the United States and several other countries. In the movement for deliberate democracy (Habermas 2006; Dryzek 2002; Fishkin 1991), the selection of citizens to participate in the consultation or decision-making process is usually by lot. These ideas are applied by Frey and Stutzer (2006) to international organizations and by Emery (1989) to decision making at workplaces. As for all decision-making processes, random selection has its advantages and disadvantages, which should be compared (for a more comprehensive discussion, see Elster 1989, Carson and Martin 1999, and Buchstein 2009).

The advantages are: First, random selection procedures guarantee the true representativeness of the discussants. Over- or underrepresentation of certain groups according to gender, race, religion, age, or other characteristics are avoided. Second, this has the additional advantage of bringing in new views often overlooked by the incumbents. It is a "search-machine" for new arguments and talents (Buchstein 2009, p. 391) and furthers "political learning" (Fishkin and Farrar 2005, p. 76; see also Dahl 1989; Ackermann and Fishkin 2004, Hendriks 2004). Third, it shields against undesired outside influences by the politicians in power as well as by entrenched interest groups, as pointed out already by Aristotle as well as by Hayek (1979). It effectively works against principal–agent conflicts and corrupting influences. Fourth, it reduces the costs of campaigning and self-promotion to achieve political goals (Burnheim 1985).

Of course there are also disadvantages. The first and most common argument against random selection is that it does not differentiate between experienced and inexperienced people. However, experts often fall victim to an oversight trap in situations of great uncertainty due to a

---

[17] The money attached to awards is less important than the reputation of the award-giving institution, see Frey and Neckermann (2008).
[18] Partly random selection is also called sortition (Dowlen, 2008). It leads to a so-called demarchy (Burnheim, 1985),

familiarity bias and overconfidence (Griffin and Tversky 1992; see Rost and Osterloh 2010, for additional empirical evidence). Second, a lack of legitimacy of the random selection process at the present time might exist. Third, there might be a lower sense of accountability by randomly selected people. Fourth, random selection might lead to less effort because candidates might build on chance rather than working hard.

For these reasons, randomly selected bodies are mostly considered not as an alternative to elected bodies but as a supplement. Accordingly, the random selection of articles or of research proposals should be used in combination with informed peer review. Nevertheless, some scholars argue for pure random selection (see Duxbury 1999, p. 89).

A first suggestion is "focal randomization" (Brezis 2007).[19] That is, papers (or R&D projects) would be immediately accepted that are unanimously ranked at the top by all reviewers. Papers not considered sufficient by all reviewers would be immediately rejected. Papers with an inconsistent vote would be selected randomly. A more moderate version of this idea proposes to spend only a certain percentage of the research budget of funding bodies on research projects that are randomly selected among those with inconsistent votes by the referees (Buchstein 2011). The disadvantage of this suggestion is that it might not give enough chances to path-breaking ideas because the correlation between reviewers' judgements is lower for papers accepted than for papers rejected (Cicchetti 1991). This means that peer reviewers are better able to identify low academic performance than excellent research (Moed 2007).

Therefore, we suggest considering a more radical proposal: All papers not rejected unanimously should be published according to random selection. The reason for this suggestion is that reviewers typically consist of mainstream scholars who often hesitate to acknowledge path-breaking ideas. Some reviewers reject work that puts their own research into question (Horrobin 1996; Armstrong 1997; Gillies 2008). As mentioned, reviewers find more methodological shortcomings in papers that contradict mainstream thought than in papers that support the mainstream (Mahoney 1977).

For the selection of articles to be published in academic journals, a minimum acceptable level of quality should be defined. If this is not done, scholars would lose part of their incentive to produce good research and to write acceptable articles. However, they would not lose this incentive completely because the articles published would be evaluated by individual readers and thus influence the writer's reputation

---

[19] Brezis (2007) considers only R&D projects. He shows that under certain conditions focal randomization leads to a higher average return than the conventional method.

in the academic community. The minimum acceptable standard could be determined in the following way:

- If all the referees think that the minimum level has not been attained, the paper is rejected.
- If the referees disagree about whether a paper meets the standard, it would be included in the set from which the papers to be published are drawn. In the case of more than two referees, one could set a qualified majority for rejecting the paper. If, say, four out of five referees state that the minimum level has not been attained, the paper would be rejected. Care should be taken not to extend the veto power too much because otherwise innovative and unorthodox but valuable papers would be excluded from publication from the outset.

The partly random selection of articles from the set of acceptable papers has various advantages over the present system of peer review and rankings: First, referees' biases play a much lesser role. Second, the tendency of referees to pursue their own agenda and their private interests no longer plays a role. Third, good connections in the scientific community, for example, working at an influential scientific institution, no longer matter. Fourth, highly original and unconventional articles that the referees find difficult to comprehend and to appreciate have a chance of being published. This corresponds well to the scientific goal of overcoming seemingly established truths or "normal science" in the sense of Kuhn (1962) and paves the way to more rapid scientific progress. Fifth, rankings based on publications in journals with high impact lose importance.

The random selection of articles for publication has three major disadvantages: First, scholars have a stronger incentive to try to publish their papers even if they are not of high quality, provided they make the cut-off point. Publication indeed becomes a random event to a certain extent. However, as noted above, there is evidence that the existing system is not far from that state anyway. Second, due to the reduced difficulty of publishing, the number of submissions to journals would increase thus putting a higher burden on referees. However, the referees' work is simpler because they only have to evaluate whether a paper meets the standard or not. As indicated above, peer reviewers are better able to identify academically low performers than excellent research (Moed 2007). Third, many "bad" papers would be published although it is not clear what "bad" really means. According to the evidence presented in the second section, the present system is not immune to what other scholars, or future scholars, consider to be "bad" papers.

The range over which papers are selected by a random procedure can be reduced, as mentioned, by editors accepting papers whose publication is supported by all referees. A further reduction is possible by accepting papers supported by a (qualified) majority of referees, for instance two out of three referees. This moves the selection process in the direction of increasing the weight of referees' opinions, that is, in the direction of the traditional method of selection. The disadvantage is that the problems with refereeing pointed out above also gain weight. In particular, it could be argued that such a decision process too drastically reduces the chance of original and unconventional papers being published.

Conclusions

Academic rankings and peer reviews have major disadvantages that tend to be disregarded or downplayed. To mitigate their negative consequences for unconventional ideas, we discuss four suggestions that could be used in combination. The first suggestion, informed peer review, is very common. Its greatest disadvantage consists in the fact that peers on average are average scholars that often do not appreciate unconventional ideas. This also is a disadvantage of the second proposal, awards. Illustrative examples are given by numerous scholars who had to wait for decades for the appreciation of their work. Therefore we discuss two radical suggestions, input control and partially random selection. Both suggestions enable creativity and foster heterogeneity of scholarly views, which is at the heart of path-breaking research. The price to pay is that the public does not get an easy to comprehend picture of scholarly activity. But it should be part of the accountability of research to the public to communicate that scholarly work has to be evaluated in a different way than football games or hit parades.

References

Abernethy, M. A. and Brownell, P. 1997. "Management control systems in research and development organizations: The role of accounting, behavior and personnel controls." *Accounting, Organizations and Society*, 22 (3/4), 233–248.

Abramo, G. D., Angelo, C. A., and Caprasecca, A. 2009. "Allocative efficiency in public research funding: Can bibliometrics help?" *Research Policy*, 38, 206–215.

Ackermann, B. A. and Fishkin, J. 2004. *Deliberation Day*. New Haven: Yale University Press.

Adler, N. J. and Harzing, A.-W. 2009. "When knowledge wins: Transcending the sense and nonsense of academic rankings." *Academy of Management Learning*, 8, 72–95.

Adler, R., Ewing, J., and Taylor, P. 2008. "Citation statistics, A report from the joint committee on quantitative assessment of research" (IMU, ICIAM, IMS). Report from the International Mathematical Union (IMU) in cooperation with the International Council of Industrial and Applied Mathematics (ICIAM) and the Institute of Mathematical Statistics (IMS).

Albers, S. 2009. "Misleading rankings of research in business." *German Economic Review*, 3, 352–363.

Amabile, T. M. 1996. *Creativity in Context: Update to the Social Psychology of Creativity*. Boulder, CO: Westview Press.

Amabile, T. M. 1998. "How to kill creativity." *Harvard Business Review*, 76, 76–87.

Amabile, T. M., Conti, R., Coon, H., Lazenby, J., and Herron, M. 1996. "Assessing the work environment for creativity." *Academy of Management Journal*, 39, 1154–1184.

Armstrong, J. S. 1997. "Peer review for journals: Evidence on quality control, fairness, and innovation." *Science and Engineering Ethics*, 3, 63–84.

Arrow, K. 1962. "Economic welfare and the allocation of resources for invention." In R. Nelson (ed.), *The Rate and Direction of Inventive Activity: Economic and Social Factors* (pp. 609–626). Princeton University Press.

Bedeian, A. G. 2003. "The manuscript review process: The proper roles of authors, referees, and editors." *Journal of Management Inquiry*, 12, 331–338.
  2004. "Peer review and the social construction of knowledge in the management discipline." *Academy of Management Learning and Education*, 3, 198–216.

Benz, M. and Frey, B. S. 2007. "Corporate governance: What can we learn from public governance?" *Academy of Management Review*, 32(1), 92–104.

Bhagwat, J. G., Ondategui-Parra, S., Zou, K. H., Gogate, A., Intriere, L. A., Kelly, P., Seltze, S. E., and Ros, P. R. 2004. "Motivation and compensation in Academic Radiology." *Journal of the American College of Radiology*, 1 (7), 493–496.

Bok, D. 2003. *Universities in the Marketplace: The Commercialization of Higher Education*. Princeton University Press.

Bornmann, L. and Daniel, H. D. 2009. "The luck of the referee draw: The effect of exchanging reviews." *Learned Publishing*, 22(2), 117–125.

Bornmann, L., Mutz, R., Neuhaus, C., and Daniel, H. D. 2008. "Citation counts for research evaluation: Standards of good practice for analyzing bibliometric data and presenting and interpreting results." *Ethics in Science and Environmental Politics*, 8, 93–102.

Brezis, E. S. 2007. "Focal randomization: An optimal mechanism for the evaluation of R&D projects." *Science and Public Policy*, 2007(Dec.), 691–698.

Brook, R. 2003. "Research survival in the age of evaluation." In *Science Between Evaluation and Innovation: A Conference on Peer Review* (pp. 61–66). München: Max-Planck-Gesellschaft.

Buchstein, H. 2009. *Demokratie und Lotterie*. Frankfurt/New York: Campus.
  2011. "Der Zufall in der Forschungsförderungspolitik." *Forschung & Lehre* 11(8), 596–597.

Buchstein, H. and Jörke, D. 2007. "Redescribing Democracy." *Redescription*, 11, 178–200.

Burnheim, J. 1985. *Is Democracy Possible? The Alternative to Electoral Politics.* London: Polity Press.

Bush, V. 1945, July. *"Science: The endless frontier." A report to the president by Vannevar Bush, Director of the Office of Scientific Research and Development.* Washington, D.C.: United States Government Printing Office. Retrieved July 1, 2010, from www.nsf.gov/od/lpa/nsf50/vbush1945.htm

Butler, L. 2003. "Explaining Australia's increased share of ISI publications—the effects of a funding formula based on publication counts." *Research Policy*, 32, 143–155.

2007. "Assessing university research: A plea for a balanced approach." *Science and Public Policy*, 34, 565–574.

Campanario, J. M. 1996. "Using citation classics to study the incidence of serendipity in scientific discovery." *Scientometrics*, 37, 3–24.

Campbell, D. T. 1957. "Factors relevant to the validity of experiments in social settings." *Psychological Bulletin*, 54, 297–312.

Campbell, P. 2008. "Escape from the impact factor." *Ethics in Science and Environmental Politics*, 8, 5–7.

Carson, L. and Martin, B. 1999. *Random Selection in Politics.* Westpoint, CN/London: Praeger.

Cicchetti, D. V. 1991. "The reliability of peer review for manuscript and grant submissions: A cross-disciplinary investigation." *Behavioral and Brain Sciences*, 14, 119–135.

Clark, B. R. 1998. *Creating Entrepreneurial Universities: Organizational Pathways of Transformation.* Surrey: Pergamon Press.

Cole, S. 1992. *Making Science: Between Nature and Society.* Cambridge, MA: Harvard University Press.

Dahl, R. A. 1989. *Democracy and its Critics.* New Haven: Yale University Press.

Dasgupta, P. and David, P. A. 1994. "Toward a new economics of science." *Research Policy*, 23, 487–521.

Deci, E. L., Koestner, R., and Ryan, R. M. 1999. "A meta-analytic review of experiments examining the effects of extrinsic rewards on intrinsic motivation." *Psychological Bulletin*, 125, 627–668.

Donoghue, F. 2008. *The Last Professors: The Corporate University and the Fate of the Humanities.* New York, NY: Fordham University Press.

Donovan, C. 2007. "The qualitative future of research evaluation." *Science and Public Policy*, 34, 585–597.

Dowlen, O. 2008. *The Political Potential of Sortition: A Study of the Random Selection of Citizens for Public Office.* Charlottesville, VA: Imprint Academic.

Dryzek, O. 2002. *Deliberative Democracy and Beyond.* Oxford University Press.

Durso, T. W. 1997. "Editor's advice to reject authors: Just try, try again." *The Scientist*, 11, 13.

Duxbury, N. 1999. *Random Justice: On Lotteries and Legal Decision Making.* Oxford University Press.

Earley, P. C., Connolly, T., and Ekegren, G. 1989. "Goals, strategy development, and task performance: Some limits on the efficacy of goal setting." *Journal of Applied Psychology*, 74, 24–33.

Ehrenberg, R. G. 2000. *Tuition Rising: Why College Costs So Much*. Cambridge, MA: Harvard University Press.

Elster, J. 1989. *Solomonic Judgements*. Cambridge University Press.

Emery, F. E. 1989. *Toward Real Democracy and Toward Real Democracy: Further Problems*. Ontario Ministery of Labour.

Eizenberger, R. and Cameron, J. 1996. "Detrimental effects of reward: Reality or myth?" *American Psychologist*, 51(11), 1153–1166.

Eizenhardt, K. M. 1985. "Control: Organizational and economic approaches." *Management Science*, 31(2), 134–149.

Espeland, W. N. and Sauder, M. 2007. "Rankings and reactivity: How public measures recreate social worlds." *American Journal of Sociology*, 113(1), 1–40.

Ethiraj, S. K. and Levinthal, D. 2009. "Hoping for A to Z while rewarding only A: Complex organizations and multiple goals." *Organization Science*, 20, 4–21.

Falk, A. and Kosfeld, M. 2006. "The hidden cost of control." *American Economic Review*, 96, 1611–1630.

Fehr, E. and Schmidt, K. M. 2004. "Fairness and incentives in a multi-task principal-agent model." *Scandinavian Journal of Economics*, 106, 453–474.

Fishkin, J. 1991. *Democracy and Deliberation*. New Haven: Yale University Press.

Fishkin, J. and Farrar, C. 2005. "Deliberative polling: From experience to community resource." In J. Gastil and P. Levine (eds.), *The Deliberative Democracy Handbook: Strategies for Effective Civic Engagement in the Twenty-First Century* (pp. 80–110). San Francisco: Jossey-Bass.

Fletcher, R. C. and Fletcher, S. W. 2003. "The effectiveness of journal peer review." In F. Godlee and T. Jefferson (eds.), *Peer Review in Health Sciences* (pp. 62–75). London: BMJ Books.

Fong, E. A. and Tosi Jr., H. L. 2007. "Effort, performance, and conscientiousness: An agency theory perspective." *Journal of Management*, 33, 161–179.

Franzoni, C., Scellato, G., and Stephan, P. E. 2010. "Changing incentives to publish and the consequences for submission patterns." (Working paper, IP Finance Institute).

Frey, B. S. 1992. "Tertium datur: Pricing, regulating and intrinsic motivation." *Kyklos*, 45, 161–185.

1997. *Not Just for the Money: An Economic Theory of Personal Motivation*. Cheltenham: Edward Elgar Publishing.

2003. "Publishing as prostitution? – Choosing between one's own ideas and academic success." *Public Choice*, 116, 205–223.

2009. "Economists in the PITS." *International Review of Economics*, 56(4), 333–346.

Frey, B. S. and Jegen, R. 2001. "Motivation crowding theory." *Journal of Economic Surveys*, 15(5), 589–611.

Frey, B. S. and Neckermann, S. 2008. "Awards – A view from psychological economics." *Journal of Psychology*, 216, 198–208.

Frey, B. S. and Osterloh, M. 2010. "Motivate people with prizes." *Nature*, 465, 871.

Frey, B. S. and Rost, K. 2010. "Do rankings reflect research quality?" *Journal of Applied Economics*, 13(1), 1–38.

Frey, B. S. and Stutzer, A. 2006. "Strengthening the citizens' role in international organizations." *Review of International Organizations*, 1, 27–43. doi:10.1007/s11558-006-6605-1

Frost, J., Osterloh, M. and Weibel, A. 2010. "Governing knowledge work: Transactional and transformational solutions." *Organizational Dynamics*, 39, 126–136.

Fuyuno, I. and Cyranoski, D. 2006. "Cash for papers: Putting a premium on publication." *Nature*, 441, 792.

Gagné, M. and Deci, E. L. 2005. "Self-determination theory and work motivation." *Journal of Organizational Behavior*, 26, 331–362.

Gans, J. S. and Shepherd, G. B. 1994. "How are the mighty fallen: Rejected classic articles by leading economists." *Journal of Economic Perspectives*, 8, 165–179.

Garfield, E. 1997. "Editors are justified in asking authors to cite equivalent references from same journal." *British Medical Journal*, 314, 1765.

    2006. "The history and meaning of the journal impact factor." *Journal of the American Medical Association (JAMA)*, 295(1), 90–93.

Gerhart, B. and Rynes, S. L. 2003. *Compensation: Theory, Evidence, and Strategic Implications*. Thousand Oaks, CA: Sage Publications, Inc.

Gillies, D. 2005. "Hempelian and Kuhnian approaches in the philosophy of medicine: The Semmelweis case." *Studies in History and Philosophy of Biological and Biomedical Sciences*, 36, 159–181.

    2008. *How Should Research Be Organised?* London: College Publications.

Gilliland, S. W. and Landis, R. S. 1992. "Quality and quantity goals in a complex decision task: Strategies and outcomes." *Journal of Applied Psychology*, 77(5), 672–681.

Gioia, D. A. and Corley, K. G. 2002. "Being good versus looking good: Business school rankings and the Circean transformation from substance to image." *Academy of Management Learning and Education*, 1, 107–120.

Gittelman, M. and Kogut, B. 2003. "Does good science lead to valuable knowledge? Biotechnology firms and the evolutionary logic of citation patterns." *Management Science*, 49(4), 366–382.

Gneezy, U. and Rustichini, A. 2000. "Pay enough or don't pay at all." *Quarterly Journal of Economics*, 115, 791–810.

Goodall, A. H. 2009. *Socrates in the Boardroom: Why Research Universities should Be Led by Top Scholars*. Princeton University Press.

Gottfredson, S. D. 1978. "Evaluating psychological research reports: Dimensions, reliability, and correlates of quality judgments." *American Psychologist*, 33, 920–934.

Griffin, D. and Tversky, A. 1992. "The weighing of evidence and the determinants of confidence." *Cognitive Psychology*, 24, 411–435.

Habermas, J. 2006. "Political communication in media society." *Communication Theory*, 16, 411–426.

Hamermesh, D. S. 2007. "Viewpoint: Replication in economics." *Canadian Journal of Economics*, 40(3), 715–733.

Handelsblatt. 2010. "Handelsblatt-Ranking schlägt hohe Wellen." Retrieved July 1, 2010, from www.handelsblatt.com/politik/vwl-ranking/

Haney, W. M. 2002. "Ensuring failure: How a state's achievement test may be designed to do just that." *Education Week*, 56–58.

Hargreaves Heap, S. P. 2002. "Making British universities accountable." In P. Mirowski and E.-M. Sent (eds.), *Science Bought and Sold: Essays in the Economics of Science* (pp. 387–411). University of Chicago Press.

Hayek, F. A. 1979. *Law, Legislation and Liberty, Volume 3: The Political Order of a Free People*. University of Chicago Press.

Heilig, J. V. and Darling-Hammond, L. 2008. "Accountability Texas-style: The progress and learning of urban minority students in high-stakes testing context." *Educational Evaluation and Policy Analysis*, 30(2), 75–110.

Heintz, B. 2008. "Governance by Numbers. Zum Zusammenhang von Quantifizierung und Globalisierung am Beispiel der Hochschulpolitik." In G. F. Schuppert and A. Voßkuhl (eds.), *Governance von und durch Wissen* (pp. 110–304).

Hendriks, C. M. 2004. "Consensus conferences and planning cells." In J. Gastil and P. Levine (eds.), *The Deliberative Democracy Handbook: Strategies for Effective Civic Engagement in the Twenty-First Century* (pp. 80–110). San Francisco: Jossey-Bass.

Hennessey, B. A. and Amabile, T. 1998. "Reward, intrinsic motivation and creativity." *American Psychologist*, 53(6), 647–675.

Hirsch, J. E. 2005. "An index to quantify an individual's scientific research output." *Proceedings of the National Academy of Sciences of the United States of America*, 102, 16569–16572. Retrieved July 1, 2010, from http://dx.doi.org/ 10.1073/pnas.0507655102

Holcombe, R. G. 2004. "The national Research Council ranking of research universities: Its impact on research in economics." *Econ Journal Watch*, 1, 498–514.

Holmstrom, B. P. and Milgrom, P. 1991. "Multitask principal-agent analyses: Incentive contracts, asset ownership, and job design." *Journal of Law, Economics, and Organization*, 7, 24–52.

Horrobin, D. F. 1996. "Peer review of grant applications: a harbinger for mediocrity in clinical research?" *Lancet*, 348, 1293–1295.

IDEAS. 2008. "IDEAS rankings." Retrieved July 2, 2010, from http://ideas. repec.org/top/

Janis, I. L. 1972. *Victims of Groupthink: A Psychological Study of Foreign-Policy Decisions and Fiascos*. Boston, MA: Houghton Mifflin.

Jimenex-Contreras, E., de Moya Anegon, F., and Delgardo Lopez-Cozar, E. 2003. "The evolution of research activity in Spain: The impact of the National Commission for the Evaluation of Research Activity (CNEAI)." *Research Policy*, 32, 123–142.

Judge, T. A., Cable, D. M., Colbert, A. E., and Rynes, S. L. 2007. "What causes a management article to be cited – article, author, or journal?" *Academy of Management Journal*, 50, 491–506.

Khurana, R. 2007. *From Higher Aims to Hired Hands: The Social Transformation of Business Schools and the Unfulfilled Promise of Management as a Profession*. Princeton University Press.

Kotiaho, J. S., Tomkin, J. L., and Simmons, L. W. 1999, July. "Unfamiliar citations breed mistakes." *Nature*, 400, 307.

Kuhn, T. 1962. *The Structure of Scientific Revolutions*. University of Chicago Press.

Laband, D. N. and Tollison, R. D. 2003. "Dry holes in economic research." *Kyklos*, 56, 161–174.

Lane, J. 2010. "Let's make science metrics more scientific." *Nature*, 464, 488–489.

Lawrence, P. A. 2002. "Rank injustice: The misallocation of credit is endemic in science." *Nature*, 415, 835–836.

2003. "The politics of publication – authors, reviewers, and editors must act to protect the quality of research." *Nature*, 422, 259–261.

Lazear, E. P. and Shaw, K. L. 2007. "Personnel economics: The economist's view of human resources." *Journal of Economic Perspectives*, 21, 91–114.

Lee, F. S. 2007. "The research assessment exercise, the state and the dominance of mainstream economics in British universities." *Cambridge Journal of Economics*, 31, 309–325.

Leibniz, G. W. 1931. "Relation de l'état présent de la république des lettres." Sämtliche Schriften und Briefe (Akademie-Ausgabe), 4. Reihe, Politische Schriften, Band 1. *Darmstadt*, 569–571.

Lindsey, D. 1991. "Precision in the manuscript review process: Hargens and Herting revisited." *Scientometrics*, 22(2), 313–325.

Locke, E. A. and Latham, G. P. 2009. "Has goal setting gone wild, or have its attackers abandoned good scholarship?" *Academy of Management Perspectives*, 21, 17–23.

Mahoney, M. J. 1977. "Publication prejudices: An experimental study of confirmatory bias in the peer review system." *Cognitive Therapy Research*, 1, 161–175.

Marginson, S. and Considine, M. 2000. *The Enterprise University: Power, Governance and Reinvention in Australia*. Cambridge University Press.

Merton, R. K. 1968. "The Matthew effect in science." *Science*, 159, 56–63.

1973. *The Sociology of Science: Theoretical and Empirical Investigation*. University of Chicago Press.

Miller, C. C. 2006. "Peer review in the organizational and management sciences: Prevalence and effects of reviewer hostility, bias, and dissensus." *Academy of Management Journal*, 49, 425–431.

Miner, L. and McDonald, S. 1981. "Reliability of peer review." *Journal of the Society of Research Administrators*, 12, 21–25.

Moed, H. F. 2002. "The impact factors debate; the ISI's uses and limits." *Nature*, 415, 731–732.

2007. "The future of research evaluation rests with an intelligent combination of advanced metrics and transparent peer review." *Science and Public Policy*, 34, 575–583.

Monastersky, R. 2005. "The number that's devouring science." *Chronicle of Higher Education*, 52(8), A12.

Mudambi, R., Mudambi, S., and Navarra, P. 2007. "Global innovation in MNCs: The effects of subsidiary self-determination and teamwork." *Journal of Product Innovation Management*, 24, 442–455.

Neckermann, S., Cueni, R., and Frey, B. S. 2010. *Awards at Work*. Working Paper No. 411, Institute for Empirical Research in Economics, University of Zurich.

Nelson, R. R. 1959. "The simple economics of basic scientific research." *Journal of Political Economy*, 67, 297–306.

—— 2004. "The market economy and the scientific commons." *Research Policy*, 33, 455–471.

—— 2006. "Reflections on the simple economics of basic scientific research: Looking back and looking forward." *Industrial and Corporate Change*, 15, 903–917.

Nichols, S. L., Glass, G. V., and Berliner, D. C. 2006. "High-stakes testing and student achievement: Does accountability pressure increase student learning?" *Education Policy Analysis Archives*, 14(1), 1–175.

Ordonez, L. D., Schweitzer, M. E., Galinsky, A. D., and Bazerman, M. H. 2009. "Goals gone wild: The systematic side effects of overprescribing goal setting." *Academy of Management Perspectives*, 23, 6–16.

Osterloh, M. 2010. "Governance by Numbers. Does it really work in Research?" *Analyse und Kritik*, 32(2), 267–283

Osterloh, M. and Frey, B. S. 2000. "Motivation, knowledge transfer, and organizational forms." *Organization Science*, 11, 538–550.

Oswald, A. J. 2007. "An examination of the reliability of prestigious scholarly journals: Evidence and implications for decision-makers." *Economica*, 74, 21–31.

Ouchi, W. G. 1977. "The relationship between organizational structure and organizational control." *Administrative Science Quarterly*, 22, 95–113.

—— 1979. "A conceptual framework for the design of organizational control mechanisms." *Management Science*, 25, 833–848.

Perrin, B. 1998. "Effective use and misuse of performance measurement." *American Journal of Evaluation*, 19, 367–379.

Peters, D. and Ceci, S. J. 1982. "Peer review practices of psychological journals: The fate of published articles, submitted again." *The Behavioral and Brain Sciences*, 5, 187–195.

Polanyi, M. 1962. "The republic of science: Its political and economic theory." *Minerva*, 1, 54–73. (Reprinted in Polanyi, M. 1969. *From Knowing and Being* (pp. 49–72). University of Chicago Press. Re-reprinted in Mirowski, P. and Sent, E. M. 2002. *Science Bought and Sold. Essays in the Economics of Science* (pp. 465–485). University of Chicago Press.)

Posner, R. A. 2010. "From the new institutional economics to organization economics: Four applications to corporate governance, government agencies, and legal institutions." *Journal of Institutional and Theoretical Economics*, 6, 1–37. doi: 10.1017/S1744137409990270

Prichard, C. and Willmott, H. 1997. "Just how managed is the McUniversity?" *Organization Studies*, 18, 287–316.

Rinia, E. J., Leeuwen, Th. N., van Vuren, H. G., and van Raan, A. F. J. 1998. "Comparative analysis of a set of bibliometric indicators and central peer review criteria: Evaluation of condensed matter physics in the Netherlands." *Research Policy*, 27, 95–107.

Roach, M. and Sauermann, H. 2010. "A taste for science? PhD scientists' academic orientation and self-selection into research career in industry." *Research Policy*, 39, 422–434.

Rost, K. and Osterloh, M. 2010. *"Opening the black box of upper echelons: Expertise and gender as drivers of poor information processing."* Corporate Governance: An International Review, 18(3), 212–233.

Rothwell, P. M. and Martyn, C. N. 2000. "Reproducibility of peer review in clinical neuroscience: Is agreement between reviewers any greater than would be expected by chance alone?" *Brain*, 123, 1964–1969.

Schimank, U. 2005. "New public management and the academic profession: Reflections on the German situation." *Minerva*, 43, 361–376.

Schreyögg, G. and Steinmann, H. 1987. "Strategic control: A new perspective." *Academy of Management Review*, 12, 91–103.

Schweitzer, M. E., Ordonez, L., and Douma, B. 2004. "Goal setting as a motivator of unethical behavior." *Academy of Management Journal*, 47, 422–432.

Shanghai Jiao Tong University 2007. "Academic Ranking of World Universities." Retrieved July 2, 2010, from www.arwu.org.

Simkin, M. V. and Roychowdhury, V. P. 2005. "Copied citations create renowned papers?" *Annals of Improbable Research*, 11(1), 24–27.

Simon, H. A. 1985. "Human nature in politics – the dialogue of psychology with political science." *American Political Science Review*, 79(2), 293–304.

Simonton, D. K. 2004. *Creativity in Science: Chance, Logic, Genius, and Zeitgeist.* Cambridge University Press.

Singh, G., Haddad, K. M., and Chow, S. 2007. "Are articles in 'top' management journals necessarily of higher quality?" *Journal of Management Inquiry*, 16, 319–331.

Smith, R. 1997. "Journal accused of manipulating impact factor." *British Medical Journal*, 314, 463.

Sokal, A. D. 1996. "A physicist experiments with cultural studies." Retrieved July 2, 2010, from www.physics.nyu.edu/faculty/sokal/lingua_franca_v4/lingua_franca_v4.html

Sorenson, O. and Fleming, L. 2004. "Science and the diffusion of knowledge." *Research Policy*, 33, 1615–1634.

Spangenberg, J. F. A., Starmans, R., Bally, Y. W., Breemhaar, B., Nijhuis, F. J. N., and van Dorp, C. A. F. 1990. "Prediction of scientific performance in clinical medicine." *Research Policy*, 19, 239–255.

Starbuck, W. H. 2005. "How much better are the most prestigious journals? The statistics of academic publication." *Organization Science*, 16, 180–200.

2006. *The Production of Knowledge: The Challenge of Social Science Research.* Oxford University Press.

2009. "The constant causes of never-ending faddishness in the behavioral and social sciences." *Scandinavian Journal of Management*, 25, 225–227.

Staw, B. M. and Boettger, R. D. 1990. "Task revision: A neglected form of work performance." *Academy of Management Journal*, 33, 534–559.

Stephan, P. E. 1996. "The economics of science." *Journal of Economic Literature*, 34, 1199–1235.

2008. "Science and the university: Challenges for future research." *CESifo Economic Studies*, 54, 313–324.

Stern, S. 2004. "Do scientists pay to be scientists?" *Management Science*, 50, 835–853.

Stokes, D. E. 1997. *Pasteur's Quadrant: Basic Science and Technological Innovation.* Washington, D.C.: Brookings Institution Press.

Strathern, M. 1966. "From improvement to enhancement: An anthropological comment on the audit culture." *Cambridge Anthropology*, 19, 1–21.

Swanson, E. 2004. "Publishing in the majors: A comparison of accounting, finance, management, and marketing." *Contemporary Accounting Research*, 21(1), 223–225.

Taylor, M., Perakakis, P., and Trachana, V. 2008, June. "The siege of science." *Ethics in Science and Environmental Politics*, 8, 17–40.

The Thomson Corporation 2008a. "ISI web of knowledge essential science indicators". Retrieved July 3, 2010, from http://esi.isiknowledge.com/home.cgi 2008b. "ISI web of knowledge journal citation report." Retrieved July 3, 2010, from http://admin-apps.isiknowledge.com/JCR/

Todd, P. A. and Ladle, R. J. 2008. "Hidden dangers of a 'citation culture'." *Ethics in Science and Environmental Politics*, 8, 13–16.

Tsang, E. W. K. and Frey, B. S. 2007. "The as-is journal review process: Let authors own their ideas." *Academy of Management Learning and Education*, 6, 128–136.

Ultee, M. 1987. "The republic of letters: Learned correspondence, 1680–1720." *Seventeenth Century*, 2(1), 95–112.

Ursprung, H. W. and Zimmer, M. 2006. "Who is the "Platz–Hirsch" of the German economics profession? A citation analysis." *Jahrbücher für Nationalökonomie und Statistik*, 227, 187–202.

Van Fleet, D., McWilliams, A., and Siegel, D. S. 2000. "A theoretical and empirical analysis of journal rankings: The case of formal lists." *Journal of Management*, 26(5), 839–861.

van Raan, A. F. J. 2005. "Fatal attraction: Conceptual and methodological problems in the rankings of universities by bibliometric methods." *Scientometrics*, 62, 133–143.

Weibel, A., Rost, K., and Osterloh, M. 2010. "Pay for performance in the public sector – benefits and (hidden) costs." *Journal of Public Administration Research and Theory*, 20(2), 387–412.

Weingart, P. 2005. "Impact of bibliometrics upon the science system: Inadvertent consequences?" *Scientometrics*, 62, 117–131.

Weller, A. C. 2001. *Editorial Peer Review: Its Strengths and Weaknesses.* Medford, NJ: American Society for Information Science and Technology.

Wenneras, C. and Wold, A. 1999. "Bias in peer review of research proposals in peer reviews in health sciences." In F. Godlee and T. Jefferson (eds.), *Peer Review in Health Sciences* (pp. 79–89). London: BMJ Books.

Willmott, H. 2003. "Commercializing higher education in the UK: The state, industry and peer review." *Studies in Higher Ecucation*, 28(2), 129–141.

Worrell, D. 2009. "Assessing business scholarship: The difficulties in moving beyond the rigor-relevance paradigm trap." *Academy of Management Learning*, 8, 127–30.

Zuckerman, H. A. 1992. "The proliferation of prizes: Nobel complements and Nobel surrogates in the reward system of science." *Theoretical Medicine*, 13, 217–231.

4 Gatekeepers of economics: the network of editorial boards in economic journals

Alberto Baccini and Lucio Barabesi

Introduction

The academic community of economics may be explored through the observation of the editorial activities of scholars engaged as members on the boards of editors of relevant scientific journals, and through the analysis of the structural properties of the network generated by the editorial activities of the members of the boards of these journals. While a lot of literature on the sociology of science uses data on editorial boards for empirical research (e.g. Braun 2004), starting at least from the seminal work of Merton and Zuckerman (1971); only recently these data, starting from Baccini (2009), have been explored with network analysis techniques (Baccini 2009; Cronin 2009; Baccini and Barabesi 2010; Ni and Ding 2010; Baccini and Barabesi 2011; Cabanac 2012).

Traditionally, the main function of editorial boards was to determine which articles were appropriate for publication. In the last two or three decades this function has changed: the spread of the anonymous referee process allows editorial boards to concentrate on selecting and evaluating referees. In every case they act as "gatekeepers of science" (Crane 1967), "holding the fate of so many papers and so many careers"; they are "a small group, although growing in numbers as specialized journals continue to launch. These people are the chaperones of submitted papers, seeing the manuscripts through the peer-review process and ultimately deciding whether a paper gets published in the journal" (Powell 2010). They control "the system of manuscript evaluation and selection" occupying a powerful strategic position in the collective activity of science (Braun 2004; Braun, Diospatonyi et al. 2007); they "exert a special influence on the orchestration of the international research activity" (Braun and Diospatonyi 2005); and they contribute to shape

Sections 2 and 3 of this paper are largely based on Baccini, A. and L. Barabesi (2010). "Interlocking Editorship. A Network Analysis of the Links Between Economic Journals." *Scientometrics* 82(2): 365–389.

the landscape of research in a discipline by encouraging or suppressing various directions through the definition of the editorial policies of their journals (Braun and Diospatonyi 2005; Braun, Diospatonyi et al. 2007; Hames 2007; Fogarty and Liao 2009). The role of editorial boards members in this respect could be stronger in the social sciences and humanities rather than in the hard sciences. Merton and Zuckerman (1971) suggested that the role of editors in this respect is stronger when the degree of consensus of scholars about a scientific paradigm is weak, as in many subfields of social sciences and humanities. According to related studies, the selection of editors in the fields where the consensus is weak tends to reflect particularistic criteria such as affiliation or the university from which a scholar graduated, rather than universalistic ones (Yoels 1974).

From a different point of view, scientific journals and their publishers are interested in assuring the presence of distinguished scholars on their boards. A cornerstone of the scientific ethos is that the selection of the editorial board members should be based on their scholarly achievements (Bedeian, Van Fleet et al. 2009). The competition between journals for talented scholars results in a partial overlapping of their editorial boards. If each member of an editorial board may influence in some measure the editorial policy of his/her journal, journals with overlapping boards may have partially overlapping editorial policies; or partially overlapping or complementary scopes. We will not be concerned with direct observations of the editorial policies adopted by the boards of journals, and of their contents – fields, subjects, and methods covered. We will infer considerations about the similarity of editorial policies and consequently of journal contents by observing the "interlocking editorship" phenomenon, that is the crossed presence of scholars on editorial boards of different journals. The interlocking editorship analysis permits us to draw exploratory elements about some questions: which are the most central journals of the network and which are the most peripheral? Which journals have the most influence over others? Who are the most influential scholars from an editorial point of view? Does the community of scientists break down into smaller groups? If so what are they?

More in general, the interlocking editorship analysis permits us to explore the existence of separate schools of thought, methodologies, or patterns of research characterizing the scientific community under scrutiny. This last feature is particularly relevant for economics where the existence of different schools of thought, characterized by different methodologies, instruments, or visions is a well-known phenomenon. The identification of different schools is generally made, so to speak, in reference to the contents of science, as for example when the Austrian school is distinguished from the neoclassical one, or when heterodox economists are distinguished from mainstream ones. The classification of macroeconomists into freshwater and saltwater, although defined in reference to the university affiliation of scholars, is ultimately based on the different approaches to macroeconomics that are used in different universities. The interlocking editorship analysis permits us to work at an exploratory level where the identification of groups is made without any reference to the contents of science. The existence of the different groups identified through network analysis may be interpreted not only from a content-based point of view, but also from an academic-power point of view. Baccini (2009) for example interpreted the interlocking editorship networks in Italian economic journals as the result of the existence of academic cliques aiming to control disciplinary fields at a national level, rather than the result of different approaches to economics.

The scientific community surrounding economic journals is represented as an affiliation or dual-mode network where the vertices are divided into two sets (scholars and journals) and the affiliation connects the vertices from the two different sets only (Wasserman and Faust 1994; de Nooy, Mrvar et al. 2005). Dual-mode networks characterize some informetric phenomena: the author–paper links result in co-authorship/ publication networks; the source–citation links result in reference– citation networks. In our case, the event of affiliation (being a member of the editorial board) connects a scholar to an economic journal. The duality specifically refers to the two alternative perspectives: on the one hand different editors are linked by their affiliation to the same journal, and on the other two journals are linked by the editors who are on their boards. Therefore, there are two different ways to view the affiliation network: as one of editors linked by journals (networks of co-membership), or as one of journals linked by editors (interlocking of events). It is possible to study the dual-mode network as a whole, or to transform it into two single-mode networks focusing only on the analysis of the network of editors or of journals.

The centre and periphery in the interlocking editorship network

There is no evidence regarding the roles of different kinds of editors in the editorial process, with the only exception of editor-in-chief (Yoels 1974). A same position such as associate editor or managing editor may often entail very different roles for different journals. As a consequence a very broad notion of editor is adopted, covering all the individuals listed as editor, co-editor, member of the editorial board, or of the advisory editorial board (Hodgson and Rothman 1999; Braun and Diospatonyi 2005; Baccini, Barabesi et al. 2009; Baccini and Barabesi 2011; Cabanac 2012).

The affiliation network database (two-mode) contains data for 746 economic journals present in the ECONLIT database and with an active editorial board in January 2006; the number of edges in the network that is the seats available in the editorial boards are 21,525; they are occupied by 15,991 scholars.[1] The database was managed by means of the package *Pajek* (de Nooy, Mrvar et al. 2005; Batagelj and Mrvar 2006).

The first step of our analysis consists in transforming the original network into the one-mode network containing only journals and their links: the interlocking editorship network. The number of lines linking the journals in the one-mode network of journals is 6,407, and the density of the interlocking directorship network (i.e. the ratio of the actual number of lines to the maximum possible number of lines in the network) is 0.023. This means that only 2.3% of the possible lines is present (Wasserman and Faust 1994); the economic journals network is much more dispersed than other known networks (Baccini, Barabesi et al. 2009; Baccini and Barabesi 2011).

The graph of the (one-mode) network of journals is reported in Figure 4.1. The vertices in the graph are automatically placed by the package Pajek on the basis of the Fruchterman–Reingold procedure. In this graph two main subsets may be roughly recognized: a giant central component composed by the majority of economic journals and a small group of isolated journals.

Table 4.1 contains the degree distribution of the journals considered; the degree of a journal is the number of lines which it shares with the other journals. The mean degree is 17.18 (while the median degree turns out to be 11) and the degree standard deviation is 17.55. The isolated journals (i.e. journals with zero degree) are 74 (10%). They are in part non-English language journals (as for example *L'impresa* or *Bancaria* in Italian, *Tahqiqat-e eqtesadi* in Arabic, *Investigación Económica* in Spanish), journals edited by national scientific societies (e.g. *Schweizerische Zeitschrift für Volkswirtschaft und Statistik/Swiss Journal of Economics and Statistics* edited by the Swiss Society of Economics and Statistics) or by institutions with a complete control of the board of editors (e.g. the *Antitrust Bulletin*)

---

[1] The data on the members of the editorial boards was directly obtained from the website of the journals or – for the few cases when the site was unavailable – from the hard copy. The data was collected from March to July 2006 considering the boards published on the websites of the journals in that period. When the hard copy was necessary, the board considered was that of the first issue in 2006 or, alternatively, that of the last issue in 2005.

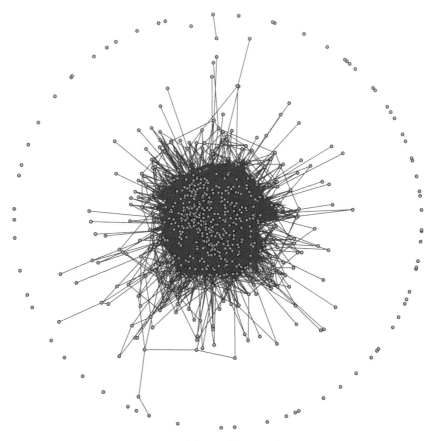

Figure 4.1 The economic journals network.

journals dedicated to very narrow topics (e.g. *Australian Commodities Forecasts and Issues* or *Agronomia Mesoamericana*; *Australian Bulletin of Labour*); journals on the boundaries with other disciplines with only a minor emphasis in economics (e.g. *American Historical Review* or *Transportation Journal*).

A main concern in our analysis is to distinguish between the economic journals which have a central position in the network and those in the periphery. As suggested by Wasserman and Faust (1994), three centrality measures for each journal in the network may be adopted. The simplest measure for the centrality of a journal is represented by its degree: indeed, the more ties a journal has to other journals, the more central is its position in the network. For example, the *Pacific Economic Review* is linked with 124 journals, while the *Journal of Development and Economic*

Table 4.1 *Degree frequency distribution of statistical journals*

Degree	Freq	Freq%	Degree	Freq	Freq%	Degree	Freq	Freq%
0	74	9.9	24	8	1.1	48	5	0.7
1	44	5.9	25	6	0.8	49	1	0.1
2	39	5.2	26	13	1.7	50	3	0.4
3	37	5.0	27	13	1.7	51	4	0.5
4	23	3.1	28	11	1.5	52	1	0.1
5	32	4.3	29	10	1.3	53	3	0.4
6	19	2.5	30	7	0.9	54	4	0.5
7	25	3.4	31	3	0.4	55	2	0.3
8	21	2.8	32	9	1.2	57	5	0.7
9	21	2.8	33	5	0.7	59	2	0.3
10	19	2.5	34	6	0.8	60	2	0.3
11	20	2.7	35	6	0.8	61	1	0.1
12	16	2.1	36	7	0.9	62	2	0.3
13	22	2.9	37	2	0.3	63	1	0.1
14	16	2.1	38	8	1.1	65	2	0.3
15	19	2.5	39	6	0.8	66	1	0.1
16	12	1.6	40	6	0.8	68	1	0.1
17	8	1.1	41	7	0.9	69	2	0.3
18	9	1.2	42	5	0.7	71	1	0.1
19	12	1.6	43	6	0.8	72	3	0.4
20	14	1.9	44	7	0.9	73	1	0.1
21	10	1.3	45	3	0.4	76	1	0.1
22	11	1.5	46	5	0.7	79	1	0.1
23	8	1.1	47	5	0.7	94	1	0.1
						124	1	0.1

Policies is linked with solely one. Hence, the first is more central in the network than the second. In addition, the normalized degree of a journal is the ratio of its degree to the maximum possible degree (i.e. the number of journals minus 1). Thus, the *Pacific Economic Review* is linked with about 16.6% of the other journals in the network, while *Statistical Modelling* is linked with only 0.001%. Table 4.A1 contains the degree and the normalized degree for the journals considered.

The second centrality measure is given by closeness centrality, which is based on the distance between a journal and all the other journals. In the network analysis, the distance between two vertices is usually based on so-called geodesic distance. Geodesic is the shortest path between two vertices, while its length is the number of lines in the geodesic (Wasserman and Faust 1994). Hence, the closeness centrality of a journal is the number of journals (linked to this journal by a path) divided by the sum of all the distances (between the journal and the linked journals).

The basic idea is that a journal is central if its board can quickly interact with all the other boards. Journals occupying a central location with respect to closeness can be very effective in communicating information (sharing research, sharing papers, and deciding editorial policies) to other journals. Table 4.A1 contains the closeness centrality for economic journals.

The third considered measure is the so-called betweenness centrality. The idea behind the index is that similar editorial aims between two non-adjacent journals might depend on other journals in the network, especially on those journals lying on the paths between the two. The other journals potentially might have some control over the interaction between two non-adjacent journals. Hence, a journal is more central in this respect if it is an important intermediary in links between other journals. From a formal perspective, the betweenness centrality of a journal is the proportion of all paths between pairs of other journals that include this journal. Table 4.A1 contains the betweenness centrality of the economic journals. For example, the *Pacific Economic Review* is in about 4% of the paths linking all other journals in the network. It is interesting to note that in the statistical journal network, the two journals with highest betweenness are each in about 12% of the paths linking all other journals (Baccini, Barabesi et al. 2009; Baccini et al. 2012).

Groups of journals in the network

We can now consider the strength of the ties linking journals: the value of a line linking two journals is the number of editors sitting on the board of the two journals linked by that line (Wasserman and Faust 1994). Table 4.2 shows the distribution of line values: 74.6% of the links are generated by journals sharing only one editor and about 94% are generated by journals sharing three or less editors. In social network analysis it is usual to consider lines with higher value to be more important since they are less personal and more institutional (de Nooy, Mrvar et al. 2005). In the case of the journal network, the basic idea is very simple: the editorial proximity between two journals can be measured by observing the degree of overlap among their boards. Two journals with no common editors have no editorial relationship. With an example: the *American Economic Review* and the *Australian Bulletin of Labour* have no common editors, so that their editorial policies can be considered independent of each other.

The opposite situation occurs when two journals have the same board; probably they have a common, or at least shared, editorial policy, i.e. they are companion journals. As an example, *Applied Economics* and *Applied*

Table 4.2 *Line multiplicity frequency distribution*

Line value	Freq	Freq (%)
1	4780	74.61
2	934	14.58
3	297	4.64
4	145	2.26
5	89	1.39
6	51	0.80
7	33	0.52
8	24	0.37
9	15	0.23
10	10	0.16
11	8	0.12
12	6	0.09
13	3	0.05
14	2	0.03
15	1	0.02
16	4	0.06
19	1	0.02
20	1	0.02
23	1	0.02
24	1	0.02
40	1	0.02

Economics Letters share all their 23 editors. In its "aims and scope" declaration for 2007, the latter explicitly stated that it is the "companion journal" of the former. In economics, there are a few journals that can be considered properly companion journals sharing all their editorial board members. The most common situation is the intermediate one in which two journals share only a part of their board members.

Starting from this basis it is possible to define cohesive subgroups, i.e. subsets of journals among which there are relatively strong ties. In a valued network a cohesive subgroup is a subset of vertices among which ties have a value higher than a given threshold. In our case, a cohesive subgroup of journals is a set of journals sharing a number of editors equal to or higher than the threshold. In our interpretation, a cohesive subgroup of journals is a subgroup with a similar editorial policy, belonging to the same subfield of the discipline or sharing a common methodological approach. Following de Nooy et al. (2005), cohesive subgroups are identified as weak components in m-slices, i.e. subsets for which the threshold value is at least m.

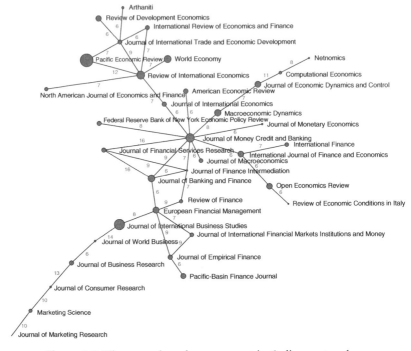

Figure 4.2 The central weak component in 6-slices network: macroeconomic, monetary and international economics journals (the dimension of vertices is proportional to betweenness centrality).

As previously remarked, the network of statistical journals is not compact: there is a big component of 670 journals and all the others are isolated. The search for cohesive subgroups strengthens this path: fixing a minimum value of threshold to $m = 2$ the big component reduces to 474 journals, 13 components emerge of 2–4 journals, and the isolated journals grow to 242. With $m = 3$ the big component reduces to 284 journals and isolated journals grow to 369. With a higher threshold value, the network gives rise to components worthy of being noticed here.

In particular we focused our attention on the weak components emerging in the 6-slices network. It is possible to isolate 41 components including 176 journals. We comment, first, on the three weak components with the biggest number of journals.

Figure 4.2 contains the representation of the central and biggest component of the network. The 36 journals in this subset of the network have at least 6 common editors. The dimension of each vertex represents the betweenness centrality of the corresponding journal in the complete network. The centre of this component is occupied by the *Journal of Money, Credit and Banking*. It is linked directly with 8 journals. Four out of eight have no other links (*American Economic Review*, *Journal of Monetary Economics*, *Journal of Macroeconomics* and *Federal Reserve Bank of New York Economic Policy Review*) and therefore they configure themselves as an efficient star at the center of the network; the other 4 out of 8 journals bridge the central star to four groups of journals. In the upper right of the figure, *Macroeconomics Dynamics* is the bridge toward journals of macroeconomic dynamics and computational economics at the boundaries of macroeconomics;[2] on the right the *International Journal of Finance and Economics* is the bridge with a small group of other policy-oriented and accessible to non-specialists journals. On the lower left the *Journal of Financial Intermediation* and the *Journal of Financial Services Research* are the bridge toward a group of financial journals; in this group the *European Financial Management* connects also a group of business and marketing journals. On the upper left the *Review of International Economics* is the bridge with a group of journals of international economics and development. So, the central component of the network contains journals of macroeconomics, monetary economics, international economics, a few journals of financial economics, and the *American Economic Review* considered by all rankings the most important journal of general economics. This configuration is probably the outcome of the (now falling) consensus achieved in monetary policy and in macroeconomics by scientists and practitioners, as discussed by Goodfriend (2007).

Figure 4.3 contains a second weak component with 12 journals devoted to economic theory, econometrics, and game and decision theory. The centre of the component is *Games and Economic Behavior*. It is linked directly to seven journals devoted to the study of mathematical and quantitative methods (*Econometrica*, *Journal of Mathematical Economics*, *International Journal of Game Theory*, *Journal of Economic Theory*, *Review of Economic Design*), of theoretical public economics (*Social Choice and Welfare*), and experimental economics (*Experimental Economics*). In this case the network is not configured as a star, because there are direct links between some of the seven journals around the central one. It is useful to note that the *Journal of Economic Behavior and Organization* presents a relatively high betweenness centrality, indicating that this controls the links of the component with the rest of the network of economic journals.

---

[2] In the aims and scope of Netnomics it is stated that "the journal also explores the emerging network-based, real-time macro economy with its own set of economic characteristics."

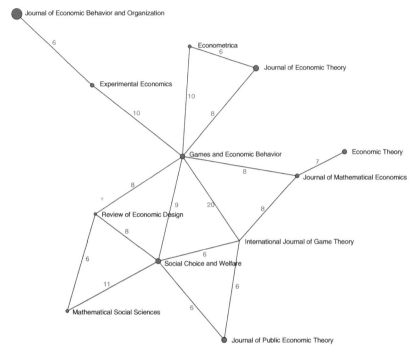

Figure 4.3 A weak component in 6-slices network: economic theory, econometrics, game and decision theory journals (the dimension of vertices is proportional to betweenness centrality).

The third weak component is drawn in Figure 4.4. It contains journals devoted to urban, spatial, and geographical economics, and to real estate economics. At the centre of the component there is a pair of journals, the *Journal of Urban Economics* and the *Journal of Regional Science*. The first is linked through the *Journal of Regional Science* to other journals of geographical economics; the second to journals of housing economics and real estate economics and finance. The journals on the right of Figure 4.4 are at the boundaries of economics, as for example the *Journal of Real Estate Literature* which is a general publication of the American Real Estate Society; but they are also relatively isolated in the network of the economic journals, as we can infer by their relatively low betweenness centrality values. The journals on the left of the Figure 4.4 are more central in the network.

The other eight weak components of the network containing more than three journals are drawn in Figure 4.5. The first component in clockwise contains five journals dedicated to insurance. The second is

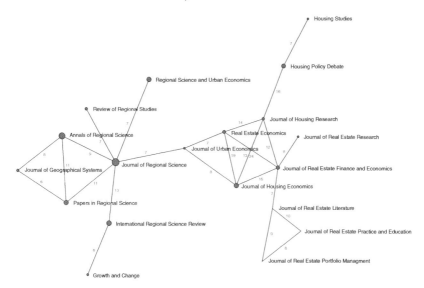

Figure 4.4 A weak component in 6-slices network: urban and regional economics journals (the dimension of vertices is proportional to betweenness centrality).

the component containing six journals of accounting research. In particular four journals out of six are linked in a complete subnetwork (*Accounting Review*, *Journal of Accounting Research*, *Journal of Accounting and Economics*, *Review of Accounting Studies*). The third group contains five journals of environmental economics; two out of five, *Journal of Environmental Economics and Management* and *Ecological Economics* are top ranked in CNRS (CNRS 2007). On the lower part of the figure there is a line network of five journals of applied finance; and another line network of four journals of finance. It is interesting to note that the journals classified by CNRS as "Finance and Insurance" when analyzed with our technique split into three specialized groups. On the left a component is drawn containing six journals of public economics: in this component there are three journals highly ranked by CNRS (*Journal of Public Economics*, *International Tax and Public Finance*, and *National Tax Journal*) and three journals published in Germany. The public choice approach to public economics defines a weak component of three journals (*Public Choice*, *European Journal of Political Economy*, and *Constitutional Political Economy*) presented in Figure 4.6. The last two components of Figure 4.5 are strongly characterized for their methodological approach. On the upper left there are six journals sharing an Austrian perspective on

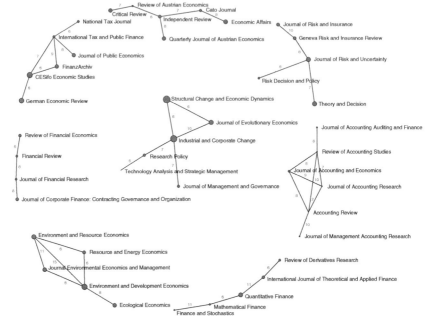

Figure 4.5 Weak components in 6-slices network with more than three journals (the dimension of vertices is proportional to betweenness centrality).

the study of political economy and political science. In the center of the figure there is a component containing journals strongly characterized for the evolutionary approach to the analysis of economics, industrial organization, and technological change.

Figure 4.6 contains the weak components with three journals. Again in clockwise, on the right there is a group of law and economics journals; then a group of business history journals; the already mentioned group of public choice journals; three journals devoted to the study of the economics of new technology; a component containing three reviews of development published by Oxford University; and finally three Brazilian economic journals.

The network of editors

We can now consider the editors sitting at the editorial tables of the economic journals. The average number of seats per journal turned out to be 28.9, while the average number of seats occupied by each scholar

Table 4.3 *Distribution of scholars according to the number of seats held*

Cluster	Freq	Freq%	CumFreq	CumFreq%
1	12742	79.68	12742	79.68
2	2052	12.83	14794	92.51
3	638	3.99	15432	96.50
4	297	1.86	15729	98.36
5	145	0.91	15874	99.27
6	57	0.36	15931	99.62
7	28	0.18	15959	99.80
8	9	0.06	15968	99.86
9	11	0.07	15979	99.93
10	5	0.03	15984	99.96
11	2	0.01	15986	99.97
12	2	0.01	15988	99.98
13	1	0.01	15989	99.99
16	1	0.01	15990	99.99
18	1	0.01	15991	100.00

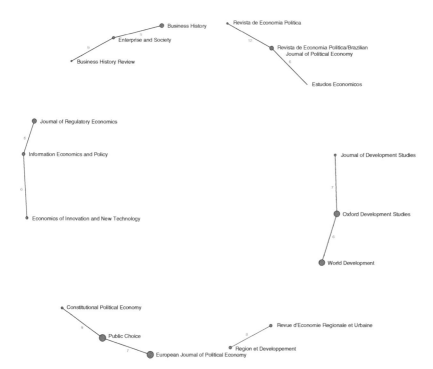

Figure 4.6 Weak components in 6-slices network with three journals (the dimension of vertices is proportional to betweenness centrality).

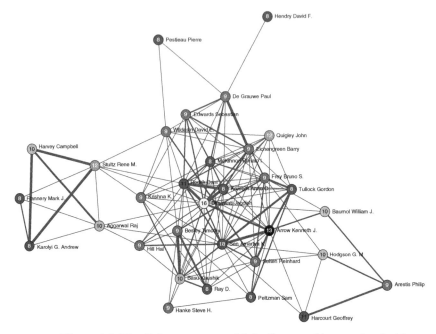

Figure 4.7 The links amongst multiple directors (the number inside each vertex is the number of boards where the director sits in the complete network).

(i.e. the mean rate of participation) is 1.35. The distribution of editorship held by scholars, which is the distribution of scholars per seats held, is described in Table 4.3. 12,742 out of 15,991 serve as editor of only one journal; 3,249 scholars are instead multiple editors. Only a small minority of scholars, less than 1%, sits in more than four different editorial boards.

It is very difficult to interpret these data. From the point of view of academic reputation, multiple editorship could be considered as a sign of distinction for those scholars serving in a plurality of editorial boards (Rost and Frey 2011). The same logic, even if reversed, applies to the ranking of academic institutions on the basis of their representation on the editorial boards of top journals (Kaufman 1984; Gibbons and Fish 1991; Braun, Diospatonyi et al. 2007). The list of multiple directors is therefore the list of the most esteemed scholars in economics.

From a more critical perspective, the attention could be focused on the editorial power of multiple editors. A first question concerns the degree of connectedness amongst multiple directors. If we consider, for the sake of simplicity, the 32 editors with more than 7 editorial positions, we can see in Figure 4.7 that all these editors are connected in a single network. In Figure 4.7 a line linking two vertices means that the two scholars sit together on one editorial board; the width of each line is proportional to the number of editorial boards in which the scholars sit together.[3]

The density of the network between multiple directors is 0.28: that is a quarter is realized of the maximum number of links in a network with 32 vertices. The diameter of the network is 4, that is the longest shortest path between two vertices is 4.[4] The average distance among reachable pairs of vertices is only 1.99. This is a very small world.

These editors, according to our hypothesis, have some power in shaping the editorial policies of the journals where they sit. It is therefore instructive to see how many journals are connected through this small group of multiple directors. Figure 4.8 draws the journals connected by this group of multiple editors. This small group of multiple editors influences 166 journals, which is about 23% of all relevant economic journals published in economics.

Legend: Dark gray vertices are journals, labeled according to Table 4.A1. Light gray vertices are the following scholars: 1 Aggarwal Raj; 2 Arestis Philip; 3 Arrow Kenneth J.; 4 Basu Kaushik; 5 Baumol William J.; 6 Besley Timothy; 7 Bhagwati Jagdish; 8 De Grauwe Paul; 9 Edwards Sebastian; 10 Eichengreen Barry; 11 Flannery Mark J.;12 Frey Bruno S.; 13 Hanke Steve H.; 14 Harcourt Geoffrey; 15 Harvey Campbell; 16 Hendry David F.; 17 Hill Hal; 18 Hodgson G. M.; 19 Karolyi G. Andrew; 20 Krishna K.; 21 Krueger Anne O.; 22 McKinnon Ronald I.;23 Peltzman Sam; 24 Pestieau Pierre; 25 Quigley John; 26 Ray D.; 27 Rodrik Dani; 28 Selten Reinhard; 29 Sen Amartya K.; 30 Stultz Rene M.; 31 Tullock Gordon; 32 Wildasin David E.

Conclusive remarks

The affiliation network generated by scholars serving on the editorial boards of economic journals is explored through network analysis technique. Editorial activity is considered a duty for scholars; an invitation to sit on an editorial board of a journal is usually considered a signal of recognition by the scientific community. When a scholar sits on an editorial board, he or she acquires some power in the definition of the editorial policy of his/her journal. Consequently, if the same scholar sits on the editorial board of two journals, those journals may have some common elements in their editorial policies. Our working hypothesis is

---

[3] In the network 91 lines have value 1; 25 value 2; 14 value 3; 6 value 2; and 2 value 5.
[4] The one between Philip Arestis and David F. Hendry.

Figure 4.8 Journals connected by multiple editors (sitting on more than 7 journals). The number inside each vertex is the label of the number of boards where the director sits in the complete network.

that it is possible to assess the proximity of the editorial policies of two scientific journals through the numbers of links generated by common editors sitting on their boards. The phenomenon of the same editor serving in the editorial boards of two different journals is called interlocking editorship. This is analogous with interlocking directorship which is the phenomenon of the same person sitting on the boards of directors of two different firms.

The editorial board members of the economic journals generated a very compact network where about 90% of the journals considered are linked directly or indirectly. If we consider the number of common editors as an indicator of proximity, it is possible to individuate into this network many different groups of journals. These different groups can be characterized in reference, so to speak, to their scientific contents. In economics competing visions or approaches to economic research prompt scholars to endorse different languages and visions about the correct view of how to conduct research. The groups of journals that emerged in the network analysis may be identified in relation to different approaches to economic scholarship: mainstream macroeconomics, mainstream microeconomics, public choice, evolutionary economics, etc. The scholars holding multiple editorships are also identified as a small group of 32 multiple directors, serving as editors in as many as 166 journals.

References

Baccini, A. 2009. "Italian economic journals. A network-based ranking and an exploratory analysis of their influence on setting international professional standards." *Rivista Italiana degli Economisti* 14(3): 491–511.

Baccini, A. and L. Barabesi 2010. "Interlocking editorship. A network analysis of the links between economic journals." *Scientometrics* 82(2): 365–389.
2011. "Seats at the table: The network of the editorial boards in information and library science." *Journal of Informetrics* 5(3): 382–391.

Baccini, A., L. Barabesi, et al. 2009. "How are statistical journals linked? A network analysis." *Chance* 22(3): 34–43.

Baccini, A., L. Barabesi, M. Marcheselli, and L. Pratelli 2012. "Statistical inference on the h-index with an application to top-scientist performance." *Journal of Informetrics* 6(4): 721–728.

Batagelj, V. and A. Mrvar 2006. *Pajek*. Lubjana.

Bedeian, A. G., D. D. Van Fleet, et al. 2009. "Scientific achievement and editorial board membership." *Organizational Research Methods* 12(2): 211–238.

Braun, T. 2004. "Keeping the gates of science journals." *Handbook of Quantitative Science and Technology Research.* H. F. Moed, W. Glanzel and U. Schmoch. Dordrecht, Kluwer Academic Publishers: 95–114.

Braun, T. and I. Diospatonyi 2005. "The counting of core journal gatekeepers as science indicators really counts. The scientific scope of action and strength of nations." *Scientometrics* 62(3): 297–319.
2005. "The journal gatekeepers of major publishing houses of core science journals." *Scientometrics* 64(2): 113–120.

Braun, T., I. Diospatonyi, et al. 2007. "Journal gatekeepers indicator-based top universities of the world, of Europe and of 29 countries – A pilot study." *Scientometrics* 71(2): 155–178.

Cabanac, G. 2012. "Shaping the landscape of research in information systems from the perspective of editorial boards: A scientometric study of 77 leading journals." *Journal of the American Society for Information Science and Technology* 63(5): 977–996.

CNRS 2007. Categorization of Journals in Economics and Management.

Crane, D. 1967. "The gatekeepers of science: Some factors affecting the selection of articles for scientific journals." *American Sociologist* 32(2): 195–201.

Cronin, B. 2009. "A seat at the table." *Journal of the American Society for Information Science and Technology* 60(12): 2387–2387.

de Nooy, W., A. Mrvar, et al. 2005. *Exploratory Social Network Analysis with Pajek*. Cambridge University Press.

Fogarty, T. J., and C. H. Liao 2009. "Blessed are the gatekeepers: A longitudinal study of the editorial boards of The Accounting Review." *Issues in Accounting Education* 24(3): 299–318.

Gibbons, J. D., and M. Fish 1991. "Rankings of economics faculties and representation on editorial boards of top journals." *Journal of Economic Education* 22(4): 361–372.

Goodfriend, M. 2007. "How the world achieved consensus on monetary policy." *Journal of Economic Perspectives* 21(4): 47–68.

Hames, I. 2007. *Peer Review and Manuscript Management in Scientific Journals. Guidelines for Good Practice*. Oxford, Blackwell.

Hodgson, G. M., and H. Rothman 1999. "The editors and authors of economics journals: A case of institutional oligopoly?" *Economic Journal* 109(453): 165–186.

Kaufman, G. G. 1984. "Rankings of finance departments by faculty representation on editorial boards of professional journals: A note." *Journal of Finance* 39(4): 1189–1197.

Merton, R. K., and H. Zuckerman 1971. "Patterns of evaluation in science: Institutionalization, structure and functions of the referee system." *Minerva* 2(1): 66–100.

Ni, C. and Y. Ding 2010. "Journal clustering through interlocking editorship information." *Proceedings of the American Society for Information Science and Technology* 47(1): 1–10.

Powell, K. 2010. "Gatekeeper's burden." *Nature* 464(31 March 2010): 800–801.

Rost, K. and B. S. Frey 2011. "Quantitative and qualitative rankings of scholars." *Schmalenbach Business Review (January)*: 63–91.

Wasserman, S. and K. Faust 1994. *Social Network Analysis: Method and Application*. Cambridge University Press.

Yoels, W. C. 1974. "The structure of scientific fields and the allocation of editorships on scientific journals: Some observations on the politics of knowledge." *Sociological Quarterly* 15(2): 264–276.

Table 4.A1 *Economic journals*

Journal	Degree	Normalized Degree	Rank Degree	Centrality	Rank Centrality	Betweenness (×100)	Rank Betweenness
Academia Economic Papers	8	0.011	433	0.323	334	0.026	470
Accounting Business and Financial History	6	0.008	479	0.303	431	0.011	523
Accounting Review	8	0.011	433	0.276	560	0.011	520
Acta Oeconomica	10	0.013	393	0.325	328	0.104	332
African Development Review/Revue Africaine de Developpement	26	0.035	189	0.351	193	0.228	229
African Economic History	0	0.000	673	0.000	673	0.000	593
African Finance Journal	21	0.028	235	0.342	237	0.307	169
Afrika Spectrum	3	0.004	553	0.282	531	0.000	593
Agenda	5	0.007	498	0.284	516	0.006	544
Agribusiness	8	0.011	433	0.282	531	0.058	399
Agricultural and Resource Economics Review	0	0.000	673	0.000	673	0.000	593
Agricultural Economics	11	0.015	373	0.293	472	0.111	322
Agricultural Finance Review	2	0.003	590	0.271	575	0.005	547
Agriculture and Human Values	0	0.000	673	0.000	673	0.000	593
Agronomia Mesoamericana	0	0.000	673	0.000	673	0.000	593
Allgemeines Statistisches Archiv/Journal of the German Statistical Society	2	0.003	590	0.258	607	0.005	552
American Economic Review	40	0.054	90	0.378	72	0.518	82
American Economist	12	0.016	357	0.328	311	0.024	474
American Enterprise	0	0.000	673	0.000	673	0.000	593
American Historical Review	0	0.000	673	0.000	673	0.000	593
American Journal of Agricultural Economics	15	0.020	300	0.321	342	0.311	165
American Journal of Economics and Sociology	3	0.004	553	0.253	614	0.000	593
American Law and Economics Review	19	0.026	259	0.341	243	0.102	335
American Political Science Review	7	0.009	454	0.285	513	0.053	409
American Prospect	5	0.007	498	0.290	487	0.005	550

Table 4.A1 (*cont.*)

Journal	Degree	Normalized Degree	Rank Degree	Centrality	Rank Centrality	Betweenness (×100)	Rank Betweenness
American Statistician	1	0.001	629	0.003	671	0.000	593
Analyse Prévision	5	0.007	498	0.282	530	0.013	513
Annales dEconomie et de Statistique	34	0.046	125	0.361	149	0.426	117
Annals of Economics and Finance	44	0.059	65	0.371	98	0.545	74
Annals of Public and Cooperative Economics	13	0.017	335	0.327	314	0.345	150
Annals of Regional Science	48	0.064	47	0.373	90	0.984	23
Annals of the American Academy of Political and Social Science	3	0.004	553	0.280	543	0.007	538
Antitrust Bulletin	0	0.000	673	0.000	673	0.000	593
Antitrust Law and Economics Review	15	0.020	300	0.329	300	0.118	315
Applied Economics	36	0.048	112	0.371	100	0.192	256
Applied Economics Letters	36	0.048	112	0.371	100	0.192	256
Applied Economics Quarterly	22	0.030	224	0.344	229	0.229	227
Applied Financial Economics	29	0.039	155	0.361	148	0.126	308
Applied Mathematical Finance	5	0.007	498	0.280	543	0.140	293
Aquaculture Economics and Management	10	0.013	393	0.305	417	0.132	301
Archives of Economic History	17	0.023	280	0.324	330	0.094	345
Arthaniti	33	0.044	131	0.367	112	0.127	304
ASEAN Economic Bulletin	13	0.017	335	0.314	372	0.025	472
Asia Pacific Business Review	21	0.028	235	0.339	255	0.251	211
Asia Pacific Journal of Economics and Business	6	0.008	479	0.306	414	0.063	386
Asian Development Review	41	0.055	83	0.372	94	0.417	121
Asian Economic Journal	52	0.070	38	0.395	20	0.421	120
Asian-Pacific Economic Literature	43	0.058	72	0.366	117	0.437	111
Asia-Pacific Development Journal	7	0.009	454	0.300	451	0.001	582
Asia-Pacific Financial Markets	7	0.009	454	0.301	435	0.002	565

Atlantic Economic Journal	44	0.059	65	0.385	43	0.763	41
Aussenwirtschaft	3	0.004	553	0.295	466	0.002	567
Australasian Journal of Regional Studies	18	0.024	271	0.330	299	0.160	279
Australian Bulletin of Labour	0	0.000	673	0.000	673	0.000	593
Australian Commodities Forecasts and Issues	0	0.000	673	0.000	673	0.000	593
Australian Economic History Review	7	0.009	454	0.318	357	0.036	435
Australian Economic Papers	30	0.040	148	0.365	121	0.177	272
Australian Economic Review	25	0.034	202	0.358	161	0.150	283
Australian Journal of Agricultural and Resource Economics	12	0.016	357	0.328	310	0.080	366
Australian Journal of Labour Economics	21	0.028	235	0.342	238	0.224	232
Australian Journal of Management	3	0.004	553	0.286	505	0.001	572
Banca Nazionale del Lavoro Quarterly Review	2	0.003	590	0.264	593	0.000	593
Bancaria	0	0.000	673	0.000	673	0.000	593
Bangladesh Development Studies	35	0.047	119	0.370	106	0.202	247
Bank of Israel Economic Review	9	0.012	412	0.325	327	0.014	511
Bank of Japan Monetary and Economic Studies	14	0.019	319	0.332	281	0.055	405
Bank of Valletta Review	1	0.001	629	0.155	670	0.000	593
Banker	1	0.001	629	0.265	588	0.000	593
Behavioral Research in Accounting	6	0.008	479	0.288	497	0.014	509
Brazilian Electronic Journal of Economics	9	0.012	412	0.317	360	0.059	394
Brazilian Review of Econometrics	22	0.030	224	0.341	241	0.258	204
British Journal of Industrial Relations	14	0.019	319	0.330	292	0.104	333
Brookings Papers on Economic Activity	0	0.000	673	0.000	673	0.000	593
Brookings-Wharton Papers on Financial Services	2	0.003	590	0.277	554	0.001	578
Brookings-Wharton Papers on Urban Affairs	2	0.003	590	0.282	528	0.000	593
Buffalo Law Review	0	0.000	673	0.000	673	0.000	593
Bulletin for International Fiscal Documentation	5	0.007	498	0.259	604	0.247	215
Bulletin of Economic Research	40	0.054	90	0.371	98	0.492	89
Bulletin of Indonesian Economic Studies	22	0.030	224	0.332	284	0.145	286
Business and Economic History	2	0.003	590	0.252	619	0.000	593
Business Economics	5	0.007	498	0.283	521	0.003	563

Table 4.A1 (*cont.*)

Journal	Degree	Normalized Degree	Rank Degree	Centrality	Rank Centrality	Betweenness (×100)	Rank Betweenness
Business History	19	0.026	259	0.340	249	0.481	93
Business History Review	7	0.009	454	0.308	404	0.056	402
Cahiers dEconomie et Sociologie Rurales	12	0.016	357	0.294	470	0.708	49
Cahiers dEconomie Politique	10	0.013	393	0.301	438	0.020	485
Cahiers Economiques de Bruxelles	1	0.001	629	0.258	605	0.000	593
California Management Review	17	0.023	280	0.330	297	0.120	312
Cambridge Journal of Economics	59	0.079	22	0.388	36	0.974	24
Canadian Business Economics	7	0.009	454	0.324	331	0.029	459
Canadian Journal of Agricultural Economics	0	0.000	673	0.000	673	0.000	593
Canadian Journal of Development Studies	3	0.004	553	0.258	605	0.009	531
Canadian Journal of Economics	16	0.021	288	0.345	224	0.120	313
Canadian Journal of Regional Science	11	0.015	373	0.295	467	0.053	410
Canadian Public Policy	6	0.008	479	0.293	471	0.030	455
Canadian Tax Journal	10	0.013	393	0.300	444	0.082	364
Cato Journal	30	0.040	148	0.360	157	0.204	245
Central European Journal of Operations Research	8	0.011	433	0.301	440	0.071	377
CESifo Economic Studies	63	0.085	16	0.400	12	1.116	16
Challenge	39	0.052	96	0.384	48	0.368	140
China Economic Review	19	0.026	259	0.345	221	0.147	284
China Quarterly	1	0.001	629	0.222	656	0.000	593
Chinese Economy	3	0.004	553	0.280	540	0.001	575
CIRIEC-España Revista de Economía Pública Social y Cooperativa	3	0.004	553	0.283	521	0.014	510
Comercio Exterior	1	0.001	629	0.227	651	0.000	593
Communications and Strategies	2	0.003	590	0.241	636	0.000	593
Comparative Economic Studies	11	0.015	373	0.325	326	0.092	350

Journal							
Computational Economics	27	0.036	176	0.363	132	0.190	261
Conceptos (Buenos Aires)	0	0.000	673	0.000	673	0.000	593
Conflict Management and Peace Science	8	0.011	433	0.309	394	0.046	424
Constitutional Political Economy	23	0.031	216	0.352	184	0.143	289
Contemporary Economic Policy	72	0.097	6	0.401	10	1.883	4
Contributions to Political Economy	1	0.001	629	0.268	581	0.000	593
Critical Review	39	0.052	96	0.376	76	0.484	92
Cuadernos de Economia	6	0.008	479	0.305	417	0.005	554
Cuadernos Economicos de I.C.E.	20	0.027	245	0.330	292	0.137	296
Cyprus Review	1	0.001	629	0.219	657	0.000	593
De Economist	38	0.051	102	0.377	73	0.290	182
Defence and Peace Economics	20	0.027	245	0.346	220	0.134	299
Demography	11	0.015	373	0.320	347	0.215	239
Desarrollo Económico	2	0.003	590	0.252	617	0.003	557
Developing Economies	38	0.051	102	0.373	90	0.347	148
Development	20	0.027	245	0.351	197	0.072	373
Development and Change	23	0.031	216	0.331	287	0.304	170
Development Southern Africa	6	0.008	479	0.299	456	0.008	537
Eastern Africa Journal of Rural Development	0	0.000	673	0.000	673	0.000	593
Eastern Economic Journal	20	0.027	245	0.335	273	0.118	316
Eastern European Economics	4	0.005	530	0.272	572	0.000	593
East-West Journal of Economics and Business	38	0.051	102	0.375	80	0.734	45
ECLAP Review	1	0.001	629	0.227	651	0.000	593
Ecological Economics	27	0.036	176	0.361	146	0.500	85
Econometric Reviews	19	0.026	259	0.339	258	0.078	367
Econometric Theory	9	0.012	412	0.308	399	0.002	568
Econometrica	40	0.054	90	0.362	143	0.239	222
Econometrics Journal	9	0.012	412	0.309	395	0.011	522
Economia (Pontifical Catholic University of Peru)	1	0.001	629	0.265	589	0.000	593
Economia Aplicada/Brazilian Journal of Applied Economics	22	0.030	224	0.333	280	0.360	144
Economia Chilena	12	0.016	357	0.320	346	0.034	442

Table 4.A1 (cont.)

Journal	Degree	Normalized Degree	Rank Degree	Centrality	Rank Centrality	Betweenness (×100)	Rank Betweenness
Economia e Lavoro	4	0.005	530	0.273	570	0.126	307
Economia Industrial	7	0.009	454	0.286	507	0.037	433
Economia Internazionale/International Economics	1	0.001	629	0.219	658	0.000	593
Economia Mexicana Nueva Epoca	11	0.015	373	0.304	425	0.571	68
Economia Politica	15	0.020	300	0.332	281	0.053	411
Economic Affairs	36	0.048	112	0.363	136	0.544	75
Economic Analysis and Policy	2	0.003	590	0.259	602	0.000	593
Economic and Business Review	13	0.017	335	0.308	405	0.435	112
Economic and Financial Modelling	12	0.016	357	0.323	335	0.044	426
Economic and Industrial Democracy	18	0.024	271	0.342	239	0.290	181
Economic and Labour Relations Review	18	0.024	271	0.340	251	0.073	370
Economic and Social Review	10	0.013	393	0.316	365	0.035	437
Economic Development and Cultural Change	14	0.019	319	0.328	307	0.030	453
Economic Development Quarterly	14	0.019	319	0.301	440	0.055	403
Economic Geography	13	0.017	335	0.313	379	0.098	342
Economic History Review	8	0.011	433	0.307	410	0.009	532
Economic Inquiry	19	0.026	259	0.344	226	0.117	317
Economic Issues	19	0.026	259	0.353	183	0.104	330
Economic Journal	21	0.028	235	0.341	243	0.069	378
Economic Modelling	34	0.046	125	0.372	95	0.738	43
Economic Notes	49	0.066	46	0.378	70	0.639	56
Economic Perspectives	0	0.000	673	0.000	673	0.000	593
Economic Policy	38	0.051	102	0.368	111	0.263	197
Economic Record	19	0.026	259	0.351	193	0.110	323
Economic Systems	27	0.036	176	0.356	172	0.804	36
Economic Systems Research	17	0.023	280	0.331	289	0.280	190

Economic Theory	41	0.055	83	0.379	67	0.414	122
Economica	28	0.038	165	0.357	167	0.257	206
Económica (National University of La Plata)	4	0.005	530	0.279	547	0.029	458
Economics and Philosophy	18	0.024	271	0.341	246	0.046	423
Economics and Politics	29	0.039	155	0.376	74	0.263	199
Economics Letters	46	0.062	57	0.376	77	0.388	131
Economics of Education Review	15	0.020	300	0.327	316	0.393	130
Economics of Governance	26	0.035	189	0.351	193	0.296	176
Economics of Innovation and New Technology	27	0.036	176	0.354	177	0.204	246
Economics of Planning (dal 9/01/06 Economic Change and Restructuring)	28	0.038	165	0.357	167	0.547	73
Economics of Transition	11	0.015	373	0.318	358	0.107	327
Economie Appliquée	14	0.019	319	0.318	356	0.263	198
Economie et Prévision	22	0.030	224	0.345	223	0.331	153
Economie et Statistique	2	0.003	590	0.222	655	0.000	593
Economie Internationale	24	0.032	208	0.362	139	0.477	94
Economie Rurale	4	0.005	530	0.226	653	0.252	210
Economies et Sociétés	7	0.009	454	0.290	487	0.059	396
Economisch en Sociaaì Tijdschrift	0	0.000	673	0.000	673	0.000	593
Economy and Society	5	0.007	498	0.273	569	0.005	549
Education Economics	11	0.015	373	0.319	350	0.058	397
Ekonomia	41	0.055	83	0.370	104	0.368	139
Ekonomiska Samfundets Tidskrift	6	0.008	479	0.313	377	0.011	519
Ekonomska Misao i Praksa	0	0.000	673	0.000	673	0.000	593
El Trimestre Economico	13	0.017	335	0.322	336	0.232	225
Emerging Markets Finance and Trade	27	0.036	176	0.362	143	0.404	125
Empirica	45	0.060	62	0.380	63	0.465	97
Empirical Economics	29	0.039	155	0.362	139	0.409	124
Energy Economics	15	0.020	300	0.331	289	0.116	319
Energy Journal	14	0.019	319	0.326	318	0.066	381
Energy Studies Review	1	0.001	629	0.264	592	0.000	593

Table 4.A1 (*cont.*)

Journal	Degree	Normalized Degree	Rank Degree	Centrality	Rank Centrality	Betweenness (×100)	Rank Betweenness
Engineering Economist	0	0.000	673	0.000	673	0.000	593
Enterprise and Society	15	0.020	300	0.305	422	0.218	237
Entrepreneurship and Regional Development	10	0.013	393	0.289	494	0.084	360
Environment and Development Economics	55	0.074	29	0.392	24	1.005	20
Environment and Planning A	13	0.017	335	0.312	382	0.102	336
Environment and Planning C: Government and Policy	13	0.017	335	0.315	370	0.437	110
Environmental and Resource Economics	47	0.063	52	0.385	43	0.725	46
Environmental Economics and Policy Studies	15	0.020	300	0.326	318	0.031	450
Environmental Values	1	0.001	629	0.233	648	0.000	593
Estudios de Economia	0	0.000	673	0.000	673	0.000	593
Estudios Económicos	15	0.020	300	0.333	278	0.317	160
Estudios Internacionales	0	0.000	673	0.000	673	0.000	593
Estudos Economicos	6	0.008	479	0.285	515	0.018	495
Eurasian Geography and Economics	7	0.009	454	0.276	564	0.122	311
EuroChoices	5	0.007	498	0.283	525	0.055	404
European Economic Review	50	0.067	43	0.383	54	0.775	38
European Financial Management	60	0.081	20	0.390	30	0.936	26
European Journal of Development Research	19	0.026	259	0.329	302	0.186	265
European Journal of Finance	47	0.063	52	0.381	58	1.001	21
European Journal of Housing Policy	12	0.016	357	0.325	323	0.009	529
European Journal of Industrial Relations	8	0.011	433	0.284	517	0.030	456
European Journal of International Relations	16	0.021	288	0.311	386	0.335	152
European Journal of Law and Economics	27	0.036	176	0.357	166	0.737	44
European Journal of Political Economy	69	0.093	10	0.402	9	1.362	10
European Journal of the History of Economic Thought	43	0.058	72	0.379	67	0.859	30

European Review of Agricultural Economics	5	0.007	498	0.277	556	0.017	499
European Review of Economic History	17	0.023	280	0.316	364	0.345	149
Experimental Economics	41	0.055	83	0.385	42	0.285	186
Explorations in Economic History	15	0.020	300	0.337	263	0.207	244
Family Economics and Nutrition Review	1	0.001	629	0.214	660	0.000	593
FDIC Banking Review	0	0.000	673	0.000	673	0.000	593
Federal Reserve Bank of Atlanta Economic Review	4	0.005	530	0.284	518	0.001	577
Federal Reserve Bank of Chicago Economic Perspectives	4	0.005	530	0.299	456	0.008	534
Federal Reserve Bank of Dallas Economic and Financial Policy Review	5	0.007	498	0.282	527	0.000	593
Federal Reserve Bank of Kansas City Economic Review	4	0.005	530	0.301	438	0.000	588
Federal Reserve Bank of Minneapolis Quarterly Review	3	0.004	553	0.297	460	0.000	593
Federal Reserve Bank of New York Economic Policy Review	44	0.059	65	0.366	117	0.439	109
Federal Reserve Bank of San Francisco Economic Review	2	0.003	590	0.287	498	0.000	592
Federal Reserve Bank of St. Louis Review	8	0.011	433	0.311	383	0.003	561
Federal Reserve Bulletin	4	0.005	530	0.286	509	0.000	593
Feminist Economics	54	0.072	31	0.385	45	1.192	13
Finance	27	0.036	176	0.339	257	0.072	375
Finance a Úver/Czech Journal of Economics and Finance	7	0.009	454	0.277	554	0.026	469
Finance and Development	5	0.007	498	0.284	518	0.074	369
Finance and Stochastics	20	0.027	245	0.326	318	0.073	371
Finance India	72	0.097	6	0.405	5	1.449	9
Financial History Review	4	0.005	530	0.266	584	0.003	560
Financial Management	6	0.008	479	0.290	491	0.000	593
Financial Markets Institutions and Instruments	5	0.007	498	0.300	451	0.000	593

Table 4.A1 (*cont.*)

Journal	Degree	Normalized Degree	Rank Degree	Centrality	Rank Centrality	Betweenness (×100)	Rank Betweenness
Financial Review	40	0.054	90	0.362	139	0.177	271
FinanzArchiv	38	0.051	102	0.371	100	0.396	128
Finnish Economic Papers	21	0.028	235	0.349	204	0.170	278
Fiscal Studies	33	0.044	131	0.358	162	0.232	226
Food Policy	6	0.008	479	0.299	455	0.023	479
Foreign Affairs	3	0.004	553	0.259	600	0.019	493
Foresight	9	0.012	412	0.293	475	0.064	383
Forum for Development Studies	0	0.000	673	0.000	673	0.000	593
Forum for Social Economics	2	0.003	590	0.264	591	0.002	566
Games and Economic Behavior	47	0.063	52	0.384	48	0.461	99
Geneva Papers on Risk and Insurance: Issues and Practice	7	0.009	454	0.306	412	0.002	570
Geneva Risk and Insurance Review	39	0.052	96	0.376	79	0.329	155
German Economic Review	65	0.087	14	0.399	16	0.884	29
Gestion 2000	2	0.003	590	0.248	624	0.003	564
Giornale degli Economisti e Annali di Economia	11	0.015	373	0.307	406	0.028	462
Global Business and Economics Review	15	0.020	300	0.332	281	0.175	274
Global Economic Review	23	0.031	216	0.359	160	0.045	425
Global Economy Quarterly	17	0.023	280	0.338	262	0.252	209
Global Environmental Politics	12	0.016	357	0.296	462	0.099	340
Global Finance Journal	23	0.031	216	0.338	261	0.027	465
Growth and Change	18	0.024	271	0.314	375	0.093	349
Harvard Business Review	0	0.000	673	0.000	673	0.000	593
Health Care Management Science	4	0.005	530	0.281	537	0.017	500
Health Economics	16	0.021	288	0.326	321	0.220	236
Health Marketing Quarterly	5	0.007	498	0.293	475	0.031	452

Journal							
Health Services Research	9	0.012	412	0.310	389	0.025	473
History of Economic Ideas	30	0.040	148	0.347	214	0.380	135
History of Economics Review	14	0.019	319	0.316	367	0.016	502
History of Political Economy	12	0.016	357	0.311	386	0.057	400
Hitotsubashi Journal of Economics	2	0.003	590	0.292	479	0.000	587
Housing Policy Debate	21	0.028	235	0.339	254	0.434	114
Housing Studies	11	0.015	373	0.291	483	0.080	365
Human Resource Development Quarterly	0	0.000	673	0.000	673	0.000	593
Humanomics	2	0.003	590	0.275	566	0.000	593
IIUM Journal of Economics and Management	3	0.004	553	0.277	552	0.000	593
Il Pensiero Economico Italiano	7	0.009	454	0.279	545	0.020	484
Il Politico	1	0.001	629	0.248	623	0.000	593
Il Risparmio	3	0.004	553	0.252	618	0.068	380
IMF Staff Papers	5	0.007	498	0.292	480	0.010	527
Independent Review	29	0.039	155	0.352	187	0.299	174
Indian Economic and Social History Review	20	0.027	245	0.347	212	0.228	228
Indian Economic Journal	28	0.038	165	0.369	109	0.362	143
Indian Economic Review	23	0.031	216	0.344	230	0.128	303
Indian Journal of Economics	2	0.003	590	0.265	589	0.000	593
Indian Journal of Gender Studies	5	0.007	498	0.305	424	0.006	545
Indian Journal of Labour Economics	10	0.013	393	0.305	422	0.041	431
Indiana Business Review	0	0.000	673	0.000	673	0.000	593
Industrial and Corporate Change	61	0.082	19	0.401	10	1.329	11
Industrial and Labor Relations Review	15	0.020	300	0.319	350	0.094	347
Industrial Development. Global Report/Unido	12	0.016	357	0.320	347	0.020	492
Industrial Relations	14	0.019	319	0.322	336	0.091	351
Industry and Innovation	24	0.032	208	0.347	216	0.286	184
Info	8	0.011	433	0.286	508	0.100	339
Informacion Comercial Española Revista de Economia	6	0.008	479	0.286	511	0.032	448
Information Economics and Policy	30	0.040	148	0.354	178	0.309	168
Innovations	33	0.044	131	0.348	205	0.430	116

Table 4.A1 (*cont.*)

Journal	Degree	Normalized Degree	Rank Degree	Centrality	Rank Centrality	Betweenness (×100)	Rank Betweenness
Inquiry	0	0.000	673	0.000	673	0.000	593
Insurance: Mathematics and Economics	11	0.015	373	0.308	401	0.084	361
Integration and Trade	7	0.009	454	0.289	492	0.072	372
International Advances in Economic Research	8	0.011	433	0.306	415	0.018	496
International Economic Journal	62	0.083	17	0.400	14	0.896	27
International Economic Review	7	0.009	454	0.310	393	0.035	438
International Economy	20	0.027	245	0.344	226	0.281	189
International Finance	48	0.064	47	0.389	33	0.319	159
International Game Theory Review	26	0.035	189	0.359	159	0.286	185
International Journal of Business	36	0.048	112	0.366	120	0.584	65
International Journal of Finance and Economics	62	0.083	17	0.390	30	0.773	40
International Journal of Forecasting	30	0.040	148	0.360	151	0.178	270
International Journal of Game Theory	20	0.027	245	0.346	218	0.017	498
International Journal of Industrial Organization	41	0.055	83	0.375	85	0.463	98
International Journal of Manpower	12	0.016	357	0.312	380	0.072	374
International Journal of Production Economics	7	0.009	454	0.308	401	0.159	280
International Journal of Social Economics	11	0.015	373	0.322	336	0.314	164
International Journal of the Economics of Business	34	0.046	125	0.370	104	0.497	88
International Journal of Theoretical and Applied Finance	32	0.043	136	0.356	170	0.259	201
International Journal of Transport Economics	9	0.012	412	0.290	490	0.283	187
International Journal of Urban and Regional Research	3	0.004	553	0.264	593	0.010	528
International Labour Review	0	0.000	673	0.000	673	0.000	593
International Organization	10	0.013	393	0.294	468	0.275	191
International Regional Science Review	31	0.042	145	0.341	246	0.616	59

Journal							
International Review of Applied Economics	35	0.047	119	0.360	151	0.255	208
International Review of Economics and Finance	57	0.077	24	0.391	26	0.440	107
International Review of Financial Analysis	41	0.055	83	0.356	175	0.315	161
International Review of Law and Economics	15	0.020	300	0.331	289	0.093	348
International Social Science Journal	2	0.003	590	0.268	582	0.001	583
International Tax and Public Finance	38	0.051	102	0.367	115	0.225	231
International Trade Journal	12	0.016	357	0.330	295	0.035	439
Investigación Económica	0	0.000	673	0.000	673	0.000	593
Investigaciones Economicas	8	0.011	433	0.309	396	0.016	504
Investment Policy	0	0.000	673	0.000	673	0.000	593
Irish Journal of Agricultural and Food Research	4	0.005	530	0.280	542	0.005	548
ISE Review	11	0.015	373	0.297	458	0.020	488
Jahrbuch für Regionalwissenschaft/Review of Regional Research	3	0.004	553	0.272	572	0.001	581
Jahrbücher für Nationalökonomie und Statistik	4	0.005	530	0.278	550	0.010	524
Japan and the World Economy	54	0.072	31	0.394	22	0.566	70
Japanese Economic Review	59	0.079	22	0.400	14	0.896	28
Japanese Economy	4	0.005	530	0.287	502	0.000	593
Journal for Studies in Economics and Econometrics	1	0.001	629	0.248	625	0.000	593
Journal of Accounting and Economics	15	0.020	300	0.320	344	0.126	309
Journal of Accounting Auditing and Finance	10	0.013	393	0.308	401	0.049	418
Journal of Accounting Research	11	0.015	373	0.309	397	0.052	414
Journal of African Business	14	0.019	319	0.322	336	0.031	451
Journal of African Economies	26	0.035	189	0.355	176	0.249	213
Journal of African Finance and Economic Development	14	0.019	319	0.324	333	0.038	432
Journal of Agricultural and Applied Economics	5	0.007	498	0.252	615	0.009	530
Journal of Agricultural and Resource Economics	9	0.012	412	0.300	447	0.047	422
Journal of Agricultural Economics	10	0.013	393	0.297	459	0.202	248
Journal of Applied Business Research	9	0.012	412	0.319	350	0.042	430
Journal of Applied Econometrics	57	0.077	24	0.384	47	0.813	34

Table 4.A1 (*cont.*)

Journal	Degree	Normalized Degree	Rank Degree	Centrality	Rank Centrality	Betweenness (×100)	Rank Betweenness
Journal of Applied Economics	20	0.027	245	0.353	179	0.064	382
Journal of Applied Finance	29	0.039	155	0.341	246	0.095	344
Journal of Applied Statistics	1	0.001	629	0.237	639	0.000	593
Journal of Asian Economics	46	0.062	57	0.382	55	0.850	31
Journal of Asian Studies	0	0.000	673	0.000	673	0.000	593
Journal of Asia-Pacific Business	19	0.026	259	0.328	307	0.064	385
Journal of Australian Political Economy	3	0.004	553	0.286	509	0.003	559
Journal of Banking and Finance	72	0.097	6	0.392	25	1.137	15
Journal of Bioeconomics	30	0.040	148	0.367	114	0.431	115
Journal of Business	6	0.008	479	0.294	469	0.026	468
Journal of Business and Economic Statistics	26	0.035	189	0.350	201	0.251	212
Journal of Business Research	27	0.036	176	0.351	192	0.498	87
Journal of Common Market Studies	15	0.020	300	0.329	302	0.188	263
Journal of Comparative Economics	8	0.011	433	0.328	309	0.053	412
Journal of Conflict Resolution	22	0.030	224	0.344	230	0.259	200
Journal of Consumer Affairs	6	0.008	479	0.265	585	0.042	429
Journal of Consumer Policy	5	0.007	498	0.288	496	0.035	436
Journal of Consumer Research	10	0.013	393	0.300	447	0.094	346
Journal of Corporate Finance: Contracting Governance and Organization	37	0.050	110	0.348	209	0.288	183
Journal of Cultural Economics	26	0.035	189	0.360	156	0.213	240
Journal of Derivatives	3	0.004	553	0.276	560	0.000	593
Journal of Developing Areas	28	0.038	165	0.353	181	0.190	260
Journal of Development and Economic Policies	1	0.001	629	0.247	626	0.000	593
Journal of Development Economics	35	0.047	119	0.363	130	0.142	290
Journal of Development Studies	26	0.035	189	0.339	258	0.182	266

Journal of East-West Business	13	0.017	335	0.309	398	0.290	180
Journal of Econometrics	36	0.048	112	0.363	132	0.323	158
Journal of Economic and Social Measurement	16	0.021	288	0.331	287	0.037	434
Journal of Economic and Social Policy	15	0.020	300	0.325	323	0.029	460
Journal of Economic and Social Research	3	0.004	553	0.285	514	0.002	571
Journal of Economic Behavior and Organization	79	0.106	3	0.417	3	2.277	3
Journal of Economic Development	26	0.035	189	0.362	137	0.117	318
Journal of Economic Dynamics and Control	51	0.068	39	0.393	23	0.805	35
Journal of Economic Education	28	0.038	165	0.364	126	0.245	218
Journal of Economic Growth	51	0.068	39	0.386	40	0.584	66
Journal of Economic History	7	0.009	454	0.296	464	0.033	445
Journal of Economic Integration	38	0.051	102	0.370	103	0.196	255
Journal of Economic Issues	3	0.004	553	0.283	521	0.000	593
Journal of Economic Literature	53	0.071	35	0.389	34	0.544	76
Journal of Economic Methodology	45	0.060	62	0.375	82	0.597	63
Journal of Economic Perspectives	29	0.039	155	0.360	154	0.098	343
Journal of Economic Psychology	26	0.035	189	0.360	151	0.301	172
Journal of Economic Studies	43	0.058	72	0.383	51	0.700	50
Journal of Economic Surveys	32	0.043	136	0.371	96	0.446	104
Journal of Economic Theory	57	0.077	24	0.388	37	0.650	54
Journal of Economics (MVEA)	0	0.000	673	0.000	673	0.000	593
Journal of Economics (Zeitschrift für Nationalökonomie)	24	0.032	208	0.352	187	0.090	353
Journal of Economics and Business	37	0.050	110	0.360	154	0.435	113
Journal of Economics and Finance	24	0.032	208	0.347	215	0.170	277
Journal of Economics and Management Strategy	26	0.035	189	0.353	181	0.384	132
Journal of Education Finance	0	0.000	673	0.000	673	0.000	593
Journal of Emerging Markets	14	0.019	319	0.317	360	0.059	393
Journal of Empirical Finance	51	0.068	39	0.381	61	0.526	79
Journal of Energy and Development	4	0.005	530	0.288	495	0.018	494
Journal of Energy Literature	6	0.008	479	0.281	539	0.023	475
Journal of Environment and Development	13	0.017	335	0.318	358	0.098	341

Table 4.A1 (*cont.*)

Journal	Degree	Normalized Degree	Rank Degree	Centrality	Rank Centrality	Betweenness (×100)	Rank Betweenness
Journal of Environmental Economics and Management	28	0.038	165	0.367	112	0.469	95
Journal of Environmental Planning and Management	10	0.013	393	0.305	417	0.244	219
Journal of European Economic History	7	0.009	454	0.286	505	0.027	466
Journal of Evolutionary Economics	47	0.063	52	0.375	80	0.723	47
Journal of Family and Economic Issues	4	0.005	530	0.281	534	0.257	207
Journal of Finance	27	0.036	176	0.351	193	0.061	390
Journal of Financial and Quantitative Analysis	32	0.043	136	0.348	205	0.142	291
Journal of Financial Economics	40	0.054	90	0.356	174	0.268	195
Journal of Financial Intermediation	25	0.034	202	0.335	271	0.108	324
Journal of Financial Management and Analysis	1	0.001	629	0.260	598	0.000	593
Journal of Financial Research	34	0.046	125	0.347	211	0.105	329
Journal of Financial Services Research	54	0.072	31	0.373	93	0.443	105
Journal of Forensic Economics	4	0.005	530	0.290	484	0.005	551
Journal of Futures Markets	3	0.004	553	0.280	540	0.000	590
Journal of Geographical Systems	20	0.027	245	0.337	263	0.189	262
Journal of Health Economics	16	0.021	288	0.325	325	0.157	282
Journal of Health Politics Policy and Law	11	0.015	373	0.329	301	0.101	337
Journal of Higher Education Policy and Management	1	0.001	629	0.243	633	0.000	593
Journal of Housing Economics	35	0.047	119	0.369	110	0.574	67
Journal of Housing Research	27	0.036	176	0.352	186	0.212	241
Journal of Human Resources	13	0.017	335	0.319	354	0.034	444
Journal of Income Distribution	9	0.012	412	0.305	421	0.023	477
Journal of Industrial Economics	26	0.035	189	0.349	202	0.297	175

Journal							
Journal of Institutional and Theoretical Economics	10	0.013	393	0.322	341	0.016	505
Journal of International Business Studies	71	0.095	9	0.406	4	2.583	2
Journal of International Development	16	0.021	288	0.331	286	0.314	163
Journal of International Economic Law	29	0.039	155	0.356	172	0.792	37
Journal of International Economics	46	0.062	57	0.384	48	0.526	80
Journal of International Financial Markets Institutions and Money	51	0.068	39	0.380	62	0.366	142
Journal of International Money and Finance	35	0.047	119	0.371	97	0.120	314
Journal of International Trade and Economic Development	60	0.081	20	0.398	17	0.466	96
Journal of Labor Economics	20	0.027	245	0.344	226	0.090	354
Journal of Labor Research	9	0.012	412	0.299	454	0.023	476
Journal of Law and Economics	8	0.011	433	0.313	376	0.059	395
Journal of Law Economics and Organization	22	0.030	224	0.340	249	0.103	334
Journal of Legal Economics	0	0.000	673	0.000	673	0.000	593
Journal of Legal Studies	2	0.003	590	0.260	596	0.001	573
Journal of Macroeconomics	44	0.059	65	0.379	67	0.381	134
Journal of Management Accounting Research	9	0.012	412	0.287	498	0.029	457
Journal of Management and Governance	18	0.024	271	0.348	210	0.191	258
Journal of Marketing	1	0.001	629	0.225	654	0.000	593
Journal of Marketing Research	5	0.007	498	0.270	577	0.003	558
Journal of Markets and Morality	9	0.012	412	0.296	463	0.005	553
Journal of Mathematical Economics	39	0.052	96	0.376	74	0.304	171
Journal of Monetary Economics	28	0.038	165	0.357	164	0.053	407
Journal of Money Credit and Banking	76	0.102	4	0.398	18	1.714	5
Journal of Multinational Financial Management	29	0.039	155	0.346	217	0.047	421
Journal of Peace Research	18	0.024	271	0.327	316	0.127	306
Journal of Pharmaceutical Finance Economics and Policy	7	0.009	454	0.314	374	0.007	540
Journal of Policy Analysis and Management	11	0.015	373	0.304	428	0.106	328
Journal of Policy Modeling	48	0.064	47	0.383	51	0.440	108
Journal of Policy Reform	43	0.058	72	0.375	82	0.412	123

Table 4.A1 (*cont.*)

Journal	Degree	Normalized Degree	Rank Degree	Centrality	Rank Centrality	Betweenness (×100)	Rank Betweenness
Journal of Political Economy	3	0.004	553	0.279	546	0.001	576
Journal of Population Economics	47	0.063	52	0.386	41	0.971	25
Journal of Portfolio Management	33	0.044	131	0.361	146	0.264	196
Journal of Post Keynesian Economics	36	0.048	112	0.365	124	0.621	58
Journal of Private Enterprise	5	0.007	498	0.287	504	0.000	591
Journal of Productivity Analysis	25	0.034	202	0.366	119	0.448	102
Journal of Public and International Affairs	0	0.000	673	0.000	673	0.000	593
Journal of Public Economic Theory	50	0.067	43	0.389	34	0.454	100
Journal of Public Economics	46	0.062	57	0.373	92	0.452	101
Journal of Public Finance and Public Choice/ Economia Delle Scelte Pubbliche	5	0.007	498	0.289	492	0.021	482
Journal of Real Estate Finance and Economics	33	0.044	131	0.364	129	0.393	129
Journal of Real Estate Literature	11	0.015	373	0.306	412	0.004	555
Journal of Real Estate Portfolio Management	10	0.013	393	0.305	416	0.016	506
Journal of Real Estate Practice and Education	8	0.011	433	0.297	460	0.006	543
Journal of Real Estate Research	21	0.028	235	0.329	302	0.089	355
Journal of Regional Analysis and Policy	5	0.007	498	0.265	586	0.051	417
Journal of Regional Science	53	0.071	35	0.385	45	1.268	12
Journal of Regulatory Economics	38	0.051	102	0.374	86	0.651	53
Journal of Risk and Insurance	32	0.043	136	0.361	150	0.369	138
Journal of Risk and Uncertainty	53	0.071	35	0.390	28	0.585	64
Journal of Social and Economic Development	8	0.011	433	0.307	409	0.182	267
Journal of Socio-Economics	39	0.052	96	0.381	58	0.614	60
Journal of Sports Economics	22	0.030	224	0.348	205	0.133	300
Journal of Taxation	1	0.001	629	0.201	666	0.000	593
Journal of Technology Transfer	12	0.016	357	0.333	278	0.061	391

Journal							
Journal of the American Statistical Association	1	0.001	629	0.003	671	0.000	593
Journal of the Asia Pacific Economy	46	0.062	57	0.388	37	0.599	62
Journal of the History of Economic Thought	16	0.021	288	0.329	305	0.114	320
Journal of the Japanese and International Economies	42	0.056	78	0.378	70	0.294	177
Journal of the Royal Statistical Society, Series A	1	0.001	629	0.270	577	0.000	593
Journal of the Social Sciences	0	0.000	673	0.000	673	0.000	593
Journal of Transnational Management	11	0.015	373	0.308	399	0.068	379
Journal of Transport Economics and Policy	20	0.027	245	0.350	199	0.174	275
Journal of Urban Economics	23	0.031	216	0.340	252	0.104	331
Journal of World Business	9	0.012	412	0.300	449	0.064	384
Journal of World Trade	1	0.001	629	0.255	609	0.000	593
Kansantaloudellinen Aikakauskirja	2	0.003	590	0.263	595	0.000	593
Keio Economic Studies	2	0.003	590	0.268	580	0.000	593
Kobe Economic and Business Review	2	0.003	590	0.281	535	0.000	589
Kredit und Kapital	0	0.000	673	0.000	673	0.000	593
Kyklos	44	0.059	65	0.383	53	0.217	238
Kyoto Economic Review	0	0.000	673	0.000	673	0.000	593
Labor History	12	0.016	357	0.302	434	0.053	408
Labour	22	0.030	224	0.346	218	0.815	33
Labour Economics	27	0.036	176	0.349	203	0.159	281
LActualité Economique/Revue DAnalyse Economique	24	0.032	208	0.341	241	0.349	147
Lahore Journal of Economics	0	0.000	673	0.000	673	0.000	593
Land Economics	5	0.007	498	0.290	484	0.063	387
Law and Contemporary Problems	0	0.000	673	0.000	673	0.000	593
Lecturas de Economia	2	0.003	590	0.259	603	0.000	593
Liiketaloudellinen Aikakauskirja	3	0.004	553	0.293	477	0.016	501
LImpresa	0	0.000	673	0.000	673	0.000	593
LIndustria, Nuova Serie	1	0.001	629	0.240	637	0.000	593
Local Economy	9	0.012	412	0.301	435	0.033	446

Table 4.A1 (*cont.*)

Journal	Degree	Normalized Degree	Rank Degree	Centrality	Rank Centrality	Betweenness (×100)	Rank Betweenness
Macroeconomic Dynamics	68	0.091	12	0.398	19	1.036	18
Management	3	0.004	553	0.244	632	0.013	512
Managerial and Decision Economics	54	0.072	31	0.395	21	1.090	17
Manchester School	25	0.034	202	0.357	167	0.082	362
Margin	2	0.003	590	0.234	646	0.001	574
Marine Resource Economics	3	0.004	553	0.265	587	0.001	580
Maritime Economics and Logistics	9	0.012	412	0.311	383	0.060	392
Maritime Policy and Management	1	0.001	629	0.246	630	0.000	593
Marketing Science	13	0.017	335	0.300	444	0.311	167
Mathematical Finance	18	0.024	271	0.324	331	0.113	321
Mathematical Methods of Operations Research	5	0.007	498	0.275	566	0.013	515
Mathematical Social Sciences	24	0.032	208	0.337	265	0.186	264
Metrika	1	0.001	629	0.237	639	0.000	593
Metroeconomica	32	0.043	136	0.363	132	0.238	224
Michigan Academician	0	0.000	673	0.000	673	0.000	593
Michigan Law Review	1	0.001	629	0.237	641	0.000	593
Middle East Journal	2	0.003	590	0.246	628	0.000	593
Middle East Technical University Studies in Development	14	0.019	319	0.344	232	0.047	420
Modern Asian Studies	4	0.005	530	0.271	575	0.021	481
Momento Económico	0	0.000	673	0.000	673	0.000	593
Moneda y Crédito	27	0.036	176	0.353	180	0.293	178
Moneta e Credito	16	0.021	288	0.327	315	0.377	136
Monthly Labor Review	1	0.001	629	0.255	609	0.000	593
Multinational Finance Journal	27	0.036	176	0.362	145	0.082	363
National Institute Economic Review	2	0.003	590	0.266	583	0.000	593

Journal						
National Tax Journal	22	0.030	224	0.345	224	0.198	253
Nationaløkonomisk Tidsskrift	3	0.004	553	0.283	526	0.001	584
Natural Resource Modeling	5	0.007	498	0.293	473	0.010	526
Natural Resources Journal	0	0.000	673	0.000	673	0.000	593
Netnomics	10	0.013	393	0.336	268	0.022	480
New Political Economy	24	0.032	208	0.342	239	0.820	32
New Zealand Economic Papers	0	0.000	673	0.000	673	0.000	593
New Zealand Geographer	0	0.000	673	0.000	673	0.000	593
Nigerian Journal of Economic and Social Studies	0	0.000	673	0.000	673	0.000	593
Nonlinear Dynamics, Psychology, and Life Sciences	7	0.009	454	0.327	313	0.011	521
Nonprofit Management and Leadership	3	0.004	553	0.259	601	0.006	546
Nordic Journal of Political Economy	0	0.000	673	0.000	673	0.000	593
North American Actuarial Journal	2	0.003	590	0.260	599	0.000	593
North American Journal of Economics and Finance	42	0.056	78	0.379	65	0.299	173
OECD Economic Studies	1	0.001	629	0.244	631	0.000	593
Okonomi og Politik	1	0.001	629	0.242	635	0.000	593
OPEC Review	0	0.000	673	0.000	673	0.000	593
Open Economies Review	57	0.077	24	0.390	32	0.775	39
OR Spectrum	13	0.017	335	0.307	408	0.544	77
Organization and Environment	6	0.008	479	0.296	465	0.026	467
Oxford Bulletin of Economics and Statistics	13	0.017	335	0.329	306	0.016	503
Oxford Development Studies	55	0.074	29	0.390	28	0.996	22
Oxford Economic Papers	25	0.034	202	0.352	187	0.137	295
Oxford Review of Economic Policy	15	0.020	300	0.330	292	0.032	447
Pacific Economic Bulletin	9	0.012	412	0.306	411	0.008	536
Pacific Economic Review	124	0.166	1	0.449	1	3.932	1
Pacific-Basin Finance Journal	50	0.067	43	0.367	115	0.631	57
Pakistan Development Review	0	0.000	673	0.000	673	0.000	593
Papeles de Economía Española	0	0.000	673	0.000	673	0.000	593

Table 4.A1 (*cont.*)

Journal	Degree	Normalized Degree	Rank Degree	Centrality	Rank Centrality	Betweenness (×100)	Rank Betweenness
Papers in Regional Science	32	0.043	136	0.351	197	0.505	83
Pesquisa e Planejamento Econômico	3	0.004	553	0.273	570	0.000	593
PharmacoEconomics	3	0.004	553	0.250	620	0.003	562
Philippine Review of Economics	5	0.007	498	0.310	388	0.002	569
Policy	2	0.003	590	0.234	647	0.000	593
Policy Review	0	0.000	673	0.000	673	0.000	593
Policy Sciences	2	0.003	590	0.249	622	0.020	486
Policy Studies	3	0.004	553	0.255	611	0.000	593
Politica Economica	11	0.015	373	0.304	425	0.034	441
Political Science Quarterly	2	0.003	590	0.236	643	0.003	556
Politická Ekonomie	13	0.017	335	0.310	389	0.085	357
Population	1	0.001	629	0.207	664	0.000	593
Population and Development Review	5	0.007	498	0.312	380	0.660	52
Population Bulletin	1	0.001	629	0.246	628	0.000	593
Population Research and Policy Review	6	0.008	479	0.285	512	0.021	483
Population Review	3	0.004	553	0.283	520	0.071	376
Population Studies	1	0.001	629	0.207	664	0.000	593
Post-Communist Economies	17	0.023	280	0.320	349	0.326	156
Post-Soviet Affairs	7	0.009	454	0.277	552	0.127	305
Prague Economic Papers	13	0.017	335	0.310	389	0.085	357
Problemas del Desarrollo	0	0.000	673	0.000	673	0.000	593
Problems of Economic Transition	2	0.003	590	0.212	663	0.000	593
Public Administration Review	0	0.000	673	0.000	673	0.000	593
Public Budgeting and Finance	0	0.000	673	0.000	673	0.000	593
Public Choice	69	0.093	10	0.405	6	1.539	7
Public Finance	0	0.000	673	0.000	673	0.000	593

Public Finance Review	16	0.021	288	0.330	297	0.259	203
Public Policy Research	0	0.000	673	0.000	673	0.000	593
Quaderni storici	1	0.001	629	0.181	669	0.000	593
Quantitative Finance	41	0.055	83	0.382	57	0.569	69
Quarterly Journal of Austrian Economics	21	0.028	235	0.343	234	0.399	127
Quarterly Journal of Business and Economics	13	0.017	335	0.343	234	0.210	243
Quarterly Journal of Economics	35	0.047	119	0.374	89	0.282	188
Quarterly Review of Economics and Finance	43	0.058	72	0.382	55	0.535	78
RAND Journal of Economics	23	0.031	216	0.339	258	0.125	310
Rassegna Economica	2	0.003	590	0.213	662	0.000	593
Real Estate Economics	32	0.043	136	0.363	131	0.272	194
Recherches Economiques de Louvain/Louvain Economic Review	24	0.032	208	0.343	233	0.274	192
Région et Développement	14	0.019	319	0.311	385	0.221	235
Regional Science and Urban Economics	45	0.060	62	0.379	66	0.562	71
Regional Studies	28	0.038	165	0.352	187	0.557	72
Regulation	28	0.038	165	0.358	163	0.200	252
Research in Economics	39	0.052	96	0.369	107	0.340	151
Research in Law and Economics	0	0.000	673	0.000	673	0.000	593
Research Policy	21	0.028	235	0.335	273	0.190	259
Research Review	1	0.001	629	0.276	563	0.000	593
Resource and Energy Economics	31	0.042	145	0.369	107	0.324	157
Resources Policy	17	0.023	280	0.333	277	0.086	356
Review of Accounting Studies	10	0.013	393	0.303	432	0.031	449
Review of African Political Economy	7	0.009	454	0.300	444	0.049	419
Review of Agricultural Economics	3	0.004	553	0.255	612	0.010	525
Review of Austrian Economics	19	0.026	259	0.326	321	0.054	406
Review of Black Political Economy	4	0.005	530	0.300	450	0.000	585
Review of Derivatives Research	32	0.043	136	0.348	205	0.173	276
Review of Development Economics	66	0.089	13	0.400	13	0.716	48
Review of Economic Conditions in Italy	8	0.011	433	0.293	477	0.029	461

Table 4.A1 (*cont.*)

Journal	Degree	Normalized Degree	Rank Degree	Centrality	Rank Centrality	Betweenness (×100)	Rank Betweenness
Review of Economic Design	34	0.046	125	0.365	123	0.138	294
Review of Economic Dynamics	29	0.039	155	0.357	165	0.179	269
Review of Economic Studies	44	0.059	65	0.374	86	0.504	84
Review of Economics and Statistics	36	0.048	112	0.362	137	0.200	250
Review of Finance	40	0.054	90	0.365	124	0.311	166
Review of Financial Economics	32	0.043	136	0.356	171	0.258	205
Review of Financial Studies	18	0.024	271	0.317	362	0.020	489
Review of Income and Wealth	16	0.021	288	0.335	271	0.422	118
Review of Industrial Organization	15	0.020	300	0.333	276	0.223	234
Review of International Economics	94	0.126	2	0.419	2	1.514	8
Review of International Political Economy	29	0.039	155	0.343	236	0.748	42
Review of International Studies	12	0.016	357	0.290	487	0.330	154
Review of Political Economy	30	0.040	148	0.352	185	0.293	179
Review of Quantitative Finance and Accounting	44	0.059	65	0.363	132	0.499	86
Review of Radical Political Economics	6	0.008	479	0.281	538	0.012	518
Review of Regional Studies	21	0.028	235	0.314	371	0.177	273
Review of Social Economy	26	0.035	189	0.345	221	0.356	146
Review of Urban and Regional Development Studies	28	0.038	165	0.352	187	0.366	141
Review of World Economics/Weltwirtschaftliches Archiv	34	0.046	125	0.365	121	0.249	214
Revista Brasileira de Economia	0	0.000	673	0.000	673	0.000	593
Revista de Analisis Economico	25	0.034	202	0.341	245	0.422	119
Revista de Economia	0	0.000	673	0.000	673	0.000	593
Revista de Economia Aplicada	10	0.013	393	0.301	443	0.034	440
Revista de Economia Institucional	13	0.017	335	0.325	328	0.144	287
Revista de Economia Politica	8	0.011	433	0.290	486	0.085	359

Revista de Economia Politica/Brazilian Journal of Political Economy	20	0.027	245	0.335	275	0.446	103
Revista de Economia y Estadistica, N.S.	2	0.003	590	0.250	621	0.000	593
Revista de Estudios Politicos	2	0.003	590	0.246	627	0.000	593
Revista de Historia Económica	9	0.012	412	0.287	498	0.062	388
Revista de Historia Industrial	7	0.009	454	0.277	551	0.034	443
Revue Canadienne des Sciences de l'Administration/Canadian Journal of Administrative Sciences	4	0.005	530	0.291	482	0.008	535
Revue de LOFCE	3	0.004	553	0.260	597	0.107	326
Revue dEconomie du Développement	2	0.003	590	0.257	608	0.000	593
Revue dEconomie Financière	9	0.012	412	0.300	451	0.014	508
Revue dEconomie Industrielle	16	0.021	288	0.317	362	0.179	268
Revue dEconomie Politique	22	0.030	224	0.340	253	0.315	162
Revue dEconomie Regionale et Urbaine	14	0.019	319	0.320	344	0.200	251
Revue dEtudes Comparatives Est-Ouest	3	0.004	553	0.278	548	0.007	541
Revue Economique	20	0.027	245	0.336	270	0.202	249
Revue Finance Contrôle Stratégie	5	0.007	498	0.282	533	0.259	202
Revue Française de Gestion	1	0.001	629	0.215	659	0.000	593
Revue Française dEconomie	13	0.017	335	0.315	369	0.136	297
Revue Tiers Monde	4	0.005	530	0.275	565	0.012	517
RISEC: International Review of Economics and Business	42	0.056	78	0.380	63	0.600	61
Risk Decision and Policy	31	0.042	145	0.364	126	0.143	288
Rivista di Politica Economica	26	0.035	189	0.362	139	0.384	133
Rivista di Storia Economica, N.S.	9	0.012	412	0.305	417	0.020	491
Rivista Internazionale di Scienze Sociali	6	0.008	479	0.304	425	0.030	454
Rivista Italiana degli Economisti	11	0.015	373	0.328	312	0.023	478
Scandinavian Economic History Review	2	0.003	590	0.252	616	0.000	586
Scandinavian Journal of Economics	17	0.023	280	0.337	267	0.061	389
Schmollers Jahrbuch: Zeitschrift für Wirtschafts- und Sozialwissenschaften	5	0.007	498	0.276	560	0.013	516

Table 4.A1 (*cont.*)

Journal	Degree	Normalized Degree	Rank Degree	Centrality	Rank Centrality	Betweenness (×100)	Rank Betweenness
Schweizerische Zeitschrift für Volkswirtschaft und Statistik/Swiss Journal of Economics	0	0.000	673	0.000	673	0.000	593
Schweizerische Zeitschrift für Wirtschafts- und Finanzmarktrecht	0	0.000	673	0.000	673	0.000	593
Science and Society	8	0.011	433	0.303	433	0.140	292
Scottish Journal of Political Economy	16	0.021	288	0.347	212	0.025	471
Seoul Journal of Economics	28	0.038	165	0.364	128	0.091	352
Singapore Economic Review	48	0.064	47	0.376	77	0.376	137
Sloan Management Review	14	0.019	319	0.332	284	0.135	298
Small Business Economics	23	0.031	216	0.360	158	0.400	126
Social and Economic Studies	2	0.003	590	0.254	613	0.007	542
Social Choice and Welfare	57	0.077	24	0.391	26	0.523	81
Social Research	0	0.000	673	0.000	673	0.000	593
Social Science Japan Journal	8	0.011	433	0.301	442	0.058	398
Social Science Quarterly	0	0.000	673	0.000	673	0.000	593
Social Security Bulletin	0	0.000	673	0.000	673	0.000	593
Society	4	0.005	530	0.282	528	0.077	368
South African Journal of Economic and Management Sciences, N.S.	5	0.007	498	0.301	435	0.008	533
South African Journal of Economics	19	0.026	259	0.350	200	0.147	285
Southern Economic Journal	0	0.000	673	0.000	673	0.000	593
Soviet Studies	10	0.013	393	0.319	353	0.101	338
Spanish Economic Review	10	0.013	393	0.303	430	0.014	507
Spoudai	1	0.001	629	0.237	638	0.000	593
Statistica	4	0.005	530	0.237	641	0.491	90
Statistica Applicata	2	0.003	590	0.188	667	0.241	221

Journal							
Statistical Journal	0	0.000	673	0.000	673	0.000	593
Statistical Papers	14	0.019	340	0.322	319	0.679	51
Strategic Finance	0	0.000	673	0.000	673	0.000	593
Structural Change and Economic Dynamics	65	0.087	7	0.404	14	1.621	6
Studi Economici	5	0.007	574	0.272	498	0.197	254
Studies in Economics and Finance	13	0.017	342	0.321	335	0.243	220
Studies in Family Planning	5	0.007	579	0.269	498	0.489	91
Studies in Nonlinear Dynamics and Econometrics	42	0.056	86	0.374	78	0.223	233
Supreme Court Economic Review	3	0.004	524	0.283	553	0.027	464
Survey of Current Business	0	0.000	673	0.000	673	0.000	593
Swiss Political Science Review	9	0.012	556	0.277	412	0.020	490
Tahqiqat-e eqtesadi (Quarterly Journal of Economic Research)	0	0.000	673	0.000	673	0.000	593
Teaching Business and Economics	0	0.000	673	0.000	673	0.000	593
Technology Analysis and Strategic Management	5	0.007	559	0.277	498	0.013	514
Technology and Culture	7	0.009	481	0.291	454	0.044	427
Telecommunications Policy	11	0.015	355	0.318	373	0.239	223
Theory and Decision	42	0.056	58	0.381	78	0.646	55
Tijdschrift voor Economie en Management	8	0.011	372	0.314	433	0.028	463
Tourism and Hospitality Management	1	0.001	668	0.186	629	0.000	593
Tourism Economics	3	0.004	644	0.235	553	0.245	216
Transnational Corporations	15	0.020	265	0.337	300	0.226	230
Transportation	12	0.016	428	0.304	357	0.052	416
Transportation Journal	0	0.000	673	0.000	673	0.000	593
Transportation Research: Part A: Policy and Practice	13	0.017	366	0.316	335	0.107	325
Transportation Research: Part B: Methodological	19	0.026	295	0.330	259	0.272	193
Transportation Research: Part D: Transport and Environment	12	0.016	367	0.316	357	0.056	401
Transportation Research: Part E: Logistics and Transportation Review	15	0.020	255	0.339	300	0.356	145
Travail et Emploi	2	0.003	473	0.293	590	0.000	593

Table 4.A1 (*cont.*)

Journal	Degree	Normalized Degree	Rank Degree	Centrality	Rank Centrality	Betweenness (×100)	Rank Betweenness
Ukrainian Economic Review	1	0.001	629	0.230	650	0.000	593
UN Chronicle	0	0.000	673	0.000	673	0.000	593
Urban Studies	8	0.011	433	0.287	502	0.018	497
Venture Capital	7	0.009	454	0.307	407	0.020	487
Vierteljahrsheftze zur Wirtschaftsforschung	7	0.009	454	0.310	392	0.042	428
Water Resources Research	3	0.004	553	0.243	634	0.052	413
Wirtschaftspolitische Blätter	0	0.000	673	0.000	673	0.000	593
WorkingUSA	13	0.017	335	0.313	378	0.132	302
World Bank Economic Review	48	0.064	47	0.388	37	0.442	106
World Bank Research Observer	13	0.017	335	0.336	269	0.210	242
World Development	43	0.058	72	0.375	82	1.030	19
World Economy	73	0.098	5	0.403	8	1.156	14
Yale Journal on Regulation	1	0.001	629	0.214	661	0.000	593
Yale Law Journal	4	0.005	530	0.281	535	0.245	217
Yapi Kredi Economic Review	1	0.001	629	0.234	645	0.000	593
Zagreb International Review of Economics and Business	3	0.004	553	0.287	501	0.001	579
Zbornik Radova Ekonomskog Fakulteta U. Rijeci/ Proceedings of Rijeka School of Econc	2	0.003	590	0.230	649	0.000	593
Zeitschrift für ArbeitsmarktForschung/Journal for Labour Market Research	3	0.004	553	0.277	556	0.007	539
Zeitschrift für Betriebswirtschaft	6	0.008	479	0.274	568	0.052	415
Zeitschrift für Wirtschaftspolitik	1	0.001	629	0.278	548	0.000	593

Part II

The individual incentives of professional economists

5 Can European economics compete with US economics? And should it?

David Colander

The European economics profession is currently in the process of changing the incentives in its research environment to more closely mimic the US economics profession so that it can perform better globally. This has led to the development and increased reliance on quantitative metrics based on "quality"-weighted journal articles and citation measures, such as the Kalaitzidakis, Mamuneas, and Stengos (2003) metric. Many top European economists are advocating that these measures be used for funding, promotion, and advancement decisions within the EU, so that the EU economics profession can compete in the global economics profession.[1] As these new global metrics become built into the European institutional incentive structure, they are changing the nature of European economics.

This chapter argues that the almost unidimensional focus on the quality-weighted journal article rankings and citations, which is advocated by "global" European economists, is misguided.[2] It further argues that, if used, these metrics will likely undermine the traditional European economics profession's strengths and will hamper European economics' development into a true global economics power. The chapter suggests a set of alternative metrics that build on the traditional European economics profession's strengths. It argues that the use of these alternative metrics will put European economics in a position to leapfrog the US economics profession in the coming decades.[3]

---

[1] A subset of European schools has already become "globalized"; they use these measures internally for hiring and promotion decisions. A majority of programs have not; they remain more traditionally European, but they are feeling strong pressure to become "globalized" as well.

[2] See, for instance, Kirman and Dahl (1994), Dreze (2001), and Neary, Mirrlees, and Tirole (2003).

[3] The arguments in this paper are based in part on a survey and interviews I have done with European graduate students and European economists in preparation for an article (Colander 2008) and two books that I am working on, *The Making of a Global European Economist* and *The Changing Face of European Economics* (together with Rick Holt and Barkley Rosser).

Formal and informal rankings

Rankings happen. Informally, economists rank other economists and programs all the time – this is a good program; this is a bad one; this is an economist who has something to say; this is one who does not. It is only natural that these informal rankings get formalized. The questions posed in this paper are: how formal does one want to make these rankings, and how much attention should the economics profession pay to them? I argue: not very, and not much.

The economics-ranking sub-industry developed in the United States in the 1970s. Initially, rankings were not given significant prominence in funding or research, and top US economists and economic programs paid little attention to it. The rankings attracted most interest among non-top-tier programs that wanted to build their programs up to become top-tier, and thought they could do it by hiring and promoting people who scored highly in the rankings. Thus, over time, the formal rankings of programs, and of economists, became used in US economics programs for promotion decisions, especially at second-tier programs.[4] Most top economists that I talk to still do not take these rankings too seriously; they make their own decisions about who is a good economist and which is a good program. The rankings are certainly not something that the AEA even implicitly endorses in the way that the EEA has done.[5]

Given this dismissive attitude by top US economists of rankings, as I turned my interest to European economics in the early 2000s, I was

---

[4] Top-tier programs tended to give far less weight to these rankings. In their view, good work leads to high rankings, not the other way around. The sense I get from economists at top programs is that if you have to think about rankings, then you probably don't have a truly top program. Few funding decisions in the United States are directly tied to these rankings although informally, rankings are used to justify funding requests. Where faculty unions exist, these formal rankings have been highly formalized and embedded in formal promotion procedures. At most non-union schools rankings of an economist's journal articles are just informally used, but they are nonetheless important.

[5] In 1989, I reviewed much of the recent literature on ranking of US departments for the AEA's Journal of Economic Perspectives. In that article I expressed a view that was shared by the top economists I spoke with, and suggested that "the ranking game has been beat to death." (Colander 1989, p. 141) I wrote: "Everyone knows that any ranking loses important dimensions and, among those active in the profession, the information about which schools rank where is known more precisely than the rankings disclose, especially in view of how quickly top individuals move from school to school and how quickly topics considered important change." Another recent survey of rankings in the US came to a similar conclusion. It found that changes in rankings methods do not change significantly the top schools, but can change significantly at the medium- and lower-ranked schools (Thursby 2000). Thursby writes, "There's not a hill of beans difference across large groups of departments" (p. 383).

surprised by the strong reliance on quantitative metrics of quality-weighted journal article output that seemed to characterize my discussions with top global European economists, and with the current reforms in European economics. I argue that this concern and focus are misplaced, both because the quantitative measures being used don't measure full output of economists, and because they don't provide a meaningful measure of future innovative cutting-edge research output, which is the type of research that can move programs into the top globally ranked set of schools.

While these top European economists advocating the use of the journal article metrics recognize the problems with formal quantitative rankings, they defend them by arguing that the need to change the institutional structure of traditional European programs is worth the costs the rankings would impose. Their goal is to make Europe competitive with US economics, and they feel that the lack of pressure to do research in traditional European programs makes that impossible. They argue that introducing quantitative measures of research, and basing funding on those admittedly imperfect measures, would increase the pressure to do quality research and should be implemented.

The argument in this paper is that the changes being imposed will likely backfire, and are unlikely to help European economics compete. While I agree that the traditional European academic economics profession needs a serious shakeup, the ranking metrics being suggested for funding and advancement are not the way to do it. Specifically, much more consideration has to be given to the limits of rankings than seems to have been given. In the absence of that consideration, the introduction of formal rankings into promotion and advancement decisions will be counterproductive. It will turn European universities into a set of perpetual second-tier global programs, like the perpetual second-tier US programs, rather than turning European programs into serious competitors for dominance of global economics.[6]

Full output ranking metrics

In theory, appropriate formal quantitative rankings can be used in promotion and funding decisions. In practice, because of principal–agent

---

[6] For all the push by various non-top-tier US programs to improve in the rankings, there has been little shift over the years in the overall rankings of programs; no program has moved into the top group that was not close to the top group initially. The problem is that when a star or group of stars develops at lower-ranked programs, they are hired away by the higher-ranked, more prestigious, and generally wealthier programs.

problems (Holmstrom and Milgrom 1991), it is not clear whether it can or not. The problem is that the appropriate formal rankings would be quite different than the existing rankings being discussed in Europe; they would have to be what I call a "full output metric." Anything less than full output metrics will bias activity away from non- or under-measured output that often makes up a large percentage of cutting-edge research activities likely to change the profession in the future.

Were formal research output rankings the only way to gather information about economists' output, the problems associated with the use of output rankings would be unavoidable. But they are not. As I will argue below, the economics profession's activities are informationally small activities, where informal knowledge that active economists have of other active economists' work provides a better measure of an economist's and a program's output than will any formal ranking. You know who responds to your paper in an email with insightful comments; you know who made an important point at a workshop. You know which program has people working on outside-the-box research that isn't showing up in the ranking metrics.[7] You know who is working on a potentially major innovation in theory or in econometrics. You know who has written a paper that is insightful, but never got around to publishing it, or who published it in an obscure journal. Thus, for example, the fact that Bill Vickrey published most of his papers in obscure journals did not stop the profession from recognizing his contribution with a Nobel Prize.

My point is that for informationally small activities, such as research in economics, formal ranking studies add little to the understanding of active professionals of other professionals' work in an operative way; they are far too imprecise for that. The measures simply create quantitative metrics that either ratify previously held views, or, if the rankings don't match one's prior, lead one to look for problems in the formal rankings. "In-the-know" economists' informal ranking supersedes any formal ranking. There is obviously an interaction, and I am not arguing that formal rankings are useless. Formal rankings can be used to refine one's informal rankings, but my claim is that the information in economists' informal rankings far exceeds the information in formal rankings.

What is economists' output?

Let me now consider what the standard journal article ranking metrics miss in measuring economists' output. Most US universities specify

---

[7] Cal Tech in the United States is an example. It ranks much higher in many top economists' rankings than it ranks in the standard ranking metrics.

economists' output as involving three components: research, teaching, and service.[8] Any meaningful ranking of economists' output must appropriately capture and weight all these elements.

Most US universities (at least those without faculty unions) leave open the relative importance of each of these measures in promotion decisions, in part because the department's weights that are used in decisions on promotion and tenure generally differ from the funder's implicit weights, especially in public universities, which are in large part government-funded. (It is an open secret in the United States that universities transfer toward research those resources given by funding agencies for teaching.) There is usually some wording in most university by-laws that all three elements contribute to promotion decisions, but in most US graduate economics departments, the sense I get from talking to economists is that about 95% of the weight is placed on research and 5% on teaching and service.[9]

Actually, teaching plays a more important role in US economics departments than the 95%/5% split would suggest. While it may not be given much weight in the formal decision, at many graduate schools economists' workmanship ethic, and their desire to be seen as good in all aspects of their job, leads professors to spend significant time on teaching – far in excess of what recognition it might provide them in the advancement process. Thus, if I had to hazard a guess about the average time spent by economics faculties at the top 50 universities on the various activities, it would be 50% teaching, 80% research, and 20% service, with much of the service coming from post-tenure faculty who have gone into government and university administration positions. (This adds up to more than 100% because most US economists believe that they are putting in more than 100% effort.) Normalizing this effort to 100%, I arrive at a relative weighting of 33% teaching, 53% research (of which 80% of research effort or 42% of total effort is for journal article publication), and 13% service for US economists, a weighting reflecting

---

[8] Each of these sub-elements of output can include many dimensions. The most ambiguous of these three is service, but it generally includes activities both within the economics profession and within the broader academic and societal community. Government, central bank, international government agency, business, and think tank economists have an even broader concept of output, and their output measure would significantly expand the areas that would fall under the service heading. Their service includes providing advice to policy makers, weighing in on public and internal debates and policy issues by writing policy briefs, and talking with, and influencing, policy makers and the general public.

[9] Where I teach, which is a liberal arts school with only undergraduates, the implicit sense I have is that after an initial high level of teaching threshold is passed, 50% of the promotion decision depends on research, 40% on teaching, and 10% on service.

the true allocation of US economists' time. So, for most US economists, a ranking based on journal article research is capturing less than half of what they would see as their output.

In traditional European universities, incentives have been quite different. As pointed out by Frey and Eichenberger (1992, 1993) there are two major differences. First, the non-journal article aspect of research gets far more importance in Europe; far less emphasis goes into preparing research for top-ranked journals. Second, in Europe, service is considered not only at the department and university level, but also at the national level; in Europe there has been a strong tradition of professors playing active formal and informal roles in advising governments and in public debates. They argue that compared to US economists, a larger percentage of European economists play the role of public intellectual and weigh in on public debates about policy issues.

In my view, contributing to the public debate is an important output of economics – it brings economic knowledge to policy. Frey and Eichenberg's argument that European economists do more of that is consistent with the incentives they face; such output is more likely to "count" in Europe, and can lead to advancement much more than is the case in the United States. My sense is that, until recently, in traditional European programs, the attitude was that if one published in an international journal – fine, but such activity was only one measure of many that lead to advancement in the European context. That means that European economists naturally focus less on publishing in international journals even if the economists in Europe are doing research that may be highly publishable in those journals.

My point is that these different incentives also lead to a different allocation of time in US and global European programs and traditional European programs. Assuming the same 20% division of time that I gave to US economists for department and university service, and adding another 10% for state-level service, I would estimate that 30% of European economists' time goes to service. Frey also states that undergraduate teaching is more important in Europe, but to be conservative, let's say that it is the same 50% input that I estimated for US economists. Research ranks lower in traditional European programs than it does in the United States. Just to put some estimate on it, say that research generally gets 30% of their time, and that 60% of that research goes toward journal-article publication. Adding these together gives a total of 110%, the lower total amount reflecting the lower incentives for work of all kinds in Europe as compared to the United States. Normalizing to 100% gives relative time spent of 45% for teaching, 28% for research, of which 60% or 17% is for journal-article publication and 28% for service.

The numbers used in these calculations are obviously debatable, but the point they make is not: these differential incentives in the US and traditional European programs make any comparison of traditional European programs and US programs highly questionable. That point holds for any reasonable choice of percentage allocation of time in Europe and the US.

If my estimates of the differential incentives for the US and traditional European programs are close to correct, this suggests that lower effort accounts for only 27% of the lower journal-article research output in Europe, and that almost 75% of the difference is simply a reflection of the differential incentive structure. By that I mean that these journal-article metrics are comparing 17% of traditional European economists' output with 42% of US economists' output, which makes it a bit like comparing European football players with US football players on the basis of their ability to pass, receive, and block a US football. If one did a full measure of output, this argument would suggest that there is much more parity between the traditional European and US economics professions than these ranking studies have suggested, and that they present a far less distressing picture than the commentators and advocates of a change in metrics suggest.[10]

What is economists' research output?

My argument against the journal-article metric is even stronger than that these metrics do not measure economists' full output. It is that they also don't measure economists' research output in an especially meaningful way. The reason they don't is that research output is a multidimensional concept, and journal-article output measures only a small part of the total; thus it biases the research done to emphasize that particular dimension. Research includes working on an idea in one's mind, taking part in an online debate, developing new ideas, writing a book, taking part in a workshop, commenting on a paper, editing a journal, refereeing, or developing some idea within a business. When Fisher Black worked on macroeconomic theory and the lack of a pricing anchor in an economy with advanced financial markets while at Goldman Sachs, or when Hal Varian worked on search algorithms while at Google, they were doing seminal research but little of it led to journal-article publication.

---

[10] As I stated earlier in this paper, my argument is not that that are no problems with academic European economics. It is simply to argue that the ranking studies comparing the programs to the United States are not a clear demonstration of those problems.

Similarly, work by economists at Yahoo Research doesn't get published. But that work influences ideas, real world policies, and discussions within economics.

Another dimension of research involves its purpose. Theoretical research is that part of research that best fits the journal-article outlets. But the majority of economists do not do theoretical research; they do applied research, which is meant to influence policy. By focusing the output metric on journal articles, economists are led to focus on what elsewhere I have called "hands-off" applied research, which I contrast with "hands-on" applied research.[11] Hands-off policy analysis is written for other economists or advisors to policy makers more than it is written for policy makers. To the degree the analysis actually comes to policy conclusions (generally it concludes with a call for more research), those conclusions are highly contingent on the implicit value judgments and goals in the models. *If* the policy maker accepts these value judgments and goals, and *if* the world works like the model, then the policy recommendations of the hands-off research are relevant, but the hands-off research papers have no discussion of these issues, which makes the research of little value to the policy maker. Hands-off researchers must leave it to an intermediary between the economic scientist and the policy maker to do the translation.

Hands-on policy analysis is different than the policy done by hands-off applied economists. Applied policy economists do work that is more econometrically sophisticated, and is written for other economists, not for policy makers. Economists' applied policy is meant to be a contribution to the scientific debate. Hands-on policy analysis is designed to contribute directly to the policy debates in a country. Whereas hands-off policy analysis concentrates on the scientific aspect of policy, hands-on policy applies scientific knowledge to policy by integrating economic knowledge and economic models into a broader framework.

Traditional European programs have given students training in both hands-on and hands-off policy analysis, but only the hands-off policy analysis has a reasonable outlet in the journals. The output of hands-on policy research is affecting policy, not economic journal articles. It is not written for other economists; it is written for policy makers and its output is useful advice to decision-makers often on a time-dependent topic of immediate importance to them. They need an answer in a short time. A "better" answer provided later than that time is useless to them. With the adoption of a journal-article metric, this hands-off research

---

[11] I develop this distinction further in Colander and Nopo (2008).

output, which well may be the most important research output of economists, is discouraged. Unless the metrics are adjusted to include this hands-on applied research, one of the major strengths of traditional European programs in training students to do such research will be undermined.

The problem becomes cumulative. Individuals who do hands-on applied research are driven from academic institutions and are replaced by researchers who do hands-off applied research. They then teach students to do hands-off applied research, even though almost all the students' primary role will be in doing hands-on applied research. Students' training becomes further and further removed from what the majority of them will actually be doing, and eventually the expertise in doing hands-on applied research is lost.

Even within hands-off applied research, quality-weighted journal article metrics miss much information about research output, which involves ideas, not articles. Because it involves ideas, economists who work in a subject area, or at a school, know who is contributing to research and who isn't regardless of whether or not those people publish. The reason is that journal publications are not the way academic researchers communicate among themselves. They talk; they email; they listen to seminars; they read. In the United States, precisely because of its use of quality-weighted journal article biased metrics, most economists who are contributing research to an area publish in journals that match the metrics, so the metrics become a better match over time, but it takes a long time and there is much noise. For example often what researchers choose to publish has to do with many issues quite separate from the quality of their paper. When a journal article research metric is used, researchers who game and play the system have an advantage over those who simply are interested in doing good work. For traditional European programs that have not previously used the metric, the metric is an especially poor way of measuring output.

The lack of correlation between true research output and journal article publication is truer today than ever before. Today, in the United States, much of the debate about an idea happens at the pre-Working Paper stage, and the research workshops at top universities are more central to the spread of ideas in economics today than are journals. If you are reading an idea for the first time when it is published in a journal, you are out of the informal research loop, and are probably at least two years behind specialists' thinking about the idea. In fact, I would argue that a paper has already had much of the influence it will have on cutting-edge researchers by the time it reaches the Working Paper stage. Publication in a journal is more often than not a tombstone, marking ownership of an idea, than it is an important method of communication among cutting-edge specialists. Today, were journal publication metrics not used for promotion and tenure decisions, many existing print, and even online, journals would disappear because they would be unnecessary.[12]

The worst effects of the metrics occur in those institutions that have most rigidly quantified them. In the United States this happens when there are faculty unions, which require carefully classified lists of what counts (and how much it counts) for tenure and promotion decisions and what does not. These lists, which can become 40 or 50 pages long, and can include weighting factors for the number of words on a page, among hundreds of other dimensions, lead to a corollary to Gresham's Law – bad research drives out good research, since faced with such a list rational researchers choose to publish in the "least costly" venue (the journals that require the least work for the highest measured gain in the metric) to them; they structure their research agenda accordingly. Researchers looking into long-range issues, advanced speculative work, or researchers setting off in new directions are selected out of the profession and are replaced by "game playing" researchers who are more focused on maximizing output as measured by the metric. It is that tendency that leads to the sense that much of what is published is of little value.[13]

My problem with the formal rankings being used to measure research is that they give zero weights to large numbers of research activities that are central to new ideas developing. That zero weighting leads researchers away from these unweighted activities and toward weighted activities. It leads rational researchers to focus on small journal-publishable ideas, and to deemphasize large ideas that might be more interesting, and have a larger research payoff. It also leads them to worry less about what their research is contributing to knowledge or society, and more about whether it is publishable. The publication of the paper becomes an end in itself. That has happened in the United States. Essentially, my conclusion of my most recent study of top US graduate economic programs (Colander 2006, 2007) is that these graduate programs have become specialists at producing highly efficient journal-article writers, but far less proficient at producing broad-based research economists and far less proficient at teaching undergraduates.

---

[12] I have discussed these issues in Colander and Plum (2004).

[13] In Colander (2007) one of the students expressed this sentiment when he stated, "In a top journal like the Quarterly Journal of Economics I'd say at least half [of the articles published] are useless. Probably 20% are useful and the rest are unclear... Fifty percent will never be cited or read again." The other students in the interview agreed.

The traditional European educational environment and research output

Traditional European programs have been far less influenced by this drive for publications. The reason is that until recently, European economists faced more informal, political, and social, incentive systems. Often, the incentive system was vague and idiosyncratic by school and country. Thus, Europe avoided the "publication at all costs" bias that characterized the US system.[14] In traditional European economics, doing good work, impressing higher-level professors, measures of publications and citations, and positively interacting with other professors are all important.[15] This continues to hold widely in traditional European programs even as the system moves into flux. Tono Puu (2006) captures this European sensibility in his assessment of publications. He writes: "We tend to look down on the previous generation as they published relatively little. This fact, however, does not imply that they worked little or were less creative. It might just signify that they were more choosy about what they regarded as being significant enough to merit publication."

Since within the traditional European academic system funding and advancement decisions were often made because of social and political factors rather than research output factors, there was little push for publication. There was no central job market that even implicitly used a journal-publication metric. From what I hear from advocates for the journal-article metrics, and from traditional European economists as

---

[14] The differential assessment system in Europe and the United States is explainable; in the US, there has long been an integrated labor market; in Europe, there was not, so in Europe there was less need to develop a generalized ranking system to compare researchers across borders. An important reason for this difference was that, until recently, European economics was fragmented by different languages and national borders, and a different promotion system that was based less on publications and more on subjective judgments that would develop over time. The smaller markets meant that all top economists in a country would meet. They could know one another personally, discuss with each other, and be able to come to an independent judgment about each other's knowledge and work. Assessments based on quantitative output measures, such as publications, would matter, but they would be only one small element in the subjective judgment. With the development of a common educational policy and a common language, that is becoming less the case, and the structure of European economics is now in the process of change, albeit slowly.

[15] We present just one example. In Britain, judgments about who was good, not publications, guided placements, with this done through established "old boys" networks. This meant, for example, that until recently, it was considered unnecessary to get a Ph.D. in order to get a job, and in fact the getting of a Ph.D. meant that the researcher was not considered good enough to be hired in the market. As Britain integrated its profession with the US profession, that is no longer the case. Indeed, today British economics may have become more "American" than American economics, slavishly following outdated orthodoxies being abandoned in the United States.

well, the results of this social advancement system were not always a pretty picture. Programs become inbred and out of touch with developments that are going on elsewhere. Programs and professors often developed fiefdoms, and a small coterie of professors often had control over hiring and research of younger professors, who then had no reason to develop an independent research program. Connections determined hiring decisions: once hired, researchers had limited flexibility. Programs were often focused on narrow issues, and many programs made little attempt to subject their ideas to the global economics discussion, in part because those discussions were in English, while the work in traditional European programs was often in the language of the country in which the work was being done.

The negative aspects of the traditional European programs are generally known and underlie the desire for change by almost all European economists; thus I am not denying that change is necessary. But when thinking about these changes, the negative aspects must be balanced against its positive aspects, and the positive aspects of the traditional European system compared to the US system have received too little discussion.

One advantage is that the traditional European system gave researchers a larger incentive to think about big questions, and to spend more time reading others' work, and to publish only when they felt they had something meaningful to say that goes beyond what others know. Put another way, it directed researchers toward *thoughtful research over publishable research*. This focus on thoughtful research allowed pockets of excellence to develop in Europe that could not develop in the United States as European researchers took long-term views of research rather than short-term views. For example, important work in cointegrated vector auto regression was done at Copenhagen, important work in general to specific econometrics was done in England, important work in behavioral and experimental economics initially developed in Germany and Switzerland, important work in non-linear dynamics and complex systems took place in Germany, Sweden, the Netherlands, and Italy, and important work in agent-based modeling was done in Italy. Most of this research reflected a deep understanding of the limitations of the current approach in economics, and was foundational work designed to change it. Aspects of this work will likely play an important role in the future development of economics.[16]

A second advantage of the traditional European system is that it left European economists free to choose the type of outlet that made most

---

[16] This argument is developed further in Colander, Holt, and Rosser (forthcoming).

sense for the idea. For example, if an idea took a book to make the point, they would write a book rather than not deal with the idea because it could not fit into a journal article. Often, ideas weren't published but simply catalogued and used in discussion and classes.

A third advantage of the European system is that it allowed for more diversity than one finds in the US programs. Since there was no single measure in Europe, there were many measures of excellence, and different countries specialized in different elements. France, with the regulation school, specialized in the integration of social and economic issues. Italy specialized in the history of economic ideas. The Netherlands specialized in econometric modeling. Some German universities specialized in policy and others specialized in the implications of non-linear dynamics for economic systems. The "sameness" of graduate programs that the COGEE commission criticized as characterizing US graduate programs was far less prevalent in Europe (Krueger et al. 1991).

Despite the push toward a global blending, the most distinctively local heterodox traditions have continued to flourish most clearly within the local-language journals and outlets. Thus, when I have met European economists from traditional European programs I have often been highly impressed with their broad knowledge of the economic literature, their technical knowledge, and their sense of what issues are important. In my judgment European economics is on a par with US economics, so not only can it compete; it is already successfully competing.

Developing a better assessment system

Let me now turn to the difficult question: how to design an assessment system that will weed out the less desirable elements of the traditional European system while not destroying the good elements. I premise this discussion on the acceptance that change in traditional European academic economics programs is needed, and that the only way to implement change is likely to involve the use of some metric that replaces the current individually subjective decision-making process. The politics and vested interests are too strong to allow the current non-metric-based system to work. Moreover, as Europe education expands from country-based education to a European education, the subjective information about who is good becomes harder to maintain and develop.

But to say that some metrics will likely be necessary is not to say that the current ones being used are the best. Indeed, my arguments suggest that they are far from the best, and that they are being used inappropriately. Let me discuss what implications I believe my arguments have.

1. *Begin from a measure of total output, and estimate what percentage of total output is being captured by the metric you are using.* If the output of economists is as complicated and multidimensional as I am arguing it is, any metric is going to capture only a small portion of that output. Thus, at the beginning of each metric study, the authors should be required by editors to estimate the percentage of output that their metric is capturing, in order to reduce the possible misuse of that metric. For example, if the recent metrics papers had stated in their conclusion that they are capturing only a small percentage (my estimate above was 17%) of European economists' total output and that there was no objective way to justify the weights they chose, their rankings would likely have not been used in the way they have been used.

2. *Use multiple metrics to judge quality of research.* All metrics are flawed, and thus one wants to use as many different measures as possible.[17] The multiple measures take account of the arbitrariness of any ranking system and better capture the multiple dimensions of research. As Zimmerman (2008) discusses, REPEC offers numerous alternative measures, which gives it a nice flexibility, and includes working papers, measures of access on the web, and other such interesting elements. The use of multiple metrics will make it easier for subjective evaluation to enter in.

3. *If you have to choose one metric to focus on, focus on an expansive output metric rather than embodying strong implicit and explicit quality weights in the metric.* In other words, the output metric should be seen as a metric measuring only the number of articles with minimal concern for where they are published. The reason is two-fold.

    a. The first reason is that the quality-weighting systems currently in use are highly biased against European economists generally. This is the case since the existing measures, based upon previous importance of journals, are highly US-centric. They rate internal US university journals (such as the *QJE* and *JPE*) highly, as well as rating AEA journals highly. This creates a bias against European economists. The problem is that the peer review process cannot be totally neutral; geographic or other proximity with the editor matters, not because of any conscious bias, but because of information flow and interests.[18] Being at the same workshops with the

---

[17] This argument is nicely developed in Henrekson and Waldenstrom, 2007.

[18] Journals are subject to real-world influences and to interactions between authors and editors in defining what a problem is, and the reasonable way of approaching it is likely to be shared by researchers in the same geographic area. JPE articles come much more

editor puts one on the same wavelength and increases chances of knowing what the editor is looking for in a paper.

Once a journal ranks high in a metric, the rankings become self-fulfilling. People send their best papers to the journals that rank the highest, and the ranking becomes built into the institutional structure. The rankings provide an institutional structure that will make it much harder for European journals to compete and will be biased against European authors. To offset that bias, at least initially, one might even consider in *European rankings giving European journals a higher ranking in the metrics for European promotion and advancement*. This would enhance their ability to attract the best papers. Giving double weights for publication in European journals can help offset that existing journal bias. It can be seen as a way of generating bottom-up European journals. I justify it by what might be called an infant journal argument. This would encourage Europeans to publish in European journals and build them up as an alternative to the established US journals.[19]

b. A second reason is that the quality-weighted systems are highly biased against traditional European economics and will likely kill off many of the strong aspects of the traditional system as well as the weak aspects. As I argued above, strengths of traditional European economics include its diversity and its pockets of excellence. These strengths have developed precisely because a ranking system was not in use, and the use of a highly qualitative ranking system will undermine that strength.

A broad-based measure – such as Coupe's (2003) measure of output – would be far less damaging, since it would give many more outlets to publish. Let me be clear; my argument is not that journal quality doesn't matter, and that a publication in the *AER* is the equivalent to an article in the *Journal of Human Resources* or *Public Finance*. It is simply to argue that the quality weights are

---

heavily from Chicago, and QJE articles come much more heavily from Harvard, than from other schools. The editors are at these schools and, even with the best of intentions about being open, which I think they have, cannot but be influenced by social interactions and discussions about what is relevant and what is not. Decisions on publication are seldom clear-cut; reviewers differ, and choice of reviewers can play an important role in whether a paper will be accepted. Thus, even in a peer review system the editor has much more influence than is often recognized. If Europe moves toward emphasizing a single peer-reviewed journal metric, it should develop its own European metric that at least initially emphasizes European-based journals (weighting such journals much more heavily) to help offset the infant-journal problem.

[19] Obviously, such an alternative weighting system should not continue forever but instead have a planned phase out over a ten-year period.

article-dependent and context-dependent, and are better made subjectively. For example, much of the initial cutting-edge research that will guide economics in the future will likely be published in non-traditional journals that are more open to new approaches; the journal article metrics will miss precisely that work that is likely to be most path-breaking.

The problem of using quality weights is that they can embody significant implicit subjective judgments under the guise of objectivity. For example, as Henrekson and Waldenstrom (2007) point out, the Kalaitzidakis, Mamuneas, and Stengos ranking, which was called "the most up-to-date set of objective journal weights available" in the introduction to a set of ranking studies published in the *JEEA* (Neary et al. 2003, p. 1247) has enormous subjective judgments hidden within it. Specifically, those authors point out that "a single article in the *American Economic Review* is valued more highly in the Kalaitzidakis, Mamuneas, and Stengos metric than 10 articles in the *Journal of Financial Economics*, or 25 articles in the *Journal of Law and Economics*, 60 articles in the *Journal of Health Economics*, or all the 400+ articles published in the *Journal of Evolutionary Economics*" (p. 5). By hiding those necessarily subjective implicit weights in the ranking metric, the subjective judgments are hidden rather than made transparent, so one can judge the metric.

4. *Develop a separate output metric to judge economists' contribution to hands-on research.* Hands-on research does not lend itself to journal articles, and should not be judged by journal article output. Often, this research will result in internal memos. Even when it does result in publication, the best publication outlets are not economic journals. Rather they include general interest magazines, newspapers, and multidisciplinary journals. Any ranking should include some measure of this form of research output, or make it clear that it is not capturing this aspect.

5. *Develop a formal subjective metric to complement and possibly replace output metrics.* If, as I argued, economics is an informationally small activity, then more information exists within the profession than can be captured in any metric. Obviously these subjective measures will be flawed, but I argue that they will be less so than the alternatives because they are more likely to include many non-quantifiable output dimensions of economists' performance.[20] There are many ways this

---

[20] One could even establish an online virtual economics academy, in which economists who join the online game can create their "dream teams of researchers." The game could

formal subjection metric could be developed. One could set up a survey sent out to specialists in a field who rank other researchers and programs in the field in terms of the dimensions that one wants to rank. Weights could be assigned to the dimensions, allowing a composite judgment to be arrived at.

Many variations of this approach are possible. For example, you could allow each researcher to write a one-page statement of her or his research agenda along with a one-page vita, which others could use to rank that research. Programs could provide two-page summaries of their research program. Then this information could be provided to all who take the survey or to a panel of experts – say US Nobel Prize winning economists – who would be asked to rank the schools based on these summaries and other knowledge of the program that they have. These formal quantified subjective measures could then be used in conjunction with the physical measures of output in the more traditional approach.

6. *Develop an input metric to supplement the output metric.* With the multidimensionality of research output, with much of it unmeasurable, even using multiple dimensions of output metrics, a lot will be missed. Essentially, what one wants in research is to have really, really bright and creative people, playing with really, really hard questions. Placing any type of measure on their output will likely hurt the process. Ideally, these really, really bright people should be given wide latitude. The problem is that all of us would like to be given that latitude. Thus some filtering device must be developed to limit those who are given that latitude. Requiring researchers to have Ph.D.s is one way in which that was done. That reduces the number of researchers significantly, and insures that they have a common core of knowledge. That filter could, and probably should, be reconsidered, and additional finer filters should be developed. For example, a set of additional difficult certification exams could be developed in specific areas, or in techniques, as is done with actuaries. Researchers could take these exams and be judged according to their knowledge, not their output. Many variations of this approach are possible; for example, before one can do research using a particular econometric technique, one could be required by a journal to have completed a difficult certification exam that demonstrated full knowledge of that technique.

___

include a trading system that would essentially value various economists. Thus a "player" in the virtual academy game would be given an objective function and allowed to "draft" and "trade" players for his virtual university.

Providing a level playing field for traditional European economists

I am realistic and I recognize that the above suggestions are unlikely to change the current use of metrics, and even if the arguments are accepted, their implementation will take many years. In the meantime the current quality-weighted journal-article metrics will likely dominate. Thus, even if one accepts none of the suggestions, I still believe that the EU should take a number of steps to offset the US bias in the existing quality-weighted journal output metrics.

1. *The EEC should subsidize the distribution of European economic journals.* As the European Economics Association has discovered, any new economics journal today faces serious problems of finding acceptance in libraries. Whereas 20 or 30 years ago new journals in economics could easily find homes in libraries, new journals today, unless they are part of a large package supplied by a journal publisher, have almost no chance of being adopted by libraries.[21] This puts new European journals, and existing European journals that are trying to expand their readership and global reach, at a considerable disadvantage to established journals with built-in library subscriptions. European journals face a strong infant journal problem.[22] By emphasizing

---

[21] The AEA journals are some of the most expensive economics journals in the world to produce, both because they pay editors well and because they have a labor-intensive quality process of review and printing. The average cost of each article is more than $8000 per article. The journals nonetheless have a low price to libraries because so many libraries subscribe. It is this advantage that is allowing the AEA to introduce four new journals at low prices. These journals will quickly move up in the rankings. The reason is twofold. First, economies of scale – the large number of library subscriptions means that the AEA can spread out the costs much more than can other journals. (They tied in their four new journals that will begin publication in 2009 to existing journals so these will also be relatively inexpensive to libraries, since very few will opt out of the total package.) The second reason is that the AEA owns EconLit, which provides a major profit (over $1,000,000 a year) to the organization, allowing it to heavily subsidize its journals.

[22] As an example of the need for such a program consider the Journal of the European Economic Association. It had hoped to become one of the top six journals in the world, but it has not achieved it, not because it is of lower quality in its reviewing process, but because it started later, which places it at a permanent disadvantage. Its lower rank is recognized by researchers and its lower position becomes self-fulfilling as the first pass of the best papers are sent to the highest-ranked journals. The problem for new journals seeking to move up is amplified by the fact that journals have proliferated, and have become very expensive to libraries, meaning that libraries are not buying new journals. The result is that all new journals are at a significant competitive disadvantage relative to established journals and even to those journals that are part of the private publisher's package of journals that is sold to libraries as a whole.

quality-weighted journal metrics, the EU is contributing to that bias and handicapping its own journals. To offset that disadvantage, if European economics chooses to give stronger emphasis to a journal ranking system, it would pay for the EEC to consider subsidizing existing European economic journals for a limited period of perhaps ten years, making them available free on the web. This subsidization would allow all libraries in the world access to these journals and showcase European researchers' work, thereby helping offset the infant journal problem. Subsidizing all European journals for a limited time period would give them a chance to develop and compete on a more level playing field. Using European research funds to do this would likely be more effective at advancing European economics than would the same funding of European research.

2. *Establish an invited peer review process for the new European journals.* Another method that European journals might use to establish their journals as top innovative journals rather than as second-tier journals is to institute an "invited peer review" section of the journal. For a young scholar, journal publishing is a crapshoot – all the more so if the author doesn't know the editor or at least is not familiar with the editor's thinking. Lack of knowledge about publishing makes it difficult for young scholars to take chances. They too often go with papers dotting i's and crossing t's.

   To offset that incentive, one can establish a system in which European editors choose highly promising young European researchers and invite them to publish a paper on a subject in the European journal. This could be competitive in the sense that it is judged on a one-page proposal of what is intended. The papers are still peer reviewed, but the presumption is that the paper will be published, and the writer will have a chance to respond to reviewers. This is essentially how some top-ranked US based journals, the *JEP* and *JEL*, work, and it allows them to get a different range of articles than shows up in other journals. Actually, in reality, journals that rely totally on submission also have aspects of these invitations since editors sometimes "encourage" economists whose work they find interesting to submit papers to their journals. The fact that that happens is one of the reasons why the geographic home of a journal matters.

Conclusion

The largest problem of European academic economics is not that it is second rate; the problem is that it sees itself as second rate, and acts second rate by trying to copy US programs rather than building on its strengths, and not worrying about how it compares to the US programs. Despite all the governance and academic institutions problems, which are considerable, its strengths are substantial. It has some of the most interesting leading-edge work taking place, and, in certain sub areas has developed pockets of excellence that match or exceed anything found in the United States. It has strength in diversity that the United States is sorely lacking; and it integrates academics into hands-on research much better than does the United States. In many ways, my goal in this paper has been a Wizard of Oz role, advising European economics to listen to European economists such as Serge-Christophe Kolm (1998), to drop that second-rate image of itself, and see its strengths. They should not be like the lion in the Wizard of Oz who needs a medal to give it courage.

So in answer to the question: Can European economics compete with US economics? the answer is yes, absolutely. I have no doubt that Europe can match the United States in terms of the journal publication and citation metrics if it changes the incentives to do that. But my answer to the second title question: Should they compete? is no, at least not in reference to any formal ranking. Just because it can compete does not mean that it should do so. Competing in reference to a formal ranking rather than competing in ideas is a tendency of a second-rate program. That's why the metrics of competition currently being used will likely do more harm to European economics than it will do good. It will put it in a permanently second-tier position as it reduces diversity and reduces work on cutting-edge ideas that may well become the economics of the future.

What European economics needs most is not a ranking metric, but a change in attitude. European economists are so sure they are second, because they are judging themselves by US-biased standards, that they develop a second-place mentality. It is time for that to end. If Europe is to move to be a leader, it must have faith in itself, and develop the mind-set of a leader. That means that it must do more than simply import US metrics to Europe and design its programs after US programs. They have to build on the strengths of the European system, and in reforming those institutions, see themselves as leapfrogging the United States, by developing a ranking metric underlying the promotion and funding mechanisms that recognizes that subjective judgments about what is good and bad must be made. The current changes being implemented will not do that; if implemented they will condemn European economics to being a second-tier set of programs. European economics can, and should, do better.

References

Colander, David 1989. "Research on the Economics Profession." *Journal of Economic Perspectives* 3:4; 137–148.

2006. "The Making of an Economist Redux." *Journal of Economic Perspectives* 19:1; 175–198.

2007. *The Making of an Economist Redux.* Princeton University Press.

2008. "The Making of a Global European Economist." *Kyklos* 61:2.

2009. *The Making of a European Economist.* Cheltenham: Edward Elgar.

Colander, David and Plum, Terry 2004. "Efficiency, Journal Publishing and Scholarly Research." Middlebury College Department of Economics Working Paper 2004–19.

Colander, David and Nopo, Hugo 2008. "The Making of a Global Latin American Economist." Middlebury College Working Paper.

Colander, David, Holt, Richard P. F., and Rosser, Jr., J. Barkley (forthcoming). *"The Changing Face of European Economics".* Cheltenham: Edward Elgar.

Coupe, Tom 2003. "Revealed Performances: Worldwide Rankings of Economists and Economic Departments, 1990–2000." *Journal of the European Economic Association* 1:6.

Dreze, Jacques 2001. "Economics and Universities in Europe." Working Paper.

Frey, Bruno and Eichenberger, Reiner 1992. "Economics and Economists: A European Perspective." *The American Economic Review* (May) 82:2; 216–220.

1993. "American and European Economics and Economists." *Journal of Economic Perspectives* 7:4; 185–193.

Henrekson, Magnus and Waldenstrom, Daniel 2007. "Can Research Performance be Measured Uni-Dimensionally?" Research Institute of Industrial Economics Working Paper.

Holmstrom, Bengt and Milgrom, Paul 1991. "Multitask Principal-Agent Analysis: Incentive Contracts, Asset Ownership, and Job Design." *Journal of Law, Economics, and Organization* 7:1.

Kalaitzidakis, Pantelis, Mamuneas, Theofanis P., and Stengos, Thanasis 2003. "European Economics: An Analysis Based on Publication in the Core Journals." *Journal of the European Economic Association.*

Kirman, Alan and Dahl, Mogens 1994. "Economic Research in Europe." *European Economic Review* 38; 505–522.

Krueger, Anne et al. 1991. "Report of the Commission on Graduate Education in Economics." *Journal of Economic Literature* 29:3 Sept.

Kolm, Serge-Christophe 1998. "Economics in Europe and the US." *European Economic Review* (January) 32:1; 207–212.

Neary, Peter, Mirrlees, James and Tirole, Jean 2003. "Evaluating Economics Research in Europe: An Introduction." *Journal of the European Economic Association* (December) 1:6; 1239–1249.

Puu, Tönu 2006. *Arts, Sciences, and Economics: A Historical Safari.* Berlin: Springer Publishing Co.

Thursby, Jerry 2000. "Yet another Look at Economics Department Research." *Journal of Economic Literature* 38:2; June 383–404.

Zimmerman, Christian 2008. "Academic Rankings with RePEc." University of Connecticut Working Paper.

6 Career patterns of economics Ph.D.s: a decade of outcomes for the class of 1997

Wendy Stock and John Siegfried

Introduction

Because economists' careers follow many paths, it is difficult to identify the ideal graduate program training, balance between theory and application, and types of knowledge, skills, and proficiencies that would best support the work of economics Ph.D.s. From as far back as 1953, when Howard Bowen cataloged for the American Economic Association (AEA) the major shortcomings in graduate economic education at the time (Bowen 1953), a perception has persisted that economics Ph.D. programs devote excessive attention to theoretical and mathematical instruction, and too little attention to real-world application and research methodology.[1] Certainly the aspects of Ph.D. education deemed most important by graduates will differ among those in different types of careers (Stock and Hansen 2004). It may also be the case that the important components of graduate training change over time.

This chapter summarizes ten years of career outcomes for a sample of 207 economists who earned Ph.D. degrees in 1996–97. We report on their employment, their salaries, their publication records, the tenure results for those in academe, and their views about the emphasis placed on various skills and proficiencies by their graduate Ph.D. programs. We relate their assessments about the importance of various skills and proficiencies to their type of employment, publication records, and other characteristics.

We find positive career outcomes among the group in terms of employment, earnings, and job satisfaction. Median nominal salaries for those in full-time jobs in the United States have doubled over the decade. Most continue to report that the emphasis given in their Ph.D. program to several economic proficiencies was about right, although gaps between the importance of various skills for success on the job

---

[1] See, e.g., Wassily Leontief (1982); David Colander and Arjo Klamer (1987); Anne O. Krueger, et al. (1991); Colander (2005) and (2007).

174

relative to success in graduate school, particularly in mathematics and communications, persist.

Background: previous research

This chapter builds primarily upon two literatures, one focusing on career outcomes for economists, and one focusing on the training of economists, and extends our earlier efforts to follow the careers of the economics Ph.D. class of 1996–97 (Stock and Siegfried 2006).

Previous research on economists' careers

Numerous studies of the relationships among salaries, productivity, age, and seniority among economists have been conducted (see Bratsberg, Ragan, and Warren 2003, Brown and Woodbury 1998, Hansen, Weisbrod, and Strauss 1978, Hoffman 1997, Moore, Newman, and Turnbull 1998, Oster and Hamermesh 1998, and Siegfried and White 1973). They generally find rising (but diminishing marginal) pay with respect to productivity, and mixed evidence on the magnitude (and even the direction) of returns to seniority once productivity, quality of job match, and union status of faculty are controlled. Ginther and Kahn (2004) and McDowell, Singell, and Ziliak (2001) have reported evidence that female economists experience slower career progress than male colleagues with similar attributes.

McMillen and Singell (1994) investigated the effect of first job choice on subsequent career patterns. Singell and Stone (1993) found that the effects of initial job placement persist throughout an economist's career. Similarly, Grimes, Millea, and Rogers (2004), using data ranging from 1968 to 1993, found that first job placements during the period 1968 through 1993 affected regional mobility. Buchmueller, Dominitz, and Hansen (1999) found that initial job placement is related to early career publication success. They did not, however, link publication success to salaries. Our work reported here adds to this literature by tracking life changes, employment history, salaries, publications, and the match between Ph.D. program training and subsequent job requirements of a cohort of economists who earned their Ph.D.s during academic year 1996–97. Based on three surveys administered to this group at three different points in time, we can evaluate their employment status, salary progression, research productivity, and assessment of the adequacy of their graduate school preparation for their jobs after their first decade as professional economists.

The Commission on Graduate Education in Economics

The types of knowledge, skills, and proficiencies taught in graduate economics programs are a matter of continuing controversy. Bowen's (1953) post-World War II AEA report identified deficiencies in graduate economics education and recommended changes to enhance the effectiveness of economics Ph.D. programs. By the 1980s, the perception that economics Ph.D. programs focused excessively on teaching theory at the expense of practice in applications had grown (Leontief 1982). The controversy induced David Colander and Arjo Klamer (1987) to conduct an interview study of graduate students at elite economics Ph.D. programs. Their findings reinforced the opinion of many, including officers of the AEA, leaders in the National Science Foundation, and several private foundations, that something was amiss. Subsequently, in 1988 the AEA established the Commission on Graduate Education in Economics (COGEE) to undertake a comprehensive review of graduate training in economics. The Commission's major finding, based on feedback from graduate students, faculty, and employers, was that graduate education in economics had successfully isolated itself from reality, i.e., real-world economic problems (Krueger et al. 1991).

The COGEE report attempted to assess the emphasis of graduate programs on cultivating various economic proficiencies and the importance of an array of skills for success in graduate school and in subsequent job performance (Hansen 1991). The proficiencies in the COGEE study included: providing rigorous training in economic theory, providing training in econometrics and measurement, applying theory to real-world problems, using economic theory in empirical applications, and conducting independent economic research. Stock and Hansen (2004) added three proficiencies to the list: understanding economic institutions and history and understanding the history of economic ideas, to capture concerns about curriculum revisions that reduced or eliminated training in these two areas, and developing teaching skills, which was ignored by the COGEE Commission.

The skills assessed in the COGEE study are: critical judgment (analyzing ideas, reviewing literature, formulating pertinent comments), analytics (understanding and solving problems, making and analyzing logical arguments), application (seeing practical implications of abstract ideas, analyzing real-world policies and processes), mathematics (constructing and analyzing proofs, manipulating mathematical abstractions), computation (effectively and quickly finding and manipulating relevant data, estimating economic relationships using statistical software), communication (speaking and writing effectively, quickly understanding spoken and written ideas of others, explaining ideas clearly), and creativity (conceiving interesting questions, finding new means of analysis). Stock and Hansen (2004) added instruction (effectiveness as a teacher) to the list.

Data sources

The evidence reported in this chapter comes from a panel of data on 207 graduates of the economics Ph.D. class of 1996–97, whom we have surveyed three times, first in late 1997 (6–18 months post-graduation), second in 2003 (5–6 years post-graduation), and the third time in 2008 (10–11 years post-graduation).

The initial population of all 1996–97 graduates was identified using the list of Ph.D. dissertations published in the December 1997 *Journal of Economic Literature*. After revising the list on the basis of survey responses that indicated some of the reported degrees were not actually earned between July 1, 1996 and June 30, 1997, we estimated that there were about 950 graduates in the 1996–97 cohort of economics Ph.D.s (for more detail, see Siegfried and Stock 1999). There were 483 responses to the first survey, conducted in fall 1997, a response rate of 51 percent. We combined the initial survey results with citizenship information we collected from the thesis advisors of 141 additional students in the class of 1997 who did not respond to the initial survey in order to project a profile of the entire graduating class of 1996–97, weighted to correct for citizenship response bias.

The second survey was conducted in spring 2003. It was distributed only to respondents to the first survey, and yielded 302 respondents. This represents 63 percent of the first wave respondents and 32 percent of the estimated Ph.D. class of 1996–97. The third survey was distributed in spring 2008 to those who responded to either the first or second survey. The third contact yielded 207 responses, or 22 percent of the original population of 950. Of these 207, 175 completed all three surveys, and 32 completed only the initial survey and the ten-year survey.

To assess response bias in our returns, we report in Table 6.1 various characteristics of the projected initial population and the respondents to each of the three surveys. There is apparent response bias along two dimensions: US citizenship and race. The fraction of respondents to each survey wave who were US citizens at the time they received their degree increases progressively from 41 percent of the initial population to 76 percent of the ten-year survey. (A further 15 of the 207 respondents in 2008 became US citizens during the decade after they earned their Ph.D.,

Table 6.1 *Characteristics of 1996–97 economics Ph.D. graduates*

	(1) 2008 Respondents (n = 207)[a]	(2) 2003 Respondents (n = 302)[a]	(3) 1997 Respondents (n = 483)[a]	(4) 1997 Projections (n = 950)[b]
Demographics				
Percent female	25.6	24.2	25.1	24.4
Percent US citizen	76.2	62.9[c]	53.4	41.3
Percent white	85.2	79.3[c]	69.4	–
Percent married in 1997	59.9	58.0[c]	62.1	–
Percent with children in 1997	30.9	30.3[c]	35.4	–
Median age at degree	31	31[c]	32	–
Median time to degree	5.3	5.3	5.3	
Ph.D. program characteristics (distribution)				
Tier 1: program ranks 1–6	21.3	21.2[c]	18.4	15.7
Tier 2: program ranks 7–15	23.2	24.8[c]	21.1	14.7
Tier 3: program ranks 16–30	13.5	16.2	15.3	21.6
Tier 4: program ranks 31–48	11.6	12.6[c]	14.3	14.3
Tier 5: program ranks >=48	30.4	25.2[c]	30.8	33.8

Source: Authors' surveys.

[a] Sample size varies by row, reported *n* is maximum. All reported data are based on at least five observations.

[b] Projection =.508(graduates' response) +.492(advisors' response) [.508 = 483/950]; 950 is the estimated number of 1996–97 US Ph.D.s in economics (Siegfried and Stock 1999).

but our analysis classifies them based on their citizenship at the time they earned their Ph.D.) This steadily increasing Americanism of the survey reflects the difficulty we have had locating many of the graduates living outside the United States. The proportion of survey respondents that is white increases from 69 percent in the first survey to 85 percent of the last survey, but we cannot assess the degree to which these proportions differ from the population of graduates because we do not have information about race for the initial population. Our survey probably contains proportionally more whites than were in the graduating class of 1997, and it surely contains proportionally more American citizens. The prevalence of other demographic characteristics among respondents remains fairly constant over the decade. All three surveys contain relatively more graduates of Tier 1 and Tier 2 (top 15 National Research Council ranked) Ph.D. programs (Goldberger et al. 1995), but there does not appear to be any meaningful differences in how response rates change over time based on the ranks of the graduates' Ph.D. programs. While 44 percent of the 2008 sample respondents received their Ph.D. from a top 15 Ph.D. program, only two of them (1 percent!) were employed at a university with a top 15 economics Ph.D. program a decade later.

Career outcomes

Changes in employment characteristics

Employment outcomes projected for the initial population and tabulated from each of the three waves of survey data are reported in Table 6.2. It is immediately apparent that the market for Ph.D. economists was healthy at the beginning of the twenty-first century. The initial three percent unemployment rate dwindled to zero for those who responded to our survey in 2008.[2] Moreover, all but a handful of the respondents were in a full-time permanent position by spring 2008. The percentage of jobs that are located in the United States creeps upward from 64 percent for the projection of the initial cohort, to 82 percent of respondents a decade later. Whether this reflects response bias favoring Americans over time, or reflects a true shift in the distribution of jobs toward those in the United States over time cannot be determined from the total responses to each survey. Thus, we tabulated column (5) of Table 6.2 which reports the 1997 responses of only those 207 economists who responded in 2008. As is evident, the apparent increase in the fraction of economists employed in the United States is entirely an artifact of the response bias favoring a higher response rate by US citizens over time.

It is evident from Table 6.2 that there is only modest net change in the distribution of jobs among employment sectors (academic, business, government, etc.) over time. However, in unpublished tabulations of the 2008 respondents, we find that 28 percent of the sample moved from a job in one sector to another sector. Although these changes across sectors largely balance out, there is a net migration over time from academe to business and government or international organizations; of the 207 respondents in 2008, 64 percent held academic appointments in 1997, but only 57 percent remained in academe by 2008. Conversely, the proportion of the 2008 respondents working in business and in government or international organizations rose from 11 to 15 percent

---

[2] To insure that the differences in employment status observed over time do not result from response bias (more successful graduates more likely to tell us about their achievements), we also report, in column (5) of Table 6.2, the 1997 employment status of just those 207 respondents to the 2008 survey. Three of them were unemployed in 1997. The comparison also reveals that those who began their careers in academe were disproportionately represented among the 207 respondents in 2008; those originally employed in the business sector were underrepresented.

Table 6.2 *Employment outcomes of 1996–97 economics Ph.D. graduates*

| | (1) | (2) | (3) | (4) | (5) 1997 Responses of 2008 |
| | | | | | |
	2008 Respondents (n = 207)[a]	2003 Respondents (n = 302)[a]	1997 Respondents (n = 483)[b]	1997 Projections (n = 950)[b]	respondents (n = 207)
Employment characteristics					
Percent unemployed	0.0	1.3	2.7	3.1	1.4
Percent of employed with full-time job	97.0	96.0	95.5	95.4	96.1
Percent of employed with permanent job	96.1	81.8	80.6	82.0	82.8
Percent of employed with job in U.S. Distribution by employment sector (percentage):	82.0	79.5	74.9	63.6	81.8
Percent of employed in academe	56.8	62.6	57.9	52.5	64.0
Percent of employed in business/industry	15.0	12.1	17.0	17.5	11.0
Percent of employed in government, international organizations, research organizations	27.1	25.3	25.1	30.0	25.0
Percent of academics with tenure	78.5	–	–	–	–

Source: Authors' surveys.

[a] Sample size varies by row, reported *n* is maximum. All reported data are based on at least five observations.

[b] Projection =.508 (graduates' response) +.492(advisors' response) [.508 = 483/950]; 950 is the estimated number of 1996–97 US Ph.D.s in economics (Siegfried and Stock 1999).

and from 25 to 27 percent, respectively, over the decade. Many more than 28 percent changed jobs, however; 64 percent of the 207 were working for a different employer in 2008 than had employed them in 1997.

Finally, we can report that among the 94 Ph.D.s who started their careers in a permanent full-time academic appointment and for whom we have information on their tenure status, 63 held tenure in 2008, including 33 of the 38 who were still at their 1997 employer in 2008, and 30 of the 56 who had changed jobs (see column (5) of Table 6.6). Of the dozen who were at the same employer in 1997 and 2003, but not in 2008, only four had tenure in 2008. Of the two dozen who changed employers between 1997 and 2003, but not thereafter, 18 had tenure in 2008. And, of the remaining 20, who either switched employers both between 1997 and 2003 and between 2003 and 2008, or switched at an unknown time (they did not complete the 2003 survey), only 8 had tenure in 2008. It appears that those who switched employers early knew what they were doing, as 18 of the 24 ended up with tenure at their new employers, a success rate not far below that of those who stayed at the same place throughout the period.

Changes in salaries

We are able to track and compare nominal salaries of 117 Ph.D. economists who were employed in the United States in full-time permanent positions at both the beginning and end of the first decade of their careers. These data are reported in Tables 6.3, 6.4, and 6.5. Although the sample contains a disproportionate fraction of economists who graduated from one of the top 15 programs (Tiers 1 and 2) (48 percent of those reporting salaries, even though they represent only 30 percent of the total population), their salaries are not out of line with the larger sample that responded in 1997. Indeed, the 255 in full-time permanent positions in the United States who reported in 1997 had a median salary of $55,000, in contrast to the $54,000 median salary reported in 1997 by the 117 respondents to the 2008 survey.

The panel of economists earned an overall median of $54,000 in October 1997, $80,000 in February 2003, and $108,000 in March 2008, implying an annual raise of 8.2 percent over the first five years and 6.2 percent over the second five years. Those on 9–10 month academic salaries, the largest single sub-category, earned a median $49,000, $66,000, and $90,000 in 1997, 2003, and 2008, respectively, implying an annual increase of 6.1 percent over the first five years, and 6.4 percent over the second five years. These rates of increase compare to an average annual inflation rate of 2.3 percent during the first five years and 3.0 percent during the second five years.

Salary growth is fastest for those economists employed in government and the private sector. While nominal permanent 9-month academic salaries grew 84 percent over the decade, nominal salaries of those with full-time jobs in business and industry rose by 125 percent, and salaries of economists working in government, research institutes, and inter-national organizations climbed by 145 percent. The dispersion of salaries grows over time. While the mean salary for all full-time jobs in the United

Table 6.3 *1996–97 Economics Ph.D. graduates' annual salaries, March 2008*

	Median	Mean	Low	High	N
All full-time jobs in the U.S.	$108,000	$144,000	$55,000	$1,500,000	117
Permanent positions	108,000	144,000	55,000	1,500,000	117
Academic	90,500	107,000	60,000	300,000	64
9–10 month	90,000	102,000	61,000	207,000	50
11–12 month	109,000	124,000	60,000	300,000	14
Business/Industry	180,000	290,000	70,000	1,500,000	18
Government, research organizations, international organizations	135,000	137,000	55,000	250,000	35
Temporary positions	–	–	–	–	0
Academic, 9–10 month	–	–	–	–	0

Source: Authors' survey. Includes only those with full-time jobs in the US in 1997, 2003, and 2008.

Table 6.4 *1996–97 Economics Ph.D. graduates' annual salaries, February 2003*

	Median	Mean	Low	High	N
All full-time jobs in the US	$80,000	$91,000	$35,000	$450,000	117
Permanent positions	80,000	92,000	35,000	450,000	113
Academic	71,000	74,000	35,000	163,000	64
9–10 month	66,000	71,000	35,000	163,000	50
11–12 month	84,000	84,000	45,000	130,000	14
Business/Industry	120,000	139,000	60,000	450,000	19
Government, research organizations, international organizations	98,000	101,000	72,000	175,000	30
Temporary positions	68,000	74,000	55,000	105,000	4
Academic, 9–10 month	66,000	66,000	55,000	78,000	2

Source: Authors' survey. Includes only those with full-time jobs in the US in 1997, 2003, and 2008.

States exceeded the median by only 4 percent in 1997, that difference had grown to 33 percent by 2008.

Publication records

The publication records of the 2008 respondents are reported in Table 6.6, divided between economists who started out in academe

Table 6.5 *1996–97 Economics Ph.D. graduates' annual salaries,*
October 1997

	Median	Mean	Low	High	N
All full-time jobs in the US	$54,000	$56,000	$30,000	$110,000	117
Permanent positions	55,000	58,000	34,000	110,000	100
Academic	51,000	53,000	34,000	93,000	63
9–10 month	49,000	52,000	34,000	93,000	52
11–12 month	60,000	58,000	34,000	78,000	11
Business/Industry	80,000	79,000	40,000	110,000	13
Government, research organizations, international organizations	55,000	58,000	35,000	93,000	24
Temporary positions	37,000	44,000	30,000	100,000	17
Academic, 9–10 month	35,000	38,000	30,000	70,000	9

Source: Authors' survey. Includes only those with full-time jobs in the US in 1997, 2003, and 2008.

and those who did not. The publication data were extracted from EconLit in August 2008. We report both total journal publications and publications in "Top-50" journals.[3] We do not use total EconLit entries because many of those are working papers that duplicate subsequent publications. This, unfortunately, means that we also are unable to include books and chapters in books.

The most striking observation from the publication data is the fact that almost half of the 99 economists with ten years of experience holding full-time permanent academic appointments in 2007–08 did not publish anything in a Top-50 journal in their career (the median number is one, but 49.49 percent of the group had zero Top-50 journal publications). The other half of the distribution includes 13 with one Top-50 publication, 25 with two to five Top-50 publications, and 12 economists with six or more publications in Top-50 journals. There are 4 individuals in the sample with 10–13 articles in Top-50 journals. It is ironic that the 63 holding tenure have a median of zero Top-50 publications, while those who do not have tenure report a median of one.

When journal articles are expanded beyond the Top-50 journals, the data show a median of five articles per full-time permanent academic, seven for those with tenure, and only two for those without tenure. As would be expected, those who started in academe (not all of whom were

[3] Journals among the Top-50 were determined from Kalaitzidakis et al. (2001).

Table 6.6 *Publication and employment outcomes*

Group	Median journal publications	Mean journal publications	Median top-50 journal publications	Mean top-50 journal publications	N
In full-time permanent academic positions in 1997	5.0	6.8	1.0	2.0	99
With tenure in 2008	7.0	7.8	0.0	2.2	63
At same employer as in 1997	5.0	6.8	0.0	1.8	33
At different employer than in 1997	7.5	8.6	1.0	2.7	30
Without tenure in 2008	2.0	4.1	1.0	1.6	31
Outside full-time permanent academic positions in 1997	1.0	4.0	0.0	1.3	108
In full-time permanent academic positions in 2008	6.0	7.8	1.0	2.8	34
In other postions in 2008	1.0	2.2	0.0	0.6	74

Source: Authors' survey. The subsample sizes for those in full-time permanent academic positions in 1997 do not sum to 99 because five individuals are missing information on their tenure status.

still there in 2008) have published more than those who began their careers elsewhere, but the publication record of the graduates who started in a sector other than academe and then moved to an academic appointment is quite similar to those who have been in academe throughout the period.

Proficiencies and skills important for career success

One goal of the COGEE study was to determine the emphasis given by economics Ph.D. programs to cultivating proficiency in an array of different areas. The COGEE study also attempted to assess the importance of an array of skills needed for success in graduate school and in later careers. The panel nature of our data allows us to ascertain graduates' perceptions regarding the relative emphasis on these proficiencies as their careers progress. One might expect perspectives to evolve as economists undertake activities over time, mitigating or exacerbating deficiencies or overtraining in various areas.

Table 6.7 *Extent of Ph.D. program emphasis on economic proficiencies*

Proficiencies	2008 Responses[1] (N= 207)			2008 Respondents 2003 Responses (N= 172)			2003 Respondents 2003 Responses (N= 316)		
	Too much[2]	Too little[2]	Mean[3]	Too much	Too little	Mean	Too much	Too little	Mean
Theory training	13	6	2.1	14	9	2	13	8	2.1
Econometrics training	6	29	1.8	5	32	1.7	6	30	1.8
Applying theory to real-world	1	63	1.4	1	59	1.4	1	62	1.4
Using theory in empirical applications	2	41	1.6	1	44	1.6	2	46	1.6
Understanding institutions and history	5	53	1.5	3	51	1.5	4	51	1.5
History of economic ideas	7	46	1.6	4	5	1.5	5	51	1.5
Conducting independent research	2	23	1.8	4	30	1.7	4	33	1.7
Developing teaching skills	1	45	1.6	2	43	1.6	3	44	1.6

[1] 2008 responses are based on survey mailed in March 2008 (i.e., roughly 10–11 years post-degree). 2003 responses are based on a survey mailed in March 2003 (i.e., roughly 5–6 years post-degree).

[2] Percent of respondents indicating that their Ph.D. program placed too much (too little) emphasis on the proficiency. Percent indicating that the emphasis was "about right" is omitted.

[3] Mean emphasis value [3 = too much, 2 = about right, 1 = too little].

Proficiencies

We track the changes in graduates' responses to questions regarding the emphasis placed on economic proficiencies in Table 6.7. The survey asked respondents to rate the emphasis placed by their Ph.D. program on each proficiency listed, using a 1–3 scale (1 = too little emphasis; 2 = about right; 3 = too much emphasis). Reported in the first panel are the responses of the cohort in 2008, 10 years into their careers. We report the percentage of respondents who reported either "too much" or "too little" emphasis; along with the mean response using the 1–3 scale. The second panel reports a summary of the 2008 survey respondents' answers to these questions in 2003 (five years into their careers). The third panel reports the responses of all of the 2003 survey respondents for comparison purposes.

Most notable in the responses is the miniscule fraction that reports too much emphasis on any particular proficiency. Instead, for five of the eight proficiencies we asked about (economic theory, econometrics and measurement, using theory in empirical applications, conducting independent research, and developing teaching skills), most graduates report that the emphasis by their graduate programs was "about right." This was also the case when these economists responded to our survey in 2003, indicating little change in their assessments over time.

Also consistent over time is that the majority of graduates report that their Ph.D. programs placed too little emphasis on applying theory to real-world problems, on understanding economic institutions and history, and understanding the history of economic ideas. Slightly more respondents in 2008 than 2003 (63 versus 59 percent) report too little emphasis on applying theory to real-world problems, while slightly fewer (46 versus 50 percent) report too little emphasis on the history of economic ideas. However, these differences are quite small, implying that ten years into their careers, economists' assessments regarding the various proficiency emphases of their graduate programs are largely unchanged relative to five years into their careers.[4]

Skills

In Table 6.8 we summarize the cohorts' assessments regarding the importance of various skills for success in their Ph.D. programs and for success in their current jobs. We also report mean differences in the graduates' ratings of the importance of the skills for success on the job versus success in graduate school, as a measure of the extent to which Ph.D. program learning and later job demands are synchronized.

As with the proficiency questions, the assessments do not appear to have changed as the cohort moved through its second five years in the profession. As was the case when the group was five years post-graduate school, almost half report that skill in analytics was the most important talent for their success in graduate school. The next rated skill in terms of its importance for success in graduate school is mathematics, with one in five respondents listing it as the most important.

The responses regarding the relative importance of the skills for success on the job are much more dispersed. Indeed, while 70 percent of respondents rate either analytics or mathematics as the most important

---

[4] We also examined differences in the proficiency questions by tier and employment sector. On neither dimension were there significant differences from those reported in Table 7.

Table 6.8 *Importance of economists' skills for success in Ph.D. program and in current job*

Skill	Importance in Ph.D. program			Importance in current job			Mean difference[4]
	Most[1]	Least[2]	Mean[3]	Most[1]	Least[2]	Mean[3]	
2008 Responses *(N = 207)*							
Critical judgment	9	3	4.2	13	3	4.5	0.3***
Analytics	48	1	4.6	15	1	4.5	−0.1*
Application	3	9	3.2	21	4	4.4	1.2***
Mathematics	22	3	4.5	1	47	2.8	−1.7***
Computation	6	2	4.1	5	10	3.7	−0.4***
Communication	1	6	3.3	18	2	4.7	1.4***
Creativity	12	9	3.6	15	2	4.1	0.5***
Instruction	0	70	2.2	12	32	3.3	1.1***
2008 Respondents' 2003 Responses *(N = 172)*							
Critical judgment	6	2	4.3	14	3	4.4	0.1
Analytics	45	0	4.6	17	2	4.5	−0.1
Application	4	9	3.2	18	4	4.4	1.2***
Mathematics	18	1	4.5	2	45	2.8	−1.7***
Computation	13	2	4.0	5	10	3.7	−0.3**
Communication	3	5	3.4	21	0	4.7	1.2***
Creativity	12	2	3.7	9	3	4.1	0.4***
Instruction	0	75	2.1	14	33	3.3	1.2***
2003 Respondents' 2003 Responses *(N = 316)*							
Critical judgment	10	2	4.2	14	3	4.4	0.2*
Analytics	41	0	4.6	17	1	4.5	−0.1*
Application	2	11	3.1	18	4	4.4	1.3***
Mathematics	20	2	4.5	2	50	2.7	−1.7***
Computation	13	3	3.9	5	10	3.7	−0.2**
Communication	3	8	3.3	20	0	4.6	1.3***
Creativity	12	4	3.7	12	3	4.1	0.4***
Instruction	0	71	2.1	12	29	3.3	1.3***

[1] Percentage distribution of cohort listing skill as most important for success.
[2] Percentage distribution of cohort listing skill as least important for success.
[3] Mean importance value [5 = very important; 1 = not very important].
[4] Reports the mean of the difference between each skill's importance on the job minus its importance in the Ph.D. program.
* = statistically significantly different from zero at the 0.10 level;
** = 0.05 level;
*** = 0.01 level.

skills for success in the Ph.D. program, only 16 percent rate these skills as the most important for success on the job. The skill most often rated most important for success on the job is application (21 percent rated this most important), followed closely by communication (18 percent).

As was the case when the group responded in 2003, mathematics dominates the list as the skill least important for success on the job (47 percent of respondents assigned this rating). This is followed by instruction, with one-third of the respondents (largely employed outside academe) listing it as the skill least important for success on their jobs.

The mean differences in the relative importance of the skills reflect the ratings above, with large positive differences (implying that the skill is more important for success on the job than for success in graduate school) emerging for application, communication, and instruction, and a large negative difference emerging for mathematics. These differences are nearly identical to what the cohort reported in 2003, again implying little evolution in economists' opinions regarding their graduate training, at least over the first decade of their careers.

We also examined whether responses to the skills questions differ among those from different graduate program tiers and those employed in different sectors. The differences in responses by tier are minimal, with the exception that graduates from Tier 1 programs have a higher mean rating for the importance of creativity for success in the Ph.D. program (4.1 vs. 3.6 for the full sample), while graduates from Tier 4 programs had lower mean ratings of creativity's importance for success in their programs (2.9 vs. 3.6). In addition, the importance of instruction for success in the Ph.D. program and for success on the job was rated lower among Tier 1 graduates (1.7 vs. 2.2 and 2.7 vs. 3.3, respectively). The only difference in the responses across those in different employment sectors is the higher rating of importance of instruction for success in the job for those in academe (4.0 vs. a mean of 3.3), and its lower rating (2.1) for those working in government, or in international or research organizations (G/IO/RO).

Attitudes regarding job fit

In Table 6.9, we report the responses over time to a series of questions asking respondents their attitudes regarding their jobs and their overall satisfaction with their decision to pursue a Ph.D. in economics. For each of the three waves of the survey, we asked about the extent of agreement with three statements regarding the respondents' current position: (1) the position is related to my field; (2) the position is commensurate with my education and training; and (3) the position is similar to what I expected to be doing when I began my Ph.D. program. For each statement, respondents were asked to report their degree of agreement or disagreement using the scale: 1 = strongly disagree; 5 = strongly agree. For the 2003 and 2008 waves, we asked respondents the yes or no question: "Had you known then what you know now would you still have enrolled in a Ph.D. program in economics?"

Table 6.9 *Economists opinions about current job*

	2008 Responses	2003 Responses	1997 Responses
All 2008 respondents *(N = 174)*			
The position is:[a]			
related to my field	4.5	4.4	4.4
commensurate with my education & training	4.4	4.4	4.4
similar to what I expected to be doing when I began my Ph.D. program	3.6	3.7	3.6
Had known[b]	0.87	0.87	–
Respondents with no employer change 1997–2008 *(N = 55)*			
The position is:			
related to my field	4.5	4.5	4.6
commensurate with my education & training	4.5	4.5	4.6
similar to what I expected to be doing when I began my Ph.D. program	3.6	3.8	3.9
Had known	0.93	0.89	–
Respondents with employer change 1997–2003 *(N = 55)*			
The position is:			
related to my field	4.5	4.5	4.2
commensurate with my education & training	4.3	4.4	4.3
similar to what I expected to be doing when I began my Ph.D. program	3.5	3.8	3.4
Had known	0.85	0.91	–
Respondents with employer change 2003–2008 *(N = 25)*			
The position is:			
related to my field	4.6	4.6	4.7
commensurate with my education & training	4.4	4.5	4.3
similar to what I expected to be doing when I began my Ph.D. program	3.7	4.1	4.0
Had known	0.88	0.88	–
Respondents with employer change 1997–2003 & 2003–2008 *(N = 39)*			
The position is:			
related to my field	4.4	4.2	4.4
commensurate with my education & training	4.4	4.0	4.4
similar to what I expected to be doing when I began my Ph.D. program	3.5	3.1	3.5
Had known	0.78	0.76	–

[a] Reports mean response to question based on the scale: 5 = strongly agree, 1 = strongly disagree

[b] Reports percent responding "yes" to: Had you known then what you know now, would you still have enrolled in a Ph.D. program in economics?

We report responses for the full set of respondents (N = 174) at the top of the table. Because the responses could differ between those who did and did not remain with their initial employer over the period, we also separate the responses based on whether the individuals had changed employers between the survey waves.

The responses indicate a remarkable degree of agreement with the "related to field" and "commensurate with my education and training" statements, averaging about 4.4 on the 1–5 scale. Only about 4 percent of the respondents either disagree or strongly disagree with the statements. In addition, there is little change in the respondents' level of agreement with the statements over time. There appears to be less agreement with the statement, "This position is similar to what I expected to be doing . . ." as the average is only 3.6 and 26 percent of respondents either disagree or strongly disagree with the statement. Finally, the level of agreement with the statements does not appear to differ substantially among those who did and did not change employers.

Among the respondents overall, a remarkable 87 percent report that had they known then what they know now, they would still have pursued their economics Ph.D. The value ranges from a low of 78 percent among those who changed employers at least twice during the decade since graduation to a high of 93 percent among those who remained at the same employer throughout the decade.

When we examined the responses separately for those employed in different sectors (academe, G/IO/RO, business/industry), the results indicate higher agreement with the statements among those in academe than those in business/industry. For example, academics rated their agreement with the statement, "This job is related to my field" at 4.6 on the 1–5 scale, while those in business/industry had a mean rating of 3.9. Similarly, academics rated their agreement with, "This job is what I expected to be doing when I began my Ph.D. program," at 3.9, versus 2.6 for those in business/industry. Although this is consistent with the commonly held notion that economics Ph.D. programs are very good at producing academics and researchers, but fare less well at training economists for jobs in business and industry, even among those in the business/industry sector, 85 percent (versus 86 percent among academics) report that had they known then what they know now, they would still have pursued their economics Ph.D.

Conclusion

Ten years after completing their Ph.D.s in economics, the class of 1996–97 continues to have good career outcomes. Their unemployment rate is zero and almost all have full-time permanent employment.

Median salaries among those in full-time jobs in the United States have doubled – rising from $54,000 in 1997 to $108,000 in 2008. Over half of the survey respondents are employed in academe, while 27 percent are employed in government, international organizations, or research organizations and 15 percent are employed in business/industry. Among the academics, more than three-fourths have earned tenure by ten years post-degree. Satisfaction with the degree is high, with 87 percent of the respondents reporting that had they known then what they know now, they would still have pursued their economics Ph.D.

On the question of the match between Ph.D. program learning and job demands, there is a substantial difference between those who teach graduate economics and those who leave their classrooms to pursue careers as economics Ph.D.s. Among our 207 sample respondents, 92 earned their Ph.D. from a top 15 Ph.D. program (Tier 1 or 2). At the start of their careers, only 8 of them found jobs in Tier 1 or 2 economics Ph.D. programs. Just 26 took jobs in Ph.D.-producing economics departments. By 2008, only 2 of the 207 were employed at a university with a Top-15 economics Ph.D. program (both in Tier 2); 21 were employed by universities with an economics Ph.D. program. Also notable is the low rate of publication in Top-50 journals ten years after completing the degree, even among those employed in academic positions and with tenure. Among the 21 employed in economics Ph.D. programs, the median number of Top-50 journal publications is two in ten years (mean 4.7); among those in academe but outside Ph.D.-producing programs, the median is just one (mean 1.8). Clearly the vast majority of economics Ph.D.s do not take jobs similar in terms of rank or publication productivity as the professors who taught them during graduate school.

The cohort continues to report a mismatch between the relative importances of skill in mathematics for success in their Ph.D. program in contrast to success in their current job.[5] They also continue to rate skill in communication as more important for success on the job than for success in their Ph.D. program.

Most of our survey respondents have reported that the emphasis placed by their Ph.D. economics programs on theory and econometrics training (including using theory in empirical applications), on conducting independent research, and on developing teaching skills was "about right." Ten years post-degree, however, a majority continue to report

---

[5] One survey respondent, who now interviews many newly-minted Ph.D.s for work in consulting, notes that his colleagues stereotype economics Ph.D. training as "long on rigor, short on relevance."

that their programs placed too little emphasis on applying economic theory to real-world problems and on understanding economic institutions and history. This outcome highlights one of the fundamental elements of economics – that life involves tradeoffs. We have shown elsewhere (Stock and Siegfried 2006) the negative relationship between the time taken to earn the Ph.D. and labor market salaries.

References

Bowen, Howard R. 1953. "Graduate Education in Economics." *American Economic Review Supplement* 43(4) (September)(part 2): 1–223.

Bratsberg, Bernt, James F. Ragan, Jr., and John T. Warren 2003. "Negative Returns to Seniority–New Evidence in Academic Markets." *Industrial and Labor Relations Review* 56(2): 306–323.

Brown, Byron and Stephen A. Woodbury 1998. "Seniority, External Labor Markets, and Faculty Pay." *Quarterly Review of Economics and Finance* 38(4): 771–98.

Buchmueller, Thomas C., Jeff Dominitz, and W. Lee Hansen 1999. "Graduate Training and the Early Career Productivity of Ph.D. Economists." *Economics of Education Review* 18(1): 65–77.

Colander, David 2005. "The Making of an Economist Redux." *Journal of Economic Perspectives* 19(1): 175–198.

2007. *The Making of an Economist Redux*. Princeton University Press.

Colander, David and Arjo Klamer 1987. "The Making of an Economist." *Journal of Economic Perspectives* 1(2) (Fall): 95–111.

Ginther, Donna K. and Shulamit Kahn 2004. "Women in Economics: Moving Up or Falling Off the Academic Career Ladder?" *Journal of Economic Perspectives* 18(3): 193–214.

Goldberger, Marvin, Brendan Maher, and Pamela Flattau, eds. 1995. *Research-Doctorate Programs in the United States: Continuity and Change*. Washington, DC: National Academy Press.

Grimes, Paul W., Meghan J. Millea, and Kevin E. Rogers 2004. "Regional Mobility of Economists: An Extension." *Journal of Labor Research* 25(1): 127–38.

Hansen, W. Lee 1991. "Education and Training of Economics Doctorates: Major Findings of the American Economic Association's Commission on Graduate Education in Economics." *Journal of Economic Literature* 29(3) (September): 1054–1087.

Hansen, W. Lee, Burton A. Weisbrod, and Robert P. Strauss 1978. "Modeling the Earnings and Research Productivity of Academic Economists." *Journal of Political Economy* 86(4): 729–741.

Hoffman, Emily P. 1997. "Effects of Seniority on Academic Salaries: Comparing Estimates." *Proceedings of the Forty-Ninth Annual Meeting of the Industrial Relations Research Association*. Madison, WI: IRRA, pp. 347–352.

Kalaitzidakis, Pantelis, Theofanis P. Mamuneas, and Thanasis Stengos 2001. "Rankings of Academic Journals and Institutions in Economics."

Department of Economics, University of Cyprus, Discussion Paper 2001–10.

Krueger, Anne O., Kenneth J. Arrow, Olivier Jean Blanchard, Alan S. Blinder, Claudia Goldin, Edward E. Leamer, Robert Lucas, John Panzar, Rudolph G. Penner, T. Paul Schultz, Joseph E. Stiglitz, and Lawrence H. Summers 1991. "Report of the Commission on Graduate Education in Economics." *Journal of Economic Literature* 29(3) (September): 1035–1053.

Leontief, Wassily 1982. "Academic Economics." *Science* 217(4555) (July): 104–107.

McDowell, John M., Larry D. Singell, Jr., and James P. Ziliak 2001. "Gender and Promotion in the Economics Profession." *Industrial and Labor Relations Review* 54(2): 224–244.

McMillen, Daniel P. and Larry D. Singell, Jr. 1994. "Gender Differences in First Jobs for Economists." *Southern Economic Journal* 60(3): 701–714.

Moore, William J., Robert J. Newman, and Geoffrey K. Turnbull 1998. "Do Academic Salaries Decline with Seniority?" *Journal of Labor Economics* 16(2): 352–366.

Oster, Sharon M. and Daniel S. Hamermesh 1998. "Aging and Productivity among Economists: Note." *Review of Economics and Statistics* 80(1): 154–156.

Siegfried, John J. and Kenneth J. White 1973. "Financial Rewards to Research and Teaching: A Case Study of Academic Economists." *American Economic Review Papers and Proceedings* 63(3): 309–315.

Siegfried, John J. and Wendy A. Stock 1999. "The Labor Market for New Ph.D. Economists." *Journal of Economic Perspectives* 13(3): 115–134.

   2001. "So You Want to Earn a Ph.D. in Economics: How Long Do You Think It Will Take?" *Journal of Human Resources* 36(2) (Spring): 364–378.

   2004. "The Market for New Ph.D. Economists in 2002." *American Economic Review Papers and Proceedings* 94(2): 272–285.

Singell, Larry D. and Joe A. Stone 1993. "Gender Differences in Ph.D. Economists' Careers." *Contemporary Policy Issues* 11(4): 95–106.

Stock, Wendy A. and W. Lee Hansen 2004. "Ph.D. Program Learning and Job Demands: How Close is the Match?" *American Economic Review Papers and Proceedings* 94(2): 266–271.

Stock, Wendy A. and John J. Siegfried 2001. "So You Want to Earn a Ph.D. in Economics: How Much Do You Think You'll Make?" *Economic Inquiry* 39(2): 320–335.

   2006. "Where Are They Now? Tracking the Ph.D. Class of 1997." *Southern Economic Journal* 73(2): 472–488.

7 Scientific norms and the values of economists: the case of priority fights in economics

Wade Hands

1 Introduction

Having the name of the person responsible for an important idea permanently attached to that idea (eponymic honor) is a common form of professional recognition in economics, as it is in other sciences. From theoretical developments like the Slutsky equation, Hotelling's lemma, or the concept of a Nash equilibrium, to the discovery of purported empirical regularities like Okun's Law, Engel's Law, or the Phillips Curve, economists systematically honor those who have made substantial discoveries by naming their discoveries after them. There is also evidence that individuals with extensive exposure to economic theory are more self-interested and behave less cooperatively than individuals who have not been exposed to disciplinary economics. Taken together these two facts would seem to suggest that the history of economic thought would be a history of rather contentious *priority fights*. If economists generally behave in self-interested and non-cooperative ways, and having your name attached to a particular result serves one's professional self-interest, then economists should be quick to fight for these eponymic honors. This means that economists should be continually involved in sordid disputes about who does, and who does not, get credit for various economic discoveries. The paradox is that such priority fights *do not exist in economics*. It is useful to begin by discussing the sociological literature on priority fights in science.

2 Priority in science

The dominant feature of the social studies of science – as opposed to most characterizations of science given by philosophers of science or by the scientists themselves – is that science, or particular sciences, have many of the same features as other "social organizations." Scientific culture is just that, a culture, and can be examined by employing the same conceptual tools that one would use to investigate any other human

194

culture. In other words science is fundamentally social – for some, social all the way down, and for others social at least where the social studies of science has something to say – and the production of scientific knowledge is a proper subject for social inquiry.

The contemporary literature on the social studies of science differs in many ways from the earlier "sociology of science" associated with the work of Robert K. Merton (1970, 1973, 1996), and yet many contemporary commentators share Merton's basic view that studying the cultural *norms* of the scientific organization is key to understanding the most important features of scientific knowledge. Many of the specific concepts that Merton introduced into the sociological literature also continue to be topics for contemporary research: for example the prevalence of "multiple discoveries" in science, the so-called "Matthew effect," and the subject here, the role of priority, and priority fights, in science.

Merton's 1935 doctoral dissertation argued that the rise of science in seventeenth-century England was a result of a particular set of cultural values, the norms and values of ascetic Protestantism. These cultural values constituted the *social preconditions* for the development of modern science. Throughout his long career Merton never abandoned the idea that unique cultural values/norms are associated with the scientific endeavor; for Merton, such norms *function* not only to reproduce the social institutions of science, they also contribute to the production of the type of reliable empirical knowledge that differentiates science from other systems of belief. These scientific norms, like any set of social norms, require social institutions for their maintenance and reproduction; those institutions must, among other things, effectively reward compliance and punish violations of these norms. According to Merton, the most important reward administered by the institutions of science is *priority*, and priority is most clearly established by the assignment of eponymic honor: having one's name attached to the discovery in question. In successful science "Eponymity, not anonymity, is the standard" (Merton 1957, p. 302).

Heading the list of the immensely varied forms of recognition long in use is eponymy, the practice of affixing the name of the scientist to all or part of what he has found, as with the Copernican system, Hooke's law, Planck's constant, or Halley's Comet. In this way, scientists leave their signatures indelibly in history; their names enter into all the scientific languages of the world. (Merton 1957, p. 298)

Given the importance of priority within the reward system of science, it is not surprising to find the history of science replete with numerous disagreements over who does, or does not, receive the proper eponymic honor. In fact the history of science seems to be strewn with such priority fights: "the history of science is punctuated by disputes, often by sordid disputes, over priority of discovery" (Merton 1957, pp. 286–287). A few of the many examples include Henry Cavendish who was engaged in a protracted priority dispute with both Lavoisier and Watt over the nature of water, Urbain Jean Le Verrier who challenged John Couch Adams over the location of Neptune, the dispute between Wollaston and Faraday over the discovery of electromagnetic induction, and more recently the disagreement between Robert Gallo and Luc Montagnier over the discovery of HIV. Even the "peerless Newton fought several battles with Robert Hooke over priority in optics and celestial mechanics and entered into a long and painful controversy with Leibniz over the invention of the calculus" (Merton 1957, p. 287). Merton even goes on to say that what "is true of physics, chemistry, astronomy, medicine, and mathematics is true also of all other scientific disciplines, not excluding the social and psychological sciences" (1957, p. 288), but the examples he offers come from sociology and psychology, not economics.

To extend the list of priority fights would be industrious and, for this occasion, superfluous. For the moment, it is enough to note that these controversies, far from being a rare exception in science, have long been frequent, harsh, and ugly. They have practically become an integral part of the social relations between scientists. Indeed, the pattern is so common that the Germans have characteristically compounded a word for it *Prioritätsstreit*. (Merton 1957, p. 289)

Although not every sociologist studying science has found priority fights to be as prevalent or as important as Merton, his two basic claims – that priority plays an essential role in the reward system of science and that major priority fights have occurred repeatedly throughout the history of science – remains a part of the conventional wisdom among sociologists of science. But it is not only sociologists who have discussed priority. Economists working in the field of the economics of scientific knowledge (Hands 2002) have also emphasized the importance of priority in the reward system of science – "To put it dramatically, priority in science is the prize" (Dasgupta and David 1994, p. 500) – as well as certain historians of modern economics (Weintraub 2011). Economists do not seem to have explicitly discussed Mertonian priority *fights*, but they certainly do insist that priority matters in science, including economic science.

3   The self-interested and non-cooperative profession

In this section I want to consider a particular aspect of the professional culture of economic science that may initially appear unrelated to the previous discussion of Merton, priority, and priority fights in science.

However disconnected the two topics may appear, they are in fact both essential to my argument and will be linked together in the following section. For now let us just put the question of priority aside and discuss some of the attitudes of professional economists and students of economics.

There seems to be substantial evidence that economics – either studying economics or being in the economics profession – makes people more self-interested and less cooperative than people who have not been influenced by the dismal science. The research that most often gets credited with initiating debate over the non-cooperativeness of economists was Maxwell and Ames (1981), a paper where the authors provided evidence that economists are particularly likely to free ride on the provision of public goods. The most cited research on the subject is Frank, Gilovich, and Regan (1993), a paper that offered a veritable litany of results from various studies indicating that in fact economists were, *ceteris paribus*, less cooperative and more self-interested than others. They discussed a wide variety of relevant evidence: the literature on economists' free riding, a variety of different experimental studies where economics students were given the chance to behave cooperatively and failed to do so relative to students in other fields, and survey data on (the absence of) charitable giving among economists. All in all the profession scored high on rational self-interest and low on cooperation and charity. As one might expect, economists found these results to be quite interesting, and an extensive literature has developed on the subject (for example Carter and Irons 1991; Frank and Günther 2000; Frank, Gilovich, and Regan 1993; Frey and Meier 2003; Hirshleifer 1994; Kirchgässner 2005; Laband and Beil 1999; Lanteri 2008; and Yeser, Goldfarb, and Poppen 1996). Some of this research offers contrary evidence; some of it lends support to the initial studies; and still other contributions focus on the question of whether one learns self-interested behavior and non-cooperation by studying economics or whether those naturally so inclined are more likely to be attracted to the profession.

Although the subject remains controversial – particularly the results from classroom experiments – the preponderance of the evidence clearly indicates that economists are, to some degree, more self-interested and less cooperative than others. Of course this should not come as a complete surprise. As is well known, economists have traditionally explained social phenomenon as the result of the rational actions of self-interested agents. And since the best response to non-cooperation is non-cooperation, it is but a short game-theoretic step to go from the fact that economists assume that others behave in self-interested and non-cooperative ways, to the result that economists themselves tend to behave in those same ways. As Frank, Gilovich, and Regan argued in response to their critics, three things seem to be evident:

First, all parties concede that economics training encourages the view that people are motivated primarily by self-interest. Second, there is clear evidence that this view leads people to expect others to defect in social dilemmas (Maxwell and Ames 1981). Third, there is also clear evidence that when people expect their partners to defect in social dilemmas, they are overwhelmingly likely to defect themselves (Frank, Gilovich and Regan 1993, p. 167). The logical implication of these three points appears to place a heavy burden of proof on those who insist that economics training does not inhibit cooperation. (Frank, Gilovich, and Regan 1996, p. 192)

Now of course, as research in the philosophy of economics makes clear, rational choice theory does *not* necessarily require self-interested behavior. As Hausman and McPherson (2006) and others have argued, economic rationality only requires two things: that agents have well-behaved preferences (complete, transitive, etc.) and that they act instrumentally on the basis of those preferences (choosing the most efficient means to satisfy them). Neither of these two things necessarily involves self-interest. Self-interest concerns the *content* of the preferences, i.e. what the person prefers, and not whether the person's preferences are rationally satisfied. Self-interested preferences are preferences that involve only the agent's own good and a self-interested agent is one who acts rationally on the basis of such preferences. One could easily act rationally to help others or to bring about some state of the world that is independent of one's own self-interest. If one has well-ordered preferences and acts in an instrumentally rational way to satisfy those preferences, then one has acted rationally, and nothing self-interested needs to be involved.

While such arguments seem to be persuasive – self-interest seems to be neither necessary nor sufficient for economic rationality – this bit of philosophical argumentation has effectively nothing to do with whether learning economics makes one behave in a more self-interested way. Even if philosophers are correct about the logical relationship between economic rationality and self-interest, it is the *culture*, not the logic, of economic science that is at issue. The fact is that economists almost always explain rational choice – and therefore social phenomena – in terms of *rational self-interest*. The folk wisdom of the profession is that people generally act in their own self-interest, and it is agreement about the explanatory adequacy of such self-interest that undergirds the profession's commitment to rational choice theory. Pick up any introductory economics text or listen in on any microeconomics lecture; the message is that people act in their own rational self-interest and that such self-interest is key to understanding economic (and perhaps all other social) behavior. It is not surprising that those conditioned by, or predisposed toward, such reasoning are more likely to behave in a self-interested way (regardless of what philosophers say about the logic of rational choice).

4   The paradox of prioritätsstreit in economics

It is now time to pull together the arguments in the previous two sections. Given that priority disputes are such a prominent feature of scientific activity, and given that economists seem to have a penchant for self-interested and non-cooperative behavior, one would expect the history of economic thought to be replete with eponymic controversy; in fact, one would expect economists to have such disagreements more frequently than other scientists. If the most important prize in science is priority, and economists are more driven by self-interest than other scientists, one would expect the discipline of economics to be in constant turmoil over who gets credit for what. While such quarrels over priority would seem to be an obvious prediction about the behavior of economists, such a prediction *would in fact be wrong*. There is not now, nor has there ever been, serious prioritätsstreit within economics. The history of economic thought is simply not a history of Mertonian priority fights over whose name is attached to important results.[1] Of course this is not to say that economists do not fight about other things, such as whether a particular discovery is right or wrong; they most certainly do fight about such things, and quite vociferously. They also argue whether particular results are useful or irrelevant, elegant or trivial, biased or unbiased, empirically supported or unsubstantiated, as well as a variety of other things; but they do not fight about whose name is attached to the result, who gets eponymic credit. All things considered, this is rather paradoxical.

---

[1] As will be discussed below in Section 5, a Mertonian priority fight is a community-social event. Two economists involved in a dispute about plagiarism or some other theft of intellectual property is not a priority fight. Priority is public honor bestowed by a particular scientific community and is negotiated within that community (Gross 1998), and any fight about it would need to take place within (at least a broad segment of) that community. If it only involves two individuals arguing with each other, or with a journal editor, or in court, it is not a priority fight in Merton's terms. Although even individual disputes about priority are somewhat rare in modern economics, there clearly have been a few. Kenneth Arrow versus Duncan Black over (Arrow's) impossibility theorem (Amadae 2003, pp. 122–28), Lionel McKenzie versus Kenneth Arrow and Gerard Debreu over the proof of existence of general equilibrium (Weintraub 2002 Ch. 6, 2011), and a number of courtroom battles over plagiarism (particularly involving textbooks) are some examples. Roy Weintraub argues there was no Mertonian priority fight over the Arrow–Debreu–McKenzie existence proof because the relevant community within economics generally agreed the credit should go to Arrow and Debreu – an example of Merton's "Matthew Effect" at work in economics (Weintraub 2011, p. 212).

One possible response to this paradox might be that economists do not fight about priority because they simply do not assign priority. If the economic profession did not regularly attach the names of economists to significant discoveries, then of course there would not be any fighting about such attachments: no priority, no priority fights. Not only would the absence of priority explain the absence of prioritätsstreit, it might also suggest an important difference between economics and other sciences. However interesting such speculation might be, it is for naught. Economists do in fact assign priority – they regularly attach the names of particular economists to significant contributions in economic science – they just don't fight about it.

Economists seem to assign eponymic credit in at least three different ways. First, the name of the economist who initially developed an important theoretical result is regularly attached to that result. This applies to major theoretical developments as well as results of lesser significance. Examples of the former include Keynesian macroeconomics, the Leontief model, Nash equilibrium, the Fisher equation, and the Solow growth model; a few examples of the latter include Hicksian compensation, the Laffer curve, Hotelling's lemma, Shephard's lemma, the Rybczynski theorem, Harberger triangles, Tobin's Q, the Tiebout hypothesis, the Slutsky effect (and decomposition, and symmetry), Granger causality, the Edgeworth Box, Knightian uncertainty, and Akerlof's lemons. Second, theoretical results are often named after a long dead economist who once suggested something similar. Although historians of economic thought seldom endorse such appellations, examples include Say's Law, Ricardian equivalence, the Pigou effect, the Hayek hypothesis, Veblen effects, Walras' Law, Gossen's Law, and Pareto optimality. Third, the names of economists are not only assigned to various theoretical contributions, they are also assigned to the discovery of significant empirical regularities. Examples of such phenomenal discoveries include Director's Law, Wagner's Law, the Phillips Curve, Engel's Law, the Giffen effect, Okun gap, Gibson's Paradox, and the Lorenz Curve.[2] It is useful to note that while all of the above examples involve the name of only one economist, there are also many cases of multiple-name appellations in each of the above categories. A few of these include the Stolper–Samuelson theorem, Cobb–Douglas production functions, Harrod–Domar growth theory, the Hawkins–Simon condition, the Sonnenschein–Debreu–Mantel results

---

[2] Economists have even been known to humorously combine such appellations: as in "It takes a lot of Harberger Triangles to fill an Okun Gap" (supposedly said by James Tobin).

on aggregate excess demand functions, the Heckscher–Ohlin theory of international trade, and Arrow–Debreu general equilibrium model.

I would like to close this section with one particularly intriguing case study of the way that individual economists seem to wave-off the whole question of priority. This example is actually a bit ironic since the economist involved is Robert C. Merton, the 1997 Nobel prize-winning economist who also happens to be the son of the sociologist Robert K. Merton. It seems that if any economist would naturally associate priority with success in science, and considers priority something worth fighting over, it would be Robert C. Merton. The discovery in question is one of the most important results in modern financial economics: the Black–Scholes equation for pricing options and other financial derivatives. It was named after Fischer Black and Myron Scholes (Black and Scholes 1972, 1973) and because it appears to be an excellent example of "performativity" in economics – where economic theory effectively creates, rather than describes, economic phenomenon – it has recently become the subject of research in the social studies of science. Donald MacKenzie's (2003, 2008) careful investigation of the history of Black–Scholes reveals that not only were there two different versions of the relationship – the Black–Scholes version which was based on the earlier discrete time capital asset pricing model (CAPM) and the Merton–Samuelson version that was more mathematical and couched in continuous time – it was actually Merton who initially called it the "Black–Scholes" model in a 1970 working paper (Jarrow 1999, p. 232; MacKenzie 2003, p. 39). As Robert C. Merton explained in his Nobel lecture:

> My principal contribution to the Black-Scholes option-pricing theory was to show that the dynamic trading strategy prescribed by Black and Scholes to offset the risk exposure of an option would provide a perfect hedge in the limit of continuous trading. ... I am also responsible for naming the model, "the Black-Scholes Option-Pricing Model."[3] (Merton 1998, p. 326)

The culture of economics somehow renders scientific priority simultaneously honorable and incontestable; and in this sense Robert C. Merton appears to be a fully enculturated economist. The first footnote of Merton's Nobel lecture thanks his father (among others) for "helpful suggestions on this lecture" (Merton 1998, p. 323); one wonders what Robert K. Merton had to say to his son about the proper response to receiving the Nobel prize for a contribution that his son had named for someone else.

---

[3] And the other possible contender, Paul Samuelson, was the first person to use the term "Black–Scholes formula" in print (Merton 1998, p. 326, n. 5).

5   Possible explanations

So how do we explain this paradox? What might account for the fact that economists do not engage in Mertonian priority disputes even though they are generally more self-interested than other scientists? What is it about the scientific culture of economics that makes it unique in this respect?

Although there are probably many different ways to explain this paradox, I will consider only two: one involving internal norms and one involving external norms. By "internal" I simply mean social norms that are internalized: socialized into the professional culture of those within the economics profession and having their influence from inside the (socialized) normative consciousness of such individuals. I will argue there is actually a professionally enculturated norm at work; that norm just seems to be peculiar because the economics profession is, well, peculiar in this respect. By "external" I mean something enforced by external sanctions – not external to the profession, but external to the individual economist. To explain the paradox, an internal norm would need to be one that says that priority fights are not honorable engagements, while an external force would indicate that bad things will happen to a person (at least professionally) who engages in such disputes. Of course these two social pressures need not be mutually exclusive; a person can resist stealing both because they believe it is wrong to do so and also because they expect to be punished if caught. Perhaps both factors have been, and are, at work within economics, but my main emphasis will be on internal values rather than external sanctions. Despite this, I will start by briefly indicating how such external forces might work, since they are frequently discussed in the literature.

Suppose that the discipline of economics were organized in the way that economists generally consider a competitive market economy to be organized: a system consisting of a large number of rational self-interested agents acting independently and where the relevant social features emerge as unintended consequences of the competitive interaction of these independent agents. If that were the case in economics, and priority was generally considered to be the most prestigious prize, then one would expect to see substantial controversy about whose name is attached to what result. Since one does not observe such controversies, perhaps it is because the economics profession is not organized like a competitive market but rather is closer to central planning. If the profession was rather tightly controlled and effective mechanisms existed for punishing deviants, then one would expect to see very little controversy about the names attached to significant results. This is of course the story that heterodox economists (Marxists, Institutionalists, Austrians, etc.) have traditionally told about the institutional structure of the discipline. It is also a view that is supported by recent methodological research arguing that the economics profession is more monopolistic than competitive in its organizational structure (I discuss some of these views in Hands 2001) – as well as by recent historical studies documenting how the mechanisms of such control emerged within the profession during the post-World War II period (Amadae 2003; Bernstein 2001; Mirowski 2002). Although there is certainly some, perhaps growing, evidence regarding such external forces, these explanations face at least two challenges with respect to the priority question. First, there really isn't much historical evidence indicating the presence of such top-down control within the profession prior to the middle of the twentieth century (the rise of "big science" in economics). And second, such control would suggest the suppression of all economic controversy which does not appear to be the case; economists seem to disagree about all sorts of things (except priority). Given these issues, I will leave consideration of external sanctions as an interesting open question and focus my attention on internal controls.

To examine how the (internal) values of economists might prevent them from engaging in priority disputes it is useful to look more carefully at Robert K. Merton's original arguments about the nature of priority controversies in science. Recall that according to Merton science is a particular type of social culture, and like any other culture, its members share certain common norms and values. In particular, scientists share a particular professional moral consensus that is captured (and internalized) in a set of implicit institutional imperatives about the proper behavior within scientific life. As Merton explained:

The ethos of science is that affectively toned complex of values and norms which is held to be binding on the man of science. The norms are expressed in the form of prescriptions, proscriptions, preferences, and permissions. They are legitimatized in terms of institutional values. These imperatives, transmitted by precept and example and reinforced by sanctions are in varying degrees internalized by the scientist, thus fashioning his scientific conscience ... (Merton 1942, pp. 268–269)

Although priority is extremely important to individual scientists, Merton argued that *the vociferousness of priority fights within science was not caused by scientists acting in their own self-interest,* i.e. acting to gain credit for themselves, but rather was caused by *moral outrage* over the injustice of scientists not receiving proper recognition: "moral indignation directed toward contraventions of the ethos" (Merton 1942, p. 269). Scientists engage in priority fights not to stake their own eponymic claims, but rather because of moral indignation over the violation of a sacred professional norm. Merton's research on priority fights demonstrated that it is frequently not the scientists themselves, or even their immediate associates, that are involved in such disputations. Often a priority fight is carried on by those who have nothing directly to gain from the outcome of the dispute. According to Merton, these bystanders are acting out of moral indignation, not self-interest.

Now these argumentative associates and bystanders stand to gain little or nothing from successfully prosecuting the claims of their candidate ... Their behavior can scarcely be explained by egotism. They do not suffer from rival claims to precedence. Their personal status is not being threatened. And yet, over and over again, they take up the cudgels in the status-battle and, uninhibited by any semblance of indulging in self-praise, express their great moral indignation over the outrage being perpetrated upon their candidate.

This is, I believe, a particularly significant fact. For ... the expression of disinterested moral indignation is a signpost announcing the violation of a social norm. Although the indignant bystanders are themselves not injured by what they take to be the misbehavior of the culprit, they respond with hostility. They want to see "fair play," to see that behavior conforms to the rules of the game. The very fact of their entering the fray goes to show that science is a social institution with a distinctive body of norms exerting moral authority and that these norms are invoked particularly when it is felt that they are being violated. (Merton 1957, pp. 292–93)

If Merton is correct that priority fights in science are driven by moral indignation over the violation of the collective norms of professional justice, then there seems to be a fairly straightforward explanation for why there are no such disputes in economics: *economists do not have such collective norms*. The discipline of economics is one that has traditionally conditioned its members to believe (or those attracted to economics have a tendency to believe) that collective benefits are best derived from rational self-interested action, not from actively championing the social good. Not only are the benefits of the "invisible hand" a key feature of the economic view of the world, the folk wisdom of the profession often emphasizes the folly of "trying" to serve the social interest and how it is generally better to rely on private incentives and self-interest to achieve collective goals. Economists share a collective ethos, but it is an ethos based on the benefits of self-interested behavior not the ethos of easy moral indignation. So of course economic scientists do not engage in priority disputes; in the field of economics the culture of the profession trumps the more normatively oriented culture of the other sciences. The paradox thus dissolves; what remains is simply a case of the content of a discipline conditioning the social behavior of those within the discipline. Since priority fights are motivated by a collective moral outrage over certain scientists being treated unfairly, and given that economists have no such sense of moral outrage, it seems perfectly reasonable that there are no priority disputes in economics. Under the circumstances, it would be the presence of such fights, not their absence that would be surprising.[4]

6   Conclusion and some reflective considerations

The absence of priority fights within economics certainly seems paradoxical. If one accepts that priority fights are common in science – and it is generally accepted that they are – and one accepts that economists tend to act in self-interested ways (a well-supported, and frankly not very surprising claim), then it appears quite obvious that prioritätsstreit should be a familiar feature of professional life within the discipline. The fact this is not the case certainly cries out for an explanation. My explanation is heavily indebted to Merton's analysis of how priority functions in science. My argument is that since priority fights in science are really about moral indignation and not rational self-interest, it is not surprising that economists would not be motivated by such indignation. People not easily outraged over eponymic injustice are people who are unlikely to engage in priority disputes. Of course if we accept Merton's overall argument about the norms of science there are other forces at work in addition to the desire for priority; in particular there is no reason to believe the Mertonian characteristics of humility and disinterestedness are any less likely to be present among economists than other scientists. The difference seems to be that in most sciences characteristics like humility and disinterestedness are in conflict with the moral imperative to see that fellow scientists are properly treated. When the moral outrage dominates disinterestedness the result is a priority fight. In economics there does not seem to be any such tension; the economics profession can hold priority (and Merton's other scientific values) in high esteem, and yet not feel any compulsion to engage in disputes about it.

While I suspect this explanation may not be very popular among economists – it is, after all, a *sociological* explanation of what goes on within economics – it need not reflect badly on the profession. Sure, to accept this story, economists must agree that they are self-interested and

---

[4] A corollary to the argument is that the type of personal one-on-one disputes (perhaps in court) mentioned in footnote 1 should be more prevalent in economics than in other disciplines for the same reasons that Mertonian priority fights are absent. This conjecture remains a footnote because I have no empirical evidence about the frequency of private intellectual property disputes among economists. It is, though, an interesting corollary.

not easily outraged, but the end result need not be so bad. Economists can still claim credit for Merton's other scientific values including disinterestedness and humility. All they lose is the disruption caused by those who take it upon themselves to go on moral crusades in professional life. Who needs that? Perhaps the individual economists who do not get their names attached to important results are not very happy about it, but if that discontent never spills over into a protest movement then it will never lead to a priority fight with all of its associated resentment, inefficiency, and negative externalities. In terms of the reward system of economic science, as long as those who get their names attached to the result are drawn from the set of legitimate candidates, then rewards will still accrue to those who deserve them: not the whole reward of course, but the right to participate in a lottery of such rewards. The incentive remains, only the inefficiency is removed. As I said, this need not be entirely unflattering to economists. The argument also turns the paradox into an example of how self-interested behavior can bring about a socially efficient (if unfair) allocation of professional resources: also something economists should be comfortable with. These things said, it is still a sociological explanation of the behavior of economists, and as such, I suspect it is not an argument that most economists will find very satisfying.

As a final point, there is some evidence that the long dominant conceptual framework of the economics profession may be changing. It has been argued that during the last decade the discipline has become substantially more fragmented (see, for example, Davis 2005a, 2005b and Colander, Holt, and Rosser 2008). Various versions of bounded rationality, behavioral economics, evolutionary modeling, computational economics, experimental economics (and psychology), and a host of other theoretical strategies that are often at odds with the profession's traditional rational choice-invisible hand catechism have emerged and are currently vying for theoretical attention. As David Colander, Richard Holt, and Barkley Rosser put it: "Economics is moving away from a strict adherence to the holy trinity – rationality, selfishness, and equilibrium – to a more eclectic position of purposeful behavior, enlightened self-interest, and sustainability" (2008, p. 31). And, it is useful to note that, unlike the heterodox theories of an earlier generation, many of these alternative ways of thinking about agency and social interaction seem to have captured the attention of those within the seats (and institutions) of disciplinary influence. It is too early to tell if these changes are the beginnings of a sea change, or just a passing squall, in the intellectual culture of economics, but it is clear that if it ends up actually being a sea change then there could be a corresponding change in the profession's behavior regarding priority fights. If there is a movement away from the self-interested and invisible-hand-based values that have long dominated the profession, then, if the argument in this chapter is correct, one would expect to see an increase in the number of Mertonian priority fights within the discipline. There is no indication this is currently happening, but I would note that if Mertonian priority fights were to start appearing within economics it would provide an excellent novel fact supporting the central thesis of this chapter.

References

Amadae, Sonja M. 2003. *Rationalizing Capitalist Democracy: The Cold War Origins of Rational Choice Liberalism*. University of Chicago Press.

Bernstein, Michael 2001. *A Perilous Progress: Economists and Public Purpose in Twentieth-Century America*. Princeton University Press.

Black, Fischer and Scholes, Myron 1972. "The Valuation of Option Contracts and a Test of Market Efficiency." *Journal of Finance*, 27, 399–418.

1973. "The Pricing of Options and Corporate Liabilities." *Journal of Political Economy*, 81, 637–654.

Carter, John R., and Irons, Michael D. 1991. "Are Economists Different, and If So Why?" *Journal of Economic Perspectives*, 5, 171–177.

Colander, David, Holt, Richard P. F. and Rosser, Barkley 2008. "The Changing Face of Mainstream Economics." *The Long Term View*, 7, 31–42.

Dasgupta, Partha and David, Paul A. 1994. "Toward a New Economics of Science." *Research Policy*, 23, 487–521 [reprinted in Mirowski, P. and Sent, E-M (2002), *Science Bought and Sold: Essays in the Economics of Science*, University of Chicago Press, 219–248].

Davis, John B. 2005a. "Heterodox Economics, the Fragmentation of the Mainstream, and Embedded Individual Analysis." In *The Future of Heterodox Economics*, G. Garnett and J. Harvey (eds.), Ann Arbor, MI: University of Michigan Press.

2005b. "The Turn in Economics: Neoclassical Dominance to Mainstream Pluralism?" Paper presented at the Allied Social Science Association Meetings, Philadelphia, PA, January 2005.

Frank, Björn and Schulze, Günther G. 2000. "Does Economics Make Citizens Corrupt?" *Journal of Economic Behavior & Organization*, 43, 101–113.

Frank, Robert H., Thomas Gilovich, and Dennis T. Regan 1993. "Does Studying Economics Inhibit Cooperation?" *Journal of Economic Perspectives*, 7, 159–171.

1996. "Do Economists Make Bad Citizens?" *Journal of Economic Perspectives*, 10, 187–192.

Frey, Bruno S. and Meier, Stephan 2003. "Are Political Economists Selfish and Indoctrinated? Evidence from a National Experiment." *Economic Inquiry*, 41, 448–462.

Gross, Alan G. 1998. "Do Disputes over Priority Tell Us Anything About Science?" *Science in Context*, 12, 161–179.

Hands, D. Wade 2001. *Reflection without Rules: Economic Methodology and Contemporary Science Theory*. Cambridge University Press.

　2002. "The Sociology of Scientific Knowledge." In *Science Bought and Sold: Essays in the Economics of Science*, P. Mirowski and E. M. Sent (eds.), University of Chicago Press, 515–548.

Hausman, Daniel and McPherson, Daniel M. 2006. *Economic Analysis, Moral Philosophy, and Public Policy*. 2nd edition, Cambridge University Press.

Hirshleifer, Jack 1994. "The Dark Side of the Force". *Economic Inquiry*, 32, 1–10.

Jarrow, Robert A. 1999. "In Honor of the Nobel Laureates Robert C. Merton and Myron S. Scholes: A Partial Differential Equation That Changed the World." *Journal of Economic Perspectives*, 13, 229–248.

Kirchgässner, Gebhard 2005. "(Why) Are Economists Different?" *European Journal of Political Economy*, 21, 543–562.

Laband, David N. and Beil, Richard O. 1999. "Are Economists More Selfish Than Other 'Social Scientists'?" *Public Choice*, 199, 85–101.

Lanteri, Alessandro 2008. "(Why) Do Selfish People Self-Select in Economics?" *Erasmus Journal for Philosophy and Economics*, 1, 1–23.

MacKenzie, Donald 2003. "An Equation and its Worlds: Bricolage, Exemplars, Disunity and Performativity in Financial Economics." *Social Studies of Science*, 33, 831–868.

　2008. *An Engine, Not a Camera: How Financial Models Shape Markets*. Cambridge, MA: MIT Press.

Maxwell, Gerald and Ames, Ruth 1981. "Economists Free Ride, Does Anyone Else?" *Journal of Public Economics*, 15, 295–310.

Merton, Robert C. 1998. "Applications of Options-Pricing Theory: Twenty-Five Years Later," *American Economic Review*, 88, 323–349.

Merton, Robert K. 1942. "The Normative Structure of Science," originally published as "Science and Technology in a Democratic Order." *Journal of Legal and Political Sociology*, 1, 115–126 [Reprinted in Merton (1973), 267–278].

　1957. "Priorities in Scientific Discovery." *American Sociological Review*, 22, 635–659 [Reprinted in Merton (1973), 286–324].

　1970. *Science, Technology and Society in Seventeenth-Century England*. New York: Harper & Row [originally published in Osiris in 1938].

　1973. *The Sociology of Science: Theoretical and Empirical Investigations*. University of Chicago Press.

　1996. *On Social Structure and Science*. University of Chicago Press.

Mirowski, Philip 2002. *Machine Dreams: Economics Becomes a Cyborg Science*. Cambridge University Press.

Weintraub, E. Roy 2002. *How Economics Became a Mathematical Science*. Durham, NC: Duke University Press.

　2011. "Lionel W. McKenzie and the Proof of Existence of a Competitive Equilibrium." *Journal of Economic Perspectives*, 25, 199–215.

Yeser, Anthony M., Robert S. Goldfarb, and Paul J. Poppen 1996. "Does Studying Economics Discourage Cooperation? Watch What We Do, Not What We Say or How We Play." *Journal of Economic Perspectives*, 10, 177–186.

Part III

Challenges and solutions

8   Why economics is on the wrong track

Deirdre McCloskey

If you will forgive me, I will be very simple here. The point I am making is simple, and does not need to be dressed up in fancy clothing. I want to state the point in a way that it cannot be evaded. I do this not to embarrass my colleagues in economics, whom I love. I do it because the science needs an answer. If I am right in my criticism of economics – I pray that I am not right – then much of what economists do is a waste of time.

What's sinful about economics is not what the average anthropologist or historian or journalist thinks. From the outside the dismal science seems obviously sinful, if irritatingly influential. But the obvious sins are not all that terrible; or, if terrible, they are committed anyway by everybody else. It is actually two particular, non-obvious, and unusual sins, two secret ones, that cripple the scientific enterprise – in economics and in a few other fields nowadays (like psychology and political science and medical science and population biology).

Yet a sympathetic critic who says these things and wishes that her own beloved economics would grow up and start focusing all its energies on doing proper science (the way physics or geology or anthropology or history or certain parts of literary criticism do it) finds herself sadly misunderstood. The commonplace and venial sins block scrutiny of the bizarre and mortal ones. Pity the poor sympathetic critic, construed regularly to be making this or that Idiot's Critique: "Oh, I see. You're one of those airy humanists who just can't stand to think of numbers or mathematics" or "Oh, I see. When you say economics is 'rhetorical' you want economists to write more warmly."

I tell you it's maddening. The sympathetic critic, herself an economist, even a Chicago-School economist, slowly during twenty years of groping came to recognize the ubiquity of the Two Secret Sins of Economics (in the end they are one, deriving from pride, as all sins do). She has developed helpful suggestions for redeeming economics from sin. And yet no one – not the anthropologist or English professor or others from the outside certainly, but least of all the economist or medical scientist – grasps her point, or acts on it.

Virtues misidentified as sins

Quantification

Quantification, though, is not a sin. Numbers came with social science at its birth. The English political arithmeticians William Petty and Gregory King and the rest in the late seventeenth century (anticipated in the early seventeenth century by, like so much of what we call English, certain Dutchmen) wanted most to know How Much. It was an entirely novel obsession. You might call it bourgeois. How much will it cost to drain the Somerset Levels? How much does England's treasure by foreign trade depend on possessing colonies? How much is this and how much that? The blessed Adam Smith a century later kept wondering how much wages in Edinburgh differed from those in London (too much) and how much the colonies by then acquired in England's incessant eighteenth-century wars against France were worth to the home country (not much). By the late eighteenth century, it is surprising to note, the statistical chart had been invented; what is surprising is that it hadn't been invented before – another sign that quantitative thinking was novel, at least in the West (the Chinese had been collecting statistics on population and prices for centuries). European states from Sweden to Naples began in the eighteenth century collecting statistics to worry about: prices, population, balances of trade, flows of gold. The word "statistics" was a coinage of German and Italian enthusiasts for state action in the early eighteenth century, pointing to a story of the state use of numbering. Then dawned the age of statistics, and everything from drug incarcerations and smoking deaths to the value of a life and the credit rating of Jane Q. Public are numbered.

It became a sort of insanity, of course. Tour guides observe that American men want to know how tall every tower is, how many bricks there are in every notable wall, how many died here, how many lived. Samuel Johnson was in 1775 typical of his age and his gender in reporting the size of everything he encountered in his tour of the West of Scotland (he used his walking stick as a measuring rod). By the 1850s the conservative critics of capitalism, such as Charles Dickens in his novel *Hard Times*, were becoming very cross about statistics:

Thomas Gradgrind, sir – peremptorily Thomas – Thomas Gradgrind. With a rule and a pair of scales, and the multiplication table always in his pocket, sir, ready to weigh and measure any parcel of human nature, and tell you exactly what it comes to. It is a mere question of figures, a case of simple arithmetic ...

"Father," she still pursued, "does Mr. Bounderby ask me to love him?"

"...[T]he reply depends so materially, Louisa, on the sense in which we use the expression. Now, Mr. Bounderby does not do you the injustice, and does not do himself the injustice, of pretending to anything fanciful, fantastic, or (I am using synonymous terms) sentimental.

... Therefore, perhaps the expression itself – I merely suggest this to you, my dear – may be a little misplaced."

"What would you advise me to use in its stead, father?"

"Why, my dear Louisa," said Mr. Gradgrind, completely recovered by this time, "I would advise you (since you ask me) to consider this question, as you have been accustomed to consider every other question, simply as one of tangible Fact. The ignorant and the giddy may embarrass such subjects with irrelevant fancies, and other absurdities that have no existence, properly viewed – really no existence – but it is no compliment to you to say, that you know better. Now, what are the Facts of this case? You are, we will say in round numbers, twenty years of age; Mr. Bounderby is, we will say in round numbers, fifty... [T]he question arises, is this one disparity sufficient to operate as a bar to such a marriage? In considering this question, it is not unimportant to take into account the statistics of marriage, so far as they have yet been obtained, in England and Wales. I find, on reference to the figures, that a large proportion of these marriages are contracted between parties of very unequal ages, and that the elder of these contracting parties is, in rather more than three-fourths of these instances, the bridegroom. It is remarkable as showing the wide prevalence of this law that among the natives of the British possessions in India, also in a considerable part of China, and among the Calmucks of Tartary, the best means of computation yet furnished us by travelers, yield similar results."

Counting can surely be a nitwit's, or the Devil's, tool. Among the more unnerving exhibits in the extermination camp at Auschwitz are the books in which Hitler's willing executioners kept records on every person who they killed.

The formal and mathematical theory of statistics was largely invented in the 1880s by eugenicists (those clever racists at the origin of so much in the social sciences) and perfected in the twentieth century by agronomists (yes, agronomists, at places like the Rothamsted agricultural experiment station in England or at Iowa State University). The newly mathematized statistics became a fetish in wannabe sciences. During the 1920s, when sociology was a young science, quantification was a way of claiming status, as it became also in economics, fresh from putting aside its old name of political economy, and in psychology, fresh from a separation from philosophy. In the 1920s and 1930s even the social anthropologists, those men and women of the fanciful, fantastic, or (I am using synonymous terms) sentimental, counted coconuts.

And the economists, oh, the economists, how they counted, and still count. Take up any copy of the *American Economic Review* to hand (surely you subscribe?) and open it at random. To perhaps Joel Waldfogel, "The Deadweight Loss of Christmas" (no kidding: December 1993; Waldfogel is arguing that since a gift is not chosen by the recipient it is

Table 8.1 *Average amounts paid and values of gifts*

Variable	Survey 1	Survey 2
Amount paid ($)	438.2	508.9
Value ($)	313.4	462.1
Percentage ratio of average value to average paid	71.5	90.8
Number of recipients	86	58

not worth what the giver spent, which leads to a loss compared with merely sending cash. Who could not love such a science of Prudence?). On p. 1331 you will find Table 8.1.

It is a mere question of figures, a case of simple arithmetic.

Refutatio: But after all, think about it. When you want to count your coconuts, or the cash value of your Christmas gifts, it makes sense to do the job right. Many of the things we wish to know come in quantitative form. It matters – not absolutely, in God's eyes, but for particular human purposes – how much it will rain tomorrow and how much it rained yesterday. For sound practical and spiritual reasons we wish sometimes to know How Much. How many slaves were driven from Africa? Perhaps 29 million (the population of Britain at the height of the slave trade was about 8 million), more than half going east, not west, across the Sahara or the Indian Ocean, not the Atlantic. How has Cuba fared under Communism and the American embargo? Income per head in Cuba has fallen by a third since 1959, while in the Dominican Republic, Chile, Mexico, Brazil, and indeed in Latin America and the Caribbean generally it has more than doubled. How big is immigration to the United States now? Smaller in proportion to population than it was in 1910. And on and on and on.

(You can see from the examples that no claim is being made here that numbers are by nature peculiarly "objective," whatever that pop-philosophical term might exactly mean, or "non-political," or "scientific." Numbers are rhetoric, which is to say humanly persuasive. We agree in a persuasive culture to assign meaning to this or that number, and then can be persuaded to this or that view of the matter. Pebbles lie around, as Richard Rorty has put it; facts of the matter do not. It is our human decision to count or weigh or mix the pebbles in constituting the pebbly facts.)

Economists are selected for their great love of numbers. The joke is "I'm an economist because I didn't have enough personality to become an accountant." A statistical argument is always honored in the Department of Economics. Many non-economists on the contrary fear numbers, dislike them, dishonor them, are confused and irritated by them. But some important questions can only be answered numerically. A great many other questions are at least helpfully illuminated by numbers. Your age number is not the only important fact about you, and is certainly nothing like your full Meaning ("You are, we will say in round numbers, twenty years of age; Mr. Bounderby is, we will say in round numbers, fifty"). But it is a number helpful for some purposes – ordinary conversation, for one thing; medical examination for another; yes, even marriage. It's humanly useful to know that you grew up in the 1950s and came of age in the liberating 1960s: age 60 on September 11, 2002 (happy birthday). Temperature is not the only measure of a good day. Wind, sunshine, human events, and human-assigned significance matter. That this is the month and this the happy morn of Christ's nativity has meaning beyond 30 °F. But it is worth knowing that the temperature on the blessed day was not 459.67 °F or 212 °F. So counting is not a sin of economics. It is a virtue.

Mathematics

Nor is mathematics a sin. Mathematics is not identical to counting or statistics. The newspapers chortle when they find a mathematician who cannot balance his checkbook, but that's just a misunderstanding of what mathematicians do. There have been some famously good calculators among mathematicians, the eighteenth-century Swiss mathematician Leonhard Euler being an instance (he also knew the entire Aeneid by heart; in Latin, I need hardly add). But odd as it sounds, most of mathematics has nothing to do with actual numbers. Euler used calculation in the same way that mathematicians nowadays use computers, for back-of-the-envelope tests of hunches on the way to developing what the mathematicians are pleased to call a real proof of such amazing facts as: $e^{\pi i} + 1 = 0$ (and therefore God exists). You can have a "real" proof, the style of demonstration developed by the Greeks (with which you became acquainted in high-school geometry, either loving or hating it), without examining a single number or even a single concrete example. Thus: the Pythagorean Theorem is true for any right triangle, regardless of its dimensions, and is proven not by induction from many or even zillions of numerical examples of right triangles, but universally and for all time, praise God, may her name be glorified, by deduction from premises. Accept the premises and you have accepted the Theorem. Quod erat demonstrandum. Statistics or other quantitative methods in science (such as accounting or experiment or simulation) answer inductively How Much. Mathematics by contrast answers deductively Why, and in a refined and philosophical version very popular among mathematicians since the early nineteenth century, whether. "Why does a stone dropped from a tower go faster and faster?" Well, $F = ma$, understand? "I wonder whether the mass, m, of the stone has any effect at all." Well, yes, actually it does: notice that there's a little m in the answer to the Why question.

Why/Whether is not the same question as How Much. You can know that forgetting your lover's birthday will have some effect on your relationship (Whether), and even understand that the neglect works through such-and-such an understandable psychological mechanism ("Don't you love me enough to know I care about birthdays?" – Why). But to know How Much the neglect will hurt the relationship you need to have in effect numbers, those ms and as, so to speak, and some notion of their magnitudes. Even if you know the Why (the proper theory of the channels through which forgetting a birthday will work; again by analogy, $F = ma$), the How Much will depend on exactly, numerically, quantitatively how sensitive this or that part of the Why is in fact in your actual beloved's soul: how much in this case the m and a are. And such sensitivity in an actual world, the scientists are always saying, is an empirical question, not theoretical. "All right, you jerk, that's the last straw: I'm moving out" or "Don't worry, dear: I know you love me" differ in the sensitivity, the How Much, the quantitative effect, the magnitude, the mass, the oomph.

Economics since its beginning has been very often "mathematical" in this sense of being interested in Why/Whether arguments without regard to How Much. For example: If you buy a loaf of bread from the super-market both you and the supermarket (its shareholders, its employees, and its bread suppliers) are made to some degree better off. How do I know? Because the supermarket offered the bread voluntarily and you accepted the offer voluntarily. Both of you must have been made better off, a little or a lot – or else you two wouldn't have done the deal.

Economists have long been in love with this simple argument. They have since the eighteenth century taken the argument a crucial and dramatic step further: that is, they have deduced something from it, namely, Free trade is neat. If each deal between you and the supermar-ket, and the supermarket and Smith, and Smith and Jones, and so forth is betterment-producing (a little or a lot: we're not talking quantities here), then (note the "then": we're talking deduction here) free trade between the entire body of French people and the entire body of English people is betterment producing, too. And therefore (note the "therefore") free trade between any two groups is neat. The economist notes that if all trades are voluntary they all have some gain. So free trade in all its forms is neat. For example, a law restricting who can get into the pharmacy business is a bad idea, not neat at all, because free trade is good, so non-free trade is bad. Protection of French workers is bad, because free trade is good. And so forth, to literally thousands of policy conclusions.

Though it is among the three or four most important arguments in economics, it is not empirical. It contains no statements of How Much. It says there exists a gain from trade – remember the phrases some gain or to some degree or a little or a lot or we're not talking quantities here. "I wonder whether there exists [in whatever quantity] a good effect of free trade?" Yes, one exists: examine this page of math; look at this diagram; listen to my charming parable about you and Dominick's. Don't ask How Much. The reasoning is Why/Whether. As stated it cannot be wrong, no more than the Pythagorean Theorem can be. It's not a matter of approximation, not a matter of How Much. It's a chain of logic from implicit axioms (which can be and have been made explicit, in all their infinite variety) to a "rigorous" qualitative conclusion (in its infinite variety). Remember those words "then," "therefore," "so." Under such-and-such a set of assumptions, A, the conclusion, C, must be that people are made better off. A implies C, so free trade is beneficial anywhere. (Please listen, and stop asking "How Much?": how many times must I remind you that the reasoning is qualitative, not quantitative?!)

The philosophers call this sort of thing "valid" reasoning, by which they do not mean "true," but "following from the axioms – if you believe the axioms, such as A, then C also must be true." If you believe that any individual exchange arrived at voluntarily is good, then with a few extra assumptions (e.g. about the meaning of "voluntarily"; or, e.g. about how one person's good depends on another's) you can get the conclusion that free international trade among nations is good.

Why/Whether reasoning, which is also characteristic of the Math Department, could be called philosophical. The Math Department and the Philosophy Department have a similar fascination with deduction, and a corresponding boredom with induction. They do not give a fig for How Much. No facts, please: we're philosophers. No numbers, please: we're mathematicians. In the Philosophy Department either relativism is or is not open to a refutation from self-contradiction. It's not a little refuted. It's knocked down, or not. In the Math Department the Goldbach Conjecture, that every even number is the sum of two prime numbers (e.g. $24 = 13 + 11$; try it), is either true or false (or, to introduce a third possibility admitted since the 1930s, undecidable). Supposing it's decidable, there's no question of How Much. You can't in the realm of Why/Whether, in the Math Department or the Philosophy Department or some parts of the Economics Department, be a little bit pregnant.

The argument for free trade is easy to express in terms that anyone would call "mathematical." Since about 1947 the front line and later the dominant and by now the arrogantly self-satisfied and haughtily intolerant if remarkably unproductive scientific program in economics has been to reformulate verbal (but still philosophical/mathematical, i.e. qualitative, i.e. Why/Whether) arguments into symbols and variables and diagrams and fixed point theorems and the like. The program is called "Samuelsonian," after the Gary, Indiana native and third person to receive the Nobel Memorial Prize in Economics, Paul Anthony Samuelson. He and his brother-in-law Kenneth Arrow (who was the fifth person out of the fifty or so from 1969 to 2001 to receive the glittering Prize) led the movement to be explicit about the math in economics, against great opposition. They were courageous pioneers (their mutual nephew Lawrence Summers, the crown prince of modern economics, became Secretary of the Treasury and President of Harvard). In 1947 Samuelson set the tone with the publication of his Ph. D. dissertation (which had been finished in 1941), the modestly entitled Foundations of Economic Analysis. In 1951 Arrow carried it to still higher realms of mathematics with his Ph.D. dissertation, Social Choice and Individual Values. Their enemies, a few of whom are still around, said, with the humanists, "Yuk. This math stuff is too hard, too inhuman. Give me words. Sentiment. Show me some verbal argumentation or some verbal history. Or even actual numbers. But none of this new x and y stuff. It gives me a headache."

Refutatio: But think again. There's nothing whatever new about deductive reasoning in economics. It didn't start in 1947. More like 1747 (in fact about this time David Hume in Scotland and the physiocrats in France were busy inventing philosophical, entirely qualitative, Why/Whether arguments about economics). Deducing sometimes surprising and anyway logically valid (if not always true) conclusions from assumptions about the economy is a game economists have always loved. And if you want to connect one thing with another, deduce conclusions C from assumptions A, free trade from characterizations of an autonomous consumer, why not do it universally and for all time? Why not, asked Samuelson and Arrow and the rest, with much justice, do it right?

True, for practical purposes of surveying grain fields it would work just as well as Pythogoras' Greek proof to have a Babylonian-style of proof-by-calculation showing that the sums of squares of the sides of zillions of triangles seem to be pretty much equal to the sums of squares of their hypotenuses. You might make a similar case for the free trade theorem, noting for example that the great internal free-trade zone called the United States still has a much higher average income (20 to 30 percent higher) than otherwise clever and hardworking countries like Japan or Germany, which insist on many more restrictions on internal trade, such as protection of small retailing. And, true, the improvement of computers is making more Babylonian-style "brute force calculations" (as the mathematicians call them with distaste) cheaper than some elegant formulas ("analytic solutions," they say, rapturously). Economics, like many other fields – architecture, engineering – is about to be revolutionized by computation.

But if beyond clumsy fact or numerical approximation there is an elegant and exact formula – $F = ma$ or $E = mc^2$ or, to give a somewhat less elegant example from economics, $1 + iusa = (eforward / espot)(1 + ifrance)$, called "covered interest arbitrage" – why not use it? Of course, any deduction depends on the validity of the premises. If a sufficiently high percentage of potential arbitrageurs in the markets for French and US bonds and currency are slothful dolts, then covered interest arbitrage will not hold. But likewise any induction depends on the validity of the data. If the sample used to test the efficacy of mammograms in preventing premature death is biased, then the statistical conclusions will not hold. Any calculation depends on the validity of the inputs and assumptions. Garbage in, garbage out. As the kids say, it all depends. Naturally: we mortals are not blessed with certitude.

So mathematics, too, is not the sin of economics, but in itself a virtue. Getting deductions right is the Lord's work, if not the only work the Lord favors. Like all virtues it can be carried too far, and be unbalanced with other virtues, becoming the Devil's work, sin. But all virtues are like that.

Libertarian politics

Nor is devotion to free markets a sin. Like quantitative induction and philosophical deduction, economics has always had a political purpose, and the purpose has usually been libertarian. Economists are freedom nuts, which is to say that they look with suspicion on lawyerly plans to solve problems with new state compulsions and longer jail sentences. Economics at its philosophical birth, among physiocrats in Paris and moral philosophers in Edinburgh, was in favor of free markets and was suspicious of overblown states. Mostly it still is. Let things be, laissez faire, has been the economists' cry against intervention. Let the trades begin.

True, not all economists are free traders. The non-free traders, often European and disproportionately nowadays French, point out that you can make other assumptions about how trade works, A', and get other conclusions, C', not so favorable to laissez faire. The free-trade theorem, which sounds so grand, is actually pretty easy to overturn. Suppose a big part of the economy – say the household – is, as the economists put it, "distorted" (e.g. suppose people in households do things for love: you can see that the economists have a somewhat peculiar idea of "distortion"). Then it follows rigorously (that is to say, mathematically) that free trade in other sectors (e.g. manufacturing) will not be the best thing. In fact it can make the average person worse off than restricted, protected, tariffed trade would. And of course normal people – I mean non-economists – are not persuaded that free trade is always and everywhere a good thing. For example most people think free trade is a bad thing for the product or service they make. By all means, let us arrange for my baker and pharmacist to compete vigorously, nay, brutally, with other bakers and pharmacists, so that I can get donuts and also vitamin E (to offset the donuts) cheaply. But I really do think we need to blockade entry into the profession of being an economist: it is, I am sure you agree, scandalous that so many unqualified quacks are bilking consumers with adulterated economics, quite unlike the pure economic ideas I offer here, at such reasonable expense.

And very many normal people of leftish views, even after communism, even after numerous disastrous experiments in central planning, even after trying to get a train ride from Amtrak or service from the Postal Service (not to mention service from the Internal Revenue Service or from the Immigration and Naturalization Service; you see I was indignant: I am, after all, a free-market economist), think Socialism Deserves a Chance. They think it obvious that socialism is after all fairer than unfettered capitalism. They think it obvious that regulation is after all necessary to restrain monopoly. They don't realize that free markets have partially broken down inequality (for example, between men and women; "partially," I said) and partially undermined monopolies (for example, local monopolies in retailing) and have increased the income of the poor over two centuries by a factor of 18. The sin of economics, the lefties think, is exactly its free-market bias.

Refutatio: But, my dearly beloved friends on the left, think again. There really is a serious case to be made against government intervention and in favor of markets. Maybe not knockdown; maybe imperfect here or there; let's chat about it; hmm, I see what you mean; but a serious case that serious people ought to take seriously. The case is not merely Country-Club Republicanism (which in fact is highly favorable to government intervention, in order you see to assist the members of the Country Club, such as its longstanding members who managed Enron, Inc.). The case in favor of markets is on the contrary populist and egalitarian and person-respecting and bad-institution-breaking libertarianism. Don't go to government to solve problems, said Adam Smith. As he didn't say, to do so is to put the fox in charge of the hen house. The golden rule is, those who have the gold rule: so don't expect a government run by men to help women, or a government run by Enron executives to help Enron employees.

Libertarianism is typical of economics, especially English-speaking economics, and most especially American economics. Most Americans if they can get clear of certain European errors, are radical libertarians under the skin. Give me liberty. Sweet land of liberty. Live free or die (a New Hampshire man who decided he didn't want the motto on his license plate and insisted on covering it up with masking tape was ... arrested: your friend the State in action).

But alas, no time, no time. Libraries of books have been written examining the numerous and weighty arguments for the market and against socialism. I urge you to go read a few such books with care, such as Thomas Friedman, *The Lexus and the Olive Tree*, or if your tastes run more academic, anything by Milton Friedman (Nobel 1976). Please, all of you, come over to my delightful, if challenging, course at UIC called "Economics for Advanced Students of the Humanities" in which I sketch the arguments. Really, that the average literary person believes the first few pages of *The Communist Manifesto* suffice for knowledge of economics and economic history, in which he professes great interest, is a bit of a scandal. It's amazing that most professors and journalists since about 1900 have not even heard of the arguments against turning the economy over to police and jailers and bureaucrats, and are scandalized when some boorish Chicago-School economist comes along and suggests that pot should be legalized and national borders opened and government schools made to compete with each other. I spoiled quite a few dinner parties early in my career blurting out such proposals. I have become cannier since then, or more polite, or just weary.

But I say, as Cromwell said wearily to the General Assembly of the Church of Scotland, August 3, 1650, "I beseech you, in the bowels of Christ, think it possible you may be mistaken."

Oh, permit me one short libertarian riff. According to the Peruvian development economist Hernando de Soto, to open a small business in Lima, Peru, getting all the forms filled out and visiting the right government offices recently took a team of researchers working six hours a day 289 days. To get the permits to build a legal house on state-owned land (land for sale, not held for the public) took nearly 7 years, with 207 administrative steps and 52 government offices. In Egypt getting the permits to build a legal house on agricultural land took from 6 to 11 years. In Haiti buying land from the government took 19 years.

Nor is such government obstruction peculiar to the present-day Third World. In one decade in the eighteenth century, according to the Swedish economist and historian Eli Heckscher in his book of 1932, *Mercantilism*, the French government sent tens of thousands of souls to the galleys and executed 16,000 (that's about 4.4 people a day over the ten years: you see the beauty of statistical thinking) for the hideous crime of. Are you ready to hear the appalling evil these enemies of the State committed, fully justifying hanging them all, every damned one of their treasonable skins? ... Importing printed calico cloth. States do not change much from age to age. Lawrence Wylie reported the attitude of a French bureaucrat in the 1950s: "If the public speaks evil of me I serenely shit on it. The complaint merely goes to show the value of my office and of my methods. The more the public is shat upon, the better the State is served."

In view of How Muches and Oh, My Gods like these – the baleful oomph of governmental intrusions worldwide crushing harmless (indeed, beneficial) exchange, from marihuana to printed calico – perhaps laissez faire does not seem so obviously sinful, does it now? Consider, my dear leftist friends. Read and reflect. I beseech you, think it possible that, like statistics and mathematics, the libertarianism of economics is a virtue.

Venial sins, easily forgiven

I am very far from wanting to defend everything about economics, even short of the Two Great Secret Sins. But you need to realize that economists do the irritating things they do for reasons, often pretty good ones.

For instance, among the most surprising and irritating features of economics (when people figure out what is going on) is its obsessive, monomaniacal focus on a prudent model of humanity. It's hard for outsiders to believe. Everything, simply everything, from marriage to murder is supposed by the modern economist to be explainable as a sort of Prudence. Human beings are supposed to be calculating machines pursuing Prudence and Price and Profit and Property and Power – "P variables," you might call them. P-obsession begins with Machiavelli and Hobbes, is continued by Bernard Mandeville (the early eighteenth-century Dutch–English spy and pamphleteer), is systematized by Jeremy Bentham (the utilitarian economist flourishing in the early nineteenth century), and is finally perfected by twentieth-century economists, including that same Paul Samuelson (b. 1915), who fully formalized the notion in a curious character known as Max U, and the great Gary Becker (b. 1930), who went about as far as he could go.

Becker (Nobel 1992), a professor of economics and sociology at the University of Chicago, asks, for example, why people have children. Answer: because children are durable goods. They are expensive to produce and maintain, over a long period of time, like a house. They yield returns over a long future, like a car. They have a poor second-hand market, like a refrigerator. They act as a store of value against future disasters, like pawnable gold or your diamond ring. So (you will sense a logical leap here; David Hume noticed the same leap in Mandeville and Hobbes), the number of children that people have is a matter of cost and benefit, just like the purchase of a house or car or refrigerator or diamond. A prudent parent decides whether to invest in many children or few, extensively or intensively, early or late, just like investing in a durable good. If you think this is funny stuff you are not alone. But think again: there's no doubt that Prudence does affect at least part of the decision to have children, to emigrate, to attend church, to go to college, to commit a murder, not to speak of buying a house or a car or a loaf of bread. In his obsessive study of the Prudential part, the economist can make some quite interesting and sometimes counter-intuitive and occasionally even factually true points For example, economists "predict" (as they always put it in their child's version of positivism) that, surprisingly, no-fault divorce should have no long-term effect on the prevalence of divorce. Why is that? Well, the law affects how the spoils from a divorce are divided up, but not their total size. Since the people on both sides have lawyers paid to collect spoils, it is the sum of spoils, not their division, which should in fact determine how much divorcing goes on. That the wife gets half instead of one quarter is offset by the necessary concomitant: the husband therefore gets half instead of three-quarters. Her increasing propensity to seek divorce (half is better than one quarter) is offset by his decreasing propensity (a half is worse than three quarters). And such a surprising claim on the basis of Prudence alone seems to be factually true in the world.

The narrowness of the scientific concern of economists has of course a cost (which is itself an economist's point: the road not traveled is the opportunity cost).

Prudence is the central ethical virtue of the bourgeoisie, but not the only one. Adam Smith's book about Prudence, *An Inquiry into the Nature and Causes of the Wealth of Nations*, published in 1776, should be read as embedded in the other virtues, especially Temperance and Justice, about which indeed Smith wrote at great length. If Smith had been statistically inclined then he would have put it this way. Take any sort of behavior you wish to understand – voting, for example, or the adoption of the Bessemer process in the making of steel. Call it B. It can be put on a scale and measured; or perhaps seen to be present or absent. You want to give an account of B. What the Prudence-only men from Machiavelli to Becker are claiming is that you can explain B with Prudence alone, the P variable – Prudence, Price, Profit, The Profane. Smith (and Mill and Keynes and quite a few other economists, if not the ones who run the discipline these days) have replied that, no, you have forgotten Love and Courage, Justice and Temperance, Faith and Hope, in a word, Solidarity, the S variable of speech, stories, shame, The Sacred. Economists have specialized in P, anthropologists in S. But most behavior, B, is explained by both:

$$B = a + bP + gS + e.$$

To include both P and S is only sensible. It is not wishy-washy or unprincipled. Of course the S variables are the conditions under which the P variables work, and of course the P variables modify the effects of S variables. It is the human dance of Sacred and Profane.

(Econometrically speaking, I remind my economist colleagues, if the P and S variables are not orthogonal, which is to say if they are not entirely independent, or the covariance, as we say, of P and S is not zero, by God's grace, bless Her holy name, or alternatively if there is reason to believe that a variable such as PS multiplied together (say) has its own influence, then an estimate of the coefficients a and b that ignores S (or PS) will give biased results. The bias is important if the S variable is important. The experiment is not properly controlled, and its conclusions are nonsense.)

It is often a mistake to rely on S alone, and to reject P, as Marshall Sahlins sometimes seems to do (shame on you, Marshall; Marshall says he doesn't, but I say he does). And vice versa, which is the point here. Most economics and most anthropology is persuasion about the mixture of Prudence and Solidarity, the Profane and the Sacred, that matters for any particular case. Without being explicit enough, some economists, and some of the best, do acknowledge S variables. Theodore Schultz argued in *Transforming Traditional Agriculture* (1964; Nobel 1979) that peasants in poor countries were Prudent. He was arguing that it was a mistake to explain their behavior anthropology-style as $B = a + gS + e$ with the S variable alone. Schultz said: Even these "traditional" peasants care about P. But Schultz did not ignore the S variables. The education of women, he argued forcefully, was crucial in making Prudence work, and doing it would depend on overcoming patriarchal objections to literate women. Robert Fogel (Nobel 1993) and Stanley Engerman argued in 1974 that American slavery was Prudential and capitalistic. But they did not entirely ignore the S variables. They measured them, by indirection, finding that for some features of slavery, such as the price of slaves, variables other than business Prudence were quantitatively not very important. And then Fogel went on to write about the influence of religious belief on slavery and abolition, and Engerman to write about the historical roots of coercion and freedom in the labor market. Many economists go through a Building of this sort, starting in graduate school as Prudence-Only guys (the guys more than the gals) and coming by age 50 or so to realize that, after all, people are motivated by more than Prudence. Even Gary Becker shows signs of such a development.

To this the academic economist who has not developed beyond his graduate-student version of the science is likely to reply, following the P-Only model, "Thanks for the advice. But I make a good living specializing in P variables." His sin is a selfish species of Ivory-Towerism. "Why do I need to concern myself with the entire argument? I do my specialty."

Well, so what? Don't you want to get the correct answer; or do you merely want to collect your paycheck? (Don't answer that.)

> *Numerous weighty sins requiring special grace*
> *to forgive but sins not peculiar to economics*

And then there are sins less easily forgiven, less easily put down to a prudent specialization that at least keeps P variables in the scientific game. The sins are shameful and scientifically damaging, I admit, having myself committed all of them at one time or another, sometimes for years and years. I am truly sorry and I humbly repent. But, goodness, if you are going to damn economics for these you are going to have to line up for damnation a considerable portion of the intelligentsia, commencing probably with your own sweet self.

Economists, for example, are Institutionally Ignorant, which is to say that they don't have much curiosity about the world they are trying to explain. For example – this will surprise you – academic economists, especially since Samuelsonianism took over, have come to think it is simply irrelevant, a waste of time, to do actual field work in the businesses they talk about. This is because (as they will explain to you patiently) people might lie, a point which is taken among economists to be a profound remark in proper scientific method. So (you will see the non sequitur) never ask a businessperson why she does something. Just observe, as though people were ants. The great economist Ronald Coase (also at the University of Chicago, Nobel 1991, but taking a different approach to P and S than Gary Becker does – Coase is no Samuelsonian), while still a student at the London School of Economics, had the startling idea of actually speaking to businesspeople. He has been trying ever since about October 1932 to get other economists to do the same thing. No soap. When two economists, Arjo Klamer and David Colander, asked economics graduate students what the skills were that made for a good economist, nearly two thirds named mathematical ability and the ability to think up quick little models of Prudence Only. How many named knowledge of the economic world as important? Go ahead, guess.

About three-and-a-half percent.

The figure was so shocking even to economists that it became part of an investigation into graduate programs by the American Economic Association. Reform was blocked by a member of the committee, also at the University of Chicago (are you seeing a pattern here?), who wants the math-with-Prudence-Only game to go on and on, undisturbed by scientific considerations.

Outsiders would likewise be amazed at the Historical Ignorance of the economist. They think that the scientific evidence about economies before the past few years would surely figure in an economist's data. It doesn't. One graduate program after another in the 1970s and 1980s cut the requirement that students become familiar with the economic past. I myself managed for twelve years to fend off the day of execution at the University of Chicago (now do you see the pattern?). The very month I left the department in disgust the barbarians inside the gates sent the economic history requirement to the guillotine, and since then Ph.D.s in economics from the University of Chicago have joined those at Minnesota, Princeton, and Columbia in ignorance of the economic past. At the same time almost all American graduate programs (my own fair Harvard was proudly among the first to do so) were abandoning the study of the past of economics itself. People call themselves economists who have never read a page of Adam Smith or Karl Marx or John Maynard Keynes. It would be like being an anthropologist who had never heard of Malinowski or an evolutionary biologist who had never heard of Darwin.

The more general Cultural Barbarism of economists is well illustrated by their Philosophical Naiveté. Few economists read outside economics. It is unnerving to gaze about the library of a distinguished professor of economics and find no books at all except on applied math and statistics: these are the worldly philosophers who run our nation? Uh-oh. So naturally the professors of economics have childish ideas about, say, epistemology. They think for example that early logical positivism (c. 1920), misunderstood because received third or fourth hand, is the latest philosophical word on meaningfulness. "Let's see now: I think I can recall from my high-school physics course. If a Hypothesis, H, does not imply materially observable Observations, O, then it is 'meaningless,' right? So that means... 'means'? Uh... well, let it go... that all ethics, introspections, accounts of mental states, metaphors, frames of meaning, literature and myths – and it would seem all of mathematics and philosophy itself, I guess; but that can't be right – are meaningless blabber. Hmm. There must be something wrong here. Well, good enough for government work."

The economists know nothing of the main finding of linguistics, philosophy, and literary criticism in the twentieth century, namely, that we have ways of world making, language games, senses of an ending that cannot be reduced to formal grammars, even in principle (economists have themselves stumbled on analogous findings in their own highly non-humanistic work, such as the finding of "rational expectations" or "the cheap talk paradox"). A famous story in linguistics illustrates the point. A very pompous linguist was giving a talk at Columbia and noted that there were languages in which a double negative meant a positive (standard English, for example: "I am not going to not speak" = "I am going to speak") and languages in which a double negative is a stronger negative (standard French and Italian, for example; or non-standard English: "You ain't got no class"). But, says he, articulating what he imagined was a universal of grammar, "There are no languages in which a double positive is a negative." Pause. Silence. Then came a loud and knowing sneer from the back of the room: "Yeah, yeah." Their high-school version of positivism means the economists depend on a high-school version of the philosophy of science. "Well, you see: if H implies O, then it follows rigorously that not-O implies not-H. So I can falsify a hypothesis simply by looking at the observable implications, O. What a wonderful simplification of my obligation to make scientific arguments! I can test the hypothesis that people vote with their pocketbooks, for example, just by looking at how a party's platform would affect voter Smith or Jones in their pocketbooks. And if it's not so falsified, it's confirmed, right?"

Never mind that Pierre Duhem pointed out as long ago as 1906 that the argument is nonsense in actual science because every experiment or observation has scientific controls (for example, S variables; or measuring devices and measuring errors) the truth or irrelevance of which needs to be assumed to make the test work. (Economists call this the specification problem.) So the specification is actually H and S1 and S2 and S3 and... implies not-O or not-S1 or not-S2 or not-S3 or ... This means that the "falsifying" observation may actually be a result of some failure of experimental control. And in fact on the frontiers of science the most usual quarrels are about just such matters: have you failed to control properly? Is your specification right? Is it rational to expect people to be rational in a voting booth when they have already shown their irrationality by showing up at the polls in the first place, considering that their (or rather, his or her) single vote is virtually certain not to change the outcome? Have you properly controlled for social solidarity and sentiment and other S variables affecting the vote, and are these uncorrelated with the included variable, P, the pocketbook effect?

The words "metaphysical" or "philosophical" are used in economics nowadays as terms of contempt: "That's rather philosophical, isn't it?" means, "What a stupid, unscientific point; only an English professor would say such a thing!" So not surprisingly economists adhere without criticism to, for instance, a high-school version of ethical philosophy. Economists believe that scientific and ethical questions are distinct, the one "positive" and the other "normative," and that real scientists ought to [hmm ...] stick to the positive. I know it's hard to believe, but most economists really do think that the positive/normative distinction lets them out of any reflection on ethics. They want to believe that: "Economics is like astronomy in having nothing to do with human affairs and therefore with the ethical universe in which humans live. No, wait, that can't be right: it has to do with human affairs – how else am I going to get paid for consulting or editorializing? – but the parts I deal with are Objective ... like who gets hurt by the imposition of free trade. Hmm. I'm having trouble with this. What I'm sure is that 'ought' and 'is' are entirely different realms and the scientist ought to ignore ... uhm... well ..."

And economists are tempted to arrogance in social engineering. Most humanists do not face the problem, since poets seldom think to ask English professors how to write poems – though of course "criticism" in the belletristic, three-star-awarding, judgments-of-Greatness sense does face the temptation, and normally yields to it; and in fact many poets have been influenced by criticism (Poe's criticism inspired Baudelaire; Emerson's inspired Whitman). Anthropologists know about the problem in their own work, and worry: am I becoming a tool of Western imperialism?

Since economists think themselves well informed about ethical philosophy if they have a muddy understanding of positive vs. normative, you can imagine the results. I would not want to accuse my colleagues of being engineers devising efficiently operating extermination chambers. At least not often. The libertarian streak in economics sometimes stays their hand. An economist would not view poor people as cattle to be herded into high-rise concentration camps – as architects in the 1950s, for example, demonstrably did; and as D. H. Lawrence and other democracy-haters earlier did. Or would they? What ethical consideration would stop them?

And economists are prone to an odd personality defect arising from their P-Only models, candid selfishness. When you ask a Chicago-School economist, "George, would you cooperate on this?" he is liable to answer, "No: it's not in my self-interest: don't you believe in economics?" When I left Chicago so long ago one of these people came up to me and said, "I suppose you aren't going to help grade the core examination – after all, you're out of here." I was astonished, and replied, "No, I'm going to fulfill my remaining obligations." He in turn was astonished. I do not think it raised his opinion of me, that I was so inconsistent in advocating a P-Only theory in economic history (as I was then) but not in everyday life. You mean you don't cheat your employer when you get a chance? You mean you don't impose burdens on your colleagues when it serves your narrow interests? Huh? What kind of an economist are you?

And I have to mention finally the very widespread opinion that economists are prone to the sin of pride – personal arrogance. Some names that come up in this connection are: Paul Krugman (gold medal in this category), Robert Lucas (Nobel 1995), and Deirdre McCloskey (bronze). Lots of intellectual professions are arrogant. Physicists, for example, are contemptuous of chemists, whom they regard as imperfect versions of themselves. In fact physicists are contemptuous of most people. But when a physicist at North Carolina named Robert Palmer went in 1989 to a conference in which physicists and economists were to educate each other he remarked, "I used to think that physicists were the most arrogant people in the world. The economists were, if anything, more arrogant." I'm afraid he's right on this score. Though of course in general he's a dope: a mere physicist.

Apologia: I have not, I realize, painted a very attractive picture of economics. But these sins are widespread; I repeat, among non-economists, too – even that odd one, candid selfishness, which you can find Nature's Economists articulating even when they aren't trained in it. But I earnestly invite you to learn by further reading in the literature the offsetting merits of economists:

Economists are for one thing serious about the public interest, and are often the only people defending it with any sort of lucidity and persuasiveness against the special interests. The model of worldly philosophy was originated in crude form by the early pamphleteers and political arithmeticians (among them Daniel Defoe). Adam Smith a half century and more later brought it to perfection.

And if you like engineers you will like many economists. Engineers are attractive people, hardworking (you have to be hardworking to absorb all that engineering math), earnest and practical, bent always on Solving the

Problem. True, they are often simpleminded. But simplicity gets the job done. Lots of economists are engineering types.

Or lawyer types. Like lawyers the economists are good arguers, which is good when you need a good argument ("How do you want it to come out?"). Economists can debate each other and yet not lose their tempers and not make irrelevant appeals to rank. Economists like lawyers are clear-minded, professionally. They are used to getting to the point and staying there. The humor of economists, unhappily, is often cynical, as it is also among lawyers, seldom generous, but that's true in many fields of the intellect.

But, above all, economics is about important matters. It would be remarkable if the economics-since-Marx that most non-economists would rather not read had nothing worthwhile in it. After all, thousands of apparently intelligent (they certainly think so) economists have labored away at it now for a century and a half.

I beseech you, dear reader; think it possible that economists, even Chicago-School economists, even Samuelsonian economists, have some important things to say about the economy.

The two real sins, almost peculiar to economics

A real science, or any intelligent inquiry into the world, whether the study of earthquakes or the study of poetry, economics or physics, history or anthropology, art history or organic chemistry, a systematic inquiry into one's lover or a systematic inquiry into the Dutch language, must do two things. If it only does one of them it is not an inquiry into the world. It may be good in some other way, but not in the double way that we associate with good science or other good inquiries into the world, such as a detective solving a case.

I am sure you will agree: An inquiry into the world must think and it must look. It must theorize and must observe. Formalize and record. Both. That's obvious and elementary. Not everyone involved in a collective intelligent inquiry into the world need do both: the detective can assign his dim-witted assistant to just observe. But the inquiry as a whole must reflect and must listen. Both. Of course.

Pure thinking, such as mathematics or philosophy, is not, however, to be disdained, not at all. Euler's equation, $e^{\pi i} + 1 = 0$, really is quite remarkable, linking "the five most important constants in the whole of analysis" (as Philip Davis and Reuben Hersh note), and would be a remarkable cultural achievement even if it had no worldly use. But certainly the equation is not a result of looking at the world. So it is not science; it is a kind of abstract art. Mathematicians are proud of the uselessness of most of what they do, as well they might be: Mozart is "useless," too; to what would you "apply" the Piano Sonata in A? I have a brilliant and learned friend who is an intellectual historian of note. He and I were walking to lunch in Iowa City one day and I said offhandedly, assuming he would of course know this, that mathematics was one of the great achievements of Western culture. He was so astonished by the claim that he stopped short and argued with me there on the sidewalk by the Old Capitol Mall: "Surely math is like plumbing: useful, but hardly in touch with deeper things; hardly a cultural achievement!" I tried to persuade him that he felt this way only because he had no acquaintance with mathematics, but I don't think I succeeded.

Nor is pure, untheorized observation to be disdained. There is something in narration, for example, that is untheorizable (though it is surprising to non-humanists how much of it can and has recently been theorized by literary critics). At some level a story is just a story, and artful choice of detail within the story is sheer observation – not brute observation, which is a hopeless ambition to record everything, but sheer. I have another brilliant and learned friend, an economist, who tells the story of how as a boy in Amsterdam he decided one day to embark in all seriousness on Social Observation. He was about ten years old when this ambition overcame him, so he equipped himself with a notebook and a pen and went to a big street and started to, well, observe. He decided to note down the license number of every car that passed. For many hours he kept it up, thrilled to be at last a real observer of society. But of course when he got home and looked at the results it occurred to him that the data were meaningless. They were brute facts unshaped by any meaningful human question, or emotion, or interest. One wishes every scholar learned this at 10 years old.

So pure mathematics, pure philosophy, the pure writing of pure fictions, the pure painting of pictures, the pure composing of sonatas are all, when done well or at least interestingly, admirable activities. I have to keep saying "pure" because of course it is entirely possible – indeed commonplace – for novelists, say, to take a scientific view of their subjects (Balzac, Zola, Sinclair Lewis among many others are well known for their self-conscious practice of a scientific literature; Roman satire is another case; or Golden Age Dutch painting). Likewise scientists use elements of pure narration (in evolutionary biology and economic history) or elements of pure mathematics (in physics and economics) to make scientific arguments. I do not want to get entangled in the apparently hopeless task of solving what is known as the Demarcation Problem, discerning a line between science and other activities. It is doubtful such a line exists. The efforts of many intelligent philosophers of science appear to have gotten exactly nowhere in solving it. I am merely suggesting that a science like many other human practices such as knitting or making a friend should be about the world, which means it should attend to the world. And it should also be something other than miscellaneous facts, such as the classification of animals in the Chinese Celestial Emporium of Benevolent Knowledge noted by Borges: (a) those that belong to the Emperor, (b) embalmed ones, (c) those that are trained, (d) suckling pigs, (e) mermaids, and so forth, down to (n) those that resemble flies from a distance. Not brute facts. And not mere theory.

So I am not dragging economics over to some implausible definition of Science and then convicting it of not corresponding to the definition. Such a move is common in economic methodology – for example in some of the less persuasive writings of the very persuasive economist Marc Blaug. I am merely saying that economists want to be involved in an intelligent inquiry into the world. If so, the field as a whole must theorize and observe, both. This is not controversial.

An economist at a leading graduate program listening to me will now burst out with: "Great! I entirely agree: theorize and observe, though of course as you admit we can specialize in one or the other as long as the whole field does both. And that, Deirdre, is exactly what we already do, on a massive scale. And we do it very well, if I don't say so myself. We do very sophisticated mathematical theorizing, such as in the Mas-Collel, Whinston, and Green textbook (1995), and then we test the theory in the world using very tricky econometrics, such as Jeffrey M. Wooldridge, *Econometric Analysis of Cross Section and Panel Data* (2001). You can see the results in any journal of economics. Some of it is pure theory, some econometrics. Theorize and observe."

To which I say: Bosh. She and her colleagues, when they are being most highbrow and Science-proud, don't really do either theorizing or observing. Economics in its most prestigious and academically published versions engages in two activities, qualitative theorems and statistical significance, which look like theorizing and observing, and have (apparently) the same tough math and tough statistics that actual theorizing and actual observing would have. But neither of them is what it claims to be. Qualitative theorems are not theorizing in a sense that would have to do with a double-virtued inquiry into the world. In the same sense, statistical significance is not observing.

This is the doubled-formed and secret sin and this the moment:

> *Eve*
> *Intent now wholly on her taste, naught else*
> *Regarded, such delight till then, as seemed,*
> *In fruit she never tasted, whether true*

Or fancied so, through expectation high
Of knowledge, nor was godhead from her
thought.   (Milton, *Paradise Lost*)

It is not difficult to explain to outsiders what is so dramatically, insanely, sinfully wrong with the two leading methods in high-level economics, qualitative theorems and statistical significance. It is very difficult to explain it to insiders, because the insiders cannot believe that methods in which they have been elaborately trained and which are used by the people they admire most are simply unscientific nonsense, having literally nothing to do with whatever actual scientific contribution (and I repeat, it is considerable) that economics makes to the understanding of society. So they simply can't grasp arguments that are plain to people not socialized in economics. (Bibliographical note to the insiders and the more adventuresome of the outsiders: see Chapters 10–13 in McCloskey 1994 and Chapters 7 and 8 in McCloskey 1998).

Hear, oh outsiders. I've told you how popular qualitative, Why/Whether reasoning is in economics. It takes this form: A implies C. Got it? Simple, huh? The crucial point is that the A and the C are indeed qualitative. They are not of the form "A is '4.8798'." They are of the qualitative form, "A is 'everyone is motivated by P-Only considerations'," say, which implies "free trade is neat." No numbers. You realize your lover will be annoyed by the neglected birthday to some degree, but we're not talking about magnitudes. Why/Whether. Not How Much. The economic "theorists" focus on what mathematicians call "existence theorems." With such and such general (or not so general, but anyway non-quantitative) assumptions A there exists a state of the imagined world C. A typical statement in economic "theory" is, "if information is symmetric, an equilibrium of the game exists" or, "if people are rational in their expectations in the following sense, buzz, buzz, buzz, then there exists an equilibrium of the economy in which government policy is useless."

Okay, now imagine an alternative set of assumptions (like the ones used earlier to "disprove" the Free Trade Theorem), A'. Look at that last item closely. If you're going to venture into the wonderful world of this really tough, macho math we economists deal in daily you are going to have to train yourself to look closely at symbols: notice that the alternative assumption has a little mark just after it, not in math called a "single quotation mark" but a "prime" (it's just a notation to distinguish one set of things – in this case assumptions – from another; it has nothing to do with prime numbers). A' is read "A prime." Naturally, if you change assumptions (introducing households who do not operate on P-Only motivations, say; or [I speak now to insiders] making information a little asymmetric; or [ditto] introduce any Second Best, such as monopoly or taxation; or [ditto] nonconvexities in production) in general the conclusion is going to change.

Natch. There's nothing deep or surprising about this: changing your assumptions changes your conclusions. Call the new conclusion C' (a test of whether you're paying attention, class: How is it read? Answer: "C single prime"). So we have the old A implies C and the fresh, publishable novelty, A' implies C'. But, as the mathematicians say, we can add another prime and proceed as before, introducing some other plausible possibility for the assumptions, A'' (read it "A double prime"), which implies its own C''. And so forth: A''' implies C'''. And on and on and on and on, until the economists get tired and go home.

What has been gained by all this? It is pure thinking, philosophy. It is not disciplined by any simultaneous inquiry into How Much. It's qualitative, not quantitative, and not organized to allow quantities into the story. It's like stopping with the conclusion that forgetting your lover's birthday will have some bad effect on one's relationship – you still have no idea how much, whether trivial or disastrous or somewhere in between. So the pure thinking is unbounded. It's a game of imagining how your lover will react endlessly. True, if you had good ideas about what were plausible assumptions to make, derived from some inquiry into the actual state of the world, the situation might be rescued for science and other inquiries into the world, such as the inquiry into the probable quantitative effect of missing a birthday on your lover's future commitment to you. But if not – and I'm telling you that such is the usual practice of "theoretical" pieces in economics, about half the items in any self-respecting journal of economic science – it's "just" an intellectual game.

I have expressed admiration for pure mathematics and for Mozart's concertos. Fine. But economics is supposed to be an inquiry into the world, not pure thinking. (If it is to be justified as pure thinking, just "fun," it is not very entertaining. No one would buy tickets to listen to a "theory" seminar in economics. Believe me on this one: as mathematical entertainment the stuff is really crummy.) The A-prime/C-prime, existence-theorem, qualitative-only "work" that economists do is like chess problems. Chess problems usually do not have anything to do even with playing real chess (since the situations are often ones that could not arise in a real game). And chess itself has nothing to do with living, except for its no doubt wonderful purity as thought, à la Mozart.

What kind of theory would actually contribute to a double-virtued inquiry into the world? Obviously, it would be the kind of theory for which actual numbers can conceivably be assigned. If Force equals Mass times Acceleration you have a potentially quantitative insight into the flight of cannon balls, say. But the qualitative theorems (explicitly advocated in Samuelson's great work of 1947, and thenceforth proliferating endlessly in the professional journals of academic economics) don't have any place for actual numbers. So the "results" keep flip-flopping, endlessly, pointlessly.

The history of economic "theory" since 1947 (and, as I said, in non-mathematical form since 1747, too) is replete with examples. Samuelson himself famously showed in the 1940s that "factor prices" (such as wages) are "equalized" by trade in steel and wheat and so forth – as a qualitative theorem, under such and such assumptions, A. It could be an argument against free trade. But shortly afterwards it was shown (by Samuelson himself, among others) that if you make alternative assumptions, A', you get very different conclusions. And so it went, and goes, with the limit achieved only in boredom, all over economics. Make thus-and-such assumptions, A, about the following game-theoretic model and you can show that a group of unsocialized individuals will form a civil society. Make another set of assumptions, A', and they won't. And so on and so forth. Blah, blah, blah, blah, to no scientific end.

Such stuff has taken over fields near to economics, first political science and now increasingly sociology. A typical "theoretical" paper in the *American Political Science Review* shows that under assumptions A the comity of nations is broken; in the next issue someone will show that under A' it is preserved. This is not theory in the sense that, say, physics uses the term. Pick up a copy of the *Physical Review* (it comes in four versions; pick any). Open it at random. You will find mind-breakingly difficult math, and physics that no one except a specialist in the particular tiny field can follow. But always, on every page, you will find repeated, persistent attempts to answer the question How Much. Go ahead: do it. Don't worry; it doesn't matter that you can't understand the physics. You will see that the physicists use in nearly every paragraph a rhetoric of How Much. Even the theorists as against the experimenters in physics spend their days trying to figure out ways of calculating magnitudes. The giveaway that something other than scientific is going on in "theoretical" economics (and, alas, political science) is that it contains not, from beginning to end of the article, a single attempt at a magnitude.

So: secret sin number one: qualitative theorems.

"But wait a minute, Deirdre," the Insider Economist breaks in (he is getting very, very annoyed because, as I told you, he Just Doesn't Get It). "You admitted that we economists also do econometrics, that is, formal testing of economic hypotheses using advanced statistical theory. You, as an economist, can hardly object to specialization: some people do theory, some empirical work."

Yes, my dear young colleague. Since I have been to your house and noted that you have not a single work on economics before your own graduate training I suppose you are not aware that the argument was first made explicit in 1957 by Tjalling Koopmans, a Dutch-American economist at Yale (Nobel 1975), who in his *Three Essays on the State of Economic Science* recommended just such a specialization. He recommended that "theorists" spend their time on gathering a "card file" of qualitative theorems attaching a sequence of axioms A′, A″, A‴, etc. to a sequence of conclusions C′, C″, C‴, etc., separated from the empirical work, "for the protection [note the word, students of free trade] of both."

Now this would be fine if the theorems were not qualitative. If they took the form that theorems do in physics (better called "derivations," since physicists are completely uninterested in the existence theorems that obsess mathematicians and philosophers), good. Then the duller wits like Deirdre McCloskey the economic historian could be assigned to mere observation, filling in blanks in the theory. But there are no blanks to fill in, no How Much questions asked, in the theory that economists admire the most and that has taken over half of their waking hours.

Still, things would not be so bad, so sunk in scientific sin, if on the lower-status empirical side of academic economics all was well. The empiricists like me in their dull-witted way could cobble together actual scientific hypotheses, simply ignoring the "work" of the qualitative theorists. Actual players of chess could ignore the "results" from chess problems. In effect this is what happens. The "theories" proffered by the "theorists" are not tested. In their stead linearized models that try crudely to control for this or that effect are used. An empiricist could therefore try to extract the world's information about the price sensitivity of demand for housing in Britain in the 1950s, say.

But the sin is double. The empirical economists also have become confused by qualitative "results." They, too, have turned away from one of the two questions necessary for a serious inquiry into the world (the other is Why), How Much. The sin sounds improbable, since empirical economics is drenched in numbers, but the numbers they acquire with their most sophisticated tools (as against their most common tools, such as simple enumeration and systems of accounting) are it turns out meaningless.

The confusion and meaninglessness arises from a particular technique in statistical studies, called "statistical significance." It has become since the cheapening of computation in the 1970s a plague in economics, in psychology, and, most alarmingly, in medical science. Consider the decades-long dispute over the prescribing of routine mammograms to screen for early forms of breast cancer. One school says, Start at age 40. The other says, No, age 50. (And still another, Never routinely. But set that aside.) Why do they differ? The American nurses' epidemiological study or the Swedish studies on which the empirical arguments are based are quite large. But there's a lot of what engineers call "noise" in the data, lots of things going on. So: although starting as early as age 40 does seem to have some effect, the samples are not large enough to be conclusive. By what standard? By the standard called "statistical significance [at the 5%, 1%, 0.1%, or whatever level]." The medical statisticians will be glad to explain to you (for example, the over-50 school will) that "significance" in this narrow and technical sense of the word tells you how likely it is the result comes just from the noise. A "highly" significant result is one in which the sample is large enough to overwhelm the noise. That is, it's unlikely – those 5%, 1%, etc. figures, successively more stringent— you'll be fooled into thinking there's an effect when in fact the effect in the real world is zero.

So the situation is this. The over-50 school admits that there is some positive effect in detecting early cancers from starting mammograms as early as age 40; but, they say with a sneer, it's uncertain. You'll be taking some chance of being fooled by chance. Nasty business. Really, something to avoid.

Huh? Are you telling me, Mr. Medical Statistician, that even though there is a life-saving effect of early mammograms in the data on average, you are uncomfortable about claiming it? I thought the purpose of medical research was to save lives. Your comfort is not, as I understand it, what we are chiefly concerned with. You find the data noisy. I'm sorry God arranged it that way. She should have been more considerate. But She's done what She's done. Now we have to decide if the cost of the test is worth the benefit. And your data shows that a benefit is there.

Mr. Medical Statistician, with some indignation: "No it's not. At conventional levels of significance there is no effect."

Deirdre, with more indignation: Nonsense. You are trying, alas, to make a qualitative judgment of existence. Compare the poor, benighted Samuelsonian "theorist." We always in science need How Much, not Whether. The effect is empirically there, whatever the noise is. If someone called "Help, help!" in a faint voice, in the midst of lots of noise, so that at the 1% level of significance (the satisfactorily low probability that you will be embarrassed by a false alarm) it could be that she's saying "Kelp, kelp!" (which arose perhaps because she was in a heated argument about a word proposed in a game of Scrabble), you wouldn't go to her rescue?

The relevant and quantitative question about routine mammograms, which has recently been reopened, is the balance of cost and benefit, since there could be costs (such as deaths from intrusive tests resulting from false positives) that offset the admittedly slight gain from starting as early as age 40. But suppose, as was long believed, that the costs do not offset the gain. That the net gain is slight is no comfort to the (few) people who die unnecessarily at 42 or 49 on account of Mr. Medical Statistician's gross misunderstanding of the proper role of statistics in scientific inquiries. A death is a death. The over-50 people are killing patients. Maybe only slightly more than zero patients. But more than zero is murder. [At this insult Mr. Medical Statistician leaps up and storms out of the room: I told you it was difficult to persuade the insiders; I wish I had a softer rhetoric to offer which would bring amoral idiots like Mr. Medical Statistician and Mr. Econometrician around gently; but as you can see it's just not in me.]

Or consider the aspirin-and-heart-attack studies. Researchers were testing the effects of administering half an aspirin a day to men who had already suffered a heart attack. To do the experiment correctly they gave one group the aspirin and the other a placebo. But they soon discovered – well short of conventional levels of statistical significance – that the aspirin reduced reoccurrences of heart attacks by about a third. What did they do? Did they go on with the study until they got a large enough sample of dead placebo-getters to be sure of their finding at levels of statistical significance that would make the referees of cardiology journals happy? Of course not: that would have been shockingly (though not unprecedentedly) unethical. They stopped the study, and gave everyone aspirin. (A New Yorker cartoon around the same time made the point, showing a tombstone inscribed, "John Smith, Member, Placebo Group.")

Or consider public opinion polls about who is going to win the next presidential election. These always come hedged about with warnings that the "margin of error is 2% plus or minus." So is the claim that prediction of a presidential election six months before it happens is only 2% off? Give me a break. What is being reported is the sampling error (and only at conventional levels of significance, themselves arbitrary). An error caused, say, by the revelation two months down the road that one of the candidates is an active child molester is not reckoned as part of "the error." You can see that a shell game is being performed here. The statement of a "probable error" of 2% is silly. A tiny part of all the errors that can afflict a prediction of a far-off political event is being elevated to the rhetorical status of The Error. "My streetlight under sampling theory is very bright, so let's search for the keys under the streetlight, even though I lost them in the dark." Get serious.

The point here is that such silliness utterly dominates empirical economics. In a study of all the empirical articles in the *American Economic Review* in the 1980s it was discovered that fully 96% of them confused statistical and substantive significance (look at McCloskey 1998; or at McCloskey and Ziliak 1996; check it out on JSTOR; we are writing a paper examining the same journal in the 1990s; bad news: the sin has gotten more prevalent, not less).

The problem is that a number fitted from the world's experiments can be important economically without being noise-free. And it can be wonderfully noise-free without being important.

On the one hand: It's completely obvious, you will agree, that a "statistically insignificant" number can be very significant for some human purpose. If you really, truly want to know how the North American Free Trade Agreement affected the average worker in the United States, then it's too bad if the data are noisy, but that's not the point. You really, truly want to know it. You have to go with what God has provided. And on the other hand: It is also completely obvious that a "statistically significant" result can be insignificant for any human purpose. When you are trying to explain the rise and fall of the stock market it may be that the fit (so-called: it means how closely the data line up) is very "tight" for some crazy variable, say skirt lengths (for a long while the correlation was actually quite good). But it doesn't matter: the variable is obviously crazy. Who cares how closely it fits? For a long time in Britain the number of ham radio operator licenses granted annually was very highly correlated with the number of people certified insane. Very funny. So?

In short, statistical significance is neither necessary nor sufficient for a result to be scientifically significant. Most of the time it is irrelevant. A researcher is simply committing a scientific error to use it as it is used in economics and the other social sciences and in medical science and (a strange one, this) population biology as an all-purpose way of judging whether a number is large enough to matter. Mattering is a human matter; the numbers figure, but after collecting them the mattering has to be decided finally by us; mattering does not inhere in a number. The point is just common sense. It is not subtle or controversial. But thousands of scientists, and among them almost all modern economists, are utterly confused about it.

Physics and chemistry, though of course highly numerical, hardly ever use statistical significance (check it out for yourself: I have in the journal *Science*, for example). Economists and those others use it compulsively, mechanically, erroneously to provide a non-controversial way of deciding whether or not a number is large. You can't do it this way. No competent statistical theorist has disagreed with me on this point since Neyman and Pearson in 1933. There is no mechanical procedure that can take over the last, crucial step of an inquiry into the world, asking How Much in human terms that matter.

My argument is not against statistics in empirical work, no more than it is against mathematics in theoretical work. It is against certain very particular and peculiar practices of economic science and a few other fields. Economics has fallen for qualitative "results" in "theory" and significant/insignificant "results" in "empirical work." You can see the similarity between the two. Both are looking for on/off findings that do not require any tiresome inquiry into How Much, how big is big, what is an important variable, how much exactly is its oomph. Both are looking for machines to produce publishable articles. In this last they have succeeded since Samuelson spoke out loud and bold beyond the dreams of intellectual avarice. Bad science – using qualitative theorems with no quantitative oomph and statistical significance also with no quantitative oomph – has driven out good.

The progress of economic science has been seriously damaged. You can't believe anything that comes out of the Two Sins. Not a word. It is all nonsense, which future generations of economists are going to have to do all over again. Most of what appears in the best journals of economics is unscientific rubbish. I find this unspeakably sad. All my friends, my dear, dear friends in economics, have been wasting their time. You can see why I am agitated about the Two Sins. They are vigorous, difficult, demanding activities, like hard chess problems. But they are worthless as science.

The physicist Richard Feynman called such activities Cargo Cult Science. Certain New Guinea tribesmen had prospered mightily during World War II when the American Air Force disgorged its cargo to fight the Japanese. After the War the tribesmen wanted the prosperity to come back. So they started a "cargo cult." Out of local materials they built mock airports and mock transport planes. They did an amazingly good job: the cargo-cult airports really do look like airports, the planes like planes. The only trouble is, they aren't actually. Feynman called sciences he didn't like "cargo cult sciences" (he was, ill-advisedly I think, going after sociology: apparently he was not acquainted with the considerable amount of good, non-statistical-significance yet quantitative and empirical and theoretically meaningful sociology, such as long ago that of C. Wright Mills). By "cargo cult" he meant that they looked like science, had all that hard math and statistics, plenty of long words; but actual science, actual inquiry into the world, was not going on.

I am afraid that my science of economics has come to the same point. Paul Samuelson, though a splendid man and a wonderful economist (honestly), is a symbol of the pointlessness of qualitative theorems. Samuelson, actually, is more than merely a symbol – he made and taught and defended the Two Sins, at one time almost singlehandedly. It was a brave stance. But it had terrible outcomes. Samuelson advocated the "scientific" program of producing qualitative theorems, developing qualitative-theorem-generating-functions (I am making an insider's statistical joke: ha, ha; such is economic humor), such as "revealed preference" and "overlapping generations models" and above all the machinery of Max U. He was involved also (it turns out somewhat surprisingly) in the early propagation of significance testing, the "scientific" method of empirical work running on statistical significance [technical remark: sans loss functions], through his first Ph. D. student, Lawrence Klein (Nobel 1980). Two sins, one scientist.

So it is only fair to call both the sins of modern economics Samuelsonian. It is rather similar to the situation in linguistics: their Great MIT Leader is Noam Chomsky (on whom views differ strongly as to whether or not he is a splendid man). Chomsky's mechanical approach to grammar, fiercely denying pragmatics and therefore the main finding of the humanities in the twentieth century, blocks progress. So too economics. Until economics stops believing, contrary to its own principles, that an intellectual free lunch is to be gotten from qualitative theorems and statistical significance it will be stuck on the ground waiting at the cargo-cult airport, at any rate in its high-end activities uninterested in (Really) How Much. High-end theoretical and econometric papers will be published. Careers will be made, thank you very much. Many outstanding fellows (and no women) will get chairs at Princeton and Chicago. But our understanding of the economic world will continue to be crippled by the spreading, ramifying, hideous sin.

Woe, woe is me. Oy vey ist mir. Pity the poor economists. The sins of economics come from pride in formalization, the making of great machines and monsters:

> ... and called me Sin, and for a sign
> Portentous held me; but familiar grown,
> I pleased, and with attractive graces won
> The most averse.   (Milton, *Paradise Lost*)

And pity, I repeat, poor old Deirdre, who appears to be doomed to keep making these arguments, showing more and more plainly that the two main methods of academic economics are nonsense, without being believed.

Cassandra, you know, was the most beautiful of the daughters of Priam, King of Troy. The god Apollo fell for her and made her a prophetess. In exchange he wanted sexual favors, which she refused. So he cursed her, in a most malicious way. He had already given her the power of prophecy, to know for example what would happen to a science that refused to ask seriously How Much. His curse was to add that though she would continue to be correct in her prophecies, no one would believe her.

Cassandra [to Trojan economists proposing to bring the wooden horse into the city]: The horse is filled with enemy soldiers! If you bring it into the city, economics is lost! Please don't!

Leading Trojan Economist: Uh, yeah, I see what you mean, Cassie. Good point. Enemy soldiers. Inside. City lost. Qualitative theorems useless for a science. Statistical significance without a loss function equally useless. Economics ruined. Thanks very much for your prophecy. Great contribution. Love your stuff. [Turning to colleagues] Okay, guys, let's bring that sucker in!

References

McCloskey, D. N. (1994). *Knowledge and Persuasion in Economics.* Cambridge University Press.

(1998). *The Rhetoric of Economics, 2nd Edition.* Madison: University of Wisconsin Press.

McCloskey, D. N. and S. Ziliak (1996) "The Standard Error of Regression," *Journal of Economic Literature,* 34, 97–114.

9   Do we try to teach our students too much?

Robert Frank

In recent months, I have been asked to speak to a variety of groups about how to improve the quality of teaching in introductory courses. Because most of these groups have been outside my home discipline of economics, I have felt apprehensive about accepting these invitations, fearing that my observations might be relevant only for introductory economics courses. Except for a freshman math course I taught during my senior year at Georgia Tech and a two-year stint as a high-school science teacher as a Peace Corps volunteer in rural Nepal, 100 percent of my teaching experience has been confined to economics.

In the course of that experience, I have discovered ways in which most principles of economics courses taught in American universities fall short of their potential. My conversations with colleagues in other departments have persuaded me that similar problems may plague introductory courses in other disciplines. But others can be the judge of that. My general message is most introductory economics courses attempt to teach students far too much.[1]

Two years after I began teaching at Cornell, several friends living in different cities mailed me copies of a New Yorker cartoon in which a woman introducing a man to a friend at a party says, "I'd like to introduce you to Marty Thorndecker. He's an economist, but he's really very nice."

Cartoons are data. If people get them, that tells us something about the world. Even before Arno's cartoon appeared, I had already begun to notice that when people I'd meet at social gatherings would ask me what I did for a living, they almost always seemed disappointed when I told them I was an economist. After a while, I began asking them why. In most cases, they appeared to think seriously about my question, and many would mention having taken an introductory economics course years ago that had had "all those horrible graphs."

---

[1] The themes of this chapter are developed more fully in Frank (2007).

About 40 percent of American undergraduates take at least one economics course, 19 percent take only one, and only 2 percent go on to major in economics. A negligible fraction of majors goes on to do Ph.D. work in economics. Yet many introductory economics courses are pitched to that negligible fraction. The result, I believe, is that most students don't learn very much in these courses. Indeed, we now have evidence that introductory economics courses leave little measurable trace on the students who take them. Thus, when these students are given tests to probe their knowledge of basic economics six months after having taken the course, they do not perform significantly better than others who never took the course at all (Hansen et al. 2002). This is scandalously bad performance. How can a university justify asking parents to spend many thousands of dollars for their children to take courses that add no value?

Even the very most basic principles of economics don't seem to be getting across. If you ever took an economics course, you have heard the term "opportunity cost." It is by consensus one of the two or three most important ideas in the introductory course. Yet we now have persuasive evidence that most students do not master this concept in any fundamental way. Even more troubling, we have evidence that the professors who are trying to teach it to them may not really understand it themselves. Opportunity cost was not well explained when they were introductory students, and in advanced courses it was simply assumed that everyone already understood the concept.

The basis for these claims is a recent study done by a former student of mine, Paul Ferraro, and his colleague Laura Taylor (Ferraro and Taylor 2005). They took an opportunity cost question from my introductory textbook and gave it to various groups of people to see whether they could answer it.

Here is the question:

You won a free ticket to see an Eric Clapton concert. You can't resell it. Bob Dylan is performing on the same night and his concert is the only other activity you are considering. A ticket to see Dylan costs $40 and on any given day you would be willing to pay $50 to see Dylan perform. There is no other cost of seeing either performer. What is the opportunity cost of attending the Clapton concert?

The opportunity cost of an activity is the value of everything you must give up to pursue it. So if you are willing to pay as much as $50 to see Dylan and the cost of a ticket to see Dylan is $40, what is the opportunity cost of seeing Clapton?

Respondents were given only these four choices:

a. $0
b. $10
c. $40
d. $50

The correct answer is $10, because the only thing of value you must sacrifice to attend the Clapton concert is seeing the Dylan concert, and the value of that sacrifice is $10. (Seeing Dylan would have been worth $50 to you, but you also would have had to buy a $40 ticket to see him, so the value of what you give up by not seeing him is just $50 – $40 = $10.)

This seems fairly straightforward, and it is. Yet when 270 undergraduates who had previously taken a course in economics were confronted with this question, only 7.4 percent of them answered it correctly. Since there were only four choices, students who just picked at random would have had a correct response rate of 25 percent. So a little bit of knowledge seems to be a dangerous thing here.

When Ferraro and Taylor posed the same question to 88 students who had never taken an economics course, 17.2 percent of them answered it correctly – more than twice the correct response rate as for former economics students, but still less than chance accuracy.

Why didn't the economics students perform much better? As Ferraro and Taylor suggest, the instructors who teach them economics do not seem to have mastered the basic opportunity cost concept very well themselves. When they posed the same question to a sample of 199 professional economists at the annual American Economic Association meeting in 2005, only 21.6 percent chose the correct answer; 25.1 percent of respondents thought the opportunity cost of attending the Clapton concert was $0; 25.6 percent thought it was $40; and 27.6 percent thought it was $50.

When Ferraro and Taylor examined the leading introductory economics textbooks, they discovered that most did not devote sufficient attention to the opportunity cost concept to enable students to answer the question they posed. They also noted that the concept receives only cursory treatment in textbooks beyond the introductory level and that the term opportunity cost does not even appear in the indexes of the leading graduate microeconomics texts.

If opportunity cost really is one of the most important ideas in economics, then we should not permit introductory students to leave the course without a firm grasp of it. To do better, we must decide up front what the most important ideas are, and then hammer away repeatedly at each of them over the course of the semester, making students use these ideas for themselves. The good news is that if we do this, students can master our most important ideas in just a single semester.

My first exposure to the less-is-more approach came in the Nepali language instruction I received in my Peace Corps training program. Prior to that experience, I had taken four years of Spanish in high school and three semesters of German in college. But when I traveled in Spain and Germany, I had great difficulty communicating even basic thoughts in those languages. Our Nepali program lasted only 13 weeks, and its teaching method was very different from the one I had experienced in my earlier courses. In those courses, we spent a lot of time on the pluperfect subjunctive tense and other grammatical arcana that professors thought important. But we didn't learn to speak. The Peace Corps program never once mentioned the pluperfect subjunctive. Its task was to teach us to speak the language, and mastering sophisticated tenses was simply not on the critical path to that goal. The program's aim was to mimic the way a child learns to speak its native language.

Our instructor began with the simplest of sentences and had us repeat them multiple times. The first was "This hat is expensive." Since one must bargain for everything one buys in Nepal, it was a useful sentence. The next step was to announce a different noun – say, "long socks" – and we would have to respond on the fly by reciting the Nepali sentence for "These long socks are expensive." The goal was to get us to be able to respond without even thinking about it.

In sum, they started with a simple example from a familiar context, had us drill it several times, then had us do slight variations on it, drilling again at each step. Once we could function on our own at the current level – but not before – they would push us a little further.

The program's responsibility was to make sure we were up and running after 13 weeks. My fellow volunteers and I had to teach science and math in Nepali shortly after arriving in the country. And starting from zero, we were able to do it. The process itself created a sense of empowerment that I had never experienced in my more traditional language courses.

Most instructors tend to ask themselves, "How much can I cover today?" And if they manage to cover a lot on a given day, they are pleased with themselves. But what we really should be asking is "How much can my students absorb?" Technology has reinforced the tendency to cover too much. We can now show students more material in an hour than ever before, but that's not a good thing.

Principles of economics courses generally try to do too much. Most are taught from encyclopedic texts that feature not only brief treatments of the opportunity cost concept, but also brief treatments of almost every other idea that economists have ever written about. With this diagnosis of the problem in hand, Ben Bernanke and I wrote an introductory economics text that focused on a short list of core principles (Frank and Bernanke 2000). This approach is especially well suited to economics, because there are really just a small number of basic ideas that do most of the heavy lifting in our discipline. Of course, not all economists would agree that ours was precisely the right list of core principles to emphasize. But the important point is that most such lists would have substantial overlap, and students would almost surely do better working from a list of this sort than with the usual encyclopedic approach.

If I could teach students only one economic principle, it would be the cost–benefit principle. It says that you should take an action if and only if the extra benefit from taking it is greater than the extra cost. Could there be a simpler sounding principle? But the cost–benefit principle turns out to be difficult to apply correctly, and I think students really master it only by seeing it in multiple familiar contexts and being repeatedly required to use it actively themselves.

I typically begin by asking them how they would make the decision posed in this example:

You are about to buy a $20 alarm clock at the campus store next door when a friend tells you that the same clock is available for $10 at the Kmart downtown. Do you go downtown and get the clock for $10? Or do you buy it at the nearby campus store?

Of course, there is no universally right answer or wrong answer. Each person has to weigh the relevant costs and benefits. But when we ask students what they would do in this situation, most say they would go downtown to buy the clock at KMart.

I then ask them a second question:

You are about to buy a laptop for $2510 at the campus store next door. You can get the very same laptop downtown at Kmart for $2500 (and it comes with the same warranty: no matter where you buy it, you have to send it to Dell if it breaks). Where would you buy the laptop?

This time, most say they would buy it at the campus store. That, by itself, isn't a wrong answer, either. But if we ask what a rational person should do in these two cases, the cost–benefit principle makes clear that the answers must be the same in both. After all, the benefit of going downtown is $10 in each case, the dollar amount you save. The cost is whatever value you assign to the hassle of going downtown, also the same in both cases. And if the costs are the same and the benefits are the same in both cases, then the answer should be the same as well.

Most people seem to think, however, that because they save 50 percent on the clock by buying downtown, that is somehow a more compelling benefit than saving only $10 on the $2510 laptop. That is not the right way to think about it. In many other contexts, thinking about things in percentage terms works reasonably well, but not here.

So weighing costs and benefits obviously is what you should do. And once people see that they don't have an automatic impulse to weigh the right costs and benefits, that grabs their attention. They go back to their dorms and pose the same questions to their friends. They seem to enjoy it when their friends, too, make inconsistent choices.

By seeing how the cost–benefit principle works in the context of a surprising example, they come away with an interesting story to tell. And in the process of telling it, their mastery of the principle is strengthened. If the example is not interesting, or if it comes from a context with which they are totally unfamiliar, they are unlikely to repeat it to others later on.

Immediately after I show students examples that illustrate a general principle, I give them an exercise that requires them to employ the principle on their own. Here's the question I pose to them after they've seen the clock and computer examples:

You have one discount coupon to use for an upcoming business trip. You can either save $90 on a $200 trip to Chicago or save $100 on a $2,000 trip to Tokyo. For which trip should you use your coupon?

Almost everybody answers correctly that you should use it for the Tokyo trip because that way you will save $100, which is better than saving $90. But the fact that everyone gets it right doesn't mean that the question wasn't worth asking. Again, our goal is for the core ideas to become part of students' working knowledge. And the only way that can happen is through active practice. If we spend all our time showing them new ideas, there is little time left for practice.

I will now describe an assignment that I stumbled onto by chance when I was participating in the "writing across the disciplines program" at Cornell some 20 years ago. The program was inspired by research showing that one of the best ways to learn about something is to write about it. As Walter Doyle and Kathy Carter, two proponents of the narrative theory of learning, have written, "At its core, the narrative perspective holds that human beings have a universal predisposition to 'story' their experience, that is, to impose a narrative interpretation on information and experience" (Doyle and Carter 2003). The psychologist Jerome Bruner, another narrative learning theorist, observes that children "turn things into stories, and when they try to make sense of their life they use the storied version of their experience as the basis for further reflection ... If they don't catch something in a narrative structure, it doesn't get remembered very well, and it doesn't seem to be accessible for further kinds of mulling over" (Bruner 1985).

In short, although the human brain can absorb information in abstract forms like equations and graphs, its specialty seems to be absorbing information in narrative form. The writing assignment I employ in my course plays directly to this strength. It is to pose an interesting question and then use some of the basic principles that we have talked about in class to answer it. The total assignment has a maximum length of one page. I call it the "economic naturalist" writing assignment, because it was inspired by the kinds of questions that an introductory course in biology enables students to answer. If you know a little biological theory, you can see things you didn't notice before. The theory identifies texture and pattern in the world that is stimulating to recognize and think about.

For example, here is a standard Darwinian question: "Why are males much bigger than females in most animal species?" Bull elephant seals, for instance, grow upwards of 20 feet long and weigh as much as 6000 pounds, whereas female elephant seals weigh only 800 to 1200 pounds.

Similar, if less pronounced, sexual dimorphism is observed in almost all sexually reproducing species. The Darwinian explanation is that because most species are polygamous – meaning that males take more than one mate, if they can (since there is usually a 50–50 sex ratio in the breeding population, if some males take more than one mate, the law of musical chairs ensures that other males won't take any mates at all) – males must battle one another for access to mates. Among elephant seals, for instance, bulls pummel one another on the beach for hours at a time, until one finally retreats, bloodied and exhausted.

The winners of these battles command nearly exclusive sexual access to harems of as many as 100 females. This is a Darwinian prize of the first order. A male with a mutant gene that coded for larger size would be much more likely to prevail in fights with other males, which means that this gene would appear with higher frequency in the next generation. In short, the reason that males are so large is that small males seldom gain access to females.

A similar explanation accounts for the large tail displays in peacocks. Experiments have demonstrated that peahens prefer peacocks with longer tail feathers, which are thought to be a signal of robust health, since parasite-ridden males simply cannot maintain a bright, long tail display.

In both of these cases – being a big elephant seal or being a peacock with a long tail display – what is advantageous to males individually is disadvantageous to them as a group. Thus, a 6000-pound seal finds it harder to escape from the great white shark, its principal predator. If seals could all cut their weight by half, that would be advantageous. The same fights would be won by the same animals, yet each would be better able to escape from predators. Similarly, if peacocks' tail displays were all reduced by half, females would still choose the same males as before, yet all peacocks would be better able to escape from predators. But elephant seals are stuck with their current size and peacocks are stuck with their long tail feathers.

The biologist's narrative is interesting. It coheres. And it seems to be right. Thus, if you look at monogamous species, ones in which males and females pair off for life, you don't see sexual dimorphism. This is the exception that proves the rule in the old-fashioned sense of the verb to prove. It tests the rule. Polygyny was what led to the prediction that males would be bigger. And when we don't have polygyny, the males are not bigger. For example, because the albatross is monogamous, theory predicts that males and females will be roughly the same size, which in fact they are.

The biologist's narrative regarding sexual dimorphism has legs. It is easy to remember and satisfying to recount to others. It is the same with narrative explanations based on principles of economics.

For several reasons, it is useful to insist that students pose the most interesting questions they can for their economic naturalist writing assignments. For one thing, to come up with an interesting question, students must usually consider numerous preliminary questions, and this itself is a useful exercise. What is more, once a student poses an interesting question, he or she is much more likely to tell others about it. If you can't actually take an idea outside the classroom and use it, then it will never become your idea. But once you use it on your own, it becomes yours forever.

Let me share with you some of the questions my students have posed and answered in recent years. My all-time favorite was submitted by Jennifer Dulski, who asked, "Why do brides spend so much money on wedding dresses – thousands of dollars in many cases – while grooms often rent cheap tuxedos, even though grooms could potentially wear their tuxedos on many other occasions and brides will never wear their dresses again?" It's a great question. There is a twist to it, a paradox. Ms. Dulski began with the assumption that on big occasions it is more important for women to make a fashion statement than for men. Most people seem comfortable enough with that assumption, and there is even some biological support for the idea that in mostly monogamous species, such as humans, displays are sometimes more pronounced for females than males.

In any event, if a woman wanted to make a distinctive fashion statement, a rental company would need to stock perhaps 30 or 40 gowns in
each size. Each gown would be rented maybe once every six or seven
years. So the rental price the company would need to charge to cover the
cost of that largely stagnant inventory would be about 20 percent more
than the purchase price. Nobody would rent at that price. If you can buy
for $1000, why rent for $1200?

So that is why women buy their wedding dresses. Men rent their
tuxedos because they are willing to settle for a standard style. That means
that the rental company can have 2 or 3 suits in each size, so each suit will
turn over seven or eight times a year. This permits the company to rent
suits for about a third of their purchase price.

I tell my students that the answer to the question they pose doesn't
have to be right; it just has to be plausible. The question has to be
interesting, and the answer has to be plausible.

Why are child safety seats required in cars but not in airplanes? This is
another of my favorites. Greg Ballet asked it. In a car, he noted, you must
put your child into a safety seat just to go to the supermarket. Yet you can
keep your child on your lap untethered when you fly from New York to
LA. Why is that? Some have suggested that it is because if the plane
crashes, you are going to die anyway, whether you are strapped in or not.
That is true, but there are many other things that happen short of a
crash – severe turbulence, for example – for which being belted in helps a
lot. The explanation he suggested was that once you have a child's safety
seat, it is free to strap your child into it in the back seat of your car,
because there is almost always room for it, and so the benefit outweighs
the cost. If you are on a full flight from New York to LA, however, you
must buy an extra ticket in order to strap your child into a safety seat. So
the cost of strapping your child in under those circumstances may run as
high as $1000. People don't feel comfortable saying it is too expensive to
provide the extra safety for their children, but that is really what it boils
down to. They hold tight to their children and hope for the best rather
than pay $1000 for an extra seat.

Another of my favorite questions was posed by Bill Tjoa, who asked
why the keypad buttons on drive-up ATMs have Braille dots. Obviously
there aren't any blind drivers. The reason, he suggested, was that because
manufacturers must make keypads with Braille dots for walk-up ATMs
anyway, it is cheaper just to make all machines the same way. The
alternative, after all, would be to hold two separate inventories and make
sure that the right machines ended up at the right destinations. If the
Braille dots caused trouble for the sighted drivers who use them, that
might be a reason to incur the extra expense. But they do not.

When Ben Bernanke and I put this example in our book, somebody sent me an angry email saying the reason for the Braille dots is that the Americans with Disabilities Act requires them. He sent me a link to a webpage documenting his claim. And sure enough, there is a requirement that all ATM keypads have Braille dots, even at drive-up locations. There are even occasions in which Braille dots on drive-up machines might be useful. For example, a blind person might visit a drive-up machine in a taxi and not want to reveal his PIN to the driver.

I wrote back to my correspondent that I tell my students that their answers don't have to be correct. But I also urged him to think about the circumstances under which the regulation was adopted. If it had been significantly more costly to require Braille dots on the drive-up machines, would they have enacted that regulation? Almost certainly not. The simple fact is that it was costless to put them there. And since they cause no harm and might occasionally be of use, regulators might well ask, why not require them (if only to be able to say they had done something useful)? I think Mr. Tjoa's explanation is much better than my angry correspondent's explanation.

Karen Hittle asked why, if you start in Kansas City and you fly to Honolulu round-trip, the fare is a lot lower than if you start the same trip in Honolulu and fly to Kansas City round-trip. Passengers travel on the same planes, consuming the same fuel, the same in-flight amenities, and so on. So why are the fares so different?

Ms. Hittle argued that if you are starting in Kansas City and going to Honolulu, you are probably going on vacation. You could go to lots of different places. You could go to Florida, to Barbados, to Cancun. Because vacationers have many destinations to choose from, airlines must compete fiercely for their business. Given economies of scale inherent in larger aircraft, carriers have a strong incentive to fill additional seats by targeting lower prices to the people who are more sensitive to price – vacationers.

But if you are starting in Honolulu on a trip to Kansas City, you are probably not a vacationer. More likely, you either have business or family reasons for traveling. So you are probably not shopping for a destination if you are going to Kansas City. And that is why the fares are different.

These are all great questions. Here is another one: Why do residents of Manhattan tend to be rude and impatient, while residents of Topeka tend to be friendly and courteous? You could argue with the premise, but most people seem to find it roughly descriptive. If you ask for directions in Topeka, people stop and help you; in Manhattan, they often don't even make eye contact. Tom Harris suggested that because Manhattan has the highest wage rate and the richest menu of things to do of any city on the planet, the opportunity cost of people's time is very high there.

So if you waste people's time in Manhattan, they are naturally quicker to show displeasure than if you waste people's time in Topeka.

Why do predominantly male legislatures enact statutes prohibiting polygamy? That is an interesting question, too. If polygamy is such a great deal for men, why do male legislators vote to prohibit it? Why do manual transmissions have six forward speeds, most automatics only four or five? The list of interesting questions is endless.

My wife and I were in Boston recently and passed a small restaurant in the Quincy Market that had one of those signs saying, "If you don't get a receipt when you pay, we will refund the price of your meal." My wife asked me, "What are those signs all about?" and I was thrilled to be able to tell her that a student last semester had posed precisely that question. The answer he suggested was that because it is difficult for restaurant owners to monitor the behavior of their employees, a cashier is in a position to charge you for your meal, then hit the no-sale button and pocket the money you gave him. If the owner offers you a free meal if you don't get a receipt, then the cashier has to run the sale through the register. The offer is just a way to keep the cashier honest.

Again, my teaching experience is almost entirely in economics. I don't have systematic evidence about the extent to which the tendency to teach too much plagues introductory courses in other disciplines. But there are hints. Both physicists and engineers, for example, have told me that this is a problem in their own introductory courses. The authors of high school biology and math texts also appear to show little restraint in the amount of material they throw at students. And I participated in a faculty seminar a few semesters ago that made me think that similar problems might exist in the humanities. Humanists and social scientists took turns leading the seminar, which meant assigning a few articles and leading that week's discussion. One of the articles we were asked by a humanist to read was "Tactical Strategies of the Streetwalker," by Maria Lugones. The following passage from this article was fairly typical of the discourse in other humanities articles we were assigned to read:

I propose to embrace tactical strategies in moving in disruption of the dichotomy, as crucial to an epistemology of resistance/liberation. To do so is to give uptake to the disaggregation of collectivity concomitant with social fragmentation and to theorize the navigation of its perils without giving uptake to its logic ...

Ms. Lugones does not seem to be trying to communicate with her readers. Rather she seems to be eager to demonstrate her erudition. The same applies to many young economists, who display their technical virtuosity by proving theorems for their freshmen. Teachers across the disciplines appear to have lost sight of the fact that the cognitive resources of students are a scarce resource. Our introductory courses are our one opportunity to persuade them that we have ideas worthy of their time and attention. To go into the introductory economics classroom and start proving theorems is to squander that opportunity.

I mentioned earlier studies showing that six months after having taken an introductory economics course, students perform no better on tests of basic economics than others who never took the course. Does an introductory course designed to emphasize the less-is-more approach work any better? I have no systematic data to report, although I hope to have some soon. But from conversations I have had with former students who come back to Cornell for class reunions, I feel confident that the economic naturalist assignment has a lasting impact. Once students learn to pose and answer interesting economic questions, many of them just keep on doing it. Their mastery of the economic way of thinking does not seem to have decayed in the years since they took the course. On the contrary, because they keep on using the ideas actively, their facility with them seems to have kept growing.

The learning curve associated with the economic naturalist writing assignment is steep. Students must submit two papers during the semester, one at mid-term, the other at term's end. Many students seem to find it difficult to pose an interesting question on the first round, but by the time their second paper comes due, the more common complaint is that they find it difficult to choose which of their several interesting questions to use.

In sum, what appears to work in the introductory economics course is to begin with a short list of the ideas we consider most important, and then imbed those ideas in the context of as many interesting examples as possible, all the while demanding that students actively use the ideas. That is the same strategy that worked so well in my Nepali language instruction class.

Don't ask how much you can cover; ask how much your students can learn. Start simple, repeat and drill. The narrative theory of learning suggests that learning economics is like learning to speak a new language. In both cases, you can't make real progress without actually doing it. The key is to provide students with tools that enable students to do something rewarding on their own.

References

Bruner, Jerome 1985. "Narrative and Paradigmatic Modes of Thought." In
    E. W. Eisner (ed.), *Learning and Teaching the Ways of Knowing*,
    84th Yearbook, Part 2, of the National Society for the Study of Education,
    University of Chicago Press, 97–115.

Doyle, Walter and Kathy Carter 2003. "Narrative and Learning to Teach:
   Implications for Teacher-Education Curriculum," *Journal of Curriculum
   Studies*, 35(2), 129–137. http://faculty.ed.uiuc.edu/westbury/JCS/Vol35/
   DOYLE.HTM
Ferraro, Paul J. and Laura O. Taylor 2005. "Do Economists Recognize an
   Opportunity Cost When They See One? A Dismal Performance from the
   Dismal Science," *The B.E. Journal of Economic Analysis & Policy*, 4(1).
Frank, Robert H. 2007. *The Economic Naturalist*, Basic Books.
Frank, Robert H. and Ben S. Bernanke 2000. *Principles of Economics*,
   McGraw-Hill.
Hansen, W. Lee, Michael. K. Salemi, and John J. Siegfried 2002. "Use It or Lose
   It: Teaching Economic Literacy," *American Economic Review (Papers and
   Proceedings)*, 92 (May), 463–472.

10 The perils of narrative teaching in economics

Jack Vromen

Introduction

With *The Economic Naturalist: In Search of Explanations for Everyday Enigmas*, Robert H. Frank has written yet another book that makes for a nice, entertaining, and at the same time also enlightening and engrossing reading experience. Unfortunately, books that are not only fun to read but that are also instructive are rare. Frank's book is primarily a report of some of the economic naturalist writing assignments that first-year students of economics over the years have written in Frank's Introductory Economics course. Underlying the assignment is what Frank calls the narrative less-is-more approach to learning. The basic idea is that freshmen are taught just a few basic economic principles and that they should pick some (preferably paradoxical) everyday phenomenon that they themselves have to explain using one or a few of these principles. The explicit goal is to acquaint freshmen with the typical economic way of thinking as quickly and as pervasively as possible so that they are hooked for the rest of their lives. There is no doubt, I think, that this goal is accomplished better by Frank's narrative less-is-more approach than by the more traditional approach. In this paper, however, I want to point out that there are also potential adverse effects to Frank's approach.

My critique will differ profoundly from the critique Stephen A. Marglin offers in his recent *The Dismal Science: How Thinking Like an Economist Undermines Community* (2008). At first sight our critiques might seem similar. Marglin also warns against adverse effects of thinking as an economist. But beyond this rather superficial similarity profound dissimilarities between our critiques prevail. Marglin focuses on the eroding effects the dismal science of economics has on communities. He argues that with its unflinching support of unfettered markets, economics undermines communal ties. By contrast, I focus on how Frank's narrative teaching of the elementary principles of economics (in his Econ 101 course) might inhibit the development of first-year economics students into open-minded scholars. For all its undeniable merits, I argue that the effect of this way of teaching economics might be that it induces a mind-set in students that favors "early closure" on the first plausible explanatory hypothesis that comes to the student's mind. Once students have hit on an economic explanation that makes sense of some initially puzzling phenomenon, they no longer tend to treat alternative explanations and possible counter-evidence in a fair, even-handed way.

There is another sense in which my critique differs from Marglin's. Marglin argues that standard economic theory is wedded to the view that economic agents are obsessively engaged in "cold" rational calculations to figure out what serves their own interest best. There is room in standard economic theory for neither intuition and "hot" emotion nor duties, obligations, and other other-regarding concerns. Ironically, Marglin takes earlier work by Frank (Frank et al. 1993) to task to buttress his point that studying economics favors self-interested behavior. As I shall argue, however, Frank does not teach his students that economic theory assumes that economic agents are self-interested "rational fools" (Sen 1977). On the contrary, he shows that the basic economic principles are general and broad enough to account for emotional non-self-interested behavior.[1] In the hands of Frank and his students, especially the cost–benefit principle, according to Frank the root explanatory principle in economics, appears as a very flexible principle that is bent and used in a variety of ways. Frank omits to tell his students that this is the case, however. Students are given the impression that the content and use of the principle is the same in all of its uses. This omission, I argue, contributes to the "early closure" effect alluded to above. It encourages a mind-set in which every new use of the principle is perceived a successful one that makes a lot of sense and is at the same time seen as yet another piece of positive evidence for the explanatory power of the principle.

One of the reasons that Frank's narrative way of teaching the elementary principles of economics leads to a better entrenched understanding of them than more traditional ways of teaching is that it plays in the hands of what is called make(s)-sense epistemology. Students are "naturally" inclined to search for explanations of phenomena that make sense to them. I argue that this natural tendency should be resisted and opposed by a "critical epistemology" in early stages of the teaching program. Part of the chapter consists of what can be seen as exercises in critical epistemology. Another label that might be attached to what I am doing here is "normatively relevant methodology" (cf. Vromen 2007). We will see normatively relevant methodology in action. Since engaging in

---

[1] For similar views, see e.g. Binmore (1998) and Gintis (2009).

critical methodological thinking goes against what students are naturally inclined to do, students should be stimulated to acquire a taste for this. Although it probably will not always make for a nice and pleasant reading, I hope to convince the reader that engaging in this sort of methodological analysis and reflection is not only needed, but also fun.

The merits

With a few exceptions, the explanations discussed in Frank (2007a) are drawn from papers Frank's students (in an introductory economics course) had to write to pass Frank's "Economic naturalist writing assignment." The assignment is "to use a principle, or principles, discussed in the course to explain some pattern or events of behavior that you personally have observed" (Frank 2006, p. 61). The students are instructed to write their short paper (word limit: 500) in accessible plain English, preferably without using algebra and graphs. In his statement of the assignment, Frank makes clear to the students that they are not required to put much effort into making sure that their explanations are correct:

This assignment is not a PhD dissertation. You are not expected to do voluminous research in support of your argument, although a relevant fact or two might help convince yourself and others that you are on the right track. It makes no difference whether your topic is "important", but try, as best as you can, to choose something interesting. A really successful paper is one that begins with a really interesting question (one that makes the listener instantly curious to learn the answer) and then uses an economic principle or principles to construct a plausible answer. You'll know you have a good paper if the first thing your roommate wants to do upon reading it is to tell friends about it. (Frank 2006, p. 61)

At the basis of the assignment is the narrative theory of learning. According to that theory, there is no better way to master and remember an idea than to write stories about it. Some studies suggest that several months after they left the regular principles course the ability of students to answer simple economic questions is not different from that of people who never took such a course. Their understanding of the really important principles and concepts, such as "opportunity costs," apparently quickly evaporates after finishing the course (or, even worse, perhaps they never came to the point of really understanding them in the first place). The reason, Frank surmises, is not only that students have to digest too much in a regular principles course but also that they have to do so in a form that does not engage them. Frank pleads for a "less-is-more" approach to learning: to get profound and lasting learning effects, it is better to teach students just a few basic principles in economics that are verbally stated than to try to get the full panoply across with the aid of algebra and graphs. It is not enough for students to learn how to explain the principles to others. They must also be trained how to actively use them themselves. Frank compares the learning of how to think as an economist with the learning of how to speak a new natural language and with the learning of how to play tennis. If the goal is to get students to communicate their thoughts in the new language as quickly as possible, then it is better not to start with a discussion of the grammar of the language but with a few single sentences having practical import that students have to repeat many times. Similarly, in learning how to play tennis it is better first to let the student practice the basic strokes (forehand and backhand) repeatedly before they turn to more complicated strokes (such as the topspin lob). The same holds for learning to think as an economist, Frank argues: it is best to start off with the most basic principles and let students apply them in multiple contexts.

I have no doubt that Frank is right that his narrative approach to teaching introductory economics is superior to more traditional ones when it comes to the speed, ease, and depth with which students master basic economic principles. Frank seems to be right also in arguing that his approach has a few more additional advantages. By making the economic way of thinking their own students are stimulated to think about things around them in interesting new ways. They come to think of hypotheses that they otherwise would have never thought of. Students start seeing general patterns they did not notice before. Phenomena that, at first seemed wholly distinct and disconnected, become instantiations of the same principles to the practiced eye of the economic naturalist. And the more skilled students become in detecting economic patterns in the world, the more they are going to like it. There will be no need any more for external incentives to motivate students. Recall the analogy with learning to play tennis. Like experienced tennis players who delight in their own skillful play, students start enjoying the sheer pleasure of being good at reading the world as an economist. A lifelong learning trajectory has begun in which their mastery of economic principles will only grow stronger: "Once students realize that they can pose and answer interesting questions on their own, they are hooked" (Frank 2006, p. 65).

Students will have become increasingly aware that thinking as an economist is fun. It is fun not only in the way that any skillful behavior gives a satisfactory feeling of craftsmanship and accomplishment. It is fun also in that students start realizing that the scope of economic principles is not limited to the often important, but also rather boring or dull traditional economic phenomena that are addressed in leading journals. They find out that the principles can be used also to shed light on issues that students find more interesting and exciting. Recall also that in the economic naturalist writing assignment students are advised to pick "interesting" questions; questions that make the listener instantly curious to learn the answer. In his assignment, Frank explains that with "listener" he has mainly fellow-students in mind. Thus the students are encouraged to answer questions that speak to their own interests, which often mean homely examples taken from everyday life. This is supposed to help overcome motivational problems in learning the basic principles of economics. Frank believes it would also boost the attractiveness of economics as a discipline if more economists addressed interesting questions.

Economics Made Fun

Frank trusts on it that after finishing his introductory course students will find out that thinking as an economist is fun. Does this make Frank (2007a) an exponent of the larger "Economics Made Fun" movement? There surely are signs that point in this direction. When discussing the intriguing questions his students came up with, Frank sighs "How much more fun it would be to be an economist if most papers published in our leading journals tackled questions as interesting as these" (Frank 2002, p. 461). Apparently Frank thinks that the questions tackled in leading economics journals are not very interesting and do not appeal to prospective economics students. This feeling arguably is a powerful impetus to the emergence of the "Economics Made Fun" movement. Frank's book has been put in the same category as such a clear product of this movement as Tim Harford's *The Logic of Life*, for example (Derbyshire 2008). And Frank's book has been discussed on the Freakonomics blog. Yet, significant differences with especially Levitt and Dubner's *Freakonomics* immediately spring to mind.

First of all, DiNardo (2005) points out, rightly I think, that there is not much explicit economics in Levitt and Dubner's *Freakonomics*. If there is economics in *Freakonomics* at all, it is the assumption that people respond to incentives. The emphasis is very much on "clean identification": the search for data that allows one to draw conclusions about causal relations. By contrast, Frank's book is rich on economic theory and poor on data. There is little else in the book doing the explanatory work than basic economic principles. What makes Frank's book stand out from other books in the "Economics Made Fun" movement such as Harford's *The Logic of Life* is also that Frank does not only discuss insights that can be obtained from standard economic theory. Under the heading of "Psychology meets Economics" key insights of behavioral economics are discussed. What is conspicuously lacking from Frank's book are data. No serious attempt is made to test the explanations empirically.

Another striking difference is that Frank does not pretend that the explanations discussed are the final words on the issues they purport to explain. There is less open disdain in Frank (2007a) about explanations offered by other social sciences than in *Freakonomics*, and less bashing of "conventional wisdom." Unlike in *Freakonomics*, with its rhetoric about letting the data speak for themselves in uncovering the hidden side of everything, the more modest claim in Frank (2007a) is that the explanations are plausible and on the right track. As we saw above, Frank tells his students explicitly that their explanations need not be right or correct. This leads me to another difference: Frank's book is primarily an attempt to engage students and readers of the book in thinking as an economist. It defends a particular didactic and pedagogical view on how to teach Introductory economics to freshmen. The ultimate goal is an in-depth understanding and mastery of basic economic principles, not the discovery of the truth about particular issues.

At the same time, it is important also not to lose sight of what Frank (2007a) has in common with other exponents of the "Economics Made Fun" movement. They all agree that economic theorizing is not just fun for its own sake, but also that it is worthwhile to try to make the larger audience more economically literate. As another "Economics Made Fun" popularizer of economics, Tim Harford (2005), puts it, the goal is to show ordinary people why they should care about becoming acquainted with economic theory and economic theorizing. Likewise, the underlying premise in Frank's book is that there is something to be gained in terms of an enhanced understanding of the world around us (and not just of what traditionally have been called economic phenomena) from an in-depth grasp and mastery of basic economic principles. Why else would Frank want to share his students' explanations with a larger audience? Furthermore, although Frank does not argue that economic explanations are necessarily superior to non-economic ones, there are passages suggesting that economic explanations can explain phenomena that non-economic explanations cannot explain. Sociological explanations of different patterns of behavior in terms of different cultural backgrounds, for example, are said to beg the question of why cultures differ (2007a, p. 149). Frank suggests that by focusing on differences between relevant costs and benefits that people face in different environments, economic theory might be able to explain why there are different cultures.

So the idea clearly is that the basic principles of economic theory can shed an illuminating light on all kinds of phenomena, including everyday ones. Does the book succeed in showing that basic economic principles really remove the enigmatic element in "everyday enigmas"? Partly, I think. In some cases, one really has the idea that applying an economic principle makes some particular paradoxical phenomenon less puzzling. But there are also explanations that do not seem to be on the right track. Let me elaborate a bit on this. Generally speaking I believe the explanations discussed in the book fall within the following four categories:

1. Really enlightening
2. Thought-provoking
3. Only paraphrasing conventional wisdom
4. Straining credulity

Let me give examples of each of these.

1. There is no shortage of examples in Frank (2007a) that I take to be genuinely illuminating. The examples given of the economics of discount pricing are a case in point. Consider the common practice of retailers selling slightly damaged refrigerators (so-called scratch 'n' dent appliance sales) for a reduced price rather than sending them back to manufacturers for repair. This practice reduces costs to retailers, Frank argues, because there will always be a few buyers who are prepared to take the hurdles first of finding out when a sale occurs, second of planning and reserving time to go at the sale, and third of coping with the idea that the refrigerator bought has a dent in it. Because of these multiple hurdles that have to be taken, there won't be many of them, thus securing that most potential buyers are prepared to pay the non-reduced full price of non-damaged refrigerators. As Frank lucidly explains, the challenge for retailers is always to find a discount scheme that gives a price break to potential buyers that are not prepared to buy at list price, while making the discount available to as few other buyers as possible.

2. There are a few examples in the book of explanations that at first do not seem to be on the right track, but that on closer inspection might be on to something. Consider for example Tobin Schilke's explanation of why many people buy larger houses when they retire and their children leave home (2007a, pp. 36–37). Schilke's answer is that the demand for visits of grandchildren has increased, while the supply has remained the same. Because divorces and remarriages have become rather common over the last decades, children typically have six grandparents or more. By buying a large and conveniently located

house, grandparents hope they are able to lure their grandchildren to visit them more often. At first sight this explanation might seem far-fetched. Isn't it more likely that elderly people buy larger houses now than they did a few decades earlier simply because elderly people always wanted to have large houses for their own comfort and social status and that new generations are more wealthy so that they can afford to buy larger houses? Perhaps, but having a larger house also brings additional costs (for cleaning and maintenance, for example) and their (conscious or unconscious) desire to have their grandchildren visit them often might make it worthwhile for them to incur these costs. Here thinking as an economist draws the attention to a possible explanatory factor that otherwise might easily be overlooked.

3. It has been observed (e.g. Derbyshire 2008), rightly I think, that some of the explanations given seem to be no more than common-sense beliefs dressed up in economic jargon. Take Digby Lock's explanation of why women endure the discomfort of high heels (Frank 2007a, pp. 97–98). The various sorts of discomfort for women wearing high heels are rather obvious. They are uncomfortable and they make walking more difficult. Wearing them often may furthermore injure the feet, knees, and the back. Women continue to wear high heels because the benefits of doing so exceed these costs. Women in high heels are more likely to attract favorable notice. It is not just that they accentuate their female forms. Wearing high heels also make women look taller, adding to their gracious presence. With Derbyshire we can ask ourselves what casting our explanation in the economic terms of costs and benefits adds to our common-sense understanding. In relabeling what we already thought anyway, economic explanation does not seem to enhance our understanding or to extend the set of possible explanations here.

Frank might retort here that this only applies to the short answer Lock gives. There is more to Lock's explanation than just a restatement of common sense. If other women did not wear high heels, wearing high heels would be clearly advantageous. But if all women start wearing high heels to reap the benefits, the comparative advantage of wearing high heels is annihilated. It is in the interest of all women then to deescalate the process by wearing lower heels. Yet women continue to wear high heels. Why? Lock's long answer is that by unilaterally deviating from wearing high heels, a single woman would be at a disadvantage by looking smaller. So even if all women wished to forgo high heels, they would still be wearing them. Only a collective decision to wear lower heels could bring solace here.

What the longer answer adds to the shorter one surely is illuminating. Frank shows what can happen when people are caught in arms races and when goods (such as appearing taller than others) are positional. This links up with other works of Robert Frank such as *The Winner-Take-All Society* (with Philip Cook) and *Luxury Fever* that also stress the inefficiencies that can result if it is relative (rather than absolute) performance that people vie for. The fact that in their explanations Frank's students pay attention to situations in which Adam Smith's invisible hand does not work I regard as one of the great merits of Frank's new book.

But it is also worth noting that the longer answer does not invalidate the shorter answer. And it also does not diminish the banality (or triviality) of the shorter explanation. The longer answer refers to the same "costs" and "benefits" as the shorter one. In both answers, the benefit of attracting favorable notice by looking taller (and, accordingly, the cost of attracting less favorable notice by wearing lower heels than other women) is emphasized. Arguably the shorter and longer answers differ mostly from each other because they are answers to slightly different questions. The question addressed by the shorter answer is: Why is it that women want to wear higher heels than other women even if doing so has certain "costs"? The shorter answer specifies the benefits that more than compensate for the costs of wearing high heels. The question addressed by the longer answer is: Why do women wear high heels even if wearing lower heels would be in the interest of all?[2] The longer answer shows that unilateral deviation from the social norm of wearing high heels is costly for women. By suggesting that it is the same question that the answers address ("Why do women endure the discomfort of high heels?"), Frank skims over this seemingly small, but significant difference.

4. There are also a few explanations in Frank's book that strain credulity. Consider Patty Yu's explanation of why the fuel filler doors are on the driver's side of some cars but on the passenger's side of others (2007a, pp. 22–23). Why don't all car manufacturers put gas caps/fuel filler doors at the same side (say the driver's side) of the car? That would save drivers of rented cars a lot of frustration. Because of the fact that fuel filler doors are placed at different sides of different (sorts of) cars, drivers of rented cars often do not know on what side of the car they are driving they are on. If such a driver pulls up at the wrong side of a gas pump, say a driver of a car with the fuel filler door on the

---

[2] This is a tricky claim: if women are used to the "beauty ideal" of wearing high heels, it might be that they would not opt for no or lower heels.

passenger's side pulls up at the right side of a gas pump, he finds out, no doubt to his dismay, that he cannot fill the tank. So why are the fuel filler doors of some cars on the driver's side, while on other cars they are on the passenger's side? Patty Yu's answer is that there are offsetting benefits to putting fuel filler doors at different sides of different cars: this reduces the waiting time at gas stations for car drivers during peak periods. Having fuel filler doors on different sides of different cars enables car drivers to fill their tanks at both sides of gas pumps rather than just on one side. As a consequence there will be less congestion at gas stations.

For several reasons Yu's explanation does not seem to be very credible. Note that several conditions have to be met for Yu's answer to make sense. Some have to do with how gas stations and in particular the gas pumps in it have to be constructed. Frank does not tell us explicitly what assumptions are made about how gas pumps are constructed. There is an illustration on p. 23 suggesting that for each available car place at a gas pump there are several pipes – presumably for different sorts of fuel – but that they are all placed on one side (the right side). But the latter suggestion cannot be true for Yu's answer to make sense. In his discussion, Frank implicitly assumes that the frustration drivers of rented cars feel when pulling up on the wrong side of a gas pump is not just the inconvenience of having to stretch the pipe in order to reach the gas cap at the other side of the car. The frustration is assumed to go deeper than that: if you pull up on the wrong side there is no way you can fill your tank. If the pipes are not long enough to reach the other side of a car, a reasonable assumption is that they are not long enough either to reach the gas caps of cars that are pulled up on the other side of the pump. Thus, if there are pipes only on the right side of gas pumps and if you pull up on the left side, you cannot fill your tank. Then there would be nothing to gain from also having cars with fuel filler doors on the right side. It would still be impossible to fill tanks simultaneously at either side of a gas pump. So there must be pipes at both sides of gas pumps. If there are different pipes for different sorts of fuel, then for each sort of fuel there should be two pipes, one on each side of the pump. Each of the pipes is not long enough, to repeat, to reach gas caps on the other side of cars.

If this is how gas pumps are constructed, will placing fuel filler doors on different sides on different cars (instead of placing all fuel filler doors say at the left side of cars) reduce waiting time during peak hours? Not necessarily. It depends. Suppose the initial situation is one in which all manufacturers put the fuel filler doors of all cars on the left side of the cars and that all drivers know this. Suppose also that all drivers know that pipes are too short to be able to fill their tanks if they pull up on the left side of a gas pump. Then they will pull up on the right side, leaving all left sides of pumps empty. Now suppose instead that manufacturers put fuel filler doors on different sides of different (types of) cars. Will this reduce waiting time during peak hours? Suppose that there is a probability of 50% that fuel filler doors are placed on the left side. If drivers knew which side the fuel filler doors are on, waiting times during peak hours would be halved. But Frank's discussion proceeds on the basis of the assumption that drivers of rented cars typically do not know which side the fuel filler doors are placed. Suppose that drivers can do no better than pulling up 50% of the time on the left side of pumps and 50% on the right side. Half of the time this works fine: instead of one car being served at a time at each gas pump, two can be served. But half of the time drivers will be disappointed, because they will find out to their dismay that cannot fill their tanks. What is the net effect? If drivers really cannot do better than flip a fair coin, it seems that the net reduction in waiting time would be small.[3]

Even if the reduction in waiting time during peak hours were considerable, it remains to be seen whether this could explain why car manufacturers decide to put fuel filler doors on different sides of different types of cars. Does an individual car manufacturer decide to put fuel filler doors on say the right side of a new type of car because it knows that most cars have their fuel filler doors on the left side and because it also knows (or expects) that placing fuel filler doors on the right side of their new type of car reduces waiting times for car drivers at gas stations during peak hours? That does not seem to be very plausible. In the next section I will discuss how Frank defends Yu's explanation against charges that it is not plausible. But before we get to that, let us first have a look at the basic economic principles students are supposed to use in their explanations. In a sense, the most basic one, Frank argues, is the cost–benefit principle. It will turn out that the cost–benefit principle is rather flexible and lacks definite content. We will see that Frank makes use of the flexibility of the cost–benefit principle in his defense of Yu's explanation.

---

[3] Of course, if the probability that they pick the correct side of the gas pump is considerably greater than 50%, net reduction in waiting time will be larger. It also obviously depends on the proportion of rental car drivers in the queue (on the assumption that non-rental drivers know which side of their car the fuel filler door is on), on whether rental car drivers typically fill the tank more than once (after the first time, they know which side of the rental car the fuel filler door is on) and on other things.

The many guises and uses of the cost–benefit principle

Thus far I talked of "basic economic principles" without specifying what they are. Frank (2006) lists seven of them:

1. The scarcity principle
2. The cost–benefit principle
3. The not-all-costs-matter-equally principle
4. The principle of comparative advantage
5. The principle of increasing opportunity cost
6. The equilibrium principle (markets leave no unexploited opportunities to individuals, but may not exploit all gains achievable through collective action)
7. The efficiency principle (efficiency is an important social goal, for everybody can benefit if the pie gets larger)

Frank notes that his list might be contested and negotiable. Other economists might come up with different lists. According to Frank, not much hinges on what specific principles are on the list. Given its central place in the economic mind-set, however, Frank is quite sure that the cost–benefit principle will be part of any list: "The mother of all economic ideas is the cost-benefit principle" (2006, p. 10). In fact, in all the specific explanations just discussed, the cost–benefit principle plays a (if not the) key role. In what follows, I will confine my attention to this principle. I will show that although Frank argues as if this were a principle with definite content and with a well-defined use, it in fact is a highly flexible and elastic principle that has many different guises and uses.

No doubt Frank knows that the cost–benefit principle is a highly flexible one that is used in many different ways. But it does not show in his discussions of the students' explanations that use the principle. Take one of Frank's favorites: Bill Tjoa's explanation of why there are Braille dots on drive-up keypads even though blind people will as a rule not make use of them. Tjoa's explanation is that ATM producers already made keypads with Braille dots for their walk-up machines anyway so that it was cheaper for them to make all machines in the same way. Since sighted users are not caused any trouble by having Braille dots on keypads it was more profitable for producers not to produce two different sorts of keypads. Note that in both Tjoa's explanation and the explanation of discount pricing the profitability of some particular strategy for some producer or seller is counted in standard financial (or monetary) units.

Tjoa's example was challenged by someone arguing that such keypads are required by the Americans with Disabilities Act. Frank does not dispute this by itself correct observation. But he argues that it is very unlikely that the regulation with this requirement would have come about if putting Braille dots on the keypads had been significantly more costly than it actually was. Apparently Frank believes that he has shown that Tjoa's explanation still stands. Tjoa's explanation in terms of costs and benefits is simply too good and powerful not to have a germ of truth in it. But in fact it is easy to see that Frank's argument differs from Tjoa's explanation. Tjao's explanation is that it would be more costly for producers of (walk-up and drive-up) cash machines to produce different keypads for drive-up machines than the ones they already produced for walk-up machines (whereas the benefits are assumed to be the same whether or not they decided to produce different keypads). Frank's response to the objection refers to costs and benefits not for the producers, however, but for the regulators. The idea is that it does not really cost regulators anything to require Braille dots on keypads (this will meet little resistance from the producers because it is costless for them), while the regulators can benefit from telling the public that they did something useful for society in general and for blind persons in particular.

Frank argues that "almost certainly" (2006, p. 12) the rule to put Braille dots on all keypads would not have been enacted if it had been more costly to put Braille dots on drive-up machines. But would that really have been the case? Is it really very unlikely for regulators to come up with regulations that are costly for private producers of goods or services? We all know of regulations that are rather costly for private producers of goods or services but that are enacted nonetheless for an allegedly good cause. The simple point is that although they might well be correlated, what is costly and beneficial for private producers might not coincide with what is costly and beneficial for public regulators. In this specific case it might make sense, of course, to argue that regulators would have had to incur costs if the rule were costly for the producers and if the regulators would have enacted the rule nevertheless. But this argument was not part of Tjoa's explanation. In order to get from Tjoa's explanation to Frank's "defense" of it, such an argument has to be added to Tjoa's explanation.

In Tjoa's explanation and in Frank's defense of it the cost–benefit principle plays a positive, explanatory role. But this is not how Frank introduces the principle. Frank starts out with a discussion of the principle in its normative use (Frank 2007a, pp. 10–11; 2006, pp. 60–61). The students are taught that it is irrational to think in percentage terms. Whether you can save €10 on buying an expensive laptop (of say €1810) or on buying a cheap alarm clock (of say €20) should not matter. It is irrational to be attracted more to the laptop bargain. For in both cases the money you can save and that you can use for alternative purposes is exactly the same. Using the cost–benefit principle as a normative principle is to tell what one should (or ought to) do (in the sense of what would be the most efficient allocation of scarce resources), or what an ideally rational individual would do.

After his brief introduction of the cost–benefit principle as a normative principle Frank continues discussing only positive explanatory uses (answering "Why" questions) without calling the readers' attention to the fact that these are two different uses of the principle. It makes quite a difference how the principle is used. As many have observed, it is possible for the cost–benefit principle to be perfectly suited for normative purposes but to fail miserably for positive purposes. The principle might state accurately what an ideally rational creature would do in some particular situation and yet be incapable of explaining actual behavior for the simple reason that "real" people often do not act in an ideally rational way.

Frank teaches his students to use the cost–benefit principle in a positive explanatory way. Does this imply that he assumes that people out there in the real world do act in a perfectly rational way? Not necessarily. It depends. Using the cost–benefit principle in an explanatory way might suggest that it is implicitly assumed that individuals consciously weigh costs and benefits flawlessly as indicated by the principle. This is what for example Derbyshire and Marglin conclude. And, indeed, this is arguably the first reading that comes to mind: in its positive use, the cost–benefit principle implies that individuals whose behavior is explained are flawless calculators who are concerned only with how to maximize their own utility.

But the explanatory use of the cost–benefit principle does not necessarily imply that individuals are such flawless calculators. Individuals might not weigh costs and benefits consciously; they might have various different motives and reasons for their actions and yet the cost–benefit principle might rightfully be used to explain behavior. The most extreme example of this possibility briefly discussed in Frank (2007a) is due to earlier work of Frank himself (Frank 1988). There Frank argued that cooperation in a non-negligible share of the population could have evolved, not despite but precisely because the cooperating people do not consciously weigh costs and benefits. Instead, these people cooperate because they are emotionally committed to cooperate in particular situations. The fact that these people do not weigh costs and benefits opportunistically provides the key to their evolutionary success: it enables them to reap benefits in so-called commitment problems that would otherwise have failed them. As Frank himself puts it succinctly: "An emotional commitment to one's spouse is valuable in the coldly rational cost-benefit calculus because it promotes fitness-enhancing investments. But note the ironic twist. These commitments work best when they deflect people from thinking explicitly about their spousal relationships in cost-benefit terms" (Frank 2007a, p. 195).

Implicit here is the assumption that there is (or has been) an evolutionary process going on that selects on cost–benefit ratios. The cost–benefit ratios in question are not ratios that individuals expect and on which they base their decisions, but actually realized ones. Behavioral strategies that have the most favorable cost–benefit ratios are assumed to spread (or to have spread) in the population at the cost of strategies with less favorable ratios. Accordingly, the type of explanation given is not intentional, but functional. Individuals are not assumed to engage in instrumental practical reasoning with the optimal cost–benefit ratio as the ultimate goal. Individuals are rather assumed to be somehow tied to particular strategies that happen to have or not have beneficial consequences. Surviving strategies are the ones that are de facto functional, i.e. that happen to have beneficial consequences. Getting back now to the issue of whether the positive, explanatory use of the cost–benefit principle implies that the people whose behavior we want to explain behave in a perfectly rational way, we could give the following answer: to survive, strategies must have a better cost–benefit ratio than alternative strategies in the population, given the prevailing frequencies of strategies in the population.

Although it is never expounded explicitly, this latter explanatory use of the cost–benefit principle looms large in Frank (2007a). Frank calls the students' writing assignment the "economic naturalist" because it was inspired by the kinds of questions that an introductory course in biology enables students to answer. Once students are trained in posing such kinds of questions and to apply principles taught to explain them, they start seeing "texture and pattern" in the world that they did not notice before (Frank 2007a, p. 6). But in fact for Frank the similarity between economics (and especially its cost–benefit principle) and evolutionary biology runs deeper than that. It is not just that biological naturalists and economic naturalists start seeing patterns in their respective domains, at root they start seeing the same sort of patterns; patterns consistent with the cost–benefit principle. Thus, when discussing the evolution of the large size of bull elephant seals or the large tail display of peacocks, Frank argues that "The balance of costs and benefits is reflected in the characteristics of surviving males" (Frank 2007a, p. 7). Frank even goes so far as to declare that "Virtually every feature of the built environment, virtually every feature of human and animal behavior, is the explicit or implicit result of the interplay of costs and benefits" (2007a, p. 204). If you want to explain some particular behavioral pattern as an economist and you have not been able so far to come up with a plausible cost–benefit explanation, try harder![4] There must be relevant costs and benefits that can rationalize the existence (or rather persistence) of the pattern.

This is also how Frank tries to defend Yu's explanation of the differential placement of fuel filler doors on cars against the objection that Yu's explanation assumes an unrealistic degree of coordination among car manufacturers. Suppose waiting time at gas stations would be maximally reduced by having fuel filler doors on the driver's side of roughly 50% of the cars and having them on the passenger's side again on roughly 50% of the cars. Suppose furthermore that this is the actual distribution of the placement of fuel filler doors in cars. Could the actual distribution be explained then by the fact that it minimizes waiting time at gas stations? The objection raised was that this would be explained only if we assume that car manufacturers coordinate their decisions, which in fact they don't. In his response (Frank 2007b), Frank agrees that car manufacturers do not coordinate on this. But he argues that the observed (allegedly approximately equal) distribution of the placement of fuel filler doors is evolutionarily stable. Frank is right that no conscious coordination is required for some distribution to be evolutionarily stable. All that is needed is that small deviations from it trigger a tendency in the distribution to move back toward the evolutionarily stable one. Suppose the evolutionarily stable distribution is one in which in half of the cars the fuel filler door is placed at the left side and in one half on the right side. Assume that at a certain point in time the car market is in this equilibrium. Now suppose that one car manufacturer, one with a market share say of 10%, decides to put the fuel filler doors on the opposite side. Say it put the doors before on the left side and after at the right side. Then the new frequencies will be that 40% of the cars have their fuel filler doors on the right side and 60% on the left side. For Frank's defense to make sense there must be a tendency for the population frequencies to return to 50% each. No conscious coordination among car manufacturers is needed for this. What might do the job is that the deviating car manufacturer finds out that switching placement of fuel filler doors did not work out fine (say the sales of its care went down) and that it therefore returns to placing the fuel filler doors on the left side of its cars.

So far so good. But note first of all that Frank's response implies that what is explained is why the observed distribution is able to survive small deviations from it. It need not explain why and how the observed

---

[4] In evolutionary biology, this is sometimes called "reverse engineering."

distribution emerged in the first place. As is well understood in evolutionary biology, what initially brings population frequencies to some evolutionarily stable equilibrium might differ from what keeps it there. The wings of birds are a famous case in point. At first the feathers of birds grew larger and thicker for reasons of thermoregulation. Only after they achieved a particular length, thickness and shape could they be used for flying. Similarly, Yu's/Frank's explanation does not explain how, historically, the distribution of fuel filler doors moved from 100% placement on the left side (or any other distribution that obtained initially in the process) to a fifty–fifty placement.

More importantly, quite a few doubtful assumptions have to be made to get from the (alleged) fact that deviations from the evolutionarily stable fifty–fifty distribution lead to longer waiting times at gas stations during peak hours to the posited evolutionary dynamics: a tendency to restore the fifty–fifty distribution. As before, suppose for the sake of argument that drivers do notice longer waiting times. For Frank's response to make sense, this discomfort should somehow prompt drivers to punish the deviating car manufacturer, for example be renting fewer cars produced by this specific manufacturer in the future. I think this is not a very credible scenario. It is most likely that the annoyance caused by longer waiting times will be directed (at least in the first instance) to others than car manufacturers (e.g. other drivers and employees and owners of gas stations). Drivers might well perceive a shortage of gas stations or the poor construction of gas pumps as the cause of the problem.[5] Thus it is doubtful whether it leads to a decrease in the number of cars rented. Even if drivers were to put the blame on car manufacturers they are not likely to be able to single out the deviating car manufacturer as the wrongdoer. They might notice for example that there are more cars with fuel filler doors on their left side than before. But they might well be ignorant of the fact that this is due to the deviating car manufacturer. And even if they do detect this and the deviating car manufacturer is facing reduced sales, the deviating car manufacturer might be unable to identify its earlier change of the placement of fuel filler doors as the cause of the reduced sales.

In short, the (alleged) relation between longer waiting times as a result of deviations from the evolutionarily stable distribution and the tendency toward the restoration of the distribution is a questionable one. It is an indirect one, dependent on several dubious links. By contrast, in evolutionary biology the link between decreased fitness of some strategy

---

[5] Note that if pipes were long enough to reach the other side of cars, waiting times would be shorter. In Europe, most gas pumps have such long pipes.

and decrease of its frequency in the population is most of the time a direct one. To take an example from Frank, in a population of bull elephant seals a mutant emerges that is smaller than the evolutionarily stable size. This mutant tends to be outcompeted by other males for access to females. As a consequence, it will be less successful in spreading its genes in the population's gene pool so that this deviation will be annihilated in due time. Compared to Frank's discussion of the distribution of fuel filler doors and waiting times at gas stations, this biological example is much more straightforward and convincing.[6]

The point I want to make with this admittedly rather lengthy discussion of Yu's explanation and Frank's defense of it is not primarily that the specific economic explanations discussed in Frank (2007a) are sometimes dubious. My main point is rather that the cost–benefit principle is used in different ways in different explanations and that no attempt is made to point this out to students and readers. We saw this already in Lock's (shorter and longer) explanation of why women endure the discomfort of high heels. And just as Tjoa's explanation turned into a slightly different explanation in Frank's defense, Yu's explanation also turns into a slightly different one in Frank's hands. In Frank's hands what is explained is no longer why the distribution of the placements of fuel filler doors arrived at its present observed state in the first place (Yu's original explanandum), but why the distribution tends to stay at this state once it got there. Here the costs and benefits for each producer (car manufacturers in this case) are assumed to depend crucially on what other producers do. This differs from Tjoa's Braille dots example in which it is assumed that for each producer it is best to put Braille dots also on drive-up cash machine keypads, regardless of what other producers do. These rather crucial changes and differences seem to be concealed rather than highlighted by Frank. The misleading impression fostered is that it is always the same cost–benefit principle used in the same way.

What is not highlighted either by Frank is the issue of who is to incur the costs and who is to reap the benefits. In the case of Tjoa's example and Frank's defense of it, we saw that the implicit assumption in Frank's defense is that if it were more costly for producers to have Braille dots on drive-up keypads, it would also have been prohibitively costly for

---

[6] Even in evolutionary biology, a widespread worry is that theorists might indulge in so-called "just-so stories" (cf. Gould and Lewontin 1979): stories in which all too easily (i.e., without proper empirical support) some phenomenon is explained as an adaptation. If I am right, such a worry is even more relevant in the sort of use of the cost–benefit principle that Frank advocates in economics.

regulators to impose regulations that make Braille dots on drive-up keypads mandatory. In the case of Yu's explanation and Frank's defense of it, the critical assumption is that the cost of longer waiting times at gas stations that drivers have to incur translates into higher costs (or lower benefits) for the "deviating" car manufacturer responsible for the longer waiting times. If it is not the "deviating" car manufacturer, but some other party, such as rental car agencies or owners of gas stations, that bear the costs of longer waiting lines, Frank's explanation might break down. But again, the main point I want to make is not that the implicit critical assumptions made are questionable. It is rather that the fact that these assumptions are made is concealed rather than highlighted.

Finally, what is not highlighted either is that both "costs" and "bene-fits" can be given (and in fact actually are given) completely different meanings in different explanations. Thus what can be said to be costly can range from out-of-pocket expenses that have to be made to psychic dissatisfactions of various sorts (enduring longer waiting times at gas stations, for example, or the inconveniences caused by wearing high heels). So flexibly or elastically can "costs" and "benefits" be interpreted that it seems possible to cast any answer to a Why question as a cost–benefit explanation. Consider Frank's "buttoning" example: Why do women's garments button from the left (whereas men's garments button from the right) even though most women are right-handers and right-buttoning garments are slightly more easy to handle for right-handers (Frank 2007a, pp. 26–28)? Frank's answer is that history really seems to matter here. In the seventeenth century, when buttons were only worn by the rich, women were buttoned by servants (whereas the custom for men was to dress themselves). Because the overwhelming majority of servants were right-handers, a social norm for left-buttoning women's garments emerged. Given the existence of this social norm, going against it will cost manufacturers of women's shirts dear.

Note that the cost–benefit principle is used twice here: first to explain the emergence of the social norm for left-buttoning women's garments and second to explain conforming behavior of manufacturers of women's shirts. The relevant "costs" and "benefits" in the first explanation are allegedly related to the (average) ease with which servants could button garments of women. The relevant "costs" and "benefits" in the second explanation are more traditional economic ones: a non-conforming manufacturer is allegedly punished by reduced sales. Note also that what could be called traditional sociological explanations of why people tend to conform to prevailing social norms can also be phrased in terms of "costs." The social disapproval or feelings of shame and guilt that norm-violation brings, and that allegedly prevent people from violating prevailing social norms, can all be called "costs." It is perhaps telling that Frank does not take issue with such traditional sociological explanations of non-conforming behavior. He only takes issue with their (alleged) inability to explain the emergence of social norms. Frank argues that sociological explanations are ultimately unsatisfactory because they beg the question of why cultures differ (2007a, p. 149).[7] Economic cost–benefit explanations are superior because they can explain that the establishment of some social norm makes perfectly good sense.

The fact that "costs" and "benefits" can be given completely different meanings should also alert us to the possibility that for each cost–benefit explanation given of some behavior or phenomenon, there might be numerous alternative cost–benefit explanations that rationalize or make sense of the behavior or phenomenon equally well. "Costs" and "benefits" might be referred to in economic explanations of why some cars have their fuel filler doors on the driver's side while others have theirs on the passenger's side that differ completely from waiting times for drivers at gas stations, for example. For example, if it turned out to be the case that car manufacturers base their decisions of where to place fuel filler doors independently of each other on historical technological grounds, this could also be cast in terms of the cost–benefit principle.

In short, the cost–benefit principle is not an unequivocal explanatory principle that gives clear guidance in the search for determinate explanations of phenomena. Contrary to what Frank suggests, it does not single out specific texture and pattern in the world. There rather are many textures and patterns in the world that are consistent with it. The cost–benefit principle is a very flexible and elastic principle that can be bent and used in many different ways.[8] It can be invoked to explain very different kinds of things, it does not pre-specify who is to bear the costs and reap the benefits and "costs" and "benefits" can be understood in many different ways. Because of this flexibility, it is quite easy to concoct a cost–benefit explanation for virtually every phenomenon. The ease with

---

[7] Seen in this light, it is a bit disappointing to see that Frank rests content with "sociological" explanations of why there is so much mathematical formalism in economics, while humanities professors excel in unclear and sometimes even obscure writing? Both explanations presuppose that the relevant social norms are already established in economics and the humanities, respectively. No attempt is made to explain why these social norms differ from each other.

[8] Indeed, so flexible is the cost–benefit principle that it is almost completely bereft of content. One is reminded of the tautology charge that has haunted utility theory ever since its inception (cf. Ross 2007 for a recent discussion and defense). It also raises the issue of what other purpose the invocation of the principle has except showing to freshmen that seemingly widely divergent behavior is amenable to treatment in the economic utility-maximizing framework.

which a cost–benefit explanation can be concocted should not be taken as an indication that the specific explanation concocted is on the right track. There are other cost–benefit explanations of the same phenomena that perhaps do not come so easily to mind but that might be more on the right track than the first cost–benefit explanation that comes to mind.

The analogy that Frank sees between learning to speak a new natural language and learning (narratively) to think as an economist might be even closer and more apt than Frank thinks. As we saw, Frank invokes this analogy primarily to stress that the best way to learn a natural language is to start with simple sentences in familiar practical contexts and drill it in practice until one is able to use them correctly without thinking about their correctness. Likewise, the best way to learn how to think as an economist is to use basic economic principles in attempts to explain everyday (preferably paradoxical) phenomena. But their similarities go further and deeper than this. Given its flexibility, using the cost–benefit principle is like speaking a natural language in that it is more a way of expressing oneself than a specific substantive proposition expressed or a specific pattern of behavior identified. Just as in natural languages, it is possible to express in a cost–benefit framework both informed and uninformed beliefs, both truths and falsehoods in a grammatically correct way. Like the rules of a natural language, the cost–benefit framework does constrain and discipline economic discourse. But when it comes to narrowing down the set of substantive hypotheses, explanations or utterances that can be expressed, the constraints seem to be quite loose in both cases.

But surely all that can wait until later?

An obvious response to my detailed discussion of the use made of the cost–benefit principle is that I take the students' assignments way too seriously. Of course all kinds of objections can be leveled against the explanations that the students come up with, one might argue. But that would be to miss the whole point of the assignment. The students are explicitly told in advance that their answers do not need to be right, correct, or the final word on the matter in question. The assignment is meant to get the students engaged with thinking as an economist, not to teach them how to tell whether some answer is correct. Frank hastens to add that the students should not take from this that rightness or truth of explanations does not matter. On the contrary, the students are told that it is a good thing to be right. Students are also reminded "that the additional step of testing a hypothesis would need to be carried out before feeling confident enough to act on it. But that is a step for another time and place" (Frank 2006, p. 62). So the idea is that teaching students how to check empirically whether explanations and hypotheses are true is best postponed until later. First things first: first students should be taught how to construct and frame economic hypotheses before they are subjected to empirical tests.

Presumably Frank also thinks that the subtleties and niceties of the different ways in which the cost–benefit principle can be used can also be better taught at a later stage in the program. Bothering students with these subtleties at a too early stage would only complicate and slow down the process of learning how to think as an economist. But should "planting a basic economic principle in the student's mind" so that it sticks (Frank 2006, p. 61) be the ultimate goal of teaching programs in economics? Or should learning how to think as an economist rather be a means that should be instrumental to the further goal of helping students develop into open-minded scholars who take into consideration whatever it needs to arrive at hypotheses about economic phenomena that are on the right track? I think the ultimate goal should be the latter. If so, it does not seem wise to postpone teaching students how to critically assess hypotheses until later stages in the program. As will be argued in more detail below, the danger is that if the introductory course is as successful as Frank wants it to be, students might already have settled on a distinctive mind-set that inhibits their development into open-minded scholars. By the time they get to later stages, in which they supposedly learn how to scrutinize hypotheses critically, they will be less open to giving negative disconfirming evidence its due. At later stages they will be less receptive in particular to alternative hypotheses and explanations that might or might not be at odds with the basic principles they have learned. My claim here might seem a bit extravagant and "over the top." Could attending Frank's ideal introductory course really spoil students as junior open-minded scholars? So let me try to explain what I mean.

Frank in fact recommends the use of the cost–benefit principle in providing explanations as both a heuristic principle and a stopping rule. The cost–benefit principle is meant to be a heuristic principle in that it is supposed to spur students to look for "costs" and "benefits" that can rationalize the pattern of behavior to be explained. The working (or default) assumption is that there must be relevant sorts of costs and benefits that can rationalize any feature or phenomenon. Recall that Frank argues that virtually every feature of human behavior is the explicit or implicit result of the interplay of costs and benefits. The challenge for economists is to discern what sorts of costs and benefits are at stake. The assignment for freshmen is: if you do not find them readily, go on searching for them. Try harder. Do not stop searching before you have found costs and benefits that do the trick. But once you have found such costs and benefits, rest content with the explanation you concocted and stick to it. This is how the cost–benefit principle is used as a stopping rule.

We saw the cost–benefit principle in action as a stopping rule in Frank's defense of Tjoa's and Yu's explanations. Both Tjoa's and Yu's explanations were challenged, and although Frank concedes the significance of the objections raised, he sets out to defend Tjoa's and Yu's explanations. Whether or not it escaped Frank's attention that both Tjoa's and Yu's explanations changed subtly in his defenses we do not know. But students are given the impression that Tjoa's and Yu's original explanations still stand. More generally, we saw that it is relatively easy to rephrase rival and even contradicting explanations in terms of the cost–benefit principle. For any cost–benefit rationalization found for some particular phenomenon, there might be many others. So the use of the cost–benefit principle by itself does not single out one specific explanation. But, to repeat, students are given the impression that it does. Especially if they had to put some effort into finding relevant costs and benefits to explain some paradoxical phenomenon, they get the feeling that the cost–benefit explanations they themselves have found are simply too good to be completely off the mark.

Every time a student encounters a new paradoxical phenomenon for which he is able to give a cost–benefit explanation, the confidence of the student in the explanatory power of the cost–benefit principle is likely to grow. Not only does skillful use of the principle become more ingrained and entrenched, the student also gets the idea that the principle provides a unifying key to understanding many different phenomena. That the unity in the phenomena thus perceived by students might be merely illusory and spurious is likely to go unnoticed. More important for the present argument is that as the number of phenomena for which cost–benefit explanations are given increases, the likelihood that students are satisfied with the first cost–benefit explanation of a new phenomenon that comes to their mind also increases.

The implicit message that the student might get from this is that this is primarily or foremost what it takes to be an economist: concoct a plausible rationalization of the phenomenon in question and your job as an economist is done. Rest content with the first explanation that does the job. When challenged defend it. Don't let it go. To be sure, they are told there must be a stage of hypothesis-testing after that, but that stage is not specific to being an economist. It is telling that all "everyday enigmas" addressed in Frank's book are couched in terms of Why questions. The assignment is to find economic rationales of the phenomena in terms of (or at least consistent with) relevant sorts of costs and benefits. In doing so, paradoxical phenomena start to make sense.

Frank argues that his narrative approach to learning fits very well with the tendency of children to make sense of their life by using the storied version of their experience as the basis for further reflection (after Jerome Brunner; Frank 2007a, p. 9). That children and adolescents tend to use things they have already learned to make sense of novel phenomena indeed seems to be well-supported in psychological research. What is more, there is also quite some evidence that if children find that some novel phenomenon fits the explanation that they formed on the basis of their previous experience reasonably well, they tend to deem the explanation true. This is argued to hold also for students: students tend to "act as though the test of truth is that a proposition makes intuitive sense, sounds right, rings true. They see no need to criticize or revise accounts that do make sense – the intuitive feel of fit suffices" (Perkins, Allen and Hafner 1983). Once a hypothesis is found that makes intuitive sense to them, students tend to consider the correctness or truth of the hypothesis to be beyond reasonable doubt. In a sense, the case is closed for them. From then on they are "hooked" on this specific hypothesis. In the words of Perkins and others, this is what it means to say that students are "natural-born" make(s)-sense epistemologists.

Frank's narrative less-is-more approach to learning the basic principles of economics seems to latch on to this "natural inclination." Students are explicitly instructed to use one or a few basic economic principles they learned in their explanation of the interesting phenomenon they selected. And, as we saw, particularly in case students use the cost–benefit principle to explain some paradoxical phenomenon, students are likely to get the feeling that their explanation makes sense. Assignment accomplished. Case closed. Objections are likely to fall on deaf ears. The way in which Frank defends Tjoa's and Yu's explanations against objections probably only further strengthens the feeling of students that the economic explanations they give are simply too good not to be true.

The drawbacks of make(s)-sense epistemology should be obvious. Though psychologically understandable, logically speaking make(s)-sense epistemology is unsound. Once one has constructed a *single hypothesis* of one's own, the possibility of interpreting evidence as supporting *alternative hypotheses* is not seriously contemplated anymore. This is considered to be a cardinal sin in particular in Bayesianism. It is easy to see why. By looking only at how well the available data support the hypothesis formed (formally, this is represented as $p(H/D)$), the possibility is ignored that the hypothesis put forward is wrong. $p(D/\sim H)$ need not be zero (it normally isn't), and in fact it might even be higher than $p(D/H)$.[9] If so, the data do not confirm H. This is tantamount to failing to take the likelihood ratio into account. One simply does not know then whether the data are diagnostic with respect to the hypothesis tested (Nickerson 1998, pp. 177–178). One does not need to be a Bayesian to appreciate that it is not enough to ascertain that the data assembled fit the explanation proposed well. In order to tell whether data confirm an explanation, one needs to take the possibility into account that the explanation proposed is not the correct one.

More generally, the danger with make(s)-sense epistemology is that once an explanation is found that is perceived to make sense, people appear to have grave problems with treating evidence even-handedly (i.e., people tend to look selectively for confirmation only) and with giving alternative explanations a fair chance. Alternative explanations only seem to get a fair chance if they are taken into consideration before a stance is taken (that is, before one's mind is set on some specific explanation). This asymmetry is sometimes called the primacy effect. Related to this is what is called "early closure" (Perkins et al. 1991, pp. 98–99). As students might sense, further examination of some phenomenon might bring to light counter-evidence or complications for their explanation. This may reinforce their tendency to close their minds about some phenomenon once they have found an explanation that makes sense to them. This tendency might be further strengthened if they have had to put a lot of effort into finding such an explanation in the first place. They then are even more inclined not to pursue the matter further, but instead to defend their explanation.

This diagnosis in terms of make(s)-sense epistemology, primacy effect, and early closure also suggests a way out of this predicament. The primacy effect and early closure can only be avoided, it seems, if students are pushed to consider different alternative explanations at the early stages of their enquiries. As Nickerson puts it: "The knowledge that people typically consider only one hypothesis at a time and often make the assumption at the outset that that hypothesis is true leads to the conjecture that reasoning might be improved by training people to think of alternative hypotheses early in the hypothesis-evaluating process" (Nickerson 1998, p. 211). Students should be trained to do this before they settle on a favored explanation, not after it. This in turn suggests that Frank's reassurance in the economic naturalist assignment that students need not conduct voluminous research before they come up with their

---

[9] In Bayesianism, for some observation to be confirming some hypothesis, the first probability needs to be smaller than the second (cf. Sober 2008, p. 15).

explanation (and yet pass the test of thinking as an economist) should be qualified at the least. Freshmen should not be required to study some phenomenon exhaustively. But they can be stimulated to find relevant data and to search for already existing alternative explanations in the literature. And if there are no other explanations available, students could be asked to articulate reasons that might be given against their own hypotheses (Narveson 1980).

In a sense, this is exactly what I did above in my critical scrutiny of Yu's explanation (and Frank's "defense" of it). In fact, what I did is that I engaged in what Perkins et al. (1991) call situation modeling. Perkins et al. themselves explain situation modeling as follows: "That is, the reasoner builds a model of a situation as it is and might be, articulating the dimensions and factors involved in an issue. Such a situation model typically involves one or more imagined scenarios and invokes a variety of common sense, causal, and intentional principles both to construct and to weigh the plausibility of alternative scenarios" (Perkins et al. 1991, p. 85). Thus in the case of Yu's explanation (and Frank's "defense" of it) I asked questions such as What if gas stations were built differently? Will drivers notice the extra delay at gas stations if one car manufacturer changes the position of the fuel filler doors on its cars (so that there is a deviation from the evolutionarily stable equilibrium)? If so, who will be the targets of their anger and frustration? Asking such questions and attempting to answer them in a plausible way might reveal some of the strengths and weaknesses of the students' explanations.

A prerequisite for comparing different explanations of the same phenomenon is that students should be trained to recognize when explanations are different and when they are essentially the same. We saw that there are examples in Frank's book in which students are reinventing the . wheel. It goes without saying that this is not very "economical" (in the sense of the search process being inefficient). The buttoning example discussed earlier is a case in point. Arguing that it is costly for individual women to go against the social norm of wearing shirts that button from the right is just relabeling the standard sociological explanation that norm-violators await social disapproval. The sociological and economic explanation here are one and the same, but the students fail to notice this. Frank does not alert students to the possibility that there might be interesting and plausible explanations already available in other disciplines that they might want to consider. Complete disregard of whatever explanations and hypotheses others, and especially non-economists, have already offered of the phenomenon in question (or of related/similar phenomena) is alas not peculiar to Frank. It is common to the broader "Economics is fun" movement. Conversely, we saw several instances of explanations (Tjoa's explanation and Frank's defense of it, for example) that are presented as one and the same, while they actually are different. How can students be expected to self-critically assess their own explanations if they are not trained to get a clear idea what exactly their explanation does and does not explain?

If only for this reason training students in distinguishing between different uses of the cost–benefit principle should not be delayed until later. I hasten to add that this is not a plea to abandon the cost–benefit principle altogether. There certainly are fruitful uses of the principle. The cost–benefit principle can inspire people to think of hypotheses and explanations that they otherwise would have never thought of. It can thus expand the set (or horizon) of possible explanations that scholars can take into consideration (cf. Aydinonat 2008). And using the cost–benefit principle can also be convenient for modeling purposes. It makes the explanation amenable for the standard constrained maximization framework in economic theory. Note, though, that the latter use does not seem to be particularly relevant for freshmen who do not want to pursue an academic career in the economics profession. Recall that Frank intended his narrative less-is-more approach to be suited precisely for freshmen who do not want to pursue such a career.

In short, training in critical thinking and in methodological analysis and reflection is to be recommended in early stages in the program. I am well aware that this can stand in the way of reaching the explicit objective of the economic naturalist writing assignment. It may slow down the process of learning how to think as an economist. Even if it does, I think it is a price worth paying. For, as I argued, the costs (sic!) of not doing this are comparatively high. Being forced to engage in critical thinking and in methodological analysis and reflection might at first also appear cumbersome and perhaps even irrelevant to freshmen. It might initially spoil the fun of learning how to think as an economist. And it goes against their natural disposition to be make-sense epistemologists. But when properly introduced and learned, students might develop an acquired taste for it. They might come to appreciate that critical thinking and methodological reflection are fun too. I can assure you that it was fun to write this chapter. I hope it shows!

Conclusions

Frank seems to overlook the perils of his narrative less-is-more approach to teaching introductory economics. I argued that his approach and especially his economic naturalist writing assignment tend to give freshmen a misleadingly simplistic impression of the basic economic principles in general and the cost–benefit principle in particular. Things could be improved by teaching students that the cost–benefit principle lacks specific content, that it can be interpreted and applied in widely different ways, and that therefore the first cost–benefit explanation that a student can think of need not be the only possible cost–benefit explanation that can be given. Students should learn to reckon with the possibility that other possible cost–benefit explanations might be closer to the truth than the cost–benefit explanation they themselves come up with.

Given the primacy effect (and related phenomena such as early closure) it would even be better that students are stimulated to go deeper into the phenomenon at issue and to consider several possible hypotheses and explanations before making up their minds. Students should be taught to suspend judgment. This might go against their "natural" impulses, but so be it!

The challenge is to familiarize students with the economic way of thinking, to let them see how it can enrich and extend their intellectual horizons, without closing their minds to other, alternative explanations. The price to be paid for this might well be that it takes longer for students before they are able to think as an economist. But if one values the correctness, rightness, or truth of explanations for their own sake, the price to be paid for the alternative program, in which the critical assessment is deferred until later, might be even higher.

References

Aydinonat, N. E. 2008. *The Invisible Hand in Economics: How Economists Explain Unintended Social Consequences.* Routledge.

Binmore, K. 1998. *Game Theory and the Social Contract, vol. 2, Just Playing.* MIT Press.

Derbyshire, J. 2008. "How to choose a sandwich." *The Guardian*, 29 March 2008.

DiNardo, J. 2005. "A review of Freakonomics." *Journal of Economics Literature*, forthcoming.

Frank, R. H. 1988. *Passions Within Reason: The Strategic Role of the Emotions.* W.W. Norton.

1999. *Luxury Fever: Why Money Fails to Satisfy in an Era of Excess.* The Free Press.

2002. "The economic naturalist: teaching introductory students how to speak economics." *American Economic Review* 92(2), 459–462.

2006. "The economic naturalist writing assignment." *Journal of Economic Education* 37(1), 58–67.

2007a. *The Economic Naturalist: In Search of Explanations for Everyday Enigmas.* Perseus Books Group.

2007b. Guest blog, in more from the "Economic Naturalist" Robert Frank, Stephen J. Dubner http://freakonomics.com/2007/07/13/more-from-the-economic-naturalist-robert-frank/

Frank, R. H. and P. J. Cook 1996. *The Winner-Take-All Society: Why the Few at the Top Get so Much More Than the Rest of Us*. Penguin Books.

Frank, R. H., T. Gilovich, and D. Regan 1993. "Does studying economics inhibit cooperation?" *Journal of Economic Perspectives* 7(2), 159–171.

Gintis, H. 2009. *The Bounds of Reason: Game Theory and the Unification of the Behavioral Sciences*. Princeton University Press.

Gould, S. J. and R. Lewontin 1979. "The spandrels of San Marco and the Panglossian paradigm: a critique of the adaptionist programme." *Proceedings of the Royal Society of London* 205, 581–598.

Harford, T. 2005. "The dawn of A-List economics." *Crooked Timber*, May 23 2005

2008. *The Logic of Life: The Rational Economics of an Irrational World*. Random House.

Levitt, S. D. and S. J. Dubner 2005. *Freakonomics: A Rogue Economist Explores the Hidden Side of Everything*. Penguin Books.

Marglin, S. A. 2008. *The Dismal Science: How Thinking Like an Economist Undermines Community*. Harvard University Press.

Narveson, R. D. 1980. "Development and learning: complementary or conflicting aims in humanities education?" In R.G. Fuller et al. (eds.), *Piagetian Programs in Higher Education*, ADAPT Program, 79–88.

Nickerson, R. S. 1998. "Confirmation bias: a ubiquitous phenomenon in many guises." *Review of General Psychology* 2(2), 175–220.

Perkins, D. N., R. Allen, and J. Hafner 1983. "Difficulties in everyday reasoning." In W. Maxwell and J. Bruner (eds.), *Thinking: The Expanding Frontier*, Franklin Institute Press, 177–189.

Perkins, D. N., M. Faraday, and B. Bushey 1991. "Everyday reasoning and the roots of intelligence." In J. F. Voss, D. N. Perkins, and J. W. Segal (eds.), *Informal Reasoning and Education*, Lawrence Erlbaum Associates, 83–105.

Ross, D. 2007. *Economic Theory and Cognitive Science*. MIT Press.

Sen, A. K. 1977. "Rational fools: a critique of the behavioral foundations of economic theory." *Philosophy & Public Affairs*, 317–344.

Sober, E. 2008. *Evidence and Evolution: The Logic Behind the Science*. Cambridge University Press.

Vromen, J. J. 2007. "In praise of moderate plurality." In J. Groenewegen (ed.), *Teaching Pluralism in Economics*, Edward Elgar, 64–94.

11 Academic women's careers in the social sciences

Donna Ginther and Shulamit Kahn

1 Introduction

Academic careers consist of a series of milestones: the doctorate, tenure track employment, and promotion through the ranks to tenured full professorships. While several researchers, including us, have examined career outcomes for women in science disciplines where they are traditionally underrepresented, few studies have examined academic careers for women in the social sciences. This chapter begins from the point when social scientists receive their Ph.D.s and investigates gender differences in career milestones as women move up the academic career ladder, getting tenure-track jobs, being granted tenure, and being promoted to full professorships.

Although women now make up the majority of US undergraduate students, as one traverses the hierarchy of academia, women make up smaller percentages of graduate students, assistant professors, and tenured faculty. This is especially true in physical science and engineering disciplines (Long 2001; Ginther 2006a, 2006b). There is a large body of literature about women and science, particularly since 1982 when Congress instructed the National Science Foundation (NSF) to report biennially on the status of women and minorities in science. The NSF reports have consistently shown that since 1982 and through the most recent report (NSF 2012), women continue to be less likely than their male colleagues to be full professors and more likely to be assistant professors. Two National Academies studies have examined women in academic science careers and the two have drawn opposite conclusions. Although the *Beyond Bias and Barriers* (National Academies 2006) report contains evidence of no gender differences in promotion to tenure in science fields (Ginther 2006a, 2006b), it concludes that discrimination and institutional barriers account for the underrepresentation of women in science careers. A subsequent study by the Academies, *Gender Differences at Critical Transitions in the Careers of Science, Engineering and Mathematics Faculty* (National Academies

2011) finds no evidence of barriers in the hiring and promotion of women in the fields that were surveyed.

When researchers have studied social sciences, they have often included them with science disciplines. Long (2001) examines the careers of women in science and social science combined from 1973–1995 and concludes that women have been successful in moving "from scarcity to visibility." This conclusion, in part, results from combining all science and social science disciplines together. Women have made great strides in representation in the social sciences and life sciences relative to anemic gains in physical science and engineering. A recent analysis by the NSF (NSF 2004) provides a comprehensive study of the factors contributing to promotion in academic careers of scientists and social scientists combined. This work uses NSF's longitudinal Survey of Doctorate Recipients (SDR), the source we use in this paper, and finds that controlling for human capital, personal characteristics, and institutional factors, there remains a significant female disadvantage in the likelihood of being in a tenure-track job, of receiving tenure, and of being promoted to full. However, in most of their specifications, they find that these gender differences become statistically insignificant when family characteristics are allowed to affect men and women differently. Ginther (2001, 2006a, 2006b) and Ginther and Kahn (2004, 2009) caution that one cannot generalize the findings from one academic discipline (science) to others (e.g. social science).

Few papers have examined gender differences in academic social science careers separately. Rudd, Morrison, Picciano, and Nerad (2008) report on data collected in the fields of anthropology, communication, geography, history, political science, and sociology. They find few gender differences in academic career milestones with the exception that men are slightly more likely to get tenure in these fields in Research I institutions. Morrison, Rudd, and Nerad (2011) use the same data as the previous study to examine gender differences in the effect of marriage and parenthood on academic career milestones. They find that women are somewhat less likely to get tenure-track jobs, but that women who are parents are more likely to get tenure-track jobs. They also find no significant gender differences in promotion. However, these two studies do not include all social science disciplines, excluding the large fields of economics and psychology.

To preview our results, we find that *ceteris paribus*, women with children are less likely than similar men to enter tenure-track jobs but not single childless women, suggesting that women's entry into tenure-track academia is dominated by choice rather than by any discrimination at hiring. Further, we find that *ceteris paribus*, gender differences in tenure award existed in the cohort of 1980s Ph.D.s but disappeared for the cohort of 1999 Ph.D.s. The exception is the field of economics, where at least the probit analysis suggests a gender difference of approximately 20% that has not disappeared and is even larger for those single and childless. Finally, we find that there does seem to be gender differences in promotion to full in social science as a whole and in economics, sociology, and anthropology/linguistics.

The remainder of the chapter is organized as follows: we first describe the present representation of women in social science academia and the trends that led to where we are now, and motivate the analysis in the rest of this chapter. We then discuss our data and methodology, before we move to the meat of our chapter: analyzing each of the three major academic milestones – starting in a tenure-track job, being awarded tenure, and being promoted to full professorship – in three separate sections. The final section concludes.

2 Social science's major improvements in women's representation

Women have made great strides in doctorates awarded in the social and behavioral sciences. The NSF conducts a census of doctorates granted in the US in its *Survey of Earned Doctorates (SED)*. Figure 11.1, based on the SED, shows that in 1974 just 33% of doctorates in social and behavioral sciences were awarded to women. Rapid increase in female representation has occurred since that point, culminating in an average 57% female in 2010 among social science Ph.D.s. Since 1990, a greater

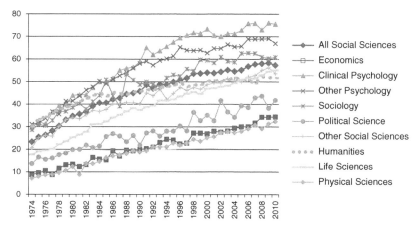

Figure 11.1 Percentage of doctorates awarded to females.
Source: Survey of Earned Doctorates 1980–2011

percentage of doctorates were awarded to women in the social sciences than in the humanities.

Have these gains carried over to women's representation in academia? To answer this, we use data from the 1981–2008 waves of the Survey of Doctorate Recipients (SDR). The SDR is a biennial, longitudinal survey of doctorate recipients from US institutions conducted by the National Science Foundation[1] and is the data source for most of the analysis in this chapter.

Figure 11.2 shows the percentage female for social science as a whole with the three key tenure-track ranks: untenured assistant professors, tenured associate professors, and tenured full professors. If men and women with recent Ph.D.s had equal likelihoods of entering social science academia, the percentage female among tenure-track assistant professors shown in Table 11.2 would mirror that of Ph.D.s in the previous six or so years. For social sciences on average, in 1981, 30% of Ph.D.s from the previous six years had been women, while 27% of assistant professors were. By 2008, 56% of Ph.D.s from the previous six years had been women, while about 50% of tenure-track assistant professors were women, so that in both of these years, both sexes had approximately equal chances of getting a tenure-track job. Moreover, both percentages female among Ph.D.s and among tenure-track assistants showed remarkable increases over the past three decades, almost doubling.

Women's representation at the tenured associate level seems to be even more in line with the Ph.D. pool feeding into it. For instance, it is reasonable to roughly assume that tenured associates tend to be from cohorts who received Ph.D.s between 6 and 15 years earlier. In 1981, 21% of tenured associate professors were women. While we do not have exact Ph.D. averages for the entire 6–15 years prior to 1981, our earliest data point of 1974 (7 years earlier) had 23% of social sciences women and rising quickly. The 21% tenured associate figure seems to match this well. In 2008, the cohort of Ph.D.s received the previous 6–15 years was 50% female, exactly matching the percentage female of tenured associate professors in 2008.

However, women are not represented in the top echelon of academia – full professors – in numbers anywhere near their representation among lower ranks. In fact, in social science as a whole, in 2008 women were only 27% of full professors. We have to go back to 1976, 32 years previously, to find a similar female percentage of Ph.D.s.

---

[1] Prior to 1993, the SDR was administered by the National Research Council. Note that there was a two-year gap from 2003 to 2006, and from then on the SDR is once again biennial, now administered in the even years.

(a)

All Social Sciences

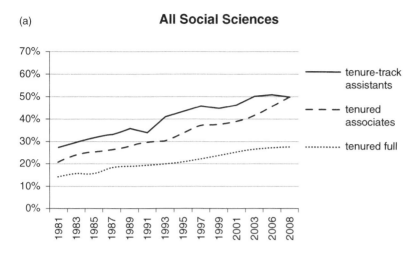

(b)

Economics

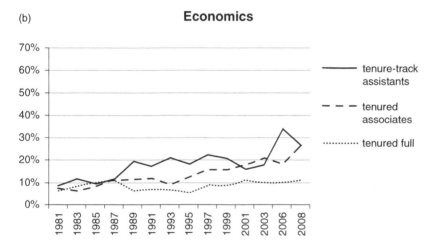

Figure 11.2 Percentage female by academic rank.
Source: Survey of Doctorate Recipients 1981–2008

There is no prima facie evidence of sex-linked differences, therefore, at the stage of appointment to tenure-track jobs or at the tenure decision, but there do seem to be sex differences at the point of promotion to full professorship. However, we cannot tell whether the former similarity or the latter differences will remain once we try to compare similar men and women, similar with respect to background ability and similar with respect to productivity. Men and women may have radically

Figure 11.2 (*cont.*)

different quality of Ph.D. education. In terms of publications, research on data from the 1980s and 1990s shows that publication rates of women in science and engineering (S&E) have been lower than men (Stack 2004; Sax et. al 2002; Xie and Shauman 1998, 2003; Levin and Stephan 1998; Bellas and Toutkoushian 1999). The gender differences are smaller once controls for teaching responsibilities are added (Bellas and Toutkoushian 1999; Xie and Shauman 1998, 2003) but it is difficult to know whether these additional responsibilities were imposed on women or chosen by them. Research on time series data finds that gender differences in publishing have narrowed substantially over time, suggesting a future convergence in women's and men's academic productivity. (Sax et. al 2002; Xie and Shauman 1998, 2003. Xie and Shauman found the male/female ratio narrowed from 58% in the late 1960s to 80% in 1993.)

Thus, a major goal of our analysis in this chapter will be to control for background and productivity characteristics to study the progression of individuals through the three major milestones of academic success in the social sciences.

Moreover, career choice and productivity may be affected by family choices. Long (2001) found that the impact of marriage and children on women's careers in sciences including social science had largely been eliminated by 1995. However, men were still four percent more likely to receive tenure. On the other hand, Wolfinger, Mason and Goulden (2008) find that in academia as a whole, children reduce the likelihood that women take tenure-track positions but have little effect on promotion to tenure. An impact of marriage and children on women's publications has been shown by Fox (2005) and Stack (2004), although not always in the direction one might expect. Fox (2005), using data from the 1990s, finds that older children slow women's research productivity but that older women with pre-school children are *more* productive than those with older children. Stack (2004) also finds that young children are positively correlated with publishing. However, Sax et. al. (2002) studying faculty at research universities find no significant impact of family characteristics on research productivity.

We revisit these issues in our study, comparing the impact of women and children on men and women's progress in their academic careers.

Finally, this chapter considers the separate fields within social science. Research by Ginther and Hayes (1999, 2003), Ginther (2001, 2003, 2004, 2006a, 2006b), and Ginther and Kahn (2004, 2009) demonstrates that employment outcomes and the impact of covariates differ by academic field. In particular, our previous work (Ginther and Kahn 2004) on economics identified substantial gender differences in promotion in economics, differences that surpassed those in the comparison fields of statistics, political science, and natural sciences.

Figure 11.1 also documents wide differences between Ph.D. fields in the percentage female even within social sciences. Economics clearly has fewest women, with just 33% female in 2010. As seen in the figure, economics is most similar to physical sciences and lies far below most other fields shown, including life sciences. The only other social science field that continues to have less than 50% of its Ph.D.s awarded to females is political science, which reached 42% female by 2010. The same underrepresentation of women in economics spills over to academic employment, where only 11% of full professors and less than 30% of assistant and associate professors were women.

Together, this evidence suggests that it is necessary to separately analyze fields within social sciences. Therefore, our analyses are estimated separately for specific fields, dividing the social sciences into economics, psychology, sociology, political science, and other social sciences (in which the largest two fields are anthropology and linguistics) as long as we had sufficient numbers of observations to do so. Further, because a relatively large percentage of Ph.D.s in clinical psychology choose clinical rather than academic careers, we analyze the tenure-track transition separately for clinical and other psychologists. Although some fields are quite small particularly as we move up the promotion ladder (see Table 11.1), our analysis shows that even within the smaller fields, many gender differences are large enough to be statistically significant.

The analysis of economics here also updates our previous 1994 work by examining SDR data from 1973–2001 to a somewhat later period – from 1981–2008. Also, of course, it performs similar analysis on all other social sciences.

3   Data and empirical methodology

As we said above, our analysis of promotion uses data from the 1981–2008 waves of the NSF's biennial, longitudinal survey, the SDR. The SDR collects detailed information on doctorate recipients including demographic characteristics, educational background, employer characteristics, academic rank, government support, primary work activity, productivity, and salary. We use the SDR from 1981 to the last year of SDR microdata available, 2008. The SDR has undergone substantial changes in the sampling frame and survey content between the 1981 and 1993 waves (Mitchell, Moonesinge, and Cox 1998). Technical reports provided by the National Science Foundation have allowed us to construct a longitudinal data set with consistent variable definitions over time.

We have selected a longitudinal extract of doctorate recipients in the social and behavioral sciences, thus including psychology, who received their Ph.D.s between the years of 1981 and 2007 (although for the analysis of promotion to full we start with the 1979 Ph.D. cohort).

Table 11.1 *Weighted means of dependent variables*

	Total	Female	Male	# Obs
The proportion of doctorates on tenure track within 6 years of Ph.D.*				
All	**0.320**	**0.271**	**0.369**	7,707
Economics	**0.491**	**0.398**	**0.520**	892
Clinical Psychology	**0.106**	**0.089**	**0.131**	1,548
Psychology	0.243	0.235	0.254	2,496
Sociology	**0.566**	**0.500**	**0.637**	733
Political Science	0.516	0.523	0.513	755
Other Social Sciences	0.384	0.376	0.392	1,283
The proportion of tenure-track professors who are promoted to tenure within 11 years of Ph.D.**				
All	**0.699**	**0.646**	**0.733**	1,906
Economics	*0.706*	*0.588*	*0.731*	336
Psychology	0.636	0.581	0.697	586
Sociology	0.763	0.748	0.774	306
Political Science	*0.733*	*0.646*	*0.771*	284
Other Social Sciences	0.722	0.731	0.715	394
The proportion of tenured professors who are promoted to full professor within 7 years of tenure receipt**				
All	**0.454**	**0.370**	**0.496**	1,130
Economics	*0.527*	*0.294*	*0.560*	210
Psychology (including Clinical)	0.439	0.434	0.444	308
Sociology	*0.410*	*0.309*	*0.475*	193
Political Science	0.456	0.378	0.481	177
Other Social Sciences	**0.425**	**0.336**	**0.501**	242

Bold: gender difference significant at 1% level; ***Bold Italics:*** at 5% level; <u>Underline</u>: at 10% level
* Sample limited to 1981 to 2003 Ph.D.s
** Sample limited to those who received a tenure-track job within 6 years of Ph.D., 1981 to 1998 Ph.D.s
*** Sample limited to those who received tenure within 11 years of Ph.D., 1979 to 1995 Ph.D.s

We exclude individuals who are not observed early enough or long enough for each specific analysis, as explained below.

Dependent variables

We estimate three career milestones. First, we examine the probability of obtaining a tenure-track job within 6 years of the Ph.D. using probit analysis. For this, we include everyone observed by the SDR at approximately 6 years[2] post-Ph.D. and consequently we limited our consideration to those who received Ph.D.s before 2003 (who were thus able to be observed 6 years post-Ph.D. in 2008.)

Next, we restrict the analysis to those who held a tenure-track job within 6 years of their Ph.D. to analyze the first award of tenure. Tenure award is modeled both using probit and Cox semi-proportional hazard methodologies. For the probit analysis, we modeled the probability of receiving tenure within approximately 11 years of Ph.D. and thus excluded those who received their Ph.D.s after 1998, those who did not hold a tenure-track job within 6 years of their Ph.D., and also those who were not observed at approximately 11 years post-Ph.D.[3] The hazard analysis models time from Ph.D. until tenure, again limiting the population to those who held a tenure-track job with 6 years.

For the probit analysis of full professorship, we model the probability that someone who had been tenured within 11 years of Ph.D. received promotion to full professorship within 7 years of being tenured. We therefore include only those who were observed at approximately 7 years post-tenure receipt and exclude those who received their Ph.D.s after 1995. In order to add observations, we extend the full analysis back to 1978 Ph.D.s.

A major difference between the hazard analyses and the probit analyses is that in the hazard analysis, we are able to include people regardless of the length of time they were observed (i.e. either since Ph.D. or since tenure receipt) because the hazard analysis merely considers everyone who drops out of the survey before that time as censored. The hazard analysis therefore allows us to include more observations, to include people from later cohorts, and to capture the entire year-by-year pattern of promotion.

---

[2] Because of the biennial nature of the SDR and the fact that respondents sometimes skipped one or two surveys, we could not only include people observed at six years exactly. Instead, we included people if they had been observed some time during years 1–6 and were observed at least once between years 5 and 10.

[3] The algorithm we used was complicated, in order to include as many people as possible since the number of social science Ph.D.s who had been on the tenure track and were interviewed by the SDR is limited. First, if the person was not observed during year 11, we looked instead at year 12. If not observed in either of those years, we looked at year 10 and then at year 13. However, because people who do not receive or did not expect to receive tenure were more likely to drop out of the SDR, we did the following. If they were last observed in the SDR any time between year 6 and year 9 post-Ph.D., we included them as tenured if they were tenured at all during that period, and as untenured if they were never observed in tenure and were in non-tenure-track academia or outside of academia when last observed. This process allowed us to categorize all but 4 people last observed between years 6 and 9 (among the set of people who had been tenure track by year 6), assuring us that we had not introduced selection bias.

From the 1981 through 1991 surveys, respondents provided the exact year that they received tenure, which adds some accuracy given the biennial nature of the survey. For later surveys, tenure year is imputed as the first year a person is observed with tenure in the sample. We impute the year a person receives full professorship as the first year a person is observed as a tenured full professor in the sample. Therefore, given the biennial nature of the survey, years until tenure and years until full professor may be measured with an error of $+/-$ one year.

Table 11.1 gives means of the dependent variables and the numbers of observations in each probit analysis. The number of observations in each hazard rate analysis is given along with hazard results in Table 11.6. All averages and analyses are weighted.

Control variables

All specifications include non-time varying control variables that describe the person's background and education: Ph.D. year, gender, race, field, whether a citizen and whether a temporary resident at Ph.D. receipt or any time within 6 years of Ph.D., and the person's Ph.D. institution's quality. The Ph.D. quality is measured by dummy variables based on rankings from the Carnegie Foundation for the Advancement of Teaching and of Comprehensive and Liberal Arts Institutions. We also include the National Resource Council's ranking of the person's Ph.D. department, although this involved some imputing and thus may be a very noisy indicator.[4] Gender-specific means of the background variables at the different stages of academic careers are given in Table 11.2.

Given the large increase in female labor force participation and in higher education rates of women over the past half-century, we wanted to test whether any gender differences we identified in social science academia were decreasing during the period of 1981 to 2008. We therefore ran additional specifications with an interaction term between Ph.D. cohort and the female dummy. For these specifications, we report the implied gender differences for both the 1981 Ph.D. cohort and the 1998 Ph.D. cohort.

Some specifications also include marriage and children variables interacted with gender. Since family characteristics vary over time, these family variables are converted into dummies for whether they equal one

---

[4] Specifically, we use 1993 Carnegie tier for those with Ph.D.s after 1987 and 1982 tiers for earlier Ph.D.s. We use 1994 NRC ratings for those with Ph.D.s after 1988 and the 1987 rankings for earlier Ph.D.s, adjusting the 1987 ratings for the overall shift in NRC rankings between 1987 and 1994 and imputing missing ratings based on other evidence.

Table 11.2 *Gender differences in mean characteristics of probit analyses (weighted)*

Variables:	Population:	All doctorates (in tenure track probit analysis)*		All tenure-track within 6 years (for tenure probit analysis)**		All tenured within 11 years (for full probit analysis)***	
		Female	Male	Female	Male	Female	Male
Background	Percent of total Population	0.498	0.502	0.395	0.605	0.331	0.618
	Age at Ph.D.	**35.473**	**34.435**	**34.039**	**33.031**	**34.531**	**32.39**
	White	0.836	0.837	0.817	0.807	0.857	0.845
	African, Native American, Mixed	**0.060**	***0.048***	***0.078***	***0.051***	0.057	0.051
	Asian	0.060	0.077	0.062	***0.100***	0.049	0.072
	Hispanic	0.042	0.035	0.042	0.043	0.037	0.032
	Citizen	**0.933**	**0.878**	**0.916**	**0.829**	**0.936**	**0.883**
	Temporary residence visa	0.030	0.048	0.039	0.057	0.031	0.044
	Year of Ph.D.	1992.6	1990.8	1989.8	1988.5	1987.0	1985.3
	Ph.D. from Research I	0.588	0.618	0.727	0.719	0.757	0.720
	Ph.D. from Research II	0.140	0.139	0.126	0.146	***0.108***	***0.159***
	Ph.D. from Doctorate I	0.142	0.143	*0.081*	*0.105*	0.082	0.096
	Ph.D. from Doctorate II	0.047	0.049	0.033	0.025	*0.033*	*0.017*
	Ph.D. department NRC rating	2.95	2.97	3.203	3.196	3.237	3.151
Family	Single no children	**0.226**	**0.181**	**0.214**	**0.113**	**0.211**	**0.091**
	Married	**0.745**	**0.812**	**0.744**	**0.884**	**0.745**	**0.891**
	Children	**0.465**	**0.561**	**0.533**	**0.695**	**0.519**	**0.749**
	Children <6	**0.349**	**0.449**	**0.421**	**0.575**	**0.348**	**0.534**
	Only older children	0.116	0.112	0.112	0.120	*0.172*	*0.214*
Employer/	% years Research I employer			8.08	7.72	8.14	8.02
Productivity	% years Research II employer			1.90	1.84	2.17	2.45
	% years Liberal Arts I employer			1.96	1.91	2.46	2.97
	% years with Government Support			5.57	5.53	6.36	6.72
	Avg. bi-annual refereed publications			***0.293***	*0.404*	0.466	0.535
	% years research primary or secondary activity			*19.20*	*19.75*	**19.16**	**20.91**
	% years teaching primary activity			15.90	14.95	20.03	18.70

Bold: gender difference significant at 1% level; ***Bold Italics:*** at 5% level; Underline: at 10% level

* Sample limited to 1981 to 2003 Ph.D.s

** Sample limited to those who received a tenure-track job within 6 years of Ph.D., 1981 to 1998 Ph.D.s

*** Sample limited to those who received tenure within 11 years of Ph.D., 1979 to 1995 Ph.D.s

at any time during the relevant period. For instance, the married variable for the tenure-track analysis equals one if the person was married anytime during the first 6 years post-Ph.D., for the tenure analysis anytime during the first 11 years, and for the full analysis anytime between tenure receipt and 7 years after. However, our category "single no children" takes a value of one only if the person was single with no children for all of the relevant period, and our category "only older children" takes on the value of one if the person has older children sometime during the period, but has no younger children (<6 years) at any time during the period. The dummy variables we create in this way are then multiplied by a female and male dummy respectively and the interactions terms are included instead of the female dummy. This allowed us to answer questions such as "What is the effect of marriage on women?" or "How do single women and men compare?" The gender-specific means of some of the family variables at the different stages of academic careers are given in the middle panel of Table 11.2. Note that family situations that are relatively rare (given the life stage being modeled) will have large standard errors for their gender difference, a point that we return to in later discussion.

We report results for what we deem to be the most important family-related questions in separate tables (Tables 11.6 and 11.8). Note that we also have estimated the promotion hazard equations using time-varying contemporaneous family dummy variables each year, rather than a dummy for whether the person fell into a specific family category anytime during the relevant time span. However, the specification with contemporaneous family variables had less predictive power and therefore is not reported here.

The last column of Table 11.4 and 11.5 (tenure and full analyses) adds to the background characteristics additional variables that relate to the person's employer type, work activities, and publications, all added to capture or proxy the productivity of the person.[5] This includes whether the employer is a Research I university, whether the employer is a Research II University, whether the employer is a Liberal Arts I college, whether the primary or secondary work activity was research, whether the primary work activity was teaching, whether the person received government support, and a limited publications measure. Measures of publications are largely missing from the SDR data, but the SDR does ask questions about refereed articles in the 1983, 1995, 2001, 2003, and 2008 surveys. The 1983 question refers to publications between 1980 and 1983 whereas the 1995–2008 questions refer to numbers of publications in the previous

---

[5] Employer and other productivity as careers unfold cannot be included in the models of whether Ph.D.s get tenure-track jobs. We have no publication data for pre-Ph.D.

five years. We use these data to create rough measures of refereed articles published per two-year period. Although this variable is clearly inaccurate since it is based on averages over several years, it nevertheless seems preferable to omitting the information altogether.

These "productivity" variables were converted to means over the relevant period for the probit analyses (for instance, for the tenure analysis, the percentage of surveys observed during the first 11 years post-Ph.D. that the person worked in a Research I university). The bottom panel of Table 11.2 gives the gender-specific means of these variables.

We realize that these variables as well as the family variables may be picking up unobserved heterogeneity rather than causality and are careful to clarify their possible interpretations in the discussion below.

Finally, note that Tables 11.3–11.8 show the gender differences but not the coefficients of other covariates. The entire equations are available upon request from the authors.

4   Stepping onto the academic career ladder

A Ph.D. in the social sciences – with the exception of clinical psychology – tends to be only absolutely necessary (as opposed to advantageous) for tenure-track faculty in institutions of higher education. Moreover, professors in these fields often socialize their Ph.D. students into believing that a tenured job in academia is the most prestigious job one could do with their Ph.D. Nevertheless, the majority of Ph.D.s do not enter a tenure-track job within six years of receiving their Ph.D. in many social science fields, as Table 11.1 shows. This section analyzes the likelihood of obtaining a tenure-track job. Of the three milestones studied here, this is the one most likely to be a complex combination of supply – the choice of the Ph.D. to enter this career track – in addition to demand – the choice of departments to hire the person.

As mentioned earlier, Figure 11.1 illustrates the continuous growth in the percentage of the Ph.D.s granted in social science going to females in all fields between 1974 and 2010, almost doubling (from 24% to 57%). The top row of Table 11.1 gives the percentage of females and males who are observed in tenure-track jobs within (approximately) the first six years post-Ph.D. for social science as a whole. Fewer women than men have tenure-track jobs within six years of Ph.D. receipt: 37 percent of men compared to 27 percent of women.[6]

---

[6] Recall that these overall average rates may be somewhat higher than observed among all doctoral recipients because of those who received doctorates after 2000, only those who were observed in a tenure-track job are included in this analysis.

Table 11.3 *Percentage point impact of being female on the probability of being in a tenure-track job (from probit analysis)*

	Background covariates	Background covariates with female*Ph.D. year interaction		Background & family covariates:
	Background covariates	Female w. 1981 Ph.D.	Female w. 1999 Ph.D.	single childless female v. similar male
ALL	−4.03	−4.02	−3.7	7.93
	(1.27)	(2.20)	(1.64)	(3.12)
Economics	−11.83	−12.46	−10.87	19.43
	(4.13)	(7.98)	(5.78)	*(9.07)*
Clinical Psychology	*−4.21*	2.04	−9.62	−2.6
	(1.70)	(3.27)	**(2.63)**	3.13
Psychology*	−1.64	1.28	−3.62	*8.73*
	(1.96)	(3.57)	(2.79)	*(4.09)*
Sociology	−15.28	−16.5	−12.66	−8.76
	(4.59)	*(7.98)*	*(6.08)*	(9.69)
Political Science	1.50	−7.05	5.65	*21.50*
	(4.42)	(9.09)	(5.28)	*(8.89)*
Other Social Sciences	−0.46	2.44	−2.09	−2.73
	(3.27)	(6.04)	(4.18)	(6.93)

Robust standard errors in parentheses. **Bold:** significant at the 1% level; ***Bold Italics:*** the 5% level; Underline: the 10% level
Sample limited to 1981 to 2003 Ph.D.s

This gender difference in the likelihood of holding a tenure-track job may not indicate that identical men and women are starting in different jobs, but instead may be picking up gender differences in background factors such as field, race, and Ph.D. quality. After all, we see in Table 11.2 that women are older at Ph.D. receipt, come from later cohorts on average, are more likely to be black and to be citizens, and are less likely to be Asian and temporary residents. Also, fewer received their degrees from major research (R1) institutions, although the (noisy) NRC rankings of Ph.D. institutions are not significantly different for men and women.

We therefore turn to our probit and hazard models of the longitudinal data to control for these factors. The first column of Table 11.3 shows the gender differences in obtaining a tenure-track job during the first six years post-Ph.D. from a probit analysis controlling for background covariates. There is a highly significant 4.0 *percentage point* female

Table 11.4 *Impact of being female on the probability of receiving tenure within 11 years of Ph.D. (from probit analysis)*

	Background covariates	Background covariates with female*Ph.D. year interaction		Background & family covariates: single childless female v. similar male	Background & productivity covariates
		Female w. 1981 Ph.D.	Female w. 1999 Ph.D.		
ALL	−7.13	−15.33	0.33	−4.60	−5.94
	(2.53)	(5.11)	(4.55)	(6.40)	(2.58)
Economics	−14.41	−13.00	−15.92	−33.89	−12.21
	(5.74)	(13.09)	(12.85)	(15.79)	(5.93)
Psychology (incl. Clinical)	−11.14	−26.23	3.77	−3.82	−9.65
	(4.47)	(8.86)	(8.48)	(11.41)	(4.34)
Sociology	−0.62	−13.83	11.90	7.29	3.76
	(5.82)	(11.45)	(10.58)	(11.62)	(5.54)
Political Science	−7.07	−11.80	−3.60	−16.51	−7.88
	(5.53)	(12.71)	(9.56)	(12.65)	(5.32)
Other Social Sciences	1.39	0.44	2.17	8.15	2.17
	(5.38)	(12.33)	(9.40)	(1.30)	(5.24)

Robust standard errors in parentheses. **Bold:** significant at the 1% level; ***Bold Italics:*** the 5% level; <u>Underline</u>: the 10% level
Sample limited to those who received a tenure-track job within 6 years of Ph.D., 1981 to 1998 Ph.D.s

disadvantage in the likelihood of obtaining a tenure-track job six years after Ph.D. receipt (which translates into women being 11% less likely than men to obtain the job). The fact that this gap is much smaller than the 10 percentage point average gender difference of Table 11.1 indicates that a great deal of the raw difference was due to different female and male background covariates.

The second and third column are based on a specification including an interaction term between female and Ph.D. year, along with background characteristic controls, in order to test whether the sex differences in the likelihood of receiving a tenure-track job changed over the decades studied. For social science overall, the interaction term is not statistically significantly different from zero and the estimated sex difference in obtaining a tenure-track job for 1981 Ph.D.s and 1999 Ph.D.s in social science as a whole is very small.

Table 11.5 *Impact of being female on the probability of achieving full professorship within 7 years of tenure receipt (from probit analysis)*

	Background covariates	Background covariates with female*Ph.D. year interaction		Background & family covariates: single childless female v. similar male	Background & productivity covariates
		Female w. 1981 Ph.D.	Female w. 1999 Ph.D.		
ALL	−11.08	−14.46	−3.21	−5.72	*−9.56*
	(3.48)	(4.93)	(8.92)	(9.16)	*(3.42)*
Economics	−24.93	*−29.27*	−16.54	19.38	*−23.03*
	(9.26)	*(12.69)*	(24.21)	(18.55)	*(9.47)*
Psychology (incl. Clinical)	−3.04	−4.05	−0.27	7.89	−0.55
	(6.05)	(8.25)	(16.78)	(14.88)	(5.80)
Sociology	*−16.55*	−9.00	−36.97	*−44.77*	−13.41
	(8.34)	(12.19)	(21.55)	*(17.45)*	(8.30)
Political Science	−5.88	−16.60	15.54	−22.82	−8.99
	(9.01)	(13.93)	(20.91)	(19.84)	(8.65)
Other Social Sciences	*−15.08*	−27.07	10.16	−19.17	−13.37
	(6.95)	*(9.87)*	(17.63)	(17.81)	(7.02)

Robust standard errors in parentheses. **Bold:** significant at the 1% level; ***Bold Italics:*** at the 5% level; Underline: at the 10% level
Sample limited to those who received tenure within 11 years of Ph.D., 1979 to 1995 Ph.D.s

The rest of the rows in the top panel of Table 11.1 and of Table 11.3 divide this analysis by social-science field and indicate wide differences between fields. The gender differences in the average rates of tenure receipt in Table 11.1 are very large for economics and sociology – each with a gender difference that represents about 24% of the average likelihood of receiving a tenure-track job (12.2 and 13.7 percentage points respectively) – and for clinical psychology, where the 4.2 percentage point gender difference represents a full 40% of the (low) average likelihood of entering a tenure-track job. The other fields have no significant female disadvantage, and in political science the point estimate even suggests that more women enter tenure-track jobs than men.

These field-specific gender differences are hardly different when controlling for background characteristics. Thus, in Table 11.2 (first column),

Table 11.6 *Probit analysis – gender differences by family situation*

	Receive tenure-track job within 6 years of Ph.D.	Receive tenure within 11 years of Ph.D.**	Receive full within 7 years of tenure receipt***
Effect of marriage on childless woman	−3.22	7.75	*14.96*
	(2.27)	(5.04)	*(7.58)*
Effect of child on woman	**−10.36**	4.51	−8.40
	(1.55)	(3.40)	(5.37)
Effect of young child on woman	**−11.47**	1.50	−9.22
	(1.62)	(3.67)	(6.20)
Effect of only older child on woman	*−6.23*	**15.87**	−6.11
	(2.53)	**(5.68)**	(7.15)
Single woman v. single man	**7.93**	−4.60	−5.72
	(3.12)	(6.40)	(9.16)
Married woman w. child v. similar man	**−11.19**	**−7.67**	**−16.43**
	(1.61)	*(3.21)*	**(4.60)**
Married woman w. young child v. similar man	**−12.42**	**−10.42**	**−19.19**
	(1.71)	**(3.50)**	**(5.53)**
Married woman w. only older child v. similar man	−5.21	7.59	−10.31
	(3.74)	(8.15)	(8.36)

Robust standard errors in parentheses. **Bold:** significant at the 1% level; ***Bold Italics:*** at the 5% level; Underline: at the 10% level

** Sample limited to those who received a tenure-track job within 6 years of Ph.D., 1981 and later Ph.D.s

*** Sample limited to those who received tenure within 11 years of Ph.D., 1979 Ph.D.s and later

Equations include background covariates and family variables.

economics and clinical psychology display only marginally smaller gender differences in the probability of entering tenure-track jobs. In sociology, adding controls actually increased the estimated gender difference. The other fields continue to have small and insignificant gender differences of varying signs.

In the field-specific equations allowing the female impact to change over time, the only field with a significant interaction term is clinical psychology, where women are becoming *less* likely to enter tenure-track jobs. In 1981, women were slightly more likely than men to enter tenure-track academia but in 1999 women were 9.6 percentage points less likely than men to enter tenure track.

Marriage and fertility decisions may be affecting women's tenure-track employment differently than men's. To investigate this possibility, we included gender-specific variables for combinations of marital status and children in additional probit analysis and report key comparisons in the first column of Table 11.6. Specifically, we report on the impact of these family choices on women, and on comparisons between otherwise

Table 11.7 *Differences in the risk ratio (female/male) from hazard of promotion*

	Background covariates	Background covariates with female*PhD year interaction		Background & family covariates: single childless female v. similar male	Background & productivity covariates	People/observations
		Female w. 1981 Ph.D.	Female w. 1999 Ph.D.			
Promotion to tenure**						
ALL	*0.889*	*0.795*	0.965	1.181	0.915	3,384/10,396
	(0.047)	*(.087)*	(.080)	(.182)	(.047)	
Economics	0.788	1.120	0.617	0.768	0.805	581/1,790
	(0.113)	(.292)	(.174)	(.275)	(.104)	
Psychology (incl. Clinical)	*0.823*	*0.561*	1.111	1.203	0.836	1,017/3,317
	(.079)	*(.106)*	(.178)	(.336)	(.077)	
Sociology	0.927	0.679	1.152	1.005	0.973	553/1,687
	(.119)	(.182)	(.218)	(.340)	(.122)	
Political Science	0.865	1.112	0.747	1.636	0.834	525/1,522
	(.124)	(.366)	(.156)	(.602)	(.114)	
Other Social Sciences	1.063	1.209	0.970	1.085	1.114	708/2,080
	(.124)	(.324)	(.166)	(.401)	(.126)	
Promotion to full (since tenure receipt)***						
ALL	*0.743*	*0.706*	0.828	0.742	*0.752*	1,936/6,324
	(.056)	*(.075)*	(.134)	(0.192)	*(.056)*	
Economics	*0.557*	*0.497*	0.709	1.368	*0.572*	318/1083
	(.138)	*(.164)*	(.328)	(.843)	*(.147)*	
Psychology (incl. Clinical)	0.939	0.943	0.929	0.813	0.944	562/1,806
	(.126)	(.173)	(.280)	(.339)	(.125)	
Sociology	*0.686*	0.674	0.720	0.520	*0.677*	334/1,104
	(.126)	(.171)	(.282)	(.358)	*(.129)*	
Political Science	0.761	0.648	0.998	0.581	0.733	310/1,008
	(.146)	(.204)	(.417)	(.304)	(.134)	
Other Social Sciences	**0.566**	**0.451**	0.900	0.487	**0.567**	412/1,323
	(0.097)	**(0.110)**	(0.325)	(0.268)	**(0.096)**	

Robust standard errors in parentheses. **Bold:** significant at the 1% level; ***Bold Italics:*** at the 5% level; <u>Underline:</u> at the 10% level

** Sample limited to those who received a tenure-track job within 6 years of Ph.D., 1981 and later Ph.D.s

*** Sample limited to those who received tenure within 11 years of Ph.D, 1979 and later

303

Table 11.8 *Hazard analysis – gender differences by family situation*

Difference in female/male risk ratio	Promotion to tenure (time since Ph.D.)**	Promotion to full (time since tenured)***
Effect of marriage on childless woman	1.200	<u>1.466</u>
	(.149)	<u>(0.314)</u>
Effect of child on woman*	0.945	0.843
	(.076)	(0.126)
Effect of young child on woman*	0.878	0.781
	(.076)	(0.136)
Effect of only older child on woman*	<u>1.242</u>	0.983
	<u>(.147)</u>	(0.200)
Single woman v. single man	1.181	0.742
	(.182)	(0.192)
Married woman w. children v. similar man	**0.787**	**0.632**
	(.056)	**(0.081)**
Married woman w. young child v. similar man	**0.737**	**0.570**
	(.058)	**(.087)**
Married woman w. only older child v. similar man	1.139	0.78
	(.192)	(.185)

Standard errors in parentheses. **Bold:** significant at the 1% level; ***Bold Italics:*** at the 5% level; <u>Underline</u>: at the 10% level
** Sample limited to those who received a tenure-track job within 6 years of Ph.D., 1981 and later Ph.D.s
*** Sample limited to those who received tenure within 11 years of Ph.D., 1979 Ph.D.s and later
Equations include background covariates and family variables.

similar men and women by family composition. Because the comparison of single childless women and single childless men arguably might be most representative of the gender differences *not* due to women's greater family responsibilities, we have estimated these for the specific fields and included them in the last column of Table 11.3.

Single childless women are actually significantly *more* likely (7.9 percentage points p=.09) than childless single men to have a tenure-track job within six years of Ph.D. for social sciences as a whole. Again, this average conceals large differences across fields. Single women have a much *greater* likelihood than men to receive tenure-track jobs in political science (21.5 percentage points), economics (19.4 ppt.), and psychology (8.7 ppt.); in sociology, the point estimate suggests that single women remain less likely than men to enter a tenure-track job but insignificantly so. In the other fields, including clinical psychology, single men and single women are statistically indistinguishable. This sheds a different light on the large gender differences in economics, clinical psychology, and perhaps sociology, suggesting that the reason women were less likely to be observed in tenure-track jobs in these fields was due to family choices.

The first column of Table 11.6 gives more details on what family characteristics deter women from entering tenure-track jobs. Marriage itself does not significantly keep women from entering tenure-track jobs. However, having a child anytime within those six years make women 11 percentage points less likely to enter a tenure-track job, with the point estimate of the impact particularly large for those with pre-kindergarten aged children. Having only a child over the age of six during this period has less than half the impact of a younger child.

The rest of the rows of Table 11.4 compare married women to married men with similar-aged children. These tell a similar story: that married women with young children are much less likely than men with young children to enter tenure-track jobs. The female–male comparisons are somewhat larger than children's impact on women alone, because in social science academia – as in the labor market more generally – marriage and children tend to occur to more successful men, which in this context means that married men with children are *more* likely than single men to get a tenure-track job. In fact, in social science academia, the male marriage and child premia is relatively small on average relative to those seen in other less educated and homogeneous populations.

In the next section, we consider gender differences in tenure receipt.

5   Moving up the career ladder: the award of tenure

Returning to Figure 11.2(a), the dashed line shows the changing percentage female among social science associate professors. The trend is increasing, most likely dominated by the increasing proportions of women among assistant professorships. This does not answer the question of whether women and men have similar likelihoods of receiving tenure. For this, we use the longitudinal aspect of the data set. We get a sense of the size of average gender differences in tenure rates for those with Ph.D.s 1981–2003 who had had a tenure-track job (within 6 years of Ph.D.) from Table 11.1. Tenure-track women in social science academia are on average 8.7 percentage points less likely than men to receive tenure within 11 years of Ph.D.

This gender difference does not control for Ph.D. year, quality of Ph.D. institution, age at Ph.D. or race/citizenship variables. The first column of Table 11.4 summarizes the impact of gender on the probability of being promoted to tenure by 11 years from the doctorate controlling for these background variables, while the first column of the top panel of Table 11.7 presents the risk ratio, the ratio of female to male likelihood of being tenured each year from the hazard analysis controlling for these same variables. To allow us to compare the hazard rates to the averages and probit analyses, in our discussion here on tenure and promotion to full we convert probit results to the gender differences as a percentage of the male average.[7]

Gender differences in social science tenure rates controlling for background characteristics are somewhat lower than they were without controls. Women are 7.1 percentage points or 9.7% less likely than men to be tenured by 11 years post-doctorate in the probit analysis; in the hazard analysis, the estimated difference is similar: women are 11.1% less likely than men to receive tenure.

The top row of the next two columns of Table 11.4 and 11.7 indicate that this gender difference is disappearing over time for social science as a whole. The interaction between female and Ph.D. year is significantly positive in both the probit and hazard analyses, leading to a large and significant gender difference for the 1981 Ph.D. cohort: 15.3 percentage points or 20% in the probit and similarly 20% in the hazard. By 1999 the gender difference in tenure had fallen to zero.

Can the gender differences in tenure receipt (averaged over the period) be explained by productivity differences and differences in the nature of the jobs? Comparing the specification with only background characteristics (column 1 of Tables 11.4 and 11.7) and the specification with productivity covariates (the fifth column of these tables respectively), we see that adding controls for publications, employer quality, government support, and work activities lowers the average female tenure disadvantage to about 8% in the probit analysis (5.9 percentage points, down from 7.1) and in the hazard analysis.

Can gender differences in tenure receipt (again, averaged over the period) be explained by family situation? The first row of the fourth columns in Tables 11.4 and 11.7 show no significant difference between tenure receipt for single childless women and men, with varying signs, suggesting that, indeed, family was a major contributor to the average gender difference.[8]

---

[7] In other words, the tables on averages and probit give the gender differences in percentage points and therefore, we divide these by the average male level. For the hazard analysis we give 1 minus the female/male risk ratio.

[8] Recall that most family variables in both the probit and hazard analysis measure whether the person was observed in a family situation at any time during the 11 years since Ph.D., but that the "single and childless" equals 1 only if the person was single and childless throughout the 11 years since Ph.D.

Tables 11.6 and 11.8 give more details on family's impact. The first rows indicate that neither marriage nor children had any significant negative impact on women's tenure receipt. Indeed, having only older children seems to have had a positive impact on women's tenure receipt by 11 years in the probit analysis. However, the comparisons of married women and men with children – particularly with young children – indicate large tenure penalties for women, which would be consistent with the other analysis only if men have a large positive marriage and child wage premium. For instance, women who had pre-K children in the first 11 years post-Ph.D. were 10.4 percentage points or 14% percent less likely to get tenure than similar men according to the probit and about 25% less likely according to the hazard analysis.

Having only older (>5 years) children does not disadvantage women in attaining tenure and instead seems to increase their likelihood of achieving tenure. Combining this with the tenure-track results in the previous section, we conclude that women who had their children before they received their Ph.D.s were much less likely to have been on the tenure track (since they had pre-K kids in the first 6 years after Ph.D.) but these children did not deter tenure receipt for those who did achieve a tenure-track job.

As was true when explaining entrance into tenure-track academia, the fields within social sciences are different. Because of the importance of the tenure decision, we discuss each field in turn.

In *economics*, with no controls the average difference in tenure rates of women and men within 11 years is 14.3 percentage points or almost 20% (Table 11.1). Adding background controls does not change the size of this tenure penalty (Table 11.4) in the probit analysis. In the hazard analysis (Table 11.7), women's disadvantage with background controls is equal in size to the disadvantage in the probit, but is not significant at conventional levels. We did not discern any changes over time in women's tenure disadvantage, as evidenced by an insignificant inter-action term between female and Ph.D. year. Controlling for our albeit limited productivity measures does little to change the gender difference, except to render it significant in the hazard analysis.

Limiting the analysis to single childless economists, in the economics probit analysis not only does the gender difference not disappear, but it actually doubles. However, the hazard analysis tells a different story, inasmuch as for single childless women, the female disadvantage does not change in size but remains. We thus have ambiguous results for economics. Gender differences in tenure receipt are large despite controls and are not limited for women who have children in the probit analysis only. They are insignificant in the hazard analysis.

Political science has the second largest raw difference in men's and women's tenure rates (12.5 percentage points or 16%). In political science, however, the size of this difference falls considerably and becomes insignificantly different from zero when background covariates are added (in both probit and hazard analysis). There are no significant time trends in the gender difference, although the sign suggests smaller differences for later cohorts. Differences between single childless men and women are also insignificant, although of opposite signs in the two analyses.

Psychology is the final field with a substantial and significant raw gender difference in tenure rates, 11.6 percentage points (16%). This gender difference remains equally large and significant when background controls are added, and has similar significance and size in the probit and hazard analyses. However, single childless women and men do not have significantly different tenure rates. How much of the gender difference is due to productivity differences depends on whether one looks at the probit analysis, where large and significant gender differences remain even with productivity controls, or at the hazard analysis, where the difference become insignificant. However, both methodologies agree that there has been significant equalization in tenure rates over time (i.e. the interaction term between female and Ph.D. year is significantly positive), so much so that while the fitted female tenure penalty in 1981 was 26 percentage points or more than 35% (in both analyses), the fitted female penalty in 1999 had fallen to zero.

Finally, both *sociology* and *other social sciences* have no significant gender differences in tenure rates without controls and in all versions with controls in both the probit and hazard analyses.

We next evaluate whether we see the same patterns in promotion to full professor.

6   Making it to the top: promotion to full professorship

Returning to Figure 11.2(a), among full professors in social science, the percentage female has been steadily increasing over the quarter century but by 2006 still had not yet achieved the level of female representation that had been achieved in assistant professorships in the early 1980s, or the level of female representation that had been achieved in Ph.D.s in 1976. Economics is the most extreme, with only 11 percent of full professors being female in 2010. Is this due to earlier career stages, where women did not take tenure-track jobs or did not receive tenure? Or are women less likely to be promoted to full? The evidence on this is presented in this section, with the caveat that the size of the sample used in the analysis of promotion to full is considerably smaller than the samples for the earlier stages, and standard errors rise accordingly.

As Table 11.1 shows, on average 45% of faculty who had been tenured within 11 years of their Ph.D. are promoted to full professors within 7 years of having received tenure. Women are about 12.6 percentage points, which translates to 25%, less likely than men to receive full professorships by 7 years post-tenure (Table 11.1). This difference is hardly ameliorated by adding background controls or even by also adding productivity controls (Tables 11.5 and 11.7), falling in the probit only to 9.6 percentage points or 20% and falling less in the hazard. The time trend in the gender difference in promotion to full is insignificant.

These differences do not remain for single, childless men and women. The probit and hazard analysis agree that single, childless are not significantly different in their promotion to full *ceteris paribus*. There are, however, not many single childless men in this older sample, making this comparison less accurate and hence indicative.

Are these differences due to family responsibilities? Marriage alone increases the likelihood that a woman gets promoted to full (Tables 11.6 and 11.8). Children's impact on women's promotion to full is not significantly different than zero, although there is some suggestion that young children do deter it (p=.15 in both analyses). However, there remains a large promotion disadvantage for married women with children compared to married men with children. Again, note that childbirth and hence young children are less likely to occur during the period one is working toward full professorships.

The different fields are not uniform in their gender differences in promotion to full. **Economics** remains the field with the largest raw gender differences, but the two other fields that indicate large differences at this career stage are sociology and other social sciences.

Economics has the highest average likelihood of promotion to full within 7 years of tenure, and the largest unadjusted female penalty difference, measuring 26.6 percentage points and making women less than half as likely as men to be promoted to full within 7 years of tenure receipt. Adding in background characteristics and productivity variables as controls does little to change the magnitude or significance of this difference (Tables 11.5 and 11.7). There is no significant time trend in the gender differences. We note that comparison of single childless women and men is particularly inaccurate in these field-specific analyses of full promotion since there are even fewer numbers who fall in this category. In economics, there are only 9 men and 14 women.

Sociology had not shown significant gender differences at the tenure decision, but women have significantly lower likelihoods of being promoted to full professors in terms of raw averages (a 16.6 percentage point or 35% difference). Again, the magnitude of the impact is not diminished when background is controlled for, but the significance in the probit (only) falls, to $p=.106$. The gender difference does not significantly change over cohorts.

Other social sciences, encompassing mostly anthropology and linguistics, also had not demonstrated significant gender differences at previous career stages but seem to indicate some differences in promotion to full. The raw magnitude is large, 16.5 percentage points or 33% of the male rate. Adding background characteristics and even productivity characteristics do not noticeably decrease the size of the effect in the probit, and in the hazard the female advantages are even larger. The interaction term between female and Ph.D. year, while not significant, has the lowest p-value of all fields in the full analysis ($p=.16$ in hazard, $p=.22$ in probit) and indicates there may have been improvement over time.

While there were gender differences in tenure receipt within *psychology*, there are none at the promotion to full stage. Probit coefficients are small and hazard risk rates are close to 1. There is also little clear evidence of gender differences in *political science*. While several of the point estimates suggest gender differences to be concerned about, most gender differences are not significant. The single exception is that with background and productivity controls, women are significantly less likely than men to be promoted to full in the probit analysis, but not in the hazard analysis.

7   Discussion and conclusion: progress, pitfalls, or plateaus?

This chapter has measured gender differences in academic social science. NSF reports (NSF 2004b and Long 2001) using the same data set considered gender differences in academic careers in all sciences, including social sciences. By separating out the natural sciences and engineering (S&E) in our previous work (Ginther and Kahn 2009) from the social sciences here, we have identified gender differences in promotion that existed in social science but not in S&E. We have found that over the period studied, there are appreciable gender differences in the probability of obtaining a tenure-track job, small differences in receiving tenure, and large gaps in promotion to full professor in social science as a whole. Despite the progress women have made in obtaining doctorates, they are less likely to take tenure-track jobs and those who achieve tenure often plateau at the associate professor rank. We find that some of these gender differences have fallen over time, that some reflect gender differences in education, ability, and productivity, and that some relate to family choices made in a world where women continue to be the main child-rearer. The differences that persist for social science as a whole that are not explained by education, ability, productivity, or family choices are at the level of promotion to full professorship. Finally, disaggregated by field, as was true in our work on earlier cohorts (Ginther and Kahn 2004), economics remains the outlier with the greatest gender differences in promotion: a 20 percent gender gap in achieving tenure and a 50 percent gap in promotion to full.

To be more specific, at the entry stage, there are raw gender differences in whether female and male social science Ph.D.s enter academic tenure-track jobs, although these mostly reflect different background characteristics. Moreover, as we found in our previous work in science (Ginther and Kahn 2009), for social science overall women seem to be facing a choice between children and an academic career, insofar as single childless women are in fact more likely than single childless men to enter a tenure-track job. Breaking this down by social science field, the lower likelihood of women to get tenure-track jobs is completely due to economics, sociology, and clinical psychology. In clinical psychology, women are increasingly choosing clinical rather than academic careers. In economics and sociology, the large raw gender difference is not attributable to differing background and education, yet only occurs for women who have children. This too suggests that supply factors and personal choices are dominating entry into tenure-track jobs.

The similarities between science and social science employment outcomes diverge at the stages of promotion to tenure. Ginther and Kahn (2009) show no gender differences in promotion to tenure – or full professor – for all science and engineering (S&E) fields combined. In the social sciences, moderate gender differences in tenure rates, on the order of 8 percent, remain even after controlling for background characteristics. However, these gender differences have fallen and indeed have disappeared over time. Moreover, there are no average gender differences in tenure receipt over the period for childless singles.

Within individual fields, we found that for one of the fields with large raw gender differences in tenure receipt – political science – the differences are simply reflecting different background characteristics (such as Ph.D. quality) while for a second field with large raw gender differences – psychology – the differences have disappeared over time. Economics is the one field where gender differences in tenure receipt seem to remain even after background and productivity controls are factored in and even for single childless women. There is ambiguity in this finding, however, because gender differences are not statistically significant in the hazard analysis.

At the top echelon, promotion to full professorships, we find persisting significant gender differences for social science as a whole and for the fields of economics, sociology and anthropology/linguistics, even after controlling for background and productivity. The gender full professor gap in social science as a whole ranges between 20 and 25 percent depending on what is controlled for and what methodology (probit, hazard) is used. Economics is again worse than all social science disciplines, where women are half as likely as men to be promoted to full professor. It is striking that the full professor promotion gaps are not readily explained by covariates including productivity measures and family characteristics. When productivity is included in the analysis, the gender promotion gap barely changes.

Dual career problems do not seem to deter women from getting a tenure-track job, from getting tenure, or from becoming a full professor. The presence of children, however, does disadvantage women in some ways. First, children and particularly pre-kindergarten children lower women's likelihood of taking a tenure-track job. Second, married women with young children are less likely to be promoted to being tenured or to full professorships than are married men with children. The interpretation of these promotion comparisons, however, is not obvious because we do *not* find that women with young children are less likely to be promoted than women without children. In fact, the story most consistent with these findings is that men are advantaged in promotion by being married and having young children. In the labor literature, there are competing explanations for why married men with children do better in general labor markets. While married men with children may feel more responsibility to their families and therefore work harder, a productivity story, another possibility is that more able men tend to get married and have children, a selection story.[9] For the highly educated men in academia, the selection story seems more applicable than the productivity story.

Similarly, the opposite selection story can be made about women: the women most committed to academic careers may choose not to have children, although would be more devoted to their careers and successful even if they did have children. We cannot know, therefore, whether the measured impact of younger children on promotion (or even on entry to academic careers) is completely selection, or whether women are being hampered by children's presence.

As economists, we remain troubled by the large, unexplained gender differences in promotion to tenure and full professor in our field.

---

[9] Much of the literature supports the selection hypothesis (e.g. Petersen et al. 2011, Rodgers and Stratton 2010) but one paper on identical twins finds the opposite (Antonovics and Town 2004).

Admittedly, our controls for academic productivity are measured with error and access to better data might explain these large differences. Nevertheless, the results indicate that professional development efforts such as the Committee on the Status of Women in the Economic Profession's CEMENT mentoring workshops remain necessary. Participants in the mentoring program are randomly assigned to the mentoring treatment. An interim assessment of CEMENT shows that it increases the number of publications, publications in top journals, and federal grants for participants (Blau, Currie, Croson and Ginther 2010). To the extent that promotion differences are being driven by productivity differences, efforts like CEMENT will help to narrow the gender promotion gap in economics.

References

Allison, Paul D. 1995. *Survival Analysis Using the SAS System*. Cary, NC: The SAS Institute, Inc.

Antonovics, Kate and Robert Town 2004. "Are All the Good Men Married? Uncovering the Sources of the Marital Wage Premium." *American Economic Review* 94(2): 317–321.

Bellas, Marcia and Robert K. Toutkoushian 1999. "Faculty Time Allocations and Research Productivity: Gender, Race and Family Effects." *Review of Higher Education* 22(4): 367–390.

Blau, Francine D., Janet M. Currie, Rachel T. A. Croson, and Donna K. Ginther 2010. "Can Mentoring Help Female Assistant Professors? Interim Results from a Randomized Trial. *American Economic Review Papers and Proceedings* 100(2): 348–352.

Brown, Prudence, Dan Pasquini, and Susan Mitchell 1997. *Methodological Report 1991 Survey of Doctorate Recipients*. Mimeo, National Research Council, Washington, DC.

Congressional Commission on the Advancement of Women and Minorities in Science, Engineering, and Technology (CAWMSET) 2000. "Land of Plenty."

Fox, Mary Frank 2005. "Gender, Family Characteristics and Publication Productivity among Scientists." *Social Studies of Science* 35(1): 131–150.

Goldberg, Carey 1999. "MIT Acknowledges Bias Against Female Professors." *The New York Times* (March 23, 1999): 1.

Ginther, Donna K. 2001. *Does Science Discriminate Against Women? Evidence From Academia 1973–1997*. Federal Reserve Bank of Atlanta Working Paper 2001–02, February 2001.

2002. *Gender Differences in Employment Outcomes for Academics in the Social Sciences*. Mimeo, University of Kansas.

2003. "Is MIT the Exception? Gender Pay Differentials in Academic Science." *Bulletin of Science, Technology, and Society* 23(1): 21–26.

2004. "Why Women Earn Less: Economic Explanations for the Gender Salary Gap in Science." *AWIS Magazine* (Winter 2004) 33(1): 6–10.

2006a. "Economics of Gendered Distribution of Resources in Academia." In *Biological, Social, and Organizational Components of Success for Women in Science and Engineering: Workshop Report.* Washington, DC: Committee on Maximizing the Potential of Women in Academic Science and Engineering, The National Academies Press. 56–60.

2006b. "The Economics of Gender Differences in Employment Outcomes in Academia." In *Biological, Social, and Organizational Components of Success for Women in Science and Engineering: Workshop Report.* Washington, DC: Committee on Maximizing the Potential of Women in Academic Science and Engineering, The National Academies Press. 99–112.

Ginther, Donna K. and Kathy J. Hayes 1999. "Salary and Promotion Differentials by Gender for Faculty in the Humanities." *American Economic Review Papers and Proceedings* 89(2): 397–402.

2003. "Gender Differences in Salary and Promotion for Faculty in the Humanities, 1977–1995." *Journal of Human Resources*, 38(1): 34–73.

Ginther, Donna K. and Shulamit Kahn 2004. "Women in Economics: Moving Up or Falling Off the Academic Career Ladder?" *Journal of Economic Perspectives* (Summer 2004) 18(3): 193–214.

2009. "Does Science Promote Women? Evidence from Academia 1973–2001". In *Science and Engineering Careers in the United States*, eds. Richard B. Freeman and Daniel F. Goroff. University of Chicago Press for NBER.

Government Accountability Office (GAO) 2004. *Women's Participation in the Sciences Has Increased, but Agencies Need to Do More to Ensure Compliance with Title IX*. Washington DC: GAO. Available at www.gao.gov/cgi-bin/getrpt?-GAO-04-639.

Kahn, Shulamit 1993. "Gender Differences in Academic Career Paths of Economists." *American Economic Review Papers and Proceedings* 93: 52–56.

1997. "Women in the Economics Profession." *Journal of Economic Perspectives* 9(4): 193–205.

Levin, Sharon G. and Paula E. Stephan 1998. "Gender Differences in the Rewards to Publishing in Academe: Science in the 1970s." *Sex Roles* 38(11/12): 1049–1064.

Long, J. Scott, Paul D. Allison, and Robert McGinnis 1993. "Rank Advancement in Academic Careers: Sex Differences and the Effects of Productivity." *American Sociological Review* 58(5): 703–722.

Long, J. Scott (ed.) 2001. *From Scarcity to Visibility.* Washington, DC: National Academy Press.

Massachusetts Institute of Technology Faculty Newsletter. 1999. March, 1999: 21(4) available at http://web.mit.edu/fnl/women/women.html.

Mitchell, Susan B., Ramal Moonesinghe, and Brenda G. Cox 1998. *Using the Survey of Doctorate Recipients in Time-Series Analyses: 1989–1997.* Mimeo, National Science Foundation, Washington, DC.

Morrison, Emory, Elizabeth Rudd, and Maresi Nerad 2011. "Onto, Up, Off the Academic Faculty Ladder: The Gendered Effects of Family on Career Transitions for a Cohort of Social Science Ph.D.s." *Review of Higher Education* 34(4): 525–553.

National Academies of Science 2006. *"Beyond Bias and Barriers: Fulfilling the Potential of Women in Academic Science and Engineering."* Washington, DC:

Committee on Maximizing the Potential of Women in Academic Science
and Engineering, The National Academies Press. 56–60.

2011. *Gender Differences at Critical Transitions in the Careers of Science,
Engineering, and Mathematics Faculty*. Washington, DC: Committee on
Gender Differences in Careers of Science, Engineering, and Mathematics
Faculty, Committee on Women in Science, Engineering, and Medicine [of]
Policy and Global Affairs [and] Committee on National Statistics, Division
of Behavioral and Social Sciences and Education, the National Research
Council of the National Academies, The National Academies Press.

National Science Foundation (NSF) 2004. *Gender Differences in the Careers of
Academic Scientists and Engineers*. NSF 04–323, Project Officer, Alan
I. Rapoport. Arlington, VA.

National Science Foundation, Division of Science Resources Statistics 2011.
*Women, Minorities, and Persons with Disabilities in Science and Engineering:
2011*. Special Report NSF 11–309. Arlington, VA. Available at www.nsf.
gov/statistics/wmpd/.

Nelson, Donna J. and Diana C. Rogers 2005. "A National Analysis of Diversity
in Science and Engineering Faculties at Research Universities." *Norman,
OK*. January, 2005. Available at http://cheminfo.chem.ou.edu/~djn/diversity/
briefings/Diversity%20Report%20Final.pdf.

Petersen, Trond, Andrew M. Penner, and Geir Hogsnes 2011. "The Male
Marital Wage Premium: Sorting vs. Differential Pay." *Industrial and Labor
Relations Review* 64(2): 283–304.

Preston, Anne E. 1994. "Why Have All the Women Gone? A Study of Exit from
the Science and Engineering Professions." *American Economic Review* 84(5):
1446–1462.

2004. *Leaving Science: Occupational Exit from Scientific Careers*. New York:
Russell Sage Foundation.

Rodgers, William M. and Leslie S. Stratton, 2010. "Male Marital Wage
Differentials: Training, Personal Characteristics, and Fixed Effects."
Economic Inquiry 48(3): 722–42

Rosser, S. V. 2004. *The Science Glass Ceiling*. New York: Routledge.

Rudd, Elizabeth, Emory Morrison, Joseph Picciano, and Maresi Nerad 2008.
"Finally Equal Footing for Women in Social Science Careers?" *CIRGE
Spotlight on Doctoral Education #1*. CIRGE: University of Washington,
Seattle, WA. www.cirge.washington.edu.

Sax, Linda J., Linda Serra Hagedorn, Maisol Arredondo, and Frank A. Dicrisi III
2002. "Faculty Research Productivity: Exploring the Role of Gender and
Family-Related Factors." *Research in Higher Education* 43(4): 423–446.

Stack, Steven 2004. "Gender, Children, and Research Productivity." *Research in
Higher Education* 45(8): 891–920.

Wolfinger, Nicholas H., Mary Ann Mason, and Marc Goulden 2008. "Problems
in the Pipeline: Gender, Marriage and Fertility in the Ivory Tower." *Journal
of Higher Education* 79(4): 389–405.

Xie, Yu and Kimberlee A. Shauman 1998. "Sex Differences in Research
Productivity: New Evidence about an Old Puzzle." *American Sociological
Review* 63(6): 847–870.

2003. *Women in Science: Career Processes and Outcomes*. Cambridge, MA:
Harvard University Press.

12 Ought (only) economists to defect? Stereotypes, identity, and the Prisoner's Dilemma

Alessandro Lanteri and Salvatore Rizzello

A trial with a moral twist has befallen the economics profession (Lanteri 2008a,b). As a consequence, it is nowadays believed "a fact beyond doubt" that "economists are more selfish than other persons" (Frey and Meier 2000, p. 2). A wide range of experimental exhibits shows, for instance, that economics students make smaller contributions to public goods (Marwell and Ames 1981, Cadsby and Maynes 1998), that they keep larger shares for themselves and offer smaller shares to their partners in ultimatum games (Carter and Irons 1991), and that more economics students defect in prisoner dilemmas (Frank et al. 1993) than non-economics ones.[1] More disputable is whether these phenomena are caused by the economic education (training) or whether selfish people voluntarily enrol in the discipline (self-selection). There are several observations that economics students differ markedly from non-economics ones from the beginning of their schooling, thus lending credit to the self-selection explanation. If the students have not yet been exposed to economic indoctrination, their unique behavior must reflect some pre-existing difference. The idea of self-selection then rests on the further speculation that their choice of studying Economics instead of another subject is a reflection of such differences. However, that they are documented on day one does not necessarily mean that these differences were also present on day zero (Lanteri 2008b).

In this chapter, we argue on theoretical grounds that claims to the pre-existence of the differences can be softened and that there exists another plausible account of the early emergence of this phenomenon. We suggest that some image of the stereotypical economist may account

[1] For an extended review and discussion of this and related evidence, see Kirchgaessner (2005). Suffice it to remind that there also exists evidence denying a difference between economists and non-economists (e.g. contributions to some public goods in Frank et al. 1993, donations to charity funds in Frey and Meier 2000, 2003, 2004, 2005), or even suggesting that the behavioral gap is reversed, i.e. that economists are less selfish than non-economists (return rate in a lost-letter experiment in Yezer et al. 1996, payments of professional association fees in Laband and Beil 1999).

for the differences in observed behavior between economists and non-economists at the earliest stages of their career. We supplement this alternative explanation with some novel experimental results.

Evidence is not lacking that individuals may assume new social roles, that they can suddenly bond or conflict with strangers, depending on whether they are introduced as team-mates or rivals, and that they adjust to stereotypes. The instructions of the experimenters modify partici-pants' dispositions toward someone, toward some choice, or toward the process of making a decision in ways that are both stable and predict-able; and that take place instantaneously.[2]

Since choices are the result of the interaction between the identity of an agent and this agent's perception of the situation (March 1994), the manipulation of experimental conditions either modify the participants' perception of the choice context or their self-perception within a fixed choice context. The research on the framing of decisions (e.g. Tversky and Kahneman 1981, 1986) is both advanced and well-known in eco-nomics; we shall hereby focus on the issue of identity.

1   Social and self-identity

Whether this happens in an aware and deliberate fashion, or unaware and unconscious, an individual's identity has a major weight in this person's decisions. Its importance in understanding several economic problems has been recently acknowledged and has stimulated research on topics as diverse as welfare policies (Alesina et al. 2001), the formation of human capital (Akerlof and Kranton 2002; Glaeser et al. 2002), poverty and exclusion (Oxoby 2004), and labor markets (Akerlof and Kranton 2005).

A longer-standing interest in studying identity, however, was present in the psychological and sociological literature (e.g. Brewer and Kramer 1986; Brewer and Silver 2000; Dawes et al 1988; Kollock 1995; Kramer and Brewer 1984; Kramer and Goldman 1995; Simpson 2006), where identity is defined with reference to a social group and is therefore explored in the relationship with other people from the same or from a different group. Two influential accounts of social groups, Social Identity Theory and Self-Categorization Theory (Tajfel 1982; Turner 1985; Tajfel

---

[2] There exists a tradition of studies on the framing of experimental settings (e.g. Tversky and Kahneman 1981; Allison and Messick 1985; Lieberman et al. 2004) in which the game description evokes behavioral norms and is the strongest predictor of individual conduct. Because the descriptions are not given in advance, they influence subjects' conduct in a very short time.

and Turner 1986; Ashfort and Mael 1989) describe how individuals delineate the boundaries of particular groups and then self-categorize themselves as belonging or not to these groups. This literature is eminently concerned with identifying the conditions under which individuals display cooperative behavior with group members and defect with non-members, and identity-as-group-membership is thus employed to explain cooperative behavior through a "shared and mutual perception by in-group members of their interests as interchangeable" (Turner et al. 1987, p. 65). A similar approach in economics has been suggested when co-members can impose sanctions on defectors (Landa 1994).

Although the very concept of identity can only be meaningful in a social environment, in what follows we do not directly refer to social entities or collective agency. We shall instead employ a more individualistic account of identity, as is customary in economics. Douglas Bernheim (1994), for instance, describes agents who care about how other individuals in specific social groups feel about them, and George Akerlof and Rachel Kranton (2000, 2002, 2005) directly incorporate identity in agents' utility function. In general, the economic literature suggests that agents form their identities by earning a reputation, by acquiring social status, or by developing some self-image (Akerlof and Kranton 2000, 2002, 2005; Benabou and Tirole 2002; Bernheim 1994). Identity "is thus explained as an extension of standard rational choice models" (Davis 2004, p. 11), in the form of "an argument in the standard Arrow-Debreu utility function" (Beaudreau 2006, p. 208). This approach has been criticized because it translates into the loss of any meaningful concept of the individual (Davis 2003, 2004, 2007).

More sophisticated views of individual identity have also been proposed from within the ranks of economics. In contrast to the standard assumptions that larger material rewards for a given action always reinforce individual incentives to perform that action, it has been observed that under identifiable conditions paying a person to perform a task is very likely to make the task more unpleasant, instead of inspiring that person to eagerly perform it in the anticipation of the compensation. When the so-called "locus of control" of a decision is moved from internal to external, the agent is likely to lose commitment to and involvement with a decision (Rotter 1966).[3] This phenomenon typically occurs when the feedback from an action takes the form of an external reward (e.g. a prize) instead of self-pride, or an external sanction (e.g. a fine)

---

[3] Locus of control refers to the beliefs concerning who or what influences or determines phenomena according to a dichotomy between oneself (internal) and external circumstances (external). See Levenson (1973) for a different classification.

instead of self-shame. To the extent that the relocation of control occurs, standard economic incentives might not only fail to achieve their original goal, but steer away from it. This problem is well-known in psychology as the "hidden cost of reward" (Deci and Ryan 1985) and has been introduced in economics by Bruno Frey (1992, 1997). Frey has shown that "intrinsic motivation" consistent with a positive self-perception may successfully replace both prices and regulations to motivate individual behavior. We sometimes react positively to material incentives but sometimes we feel offended by them; and sometimes we are willing to do something for intrinsic motivation but sometimes we are not.

These variations are not a reflection of our capricious and erratic nature. Instead, they indicate that each of us has a plurality of identities, crucial to our view of ourselves and to the decisions we make. In economics, the idea of multiple identities has been advocated by Amartya Sen (1985, 2002), who also explained how our identities bear important consequences on individual welfare, goals, and norms of conduct. Nancy Folbre (1994) acknowledges that individuals are endowed with multiple social identifications because they operate within a plurality of groups. Deirdre McCloskey (2006) even suggests that one way in which our lives are made richer in a market economy is by being entitled to a broader set of identities than has ever been possible under other political and economic systems.

This interpretation of identity seems closer to a so-called "personality approach" in psychology (Bosma 1995; Oosterwegel and Wicklund 1995, cited in Beaudreau 2006). According to this approach, although both help defining oneself and creating meaning in one's life, personal and social identities are kept separate and "distinction is typically drawn between identity as a cumulative concept of self, and identity as it is situated or conceived of in relation to other people in particular situations" (Beaudreau 2006, p. 209).

In what follows we refer to the concept of identity in its meaning that people are capable of scrolling through the social components (both authentic and experimentally activated) of their identity.[4] We therefore expect that, as one joins an institution for the first time or fills a new role, one changes in harmony with one's perceptions of the new institution or role. In the case of economists, the image of the role may not be very flattering.

---

[4] A large body of literature on "entatitivity" shows that there may exist substantial differences in the processing of information about groups and about individuals, and that groups may vary in their "groupiness," with critical consequences for social perception, memory, and judgment (e.g. Hamilton and Sherman 1996; McConnell et al. 1997; Yzerbyt et al. 1998).

2   Earlier investigations

Experimental results seem to show that economists are not very nice people, because in game-theoretical settings students of economics behave more in accordance with the prediction of economic theory (i.e. more selfishly) than students of other disciplines. The evidence is gathered by means of game-theoretical applications for which it is easiest to make a pointed prediction and to compare it to observed behavior.

In a public good game, for example, individuals are endowed with a fixed amount of tokens, which they can invest in either of two goods. There is a "private exchange," which is a private good, and grants a fixed return on the investment. Alternatively there is a "common exchange," which grants a larger return on the investment once an investment threshold is reached, but this return is then equally shared among every player of the game, regardless of who actually invested in it. This makes the common exchange a public good, in that it benefits everyone (its consumption is non-rival and non-excludable) and it is provided after a threshold is reached (the marginal cost to additional investors is zero). Economic theory purports that a rational and self-interested agent does not contribute to the investment (strong free-riding) or that she contributes only insofar as the expected return from the public good is larger than the cost of financing its provision all by herself (Olson 1965; Hardin 1968). A more moderate version allows for the possibility that economic agents contribute positive, but suboptimal amounts (weak free-riding). This is unfortunate, because the social optimum is reached when everybody contributes all their tokens to the common exchange. The individual optimum, on the other hand, obtains when everybody else invests in the common exchange but oneself. In experiments constructed around public goods, one could expect contributions in the 40% to 60% of collective optimum (Ledyard 1995, p. 113). When these experiments were set-up by Marwell and Ames (1981), non-economists invested 49% of their tokens in the public good; economists only 24%. Although nobody behaved as economic theory predicts, economists came closer.

In a ultimatum bargaining game, there are two players: a proposer and a receiver. The proposer is given an amount of tokens, which he has to divide between himself and the co-player. If the responder agrees to the split, the tokens are divided as proposed, otherwise nobody receives anything. Once again economic rational and self-interested agents should offer the minimum positive amount possible (e.g. 0.001%) so as to keep the fattest share for themselves (e.g. 99.999%). An economic agent, when offered even that small amount, accepts it because it is better than nothing. In actual experiments, respondents are very likely to refuse offers below 25% and the proposers make offers round about 40% of the initial sum (Oosterbeek et al. 2004). In an experiment by Carter and Irons (1991), non-economists would keep 54.4% and would accept 24.4%. But economists wish to keep 61.5% and would accept a mere 17%.

In a Prisoner's Dilemma, two players have an independent choice between cooperation and defection, but their payoff is determined both by their response and that of their co-player. If both cooperate, their outcome is high. If one cooperates and the other defects, however, the defector achieves the highest result, while the cooperator loses big. When both players defect, they are not as well off as when both cooperate. A typical payoff matrix for prisoner dilemmas is reported in Table 12.1. In a situation of this kind, defection is a dominant strategy, because it is always advantageous and, no matter what the co-player does, it always yields a higher payoff. Though when both players defect, they are worse off than they would be if both cooperated, economic theory predicts defection in one-shot prisoner dilemmas. In practice, 38.8% non-economists and 60.4% economists defect (Frank et al. 1993).

These findings raise the question of whether the difference is due to the choice of selfish individuals to study economics (self-selection) or to the effect of attending Econ classes (training). Though there are indications that training matters (Frank et al. 1993, 1996), most experiments indicate that the difference between economists and non-economists can be observed on subjects at the very beginning of their training. If the gap is already present among freshmen, quite obviously it cannot be brought about by Econ teachers. But does this unavoidably mean "economists are born, not made" (Carter and Irons 1991, p. 174)?

If Econ training matters so little, one wonders what has happened to the Nobel Prize winner Friedrich von Hayek (1944, p. vii), who wrote in an autobiographical note: "my opposition to [socialist] views is not due to their being different from those with which I have grown up, since they are the very views which I held as a young man and which have led me to make the study of economics my profession." He self-selected in economics as a socialist and then grew to become a herald of Thatcherism and Reaganomics. Another puzzle would be the master economic historian Angus Maddison, who had been inspired to study economics by his uncle's spirited speeches advocating socialism (Maddison 1994), and who then dug out an astounding amount of data showing that economic growth and development are in good part the result of free trade. These two are just anecdotes and only provide circumstantial evidence. There exist, however, no systematic studies comparing the behavior of economics students with that of high school students and economics graduates. Should such studies be conducted, if self-selection is sound, one would observe that the behavior of the three categories is very similar on the grounds that they are all economists-at-heart and that, if anything, selfish conduct increases over time as more and more economic dogma is absorbed.

In the absence of a direct comparison, we look for answers in a recent experiment by Ariel Rubinstein (2006). The participants are presented with a scenario in which they are the vice-president of a small business facing a recession. Though the firm is still in the black, it is possible to improve profitability by firing some workers. A forecast informs the participants that the profits will be higher the more numerous the layoffs, up to about half of the 196 employees, after this threshold profits go down again. On average, economics students lay off more workers (circa 65) than non-economics ones (c. 48). About 50% Econ students lay off enough workers (96) to pursue profit maximization, compared with about 30% Business and Law students, and about 15% Maths and Philosophy students. Such results are not quite unexpected.[5] The same questionnaire was also administered to the readers of a major business newspaper. Among these, the participants with a background in Economics laid off 56 workers on average, and 36% of them maximized, only 25% of those with neither Economics nor Business background maximized, and they laid-off 47 employees on average. A difference is surely noticeable, but not nearly as large as that observed among students.

Another study (Laband and Beil 1999) shows that fewer professors of economics than professors of sociology and political science free ride on their fees to professional associations, which are public goods. A survey on the contributions to charity and to a number of other public goods (Frank et al. 1993, p. 162) shows that the behavior of economists was "little different" from that of professors of other disciplines.[6]

If one were born "selfish" or "economist" we would expect such nature to endure Economics training. Otherwise, why would selfish individuals self-select in the discipline? If such nature is at all affected by Econ training, indeed, it should be strengthened, not diminished. It is implausible that economists are born selfish and only begin losing this

---

[5] A sub-sample of the students of Economics, Mathematics, and Business Administration were assigned a formula to calculate the increase in profits at various levels of lay-offs instead of the explicit forecast. The differences among them are virtually non-existent, and about 75% in each group maximize profits (Rubinstein 2006: C4–C5).

[6] According to this study, however, Economics professors are roughly twice as likely to be pure free riders than non-Economics ones.

inclination after they are handed a degree, or at least it is implausible that this happens to large numbers of them. The behavioral gap between adults trained in Economics and those trained otherwise, nonetheless, seems to be much smaller – when present at all – than that observed among students.

In what follows we argue for the possibility that the differences among first-year students originate elsewhere than in a selfish nature that manifests itself in self-selection.

3   Values and stereotypes

Newly enrolled economics students are not born on the first day of college. They have experienced a number of situations, gone through high school, made friends, constructed some sort of image of themselves, and developed a set of values that characterize them as young men and women. They must also have developed aspirations about their future, some idea of what economics and other trainings are like, and what kind of people economists and other professionals are. In this sense, economics students are just like everyone else, and understanding the idiosyncrasies in the individual paths that led to their decision is a thankless pursuit. Eventually, on that faithful day, they ticked the Econ 101 box. In this sense, no doubt, they are different from the students who chose Literature or Physics.

What is this difference?

3.1   Values of economists and economics

One major element that characterizes people can be found in the values they hold. Values are social representations of basic motivations in the pursuit of goals that globally guide a person's life; and they can be usefully classified according to those goals (Gandal and Roccas 2002; Gandal et al. 2005; Schwartz 1992).[7] Neil Gandal and his colleagues, for instance, cluster some of them under the label of "self-enhancement" values: achievement, hedonism, and power. These are self-directed aspirations. Achievement refers to the goal of personal accomplishments and it evokes concepts like success, capacity, ambition, influence; hedonism is concerned with aesthetic gratification in the form of pleasure or

---

[7] For a full taxonomy of values and cross-cultural empirical confirmation, see Schwartz (1992). Here we follow Schwartz's formulation of values as reported by Gandal and colleagues (Gandal and Roccas 2002, Gandal et al. 2005) and quote from these sources.

enjoyment; power amounts to striving for social status and control over people and resources, as in wealth, prestige, authority. Other values – universalism and benevolence – are other-directed and they are classified as "self-transcendence" values. Universalism aims at the understanding, appreciation, and protection of people and nature, it is associated with ideas like social justice, equality, unity with nature, and peace; benevolence addresses the preservation and enhancement of the welfare of people with whom one is in frequent personal contact and it manifests itself through helpfulness, honesty, loyalty, and responsibility.

Broadly speaking, values convey beliefs about desirability and despicability, goodness and badness, and therefore constitute criteria for individuals to select actions, evaluate people and events, and explain their actions and evaluations. Yet, even a life guided by strong adherence to certain values is not free of testing decisions. One may want to preserve the employment of several workers, but feel compelled to ensure the highest remuneration for the shareholders or one may want to obtain the largest return for the shareholders' investment and yet be prevented by one's sympathy for the workforce. Because one often holds several values at the same time, the pursuit of the goals represented by each of them may force one to negotiate between alternative choices. Which values ultimately prevail depends on their relative weights.

In a comparative study on the importance of various values, Gandal and colleagues find that economics students ranked achievement, hedonism, and power higher than other students. Conversely, they put less importance on universalism. There was, however, no difference in the value attributed to benevolence. In a further study they also compare the responses of freshmen in their first week of studies and at the end of their first year, with the result that "[t]here were virtually no differences between the value priorities of the two samples, and none of the differences were statistically significant" (Gandal et al. 2005, p. 1236). It appears, once again, that economics students differ from others from day one. And they differ in terms of the values they deem important. But do these values explain why they choose Economics and not Anthropology or Chemistry?

First week economists were also asked to list five characteristics they believed to be the most important to economists in general. Ambitious, intelligent, and successful topped the ranking,[8] and 72% of the students also reported at least one of the other self-enhancement values. Only 55%

---

[8] Note, moreover, that ambition, intelligence, and success are all concepts associated with the value of achievement, and not with power or hedonism.

of the respondents included at least one of the self-transcendence values.[9] Ideally, one would like to also ask non-Economics students which ones would they rank as the top-5 Econ values, and as top-5 values of their disciplines. There does not seem to exist a specific reason to reject a priori the possibility that students in Architecture or Medicine believe that architects or medics are ambitious, intelligent, and successful.

At any rate, if freshmen are aware of the dominant values of their profession, their career choice may be interpreted as a (spelled out in more detail than usual) form of self-selection into a field that meets their tastes. But how, one wonders, did they discover what economics is like?

3.2   Stereotypes (and accuracy thereof)

One way to form an image of economists would be to gather several of them and thoroughly investigate their profile. Most people shirk from such burden and rely instead on some stereotypical image of "the economist" derived from a combination of gossip, personal acquaintance, and pure myth: both the media and personal experience contribute to the creation and diffusion of stereotypes of this kind. Stereotypes are ideas and opinions about the members of some groups based on their belonging to those groups instead of their individual characteristics.

These opinions may be positive (i.e., Asians are skilled at Math) or negative (i.e., women are poor at Math) and they have several beneficial functions for both individuals and societies. Direct acquaintance with someone before making a judgment or a decision may be too costly or time-consuming. Because humans have a limited capacity to acquire and process information, we may do best by selectively focusing on some general traits that are enough to attach to our target a rough "image" or "label," which quickly pops up in the right circumstances. We then supplement this approximate datum with information derived from past experience in a path-dependent way (Rizzello 1999, 2004), and in this way we fill in the gaps (Macrae and Bodenhausen 2000; Patalano 2005) in a cost-efficient fashion (Newell and Simon 1972; Britton and Tesser 1982). Arguably, the main function of categorical representations like stereotypes is to provide the decision maker with expectancies that help processing future information (Olson et al. 1996). In standard economic jargon, they reduce transaction costs.

---

[9] "This result is particularly striking because in nearly all studies on values, individuals attribute more importance to self-transcendence values than to self-enhancement values" (Gandal and Roccas 2002, p. 7).

The capacity to make a timely assessment about individuals uniquely based on their group memberships can be of great help in navigating complex social ecosystems, and stereotypes are among the tools that empower such navigation (Lee et al. 1995; Pinker 2002). Testifying to the speed and unawareness (which may be taken as hints of cognitive inexpensiveness) of the process, several empirical investigations have shown, although the exact reasons and detailed mechanics are not fully understood, that when stereotypical representations of agency or behavior are displayed, relevant behavior becomes activated (Wheeler and Petty 2001). It has thus been shown how stereotypes often prove self-fulfilling and self-propagating. For instance, when Asian women were made aware of their gender they performed much worse at a mathematical test than when they were made aware of their ethnicity, because there exist stereotypes about Asians being skilled at math and about women being poor at it (Shih et al. 1999).[10] Stereotypes affect individual expectations in a way that critically alters subsequent behavior. The stereotype of black people being aggressive made white students exposed to the pictures of black people more hostile to co-players in a game. This attitude made the co-players respond with hostility and aggressiveness (Chen and Bargh 1997). Stereotypes may thus backfire, either because they cause the outcome they presumably serve to guard us from, or because – though they rest on a kernel of truth – their intrinsic imprecision may lead to inaccurate predictions.

We see stereotype-driven biases all the time, but the case has been made especially convincingly with the case of Miss Linda (Kahneman 2003, p. 1462).

Linda is 31 years old, single, outspoken and very bright. She majored in philosophy. As a student she was deeply concerned with issues of discrimination and social justice and also participated in antinuclear demonstrations.

Two groups of subjects were asked about Linda's present employment. The first group was required to rank the probability that she corresponds to eight alternatives (probability treatment). The second group was required to rank the same alternatives by the degree to which Linda resembles a typical representative of the job (representativeness treatment). Some alternatives seemed only marginally related to the description, but two items were crucial:

[#6] Linda is a bank teller;
[#8] Linda is a bank teller and active in the feminist movement.

---

[10] An analogous phenomenon has been identified with African-Americans (Steele and Aronson 1995).

Though there is no doubt that #8 is a subset of #6, and therefore the probability that <#6 is true> is necessarily larger than <#8 is true>, Linda resembles more a stereotypical feminist bank teller than a bank teller tout court. The proportion of respondents who ranked #8 above #6 is very large and it is about the same for both the probability (89%) and the representativeness (85%) treatments.

While there may be some hint that she could be a feminist, there is no element in Linda's portrait suggesting that she could not be a bank teller, a psychiatric social worker, or an elementary school teacher: she simply is not the stereotypical one. When asked about the probability that Linda is #6 or #8, therefore, subjects seem to offer a reasonable answer to a different question – namely, the representativeness question.[11] The reason for the mismatch between question and answer does not appear to be that respondents confuse concepts of similarity and probability – though it may be reasonable to do so in various circumstances. "A more plausible hypothesis is that an evaluation of the heuristic attribute [i.e. representativeness] comes immediately to mind, and that its associative relationship with the target attribute [i.e. probability] is sufficiently close to pass the monitoring" of our conscious reflections (Kahneman 2003b, p. 709).

A little reflection might have instead suggested that Linda cannot be more likely to be a feminist bank teller than just a bank teller and that one ought to keep this in mind in one's rankings. A corrective thought of this kind, unquestionably within the intellectual reach of graduate students, is a "statistical heuristic" (Nisbett et al. 2002). It occurred to very few respondents because the substitution of a target attribute with a heuristic one is a subtle and unaware process. The heuristic attribute "is pertinent to the task, and its value comes to mind with little or no effort and with high confidence" (Kahneman 2003a, p. 472). Although statistical heuristics are usually not very accessible, they can be triggered by the context – e.g. they are more common in games of chance than in situations involving the psychology of individuals – or by wording – e.g. by the explicit mentioning of sampling procedures (Nisbett et al. 2002). Also who (you think) you are matters: statistical reasoning is activated more often when the respondents are required to "think as statisticians" than when they "think as psychologists" (Zukier and Pepitone 1984, reported in Sedikides and Skowronski 1991, p. 174), and it results in a significant reduction of the mistakes. Zukier and Pepitone also show that the people for whom the activation of statistical heuristics is habitual – therefore "chronically accessible" – are immune from the fallacy and, if anything,

---

[11] This phenomenon has been dubbed base-rate fallacy (Kahneman and Tversky 1973) or conjunction fallacy (Tversky and Kahneman 1983).

they seem to "overutilize" base-rate information. Thus, Constantine Sedikides and John Skowronski (1991, p. 174) comment that "both cognitive structures that are momentarily activated through experimental instructions or problem formulation and cognitive structures that are chronically active determine people's susceptibility to the base-rate fallacy and, hence, their success in problem solving."

A cognitive structure is a mental representation, such as the representation of general semantic categories (e.g. selfishness), of behavioral scripts (e.g. playing a Prisoner's Dilemma), of procedures (e.g. solving a problem), of specific event memories (e.g. the day of enrolment in Economics), and of specific people or objects (e.g. one's cousin who studied economics) (p. 169). Within a given cognitive structure, everything seems to have a proper place and a specific meaning, which are rarely questioned – in part because, although we have numerous cognitive structures that can be applied on each occasion, we tend to employ only one or two at a time (p. 170). For instance, when some (presumably) healthy psychologists secretly enrolled into a psychiatric hospital to conduct research, though they behaved as they would have behaved outside, the personnel treated them as patients. When he explained that as a little child he was more attached to his mother but later became more attached to his father, therefore, one researcher-patient was described as having "unstable relationships in childhood" (Rosenham 1975, quoted in Rachels 2003, p. 73). Just the same way, when one researcher took notes on the goings-on of the clinic as his job required, the nurses worriedly drafted a report describing how "the patient engages in writing behaviour." Such were the judgments expressed by someone whose – so to speak – "psychiatric illness cognitive structure" is active. Besides statistical and psychiatric ones, there exist many more cognitive structures, which may be activated in many situations.[12]

It thus seems natural to wonder: does there exist something akin to an "economics heuristic" or a "economist's cognitive structure," too? And, if so, can it be activated in non-economists? The two questions are conditional on people having at least a rough image of economists or economics, otherwise they would be puzzled rather than inspired by the suggestion to think or act like an economist. Do people, as it seems plausible, hold stereotypes about economists? And, if so, what are these stereotypes like? Let us turn to some experimental evidence inspired by these questions.

---

[12] A large body of sociological research investigates the closely related theme of "professionalization," which refers to the development of certain sets of identities, skills, cognitions, norms and values, but also biases and idiosyncrasies (i.e., déformation professionnelle) associated with becoming a member of a professional group.

4   The experiments

The experiments were conducted with a total of 68 subjects, recruited among students of Occupational Therapy (N=40) at the Università Cattolica del Sacro Cuore (Italy) and students of Economics (N=28) at the University of Eastern Piedmont (Italy).[13] In the basic treatment, participants are confronted with a standard version of the Prisoner's Dilemma, based on the same payoff matrix as that in Table 12.1 (see Appendix). They answered whether they would cooperate or defect and whether they expected the majority of other players to cooperate or defect.

Since all the Econ students and a sub-sample of the students from Occupational Therapy (N=19) played the basic version, it is possible to verify whether their responses differ. Predictably, more Econ students defect than non-Econ students. The difference, however, is not statistically significant (possibly as a consequence of the relatively small number of observations).[14] A comparable difference, but statistically significant, can also be observed in terms of the expectations about the behavior of others, with Economics students revealing more cynical expectations. These responses may be determined by the experimental procedure. Though this is not explicitly mentioned in the instructions, it is plausible that the subjects believe they are about to play with fellow students present in the room – i.e. students of the same discipline. Such belief would certainly affect the responses. To the extent that this is the case, the expectations about fellow students reveal that, according to their fellows, Economics students are those most likely to defect.

Occupational Therapy students share such expectations. They were later told to play the same game with a person, of whom they only know that she or he is a student of Economics (vs. ECON treatment). Again they were asked whether they would cooperate or defect and whether they expected this Economics student to cooperate or defect. Cooperation

---

[13] In addition to a show-up fee of €4 (c. $5.5) paid to all participants, 6 of the 19 students of Occupational Therapy who played the standard version of the game and 4 students of Economics were randomly selected and paired, and then paid an additional amount of €1 per point, based on their responses. Also 6 of the 21 students of Occupational Therapy who did not play the standard game, instead, were randomly selected and paid an additional amount of €1 per point, calculated as if they played against a player who behaved as they predicted. For bureaucratic reasons the participants have been paid not with cash, but with vouchers to be redeemed at a local canteen. At the end of the experiment, each player also answered two questions to verify her understanding of the game. Since all responded correctly, we did not drop any observation.

[14] See Table 12.2 in the Appendix for statistical testing of independence, with parametric (t-test) and non-parametric (Mann–Whitney) tests.

drops significantly, and expectations of cooperative behavior from students of Economics are virtually non-existent.

Why is there a gap between the expectations in the standard treatment and in the VS-ECON treatment? It is not the percentage of defectors per se that matters here, but what it represents. Such a percentage may be seen as an indication of how widespread is the belief that economics students in general are defective. With some caveats about the comparison of results across treatments, one could regard the difference between expected defection when playing against Econ students and expected defection under normal conditions as a signal that a stereotype (of an unflattering kind) is probably present. The figure is over 52%.

In general, unless one has some reasons to form the expectation that one's co-player will behave in a specific manner, one should play under the auspices of a standard theory of the co-player's behavior – namely, the expectations should be in accordance with the base-rate, if known, or should roughly mirror the expectations about the rest of the population, although these expectations may in actual fact turn out to be inaccurate. And indeed they are: predictions about the conduct of the population at large (for which we do not have complete observations and which includes economists) overestimate cooperation. With the predicted behavior of Econ students the mistake gets corrected, only to result in an unwarranted estimate of high defection.

As a further confirmation that a stereotype of this kind might play a role in the observed behavioral differences between Economics and non-Economics students, we conducted an additional, separate treatment, in which some students of Occupational Therapy (N=21) who had not participated in the standard treatment played as "imaginary Economics students." In other words, they were asked to wear the shoes of Economics students being administered a test, corresponding to the Prisoner's Dilemma with the standard payoffs (AS ECON treatment). These subjects were thus asked whether they would cooperate or defect and whether they expected the majority of other players to cooperate or defect. Again, we observe an evident difference between the way non-Econ students respond "normally" and they way they respond "as Economics students," the latter being more defective.[15] This shows that non-Econ students can simulate and that, without being explicitly told to or how, they significantly alter what would have presumably been their standard behavior. Moreover simulated behavior quite accurately maps the authentic conduct of Economics students. This result is new in that, to

---

[15] This difference is statistically significant with parametric testing, but not with the Mann–Whitney test.

our knowledge, conduct of non-Econ students has never been observed before, which surpasses that of Econ students in the way of rational self-interest in a Prisoner's Dilemma.

It is also remarkable that simulators exaggerate it. But this result can be understood by considering that our subjects do not play as if each of them were a student of Economics and they were supposed, as a group, to respond as a group of Economic students would. Instead they answer as if each, individually, was to give the most likely response from the Econ-group. Because the most likely response for the sample in question is defection, it also makes sense that defection is the most common response for each participant in this treatment. To be sure, also OT students and people in general should be expected to defect – because in these prisoner dilemmas defectors are always more numerous than cooperators. Not everyone, however, is associated with a stereotype like that of economists.

Perhaps (at least some) students of Economics' conduct is in accordance with some cognitions hard-wired or otherwise imprinted unto them by nature and these cognitions are of a selfish kind. They may be born economists and consistently behave as economists throughout their lives. The question remains begging, however, why would a natural born egoist choose to major in Economics and not in the Humanities, in Psychology, or in the far better paying Business, Law, and Medicine. At any rate, our findings might help relax this interpretation.

The evidence above indicates that the usual higher percentage of defective players among Economics students than among non-Econ ones is not constant or irreversible, but may be tacitly triggered by experimental instructions. Since what one could regard as students of Economics' unique response pattern can be replicated among non-Economics students, by simply asking them to act as economists, we conclude that defection or otherwise selfish behavior need not be regarded as the manifestation of a hard-wired cognition (and one whose owner will probably become an economist), but may easily be triggered by experimental instructions. Consequently, the common interpretation of the experimental literature on the ethics of economists as proof of self-selection can be relaxed. Note, however, that ruling out self-selection is not our goal: suffice it here to observe that it is possible to describe Economics students' conduct, without positing a specific ex-ante behavioral difference from non-Econ students, and without positing a corresponding self-selection.

5   Identity and cognitive dissonance

That they find joining the Economics ranks in line with their self-perceptions, one could speculate, still separates Econ students from non-Econ ones. Quite possibly so. Yet, in actual fact, Economics training is defined along a variety of attributes beyond the stereotypical character who populates the field. Given the central social-coordination role of stereotypes, they are possibly the single most important attribute of a profession. On the other hand, such importance might be confined to problems of social coordination, whereas here the issue is an individual self-relevant decision about his professional future.

Do Econ students choose their major because of the stereotype? If it were validated, this hypothesis would deepen our understanding of self-selection. Or do Economics students enrol in the discipline, regardless of the stereotype? They could choose to do so because of and in spite of a number of features, beside the stereotype. Finally, Econ students could choose Economics in spite of the stereotype. They may dislike it, like some of their fellows in other majors, but still pick Econ 101.[16]

Even then, students of Economics would have to cope with the stereotype. We admit to the possibility that they hold a stereotype in some respect different from that held by non-Econ students, but in what follows we proceed by the assumption that there exists but one Econ stereotype.[17] One trick would be to redefine the stereotype by means of "language euphemisms" – e.g. "ambitious, intelligent, and successful" instead of "calculative and greedy." Even if one dislikes Economics because of the stereotype, one may find it easier to behave in accordance with such a stereotype after he has already enrolled in Econ 101, through what might be called "the slippery slope of decision-making." These two effects, together with errors in perceptual causation and constraints induced by representations of the self, are some recognized enablers of self-deception in connection with morally poor choices (Tenbrunsel and Messick 2004, pp. 225–231). We cannot, indeed, take for granted that the same piece of information is treated in a predetermined way by everyone, because the production of novel knowledge depends – among other things – on previous beliefs and cognitive structures. One may believe that defection in a Prisoner's Dilemma is an indication of selfishness, but also that one's profession is all right. One could then observe defection among one's colleagues and comment that it is a legitimate self-defense against the threat of defection from the co-player or perhaps a sign of wits, and not a manifestation of greed. Some form of self-deception, either conscious or unconscious, seems therefore to

---

[16] Note, again that none of these explanations necessarily rules out self-selection: all are compatible with it.

[17] Our comments below, however, would still hold if we dropped this assumption.

be "the only way to explain ... a person's failure to acknowledge what is too obvious to miss" (Bok 1989, p. 60).

As a matter of fact, when two pieces of information contradict each other, we feel uncomfortable and try to contain this feeling by adjusting our interpretation of the incompatible elements. Although the motivation for such tuning of one's perception is still much debated (Harmon-Jones and Mills 1999), it is generally agreed that the attempt to reduce discomfort and to preserve a "sense of the self" is one of the strongest motivators of human action, both aware and unaware. This preservation often happens through the dismissal or the reinterpretation of available information so as to reduce "cognitive dissonance" (Festinger 1957). On the one hand, therefore, people incur in "belief-disconfirmation" dissonance, leading to the misperception and misinterpretation of information. On the other hand, people also face "induced-compliance" dissonance (Harmon-Jones and Mills 1999, p. 8), which

is aroused when a person does or says something that is contrary to a prior belief or attitude. From the cognition of the prior belief or attitude, it would follow that one would not engage in such behaviour. On the other hand, inducements to engage in such behaviour, promises of reward or threats of punishment provide cognitions that are consonant with the behaviour. Such cognitions provide justifications for the behaviour. The greater the number and importance of the cognitions justifying the behaviour, the less the dissonance aroused.

It might thus be the case that some of the students in the experiments answered as they thought made sense from the point of view of someone enrolled in Economics. Once a teenager becomes (for whatever reason) an Economics student, it is plausible that she tries to speak and act the way she believes an Economics student speaks and acts: it most certainly is a way to preserve her sense of the self. Gandal and Roccas (2002, 7n) reject this explanation. Such pattern of responses, they correctly point out, would correspond to a high importance placed on the value of conformity.[18] Two regressions run on the results of economics students show that there is no correlation between higher self-enhancing values and higher (revealed) conformity values. But, of course, the students who respond "as they think they should" would not admit to being admirers of conformity! If, moreover, Econ freshmen genuinely take up the stereotypical role of economist, they won't even be *aware* of being anything but ambitious, intelligent, and successful. Identity is best seen not as who we are, but as who we *think* we are.

---

[18] The value of conformity aims at restraining actions that are likely to upset or harm others or violate social norms and expectations and it takes manifestations like obedience, politeness, self-discipline, and respect.

Rubinstein's experiment above does not suggest that relatively more students of Economics prioritize profit maximization, in an abstract sense. It shows that they do so when acting in their (artificially induced) capacity as vice president of a private company.[19] The subjects could, however, be instructed to act as Labour Union representatives or management consultants. How would they act, then? There would still presumably emerge a behavioral difference between Econ and non-Econ, but also a – probably larger – difference between executives and worker unions' delegates.

Freshmen Econ students differ from non-Econ ones at least in that they study Economics and not some other subject, but this then brings about many more differences. Graduate students in Economics, for example, hope to be hired by prestigious universities and refuse good job offers from private firms (Stigler 1959). Some may be willing to teach at liberal arts colleges or to join governmental or international agencies, but very few openly admit to this (Klamer and Colander 1990). Nor do they spurn or abjure private enterprises or public service per se. More simply, Econ Ph.D.s (ought to) want to do research at high-profile universities. This is who they think they are. Perhaps this is one example of the way in which some institutions alter individual perceptions of meaning and appropriateness, and thus the personal tastes of their members (Denzau and North 1994; Hodgson 2003; Rizzello and Turvani 2000, 2002). And institutions also affect the perceptions and expectations others have about their members.

6   Some consequences of economics stereotypes

The agreement about Econ students' expected behavior and the way most people respond to that, at any rate, is not telling much about those students, but about the beliefs others hold about them. These stereotypes seem quite correct, if incomplete. Expectations based on such stereotypes, on the other hand, might be incorrect.

Though we do not expect them to, and though they believe nobody would do so, a larger proportion of Economics students return lost letters filled with cash to unknown owners than non-Econ students (Yezer et al. 1996). The life of an economist can indeed be rich in selfless generosity, both done unto others by him and unto himself by others, although such stories do not prevail in gossip. For instance, Steven Levitt (Levitt and Dubner 2005, pp. 145–146)

---

[19] Though many believe real managers would behave differently (Rubinstein 2006, C5).

found that the support at the University of Chicago went beyond the scholarly ... Amidst the shock and grief [for having suddenly lost his two years old son Andrew], Levitt had an undergraduate class that needed teaching. It was Gary Becker – a Nobel laureate nearing his seventieth birthday – who sat in for him. Another colleague, D. Gale Johnson, sent a condolence card that so moved Levitt that he can still cite it from memory ... The Levitts have become close friends with the family of the little girl to whom they donated Andrew's liver [... And they] joined a support group for grieving parents.

None of these sounds quite like the kind of people and manners we typically expect to find in the Economics Department. (Again, the problem need not be in the people and manners, but perhaps in the expectations.)

In the study by Gandal and colleagues, for instance, the high subjective importance attributed to the value of benevolence by Economics students (equal to that of others) is not matched in the alleged values prevalent in the discipline at large. Those values correctly include power, hedonism, and achievement, but they undeservedly leave out benevolence. One weakness of the values studies is thus that students who declare the importance of self-enhancing values might have chosen Economics regardless of those, and might not have held in very high regard those values before, nor would they if they had not chosen Economics.

The economist's stereotype, therefore, if quite understandable to some extent, does not produce an accurate description of the actual characteristics of real economics students. Instead, it may create these students by means of self-fulfilling prophecies. In game-theoretical experiments, expectations shape conduct to a large extent. If I believe my co-player anticipates defection from me, I also expect her to defect. In response, I defect and make my co-player's anticipation correct. Many people (including other economists) treat economists as if we were non-cooperative in social dilemmas, thus possibly induce us to defect in response. As said, this happens to the extent that there exists some shared stereotypical belief about what economists are like.

When such belief exists, moreover, Econ students are probably informed about at least some of its defining features. It is thus likely that students of Economics adjust their behavior in game-theoretical experiments and responses to values surveys, in a way that is consistent with their image of the "stereotypical economists," because that is who they think they are and because the mental structures that are most accessible to them are probably those of an economist.

Yet, it is not granted that the mental processes behind those answers and actions are the same. Whether one is somehow pressed to activate a certain cognitive structure (by being explicitly requested to act as an economist or by autonomously trying to act like one) or one is so accustomed (by habitually thinking like an economist), one's conduct can be expected to approximate some benchmark behavior that is connected to the cognitive structure in question (in the case at hand, defection). It may not be very easy, however, to uncover precisely which type of activation – chronic or contingent, context- or identity-related – is at play on specific occasions for specific individuals. It is therefore also not very easy to tell whether two economics students, the one on his first day and the one on the eve of graduation, provide similar responses and behave the same way in some tasks because they have been that way all along or because each follows their own, very different, decision-making processes which happen result in the same choice. (This may sound unlikely in those choice settings that present participants with several options, but it is less so in a game-theoretical experiment for which there exists only two possible answers.) Different effects probably play out at different levels of seniority. As they become more mature, Economics students should stop behaving in certain ways because it is the stereotypical way to behave. In the meanwhile, however, they have perhaps been indoctrinated to behave precisely that way. It is thus possible that, when we observe defection among freshmen, we may be observing the same outcome, but not exactly the same choice we observe when senior students defect.

References

Akerlof, G. and R. Kranton 2000. "Economics and Identity." *Quarterly Journal of Economics*. 115 (3): 715–753

2002. "Identity and Schooling: Some Lessons from the Economics of Education." *Journal of Economic Literature*. 40 (4): 1167–1201

2005. "Identity and the Economics of Organizations." *Journal of Economic Perspectives*. 19 (1): 9–32

Alesina, A., E. Glaeser, and B. Sacerdote 2001. "Why doesn't the U.S. have a European style Welfare State?" *Brookings Papers on Economic Activity*. 187–278

Allison, S. and D. Messick 1985. "Effects of Experience on Performance in a Replenishable Resource Trap." *Journal of Personality and Social Psychology*. 49 (4): 943–948

Ashfort, B. and F. Mael 1989. "Social Identity Theory and the Organization." *Academy of Management*. 14: 20–39

Beaudreau, B. C. 2006. "Identity, Entropy, and Culture." *Journal of Economic Psychology*. 27: 205–223

Benabou, R. and J. Tirole 2002. "Self-Confidence and Personal Motivation." *Quarterly Journal of Economics*. 117 (3): 871–915

Bernheim, B. 1994. "A Theory of Conformity." *Journal of Political Economy*. 102 (5): 841–877

Bok, S. 1989. *Secrets: On the Ethics of Concealment and Revelation*. New York, NY: Vintage Books

Bosma, H. A. 1995. "Identity and Identity Process: What are We Talking About?" In A. Oosterwegel and R. A. Wicklund (eds.), *The Self in European and North American Culture: Development and Processes*. Dordrecht: Kluwer Academic Publishers

Brewer, M. and M. Silver 2000. "Group Distinctiveness, Social Identification, and Collective Mobilization." In S. Stryker, T. Owens, and R. White (eds.), *Self, Identity and Social Movements*. University of Minnesota Press. pp. 153–171

Brewer, M. and R. Kramer 1986. "Choice Behavior in Social Dilemmas: Effects of Social Identity, Group Size and Decision Framing." *Journal of Personality and Social Psychology*. 3: 543–549

Britton, B. and A. Tesser 1982. "Effects of Prior Knowledge on Use of Cognitive Capacity in Three Complex Cognitive Tasks." *Journal of Verbal Learning and Verbal Behavior*. 21: 421–436

Cadsby, C. and E. Maynes 1998. "Choosing Between a Socially Efficient and Free-Riding Equilibrium: Nurses versus Economics and Business Students." *Journal of Economic Behavior and Organization*. 37 (2): 183–192.

Carter, J. and M. Irons 1991. "Are Economists Different, and If So, Why?" *Journal of Economic Perspectives*. 5: 171–177

Chen, M. and J. Bargh 1997. "Nonconscious Behavioral Confirmation Processes: The Self-Fulfilling Consequences of Automatic Stereotype Activation." *Journal of Experimental Social Psychology*. 33 (5): 541–560

Denzau, A. and D. North 1994. "Shared Mental Model: Ideologies and Institutions." *Kyklos*. 47 (1): 3–31

Davis, J. 2003. *The Theory of the Individual in Economics*. London: Routledge
2004. "Identity and Commitment: Sen's Conception of the Individual." Tinbergen Institute Discussion Paper. *TI 055/2*
2007. "Akerlof and Kranton on Identity in Economics: Inverting the Analysis." *Cambridge Journal of Economics*. 31 (3): 349–362

Dawes, R. , A. Van de Kragt, and J. Orbell 1988. "Not Me or Thee but We: The Importance of Group Identity in Eliciting Cooperation in Dilemma Situations: Experimental Manipulations." *Acta Psychologica*. 68: 83–97

Deci, E. and R. Ryan 1985. *Intrinsic Motivation and Self Determination in Human Behavior*. New York: Plenum Press

Festinger, L. 1957. A Theory of Cognitive Dissonance. *Stanford University Press*

Folbre, N. 1994. *Who Pays for the Kids: Gender and the Structure of Constraint*. London: Routledge

Frank, R., T. Gilovich, and D. Regan 1993. "Does Studying Economics Inhibit Cooperation?" *Journal of Economic Perspectives*. 7: 159–71

Frey, B. 1992. "Tertium Datur: Pricing, Regulating, and Intrinsic Motivation." *Kyklos*. 45 (2): 161–184
1997. *"Not Just for the Money: An Economic Theory of Personal Motivation"*. Cheltenham: Edward Elgar

Frey, B. and S. Meier 2000. "Political Economists are Neither Selfish Nor Indoctrinated." *IEW – Working Paper*. 69

    2003. "Are Political Economists Selfish and Indoctrinated? Evidence from a Natural Experiment." *Economic Inquiry*. 41(3): 448–62

    2004. "Do business students make bad citizens?" *International Journal of the Economics of Business*. 11(2): 141–63

    2005. "Selfish and indoctrinated economists?" *European Journal of Law and Economics*. 19: 165–71

Gandal, N. and S. Roccas 2002. "Good Neighbours/Bad Citizens: Personal Value Priorities of Economists." *CEPR Discussion Papers*. 3660

Gandal, N., S. Roccas, L. Sagiv, and A. Wrzesniewsky 2005. "Personal Value Priorities of Economists." *Human Relations*. 58 (10): 1227–1252

Glaeser, E., D. Laibson, and B. Sacerdote 2002. "An Economic Approach to Social Capital." *The Economic Journal*. 112: F437–F458

Hamilton, D. and S. Sherman 1996. "Perceiving Individuals and Groups." *Psychological Review*. 103: 336–355

Hardin, G. 1968. "The Tragedy of the Commons." *Science*. 162: 1243–48

Harmon-Jones, E. and J. Mills 1999. "An Introduction to Cognitive Dissonance Theory and an Overview of Current Perspectives on the Theory." In E. Harmon-Jones and J. Mills (eds.), *Cognitive Dissonance: Progress of a Pivotal Theory in Social Psychology*. Washington, D.C.: Braun-Brumfield

Hayek, F. 1944. *The Road to Serfdom*. London: Routledge

Hodgson, G. 2003. "The Hidden Persuaders: Institutions and Individuals in Economic Theory." *Cambridge Journal of Economics*. 27 (2): 159–175

Kahneman, D. 2003a. "Maps of Bounded Rationality: Psychology for Behavioral Economics." *American Economic Review*. 93 (5): 1449–1475

    2003b. "A Perspective on Judgement and Choice: Mapping Bounded Rationality." *American Psychologist*. 58 (9): 697–720

Kahneman, D. and A. Tversky 1973. "On the Psychology of Prediction." *Psychological Review*. 80: 237–251

Kirchgaessner, G. 2005. "(Why) Are economists different?" *European Journal of Political Economy*. 21: 543–562

Klamer, A. and D. Colander 1990. *The Making of an Economist*. Boulder, CO: Westview Press

Kollock, P. 1995. "Transforming Social Dilemmas: Group Identity and Cooperation." In P. Danielson (ed.), *Modelling Rational and Moral Agents*. Oxford University Press

Kramer, R. and L. Goldman 1995. "Helping the Group or Helping Yourself? Social Motives and Group Identity in Resource Dilemmas." In D.A. Schroeder (ed.), *Social Dilemmas: Perspectives on Individuals and Groups*. Westport, CT: Praeger. pp. 49–67

Kramer, R. and M. Brewer 1984. "Effects of Group Identity on Resource Use in a Simulated Commons Dilemma." *Journal of Personality and Social Psychology*. 46: 1044–1057

Laband, D. N. and R. O. Beil 1999. "Are Economists more Selfish than Other 'Social' Scientists?" *Public Choice*. 100 (1–2): 85–101

Landa, J. 1994. *Trust, Ethnicity, and Identity: Beyond the New Institutional Economics of Trading Networks*. Ann Arbor: University of Michigan Press

Lanteri, A. 2007. "The Moral Trial: Economics' Socratic Problem." *ICER Working Papers*. 44/07

  2008a. "The Moral Trial. On Ethics and Economics." Unpublished doctoral dissertation. Erasmus University Rotterdam.

  2008b. "(Why) Do Selfish People Self-Select in Economics?" *Erasmus Journal of Philosophy and Economics*. 1 (1): 1–23.

Ledyard, J. 1995. "Public Goods: A Survey of Experimental Research." In J. Kagel and A. Roth (eds.), *The Handbook of Experimental Economics*. Princeton University Press. pp. 111–194

Lee, Y., L. Jussim and C. McCauley 1995. *Stereotype Accuracy: Toward Appreciating Group Differences*. Washington, DC: The American Psychological Association.

Levenson, H. 1973. "Multidimensional Locus of Control in Psychiatric Patients." *Journal of Consulting and Clinical Psychology*. 41: 397–404

Levitt, S. and S. Dubner 2005. *Freakonomics: A Rogue Economist Explores the Hidden Side of Everything*. New York: William Morrow (Harper Collins)

Lieberman, V., S. Samuels, and L. Ross 2004. "The Name of the Game: Predictive Power of Reputation versus Situational Labels in Determining Prisoner's Dilemma Game Moves." *Personality and Social Psychology Bulletin*. 30 (9): 1175–1185

Macrae, N. and G. Bodenhausen 2000. "Social Cognition: Thinking Categorically about Others." *Annual Review of Psychology*. 51: 93–120

Maddison, A. 1994. "Confessions of a Chiffrephile." *Banca Nazionale del Lavoro Quarterly Review*. 189: 1–27

March, J. 1994. *Primer on Decision Making: How Decisions Happen*. New York: Free Press

Marwell, G. and R. Ames 1981. "Economists Free Ride, Does Anyone Else?" *Experiments on the Provision of Public Goods, IV, Journal of Public Economics*. 15

McCloskey, D. N. 2006. *Bourgeois Virtues. Ethics for an Age of Commerce*. Chicago University Press

McConnell, A., S. Sherman, and D. Hamilton 1997. "Target Entatitivity: Implications for Information Processing about Individual and Group Targets." *Journal of Personal and Social Psychology*. 72: 750–762

Newell, A. and H. Simon 1972. *Human Problem Solving*. New Jersey: Prentice-Hall.

Olson, J., N. Roese, and M. Zanna 1996. "Expectancies." In E. Higgins (ed.), *Social Psychology: Handbook of Basic Principles*. New York: Guilford. pp. 211–238

Olson, M. 1965. *The Logic of Collective Action: Public Goods and the Theory of Groups*. Schocken Books

Oosterbeek, H., R. Sloof, and G. van de Kuilen 2004. "Cultural Differences in Ultimatum Game Experiments: Evidence from a Meta-Analysis." *Experimental Economics*. 7 (2): 171–188

Oosterwegel, A. and R. A. Wicklund (eds.) 1995. *The Self in European and North American Culture: Development and Processes*. Dordrecht: Kluwer Academic Publishers

Oxoby, R. 2004. "Cognitive Dissonance, Status, and Growth of the Underclass." *The Economic Journal*. 114: 729–749

Patalano, R. 2005. *La Mente Economica. Immagini e Comportamenti di Mercato*. Rome: Laterza

Pinker, S. 2002. *The Blank Slate. The Modern Denial of Human Nature*. New York: Viking

Rachels, J. 2003. *The Elements of Moral Philosophy, 4th Edition*. New York: McGraw-Hill

Rizzello, S. 1999. *The Economics of the Mind*. Routledge
    2004. "Knowledge as a Path Dependence Process." *Journal of Bioeconomics*. 6

Rizzello, S. and M. Turvani 2000. "Institutions Meet Mind: The Way out of a Deadlock." *Constitutional Political Economy*. 11 (2): 165–180
    2002. "Subjective Diversity and Social Learning: A Cognitive Perspective for Understanding Institutional Behavior." *Constitutional Political Economy*. 13 (2): 197–210

Rotter, J. 1966. "Generalized Expectancies for Internal versus External Control of Reinforcement." *Psychological Monographs: General and Applied*. 80 (1): 1–28

Rubinstein, A. 2006. "A Sceptic's Comment on Studying Economics." *Economic Journal*. 116: C1–C9

Schwartz, S. H. 1992. "Universals in the Content and Structure of Values: Theory and Empirical Tests in 20 Countries." In M. Zanna (ed.), *Advances in Experimental Social Psychology. Vol. 25*. New York: Academic Press. pp. 1–65

Sedikides, C. and J. Skowronski 1991. "The Law of Cognitive Structure Activaton." *Psychological Inquiry*. 2 (2): 169–184

Sen, A. 1985. "Goals, Commitment, and Identity." *Journal of Law, Economics, and Organization*. 1 (2): 341–355
    2002. *Rationality and Freedom*. Cambridge, MA: Belknap Press

Shih, M., T. Pittinsky, and N. Ambady 1999. "Stereotype Susceptibility: Identity Salience and Shifts in Quantitative Performance." *Psychological Science*. 10: 80–83

Simpson, B. 2006. "Social Identity and Cooperation in Social Dilemmas." *Rationality and Society*. 18 (4): 443–470

Steele, C. and J. Aronson 1995. "Stereotype Threat and the Intellectual Test Performance of African-Americans." *Journal of Personality and Social Psychology*. 69 (5): 797–811

Stigler, G. 1959. "The Politics of Political Economists." *Quarterly Journal of Economics*. 73: 522–532

Tajfel, H. 1982. "Social Psychology of Intergroup Relations." *Annual Review of Psychology*. 33: 1–39

Tajfel, H. and J. Turner 1986. "An Integrative Theory of Intergroup Conflict". In W. Austin and S. Worchel (eds.), *The Social Psychology of Intergroup Relations*. Chicago, IL: Nelson-Hall Publishers. pp. 7–24

Tenbrunsel, A. E. and D. M. Messick 2004. "Ethical Fading: The Role of Self-Deception in Unethical Behavior." *Social Justice Research*. 17 (2)

Turner, J. 1985. "Social Categorization and the Self-Concept: A Social Cognitive Theory of Group Behavior." *Advances in Group Processes*. 2: 77–121

Turner, J., M. Hogg, P. Oakes, S. Reicher, and M. Wetherell 1987. *Redescovering the Social Group: A Self-Categorization Theory*. Oxford: Basil Blackwell

Tversky, A. and D. Kahneman 1981. "The Framing of Decisions and the Psychology of Choice." *Science*. 211 (4481): 453–458

   1983. "Extensional versus Intuitive Reasoning: The Conjunction Fallacy in Probability Judgement." *Psychological Review*. 90: 293–315

   1986. "Rational Choice and the Framing of Decisions." *Journal of Business*. 59 (4): s251–s278

Wheeler, S. and R. Petty 2001. "The Effects of Stereotype Activation on Behavior: A Review of Possible Mechanisms." *Psychological Bulletin*. 127(6): 797–826

Yezer, A., R. Goldfarb, and P. Poppen 1996. "Does Studying Economics Discourage Cooperation? Watch What We Do, Not What We Say or How We Play." *Journal of Economic Perspectives*. 10: 177–86

Yzerbyt, V., A. Rogier, and S. Fiske 1998. "Group Entatitivity and Social Attribution: on Translating Situational Constraints into Stereotypes." *Personal Socio-Psychological Bulletin*. 24: 1089–103

Zukier, H. and A. Pepitone 1984. "Social Roles and Strategies in Prediction: Some Determinants of the Use of Base Rate Information." *Journal of Personality and Social Psychology*. 47: 349–360

Appendix

Task instructions

[Game Description]

If you play A and your co-player plays A, you earn 3 points and your co-player earns 3 points;

If you play A and your co-player plays B, you earn 0 points and your co-player earns 5 points;

If you play B and your co-player plays A, you earn 5 points and your co-player earns 0 points;

If you play B and your co-player plays B, you earn 1 point and your co-player earns 1 point;

[Standard]

You and another person play a game. In this game you can choose either A or B. Similarly, your co-player can choose A or B. Your final score will depend both on your and your co-player's choices, as follows: *[Game Description]*.

★ What do you choose?

★ What do you expect the majority of people to choose?

[Versus Economics Student]

Now imagine you play the game with a person, of whom you know that she or he is a student of Economics.

★ What do you choose?

★ What do you expect she or he to choose?

[As an Economics Student]

Imagine you are a student of Economics. You are about to take a test. The test score system works according to the following rules: *[Game Description]*.

★ What do you choose?

★ What do you expect the majority of people to choose?

[Consistency Test]

★ In the game you just played, which would be the combination of responses, both yours and your co-player's, which ensures the highest collective outcome?

You choose _____ and your co-player chooses _____

★ Which would be the combination of responses, yours and your co-player's, which ensures the highest individual outcome to you?

You choose _____ and your co-player chooses _____

Detailed results

Table 12.1 *Results*

	Decision		Expectation	
	cooperate	defect	cooperate	defect
OT	47.37%	52.63%	57.89%	42.11%
vs-Econ	15.79%	84.21%	5.26%	94.74%
as Econ	19.05%	80.95%	19.05%	80.95%
Econ	35.71%	64.29%	28.57%	71.43%

Table 12.2 *Independence*

	Decision			
	OT	vs-Econ	as Econ	Econ
	Parametric test (t-test)★			
OT	–	yes	yes	no
vs-Econ	yes	–	–	no
as Econ	no	–	–	no
Econ	no	no	no	–
	Non-parametric test (Mann-Whitney)★			

★ At the 90% confidence level

	Expectation			
	OT	vs-Econ	as Econ	Econ
	Parametric test (t-test)★			
OT	–	yes	yes	yes
vs-Econ	yes	–	–	yes
as Econ	yes	–	–	no
Econ	yes	yes	no	–
	Non-parametric test (Mann-Whitney)★			

★ At the 90% confidence level

13 The financial crisis and the systemic failure of academic economics

David Colander, Hans Follmer, Armin Haas, Michael Goldberg, Katarina Juselius, Alan Kirman, Thomas Lux, and Brigitte Sloth

This opinion paper is the outcome of one week of intense discussions within the working group on "Modeling of Financial Markets" at the 98th Dahlem Workshop, 2008. David Colander served as moderator of this group and Thomas Lux served as Rapporteur. We are grateful to Carlo Jaeger and Rupert Klein for organizing this stimulating meeting and to Deirdre McCloskey and Peter Sørensen and other participants for helpful comments. The present version is the reprint of Kiel Working Paper, 1489, Institute for the World Economy, Kiel, 2009, that also appeared in electronic format in many other places. A revised version of this manuscript appeared in print as Colander, D., Haas, A., Goldberg, M., Juselius, K., Kirman, A., Lux, T., Sloth, B. (2009). "The Financial Crisis and the Systemic Failure of the Economics Profession." *Critical Review*, 21 (2–3), 249–267.

Introduction

The global financial crisis has revealed the need to rethink fundamentally how financial systems are regulated. It has also made clear a *systemic failure of the economics profession.* Over the past three decades, economists have largely developed and come to rely on models that disregard key factors – including heterogeneity of decision rules, revisions of forecasting strategies, and changes in the social context – that drive outcomes in asset and other markets. It is obvious, even to the casual observer that these models fail to account for the actual evolution of the real-world economy. Moreover, the current academic agenda has largely crowded out research on the inherent causes of financial crises. There has also been little exploration of early indicators of system crisis and potential ways to prevent this malady from developing. In fact, if one browses through the academic macroeconomics and finance literature, "systemic crisis" appears like an otherworldly event that is absent from economic models. Most models, by design, offer no immediate handle on how to think about or deal with this recurring phenomenon.[1] In our hour of greatest need, societies around the world are left to grope in the dark without a theory. That, to us, is a systemic failure of the economics profession.

The implicit view behind standard equilibrium models is that markets and economies are inherently stable and that they only temporarily get off track. The majority of economists thus failed to warn policy makers about the threatening system crisis and ignored the work of those who did. Ironically, as the crisis has unfolded, economists have had no choice but to abandon their standard models and to produce hand-waving common-sense remedies. Common-sense advice, although useful, is a poor substitute for an underlying model that can provide much-needed guidance for developing policy and regulation. It is not enough to put the existing model to one side, observing that one needs, "exceptional measures for exceptional times." What we need are models capable of envisaging such "exceptional times."

The confinement of macroeconomics to models of stable states that are perturbed by limited external shocks and that neglect the intrinsic recurrent boom-and-bust dynamics of our economic system is remarkable. After all, worldwide financial and economic crises are hardly new and they have had a tremendous impact beyond the immediate economic consequences of mass unemployment and hyperinflation. This is even more surprising, given the long academic legacy of earlier economists' study of crisis phenomena, which can be found in the work of Walter Bagehot (1873), Axel Leijonhuvfud (2000), Charles Kindleberger (1989), and Hyman Minsky (1986), to name a few prominent examples. This tradition, however, has been neglected and even suppressed.

The most recent literature provides us with examples of blindness against the upcoming storm that seem odd in retrospect. For example, in their analysis of the risk management implications of CDOs, Krahnen (2005) and Krahnen and Wilde (2006) mention the possibility of an increase of "systemic risk." But, they conclude that this aspect should not be the concern of the banks engaged in the CDO market, because it is the governments' responsibility to provide costless insurance against a system-wide crash. We do not share this view. On the more theoretical side, a recent and prominent strand of literature essentially argues that

---

[1] Reinhart and Rogoff (2008) argue that the current financial crisis differs little from a long chain of similar crises in developed and developing countries. We certainly share their view. The problem is that the received body of models in macro finance to which the above authors have prominently contributed provides no room whatsoever for such recurrent boom-and-bust cycles. The literature has, therefore, been a major source of the illusory "this time it is different" view that the authors themselves criticize.

consumers and investors are too risk averse because of their memory of the (improbable) event of the Great Depression (e.g. Cogley and Sargent 2008). Much of the motivation for economics as an academic discipline stems from the desire to explain phenomena like unemployment, boom-and-bust cycles, and financial crises, but dominant theoretical models exclude many of the aspects of the economy that will likely lead to a crisis. Confining theoretical models to "normal" times without consideration of such defects might seem contradictory to the focus that the average taxpayer would expect of the scientists on his payroll.

This failure has deep methodological roots. The often heard definition of economics – that it is concerned with the "allocation of scarce resources" – is short-sighted and misleading. It reduces economics to the study of optimal decisions in well-specified choice problems. Such research generally loses track of the inherent dynamics of economic systems and the instability that accompanies its complex dynamics. Without an adequate understanding of these processes, one is likely to miss the major factors that influence the economic sphere of our societies. This insufficient definition of economics often leads researchers to disregard questions about the coordination of actors and the possibility of coordination failures. Indeed, analysis of these issues would require a different type of mathematics than that which is generally used now by many prominent economic models.

Many of the financial economists who developed the theoretical models upon which the modern financial structure is built were well aware of the strong and highly unrealistic restrictions imposed on their models to assure stability. Yet, financial economists gave little warning to the public about the fragility of their models,[2] even as they saw individuals and businesses build a financial system based on their work. There are a number of possible explanations for this failure to warn the public. One is a "lack of understanding" explanation – the researchers did not know the models were fragile. We find this explanation highly unlikely; financial engineers are extremely bright, and it is almost inconceivable that such bright individuals did not understand the limitations of the models. A second, more likely explanation, is that they did not consider it their job to warn the public. If that is the cause of their failure, we believe that it involves a misunderstanding of the role of the economist, and involves an ethical breakdown. In our view, economists, as with all scientists, have an ethical responsibility to communicate the limitations of their models and the potential misuses of their research. Currently,

---

[2] Indeed, few researchers explored the consequences of a breakdown of their assumptions, even though this was rather likely.

there is no ethical code for professional economic scientists. There should be one.

In the following pages we identify some major areas of concern in theory and applied methodology and point out their connection to crisis phenomena. We also highlight some promising avenues of study that may provide guidance for future researchers.

Models (or the use of models) as a source of risk

The economic textbook models applied for allocation of scarce resources are predominantly of the Robinson Crusoe (representative agent) type. Financial market models are obtained by letting Robinson manage his financial affairs as a sideline to his well-considered utility maximization over his (finite or infinite) expected lifespan taking into account with correct probabilities all potential future happenings. This approach is mingled with insights from Walrasian general equilibrium theory, in particular the finding of the Arrow–Debreu two-period model that all uncertainty can be eliminated if only there are enough contingent claims (i.e., appropriate derivative instruments). This theoretical result (a theorem in an extremely stylized model) underlies the common belief that the introduction of new classes of derivatives can only be welfare increasing (a view obviously originally shared by former Fed Chairman Greenspan). It is worth emphasizing that this view is not an empirically grounded belief but an opinion derived from a benchmark model that is much too abstract to be confronted with data.

On the practical side, mathematical portfolio and risk management models have been the academic backbone of the tremendous increase of trading volume and diversification of instruments in financial markets. Typically, new derivative products achieve market penetration only if a certain industry standard has been established for pricing and risk management of these products. Mostly, pricing principles are derived from a set of assumptions on an "appropriate" process for the underlying asset, (i.e., the primary assets on which options or forwards are written) together with an equilibrium criterion such as arbitrage-free prices. With that mostly comes advice for hedging the inherent risk of a derivative position by balancing it with other assets that neutralize the risk exposure. The most prominent example is certainly the development of a theory of option pricing by Black and Scholes that eventually (in the eighties) could even be implemented on pocket calculators. Simultaneously with Black–Scholes option pricing, the same principles led to the widespread introduction of new strategies under the heading of portfolio insurance and dynamic hedging that just tried to implement a theoretically risk-free portfolio composed of both assets and options and keep it risk-free by frequent rebalancing after changes of its input data (e.g. asset prices). For structured products for credit risk, the basic paradigm of derivative pricing – perfect replication – is not applicable so that one has to rely on a kind of rough-and-ready evaluation of these contracts on the base of historical data. Unfortunately, historical data were hardly available in most cases which meant that one had to rely on simulations with relatively arbitrary assumptions on correlations between risks and default probabilities. This makes the theoretical foundations of all these products highly questionable – the equivalent to building a building of cement of which you weren't sure of the components. The dramatic recent rise of the markets for structured products (most prominently collateralized debt obligations and credit default swaps – CDOs and CDSs) was made possible by development of such simulation-based pricing tools and the adoption of an industry-standard for these under the lead of rating agencies. Barry Eichengreen (2008) rightly points out that the "development of mathematical methods designed to quantify and hedge risk encouraged commercial banks, investment banks and hedge funds to use more leverage" as if the very use of the mathematical methods diminished the underlying risk. He also notes that the models were estimated on data from periods of low volatility and thus could not deal with the arrival of major changes. Worse, it is our contention that such major changes are endemic to the economy and cannot be simply ignored.

What are the flaws of the new unregulated financial markets which have emerged? As we have already pointed out in the introduction, the possibility of systemic risk has not been entirely ignored but it has been defined as lying outside the responsibility of market participants. In this way, moral hazard concerning systemic risk has been a necessary and built-in attribute of the system. The neglect of the systemic part in the "normal mode of operation," of course, implies that external effects are not taken properly into account and that in tendency, market participants will ignore the influence of their own behavior on the stability of the system. The interesting aspect is more that this was a known and accepted element of operations. Note that the blame should not only fall on market participants, but also on the deliberate ignoring of the systemic risk factors or the failure to at least point them out to the public amounts to a sort of academic *"moral hazard."*

There are some additional aspects as well: asset-pricing and risk management tools are developed from an individualistic perspective, taking as given (*ceteris paribus*) the behavior of all other market participants. However, popular models might be used by a large number or even the majority of market participants. Similarly, a market participant (e.g. the notorious Long-Term Capital Management) might become so dominant in certain markets that the *ceteris paribus* assumption becomes unrealistic. The simultaneous pursuit of identical micro strategies leads to synchronous behavior and mechanic contagion. This simultaneous application might generate an unexpected macro outcome that actually jeopardizes the success of the underlying micro strategies. A perfect illustration is the US stock market crash of October 1987. Triggered by a small decrease of prices, automated hedging strategies produced an avalanche of sell orders that out of the blue led to a fall in US stock indices of about 20 percent within one day. With the massive sales to rebalance their portfolios (along the lines of Black and Scholes), the relevant actors could not realize their attempted incremental adjustments, but rather suffered major losses from the ensuing large macro effect.

A somewhat different aspect is the danger of a control illusion: The mathematical rigor and numerical precision of risk management and asset pricing tools has a tendency to conceal the weaknesses of models and assumptions to those who have not developed them and do not know the potential weakness of the assumptions and it is indeed this that Eichengreen emphasizes. Naturally, models are only approximations to the real-world dynamics and partially built upon quite heroic assumptions (most notoriously: Normality of asset price changes which can be rejected at a confidence level of 99. 9999... Anyone who has attended a course in first-year statistics can do this within minutes). Of course, considerable progress has been made by moving to more refined models with, e.g. "fat-tailed" Lévy processes as their driving factors. However, while such models better capture the intrinsic volatility of markets, their improved performance, taken at face value, might again contribute to enhancing the control illusion of the naïve user.

The increased sophistication of extant models does, however, not overcome the robustness problem and should not absolve the modelers from explaining their limitations to the users in the financial industry. As in nuclear physics, the tools provided by financial engineering can be put to very different uses so that what is designed as an instrument to hedge risk can become a weapon of "financial mass destruction" (in the words of Warren Buffet) if used for increased leverage. In fact, it appears that derivative positions have been built up often in speculative ways to profit from high returns as long as the downside risk does not materialize. Researchers who develop such models can claim they are neutral academics – developing tools that people are free to use or not. We do not find that view credible. Researchers have an ethical responsibility to point out to the public when the tool that they developed is misused. It is the responsibility of the researcher to make clear from the outset the limitations and underlying assumptions of his models and warn of the dangers of their mechanic application.

What follows from our diagnosis? Market participants and regulators have to become more sensitive toward the potential weaknesses of risk management models. Since we do not know the "true" model, robustness should be a key concern. Model uncertainty should be taken into account by applying more than a single model. For example, one could rely on probabilistic projections that cover a whole range of specific models (cf. Föllmer 2008). The theory of robust control provides a toolbox of techniques that could be applied for this purpose, and it is an approach that should be considered.

Unrealistic model assumptions and unrealistic outcomes

Many economic models are built upon the twin assumptions of "rational expectations" and a representative agent. "Rational expectations" instructs an economist to specify individuals' expectations to be fully consistent with the structure of his own model. This concept can be thought of as merely a way to close a model. A behavioral interpretation of rational expectations would imply that individuals and the economist have a complete understanding of the economic mechanisms governing the world. In this sense, rational expectations models do not attempt to formalize individuals' actual expectations: specifications are not based on empirical observation of the expectations formation process of human actors. Thus, even when applied economics research or psychology provide insights about how individuals actually form expectations, they cannot be used within rational expectations models. Leaving no place for imperfect knowledge and adaptive adjustments, rational expectations models are typically found to have dynamics that are not smooth enough to fit economic data well.[3]

Technically, rational expectations models are often framed as dynamic programming problems in macroeconomics. But, dynamic programming models have serious limitations. Specifically, to make them analytically tractable, not more than one dynamically maximizing agent can be considered, and consistent expectations have to be imposed. Therefore, dynamic programming models are hardly imaginable without the assumptions of a representative agent and rational expectations. This has generated a vicious cycle by which the technical tools developed on

---

[3] For a critique of rational expectations models on epistemological grounds, see Frydman and Goldberg (2007, 2008) and references therein.

the base of the chosen assumptions prevent economists from moving beyond these restricted settings and exploring more realistic scenarios. Note that such settings also presume that there is a single model of the economy, which is odd given that even economists are divided in their views about the correct model of the economy. While other currents of research do exist, economic policy advice, particularly in financial economics, has far too often been based (consciously or not) on a set of axioms and hypotheses derived ultimately from a highly limited dynamic control model, using the Robinson approach with "rational" expectations.

The major problem is that despite its many refinements, this is not at all an approach based on, and confirmed by, empirical research.[4] In fact, it stands in stark contrast to a broad set of regularities in human behavior discovered both in psychology and what is called behavioral and experimental economics. The cornerstones of many models in finance and macroeconomics are rather maintained *despite* all the contradictory evidence discovered in empirical research. Much of this literature shows that human subjects act in a way that bears no resemblance to the rational expectations paradigm and also have problems discovering "rational expectations equilibria" in repeated experimental settings. Rather, agents display various forms of "bounded rationality" using heuristic decision rules and displaying inertia in their reaction to new information. They have also been shown in financial markets to be strongly influenced by emotional and hormonal reactions (see Lo et al. 2005, and Coates and Herbert 2008). Economic modeling has to take such findings seriously.

What we are arguing is that as a modeling requirement, internal consistency must be complemented with external consistency: Economic modeling has to be compatible with insights from other branches of science on human behavior. It is highly problematic to insist on a specific view of humans in economic settings that is irreconcilable with evidence.

The "representative agent" aspect of many current models in macroeconomics (including macro finance) means that modelers subscribe to the most extreme form of conceptual reductionism (Lux and

---

[4] The historical emergence of the representative agent paradigm is a mystery. Ironically, it appeared over the 1970s after a period of intense discussions on the problem of aggregation in economics (that basically yielded negative results such as the impossibility to demonstrate "nice" properties of aggregate demand or supply functions without imposing extreme assumptions on individual behavior). The representative agent appeared without methodological discussion. In the words of Deirdre McCloskey: "It became a rule in the conversation of some economists because Tom and Bob said so" (personal communication). Today, this convention has become so strong that many young economists wouldn't know of an alternative way to approach macroeconomic issues.

Westerhoff 2009): by assumption, all concepts applicable to the macro sphere (i.e., the economy or its financial system) are fully reduced to concepts and knowledge for the lower-level domain of the individual agent. It is worth emphasizing that this is quite different from the standard reductionist concept that has become widely accepted in natural sciences. The more standard notion of reductionism amounts to an approach to understanding the nature of complex phenomena by reducing them to the interactions of their parts, allowing for new, emergent phenomena at the higher hierarchical level (the concept of "more is different," cf. Anderson 1972).

Quite to the contrary, the representative agent approach in economics has simply set the macro sphere equal to the micro sphere in all respects. One could, indeed, say that this concept negates the existence of a macro sphere and the necessity of investigating macroeconomic phenomena in that it views the entire economy as an organism governed by a universal will.[5] Any notion of "systemic risk" or "coordination failure" is necessarily absent from, and alien to, such a methodology.

For natural scientists, the distinction between micro-level phenomena and those originating on a macro, system-wide scale from the interaction of microscopic units is well-known. In a dispersed system, the current crisis would be seen as an involuntary emergent phenomenon of the microeconomic activity. The conceptual reductionist paradigm, however, blocks from the outset any understanding of the interplay between the micro and macro levels. The differences between the overall system and its parts remain simply incomprehensible from the viewpoint of this approach.

In order to develop models that allow us to deduce macro events from microeconomic regularities, economists have to rethink the concept of micro foundations of macroeconomic models. Since economic activity is of an essentially interactive nature, economists' micro foundations should allow for the interactions of economic agents. Since interaction depends on differences in information, motives, knowledge, and capabilities, this implies heterogeneity of agents. For instance, only a sufficiently rich structure of connections between firms, households, and a dispersed banking sector will allow us to get a grasp on "systemic risk," domino effects in the financial sector, and their repercussions on consumption and investment. The dominance of the extreme form of conceptual reductionism of the representative agent has prevented economists from

---

[5] The conceptual reductionist approach of the representative agent is also remarkably different from the narrative of the "invisible hand" which has more the flavor of "more is different."

even attempting to model such all important phenomena. It is the flawed methodology that is the ultimate reason for the lack of applicability of the standard macro framework to current events.

Since most of what is relevant and interesting in economic life has to do with the interaction and coordination of ensembles of heterogeneous economic actors, the methodological preference for single actor models has extremely handicapped macroeconomic analysis and prevented it from approaching vital topics. For example, the recent surge of research in network theory has received relatively scarce attention in economics. Given the established curriculum of economic programs, an economist would find it much more tractable to study adultery as a dynamic optimization problem of a representative husband, and derive the optimal time path of marital infidelity (and publish his exercise) rather than investigating financial flows in the banking sector within a network theory framework. This is more than unfortunate in view of the network aspects of interbank linkages that have become apparent during the current crisis.

In our view, a change of focus is necessary that takes seriously the regularities in expectation formation revealed by behavioral research and, in fact, gives back an independent role to expectations in economic models. It would also be fallacious to only replace the current paradigm by a representative "non-rational" actor (as it is sometimes done in recent literature). Rather, an appropriate micro foundation is needed that considers interaction at a certain level of complexity and extracts macro regularities (where they exist) from microeconomic models with dispersed activity.

Once one acknowledges the importance of empirically based behavioral micro foundations and the heterogeneity of actors, a rich spectrum of new models becomes available. The dynamic co-evolution of expectations and economic activity would allow one to study out-of-equilibrium dynamics and adaptive adjustments. Such dynamics could reveal the possibility of multiplicity and evolution of equilibria (e.g. with high or low employment) depending on agents' expectations or even on the propagation of positive or negative "moods" among the population. This would capture the psychological component of the business cycle which – though prominent in many policy-oriented discussions – is never taken into consideration in contemporary macroeconomic models.

It is worth noting that understanding the formation of such low-level equilibria might be much more valuable in coping with major "efficiency losses" by mass unemployment than the pursuit of small "inefficiencies" due to societal decisions on norms such as shop opening times. Models with interacting heterogeneous agents would also open the door to the incorporation of results from other fields: network theory has been mentioned as an obvious example (for models of networks in finance see Allen and Babus 2008). "Self-organized criticality" theory is another area that seems to have some appeal for explaining boom-and-bust cycles (cf. Scheinkman and Woodford 1994). Incorporating heterogeneous agents with imperfect knowledge would also provide a better framework for the analysis of the use and dissemination of information through market operations and more direct links of communication. If one accepts that the dispersed economic activity of many economic agents could be described by statistical laws, one might even take stock of methods from statistical physics to model dynamic economic systems (cf. Aoki and Yoshikawa 2007; Lux 2009, for examples).

Robustness and data-driven empirical research

Currently popular models (in particular dynamic general equilibrium models) do not only have weak micro foundations, their empirical performance is far from satisfactory (Juselius and Franchi 2007). Indeed, the relevant strand of empirical economics has more and more avoided testing their models and has instead turned to calibration without explicit consideration of goodness-of-fit.[6] This calibration is done using "deep economic parameters" such as parameters of utility functions derived from microeconomic studies. However, at the risk of being repetitive, it should be emphasized that micro parameters cannot be used directly in the parameterization of a macroeconomic model. The aggregation literature is full of examples that point out the possible "fallacies of composition." The "deep parameters" only seem sensible if one considers the economy as a universal organism without interactions. If interactions are important (as it seems to us they are), the restriction of the parameter space imposed by using micro parameters is inappropriate.

Another concern is non stationarity and structural shifts in the underlying data. Macro models, unlike many financial models, are often calibrated over long time horizons which include major changes in the regulatory framework of the countries investigated. Cases in question are the movements between different exchange rate regimes and the deregulation of financial markets over the 1970s and 1980s. In summary, it seems to us that much of contemporary empirical work in

---

[6] It is pretty obvious how the currently popular class of dynamic general equilibrium models would have to "cope" with the current financial crisis. It will be covered either by a dummy or it will have to be interpreted as a very large negative stochastic shock to the economy, i.e. as an event equivalent to a large asteroid strike.

macroeconomics and finance is driven by the pre-analytic belief in the validity of a certain model. Rather than (mis)using statistics as a means to illustrate these beliefs, the goal should be to put theoretical models to scientific test (as the naïve believer in positive science would expect).

The current approach of using pre-selected models is problematic and we recommend a more data-driven methodology. Instead of starting out with an ad-hoc specification and questionable *ceteris paribus* assumptions, the key features of the data should be explored via data-analytical tools and specification tests. David Hendry provides a well-established empirical methodology for such exploratory data analysis (Hendry 1995, 2009) as well as a general theory for model selection (Hendry and Krolzig 2005); clustering techniques such as projection pursuit (e.g. Friedman 1987) might provide alternatives for the identification of key relationships and the reduction of complexity on the way from empirical measurement to theoretical models. Cointegrated VAR models could provide an avenue towards identification of robust structures within a set of data (Juselius 2006), for example, the forces that move equilibria (pushing forces, which give rise to stochastic trends) and forces that correct deviations from equilibrium (pulling forces, which give rise to long-run relations). Interpreted in this way, the "general-to-specific" empirical approach has a good chance of nesting a multivariate, path-dependent data-generating process and relevant dynamic macroeconomic theories. Unlike approaches in which data are silenced by prior restrictions, the Cointegrated VAR model gives the data a rich context in which to speak freely (Hoover et al. 2008).

A chain of specification tests and estimated statistical models for simultaneous systems would provide a benchmark for the subsequent development of tests of models based on economic behavior: significant and robust relations within a simultaneous system would provide empirical regularities that one would attempt to explain, while the quality of fit of the statistical benchmark would offer a confidence band for more ambitious models. Models that do not reproduce (even) approximately the quality of the fit of statistical models would have to be rejected (the majority of currently popular macroeconomic and macro finance models would not pass this test). Again, we see here an aspect of ethical responsibility of researchers: Economic policy models should be theoretically and empirically sound. Economists should avoid giving policy recommendations on the base of models with a weak empirical grounding and should, to the extent possible, make clear to the public how strong the support of the data is for their models and the conclusions drawn from them.

A research agenda to cope with financial fragility

The notion of financial fragility implies that a given system might be more or less susceptible to produce crises. It seems clear that financial innovations have made the system more fragile. Apparently, the existing linkages within the worldwide, highly connected financial markets have generated the spillovers from the US subprime problem to other layers of the financial system. Many financial innovations had the effect of creating links between formerly unconnected players. All in all, the degree of connectivity of the system has probably increased enormously over the last decades. As is well known from network theory in natural sciences, a more highly connected system might be more efficient in coping with certain tasks (maybe distributing risk components), but will often also be more vulnerable to shocks – and systemic failure! The systematic analysis of network vulnerability has been undertaken in the computer science and operations research literature (see e.g. Criado et al. 2005). Such aspects have, however, been largely absent from discussions in financial economics. The introduction of new derivatives was rather seen through the lens of general equilibrium models: more contingent claims help to achieve higher efficiency. Unfortunately, the claimed efficiency gains through derivatives are merely a theoretical implication of a highly stylized model and, therefore, have to count as a hypothesis. Since there is hardly any supporting empirical evidence (or even analysis of this question), the claimed real-world efficiency gains from derivatives are not justified by true science. While the economic argument in favor of ever new derivatives is more one of persuasion rather than evidence, important negative effects have been neglected. The idea that the system was made less risky with the development of more derivatives led to financial actors taking positions with extreme degrees of leverage and the danger of this has not been emphasized enough.

As we have mentioned, one neglected area is the degree of connectivity and its interplay with the stability of the system (see Boesch et al. 2006). We believe that it will be necessary for supervisory authorities to develop a perspective on the network aspects of the financial system, collect appropriate data, define measures of connectivity, and perform macro stress testing at the system level. In this way, new measures of financial fragility would be obtained. This would also require a new area of accompanying academic research that looks at agent-based models of the financial system, performs scenario analyses, and develops aggregate risk measures. Network theory and the theory of self-organized criticality of highly connected systems would be appropriate starting points.

The danger of systemic risk means that regulation has to be extended from individualistic (regulation of single institutions which, of course, is still crucial) to system-wide regulation. In the sort of system which is prone to systemic crisis, regulation also has to have a systemic perspective. Academic researchers and supervisory authorities thus have to look into connections within the financial sector and to investigate the repercussions of problems within one institute on other parts of the system (even across national borders). Certainly, before deciding about the bail-out of a large bank, this implies an understanding of the network. One should know whether its bankruptcy would lead to widespread domino effects or whether contagion would be limited. It seems to us that what regulators provide currently is far from a reliable assessment of such after effects.

Such analysis has to be supported by more traditional approaches: Leverage of financial institutions rose to unprecedented levels prior to the crisis, partly by evading Basle II regulations through special investment vehicles (SIVs). The hedge fund market is still entirely unregulated. The interplay between leverage, connectivity, and system risk needs to be investigated at the aggregate level. It is highly likely, that extreme leverage levels of interconnected institutions will be found to impose unacceptable social risk on the public. Prudent capital requirements would be necessary and would require a solid scientific investigation of the above aspects rather than a pre-analytic laissez-faire attitude.

We also have to re-investigate the informational role of financial prices and financial contracts. While trading in stock markets is usually interpreted as at least in part transmitting information, this information transmission seems to have broken down in the case of structured financial products. It seems that securitization has rather led to a loss of information by anonymous intermediation (often multiple) between borrowers and lenders. In this way, the informational component has been outsourced to rating agencies and typically, the buyer of CDO tranches would not have spent any effort himself on information acquisition concerning his far away counterparts. However, this centralized information processing instead of the dispersed one in traditional credit relationships might lead to a severe loss of information. As it turned out, standard loan default models failed dramatically in recent years (Rajan et al. 2008). It should also be noted that the price system itself can exacerbate the difficulties in the financial market (see Hellwig 2008). One of the reasons for the sharp fall in the asset valuations of major banks was not only the loss on the assets on which their derivatives were based, but also the general reaction of the markets to these assets. As markets became aware of the risk involved, all such assets were written down and it was in this way that a small sector of the market "contaminated" the rest. Large parts of the asset holdings of major banks abruptly lost much of their value. Thus the price system itself can be destabilizing as expectations change.

On the macroeconomic level, it would be desirable to develop early warning schemes that indicate the formation of bubbles. Combinations of indicators with time series techniques could be helpful in detecting deviations of financial or other prices from their long-run averages. Indication of structural change (particularly toward non-stationary trajectories) would be a signature of changes of the behavior of market participants of a bubble-type nature.

Conclusions

The current crisis might be characterized as an example of the final stage of a well-known boom-and-bust pattern that has been repeated so many times in the course of economic history. There are, nevertheless, some aspects that make this crisis different from its predecessors: First, the preceding boom had its origin – at least to a large part – in the development of new financial products that opened up new investment possibilities (while most previous crises were the consequence of overinvestment in new physical investment possibilities). Second, the global dimension of the current crisis is due to the increased connectivity of our already highly interconnected financial system. Both aspects have been largely ignored by academic economics. Research on the origin of instabilities, overinvestment, and subsequent slumps has been considered as an exotic side track from the academic research agenda (and the curriculum of most economics programs). This, of course, was because it was incompatible with the premise of the rational representative agent. This paradigm also made economics blind with respect to the role of interactions and connections between actors (such as the changes in the network structure of the financial industry brought about by deregulation and introduction of new structured products). Indeed, much of the work on contagion and herding behavior (see Banerjee 1992, and Chamley 2002) which is closely connected to the network structure of the economy has not been incorporated into macroeconomic analysis.

We believe that economics has been trapped in a suboptimal equilibrium in which much of its research efforts are not directed toward the most prevalent needs of society. Paradoxically self-reinforcing feedback effects within the profession may have led to the dominance of a paradigm that has no solid methodological basis and whose empirical performance is, to say the least, modest. Defining away the most prevalent economic problems of modern economies and failing to communicate the limitations and assumptions of its popular models, the economics profession bears some responsibility for the current crisis. It has failed in its duty to society to provide as much insight as possible into the workings of the economy and in providing warnings about the tools it created. It has also been reluctant to emphasize the limitations of its analysis. We believe that the failure to even envisage the current problems of the worldwide financial system and the inability of standard macro and finance models to provide any insight into ongoing events make a strong case for a major reorientation in these areas and a reconsideration of their basic premises.

References

Allen, F. and A. Babus 2008. "Networks in finance." Wharton Financial Institutions Center Working Paper No. 08-07. Available at SSRN: http://ssrn.com/abstract=1094883

Anderson, P. W. 1972. "More is different." *Science*, 177, 393–396.

Aoki, M. and H. Yoshikawa 2007. *Reconstructing Macroeconomics: A Perspective from Statistical Physics and Combinatorial Stochastic Processes.* Cambridge University Press.

Bagehot, W. 1873. *Lombard Street: A Description of the Money Market.* Henry S. King and Co.: London.

Banerjee, A. 1992. "A simple model of herd behavior." *Quarterly Journal of Economics*, 108, 797–817.

Boesch, F. T., F. Harary, and J. A. Kabell 2006. "Graphs as models of communication network vulnerability: Connectivity and persistence." *Networks*, 11, 57–63.

Brigandt, I. and A. Love. "Reductionism in Biology" in the *Stanford Encyclopedia of Philosophy.* Available at http://plato.stanford.edu/entries/reduction-biology/

Campos, J., N. R. Ericsson, and D. F. Hendry 2005. "Editors' Introduction" in *General to Specific Modelling*, 1–81. Edward Elgar: London.

Chamley, C. P. 2002. *Rational Herds: Economic Models of Social Learning.* Cambridge University Press.

Coates, J. M. and J. Herbert 2008. "Endogenous steroids and financial risk taking on a London trading floor." *Proceedings of the National Academy of Sciences*, 6167–6172.

Cogley, T. and T. Sargent 2008. "The market price of risk and the equity premium: A legacy of the Great Depression?" *Journal of Monetary Economics*, 55, 454–476.

Criado, R., J. Flores, B. Hernández-Bermejo, J. Pello, and M. Romance 2005. "Effective measurement of network vulnerability under random and intentional attacks." *Journal of Mathematical Modelling and Algorithms*, 4, 307–316.

Eichengreen, B. 2008. "Origins and Responses to the Crisis." Unpublished manuscript, University of California, Berkeley.

Föllmer, H. 2008. "Financial uncertainty, risk measures and robust preferences." In Yor, M, ed., *Aspects of Mathematical Finance*, Springer: Berlin.

360   *David Colander, Hans Follmer, Armin Haas et al.*

Friedman, J. 1987. "Exploratory projection pursuit." *Journal of the American Statistical Association*, 82, 249–266

Frydman, R. and M. D. Goldberg 2007. *Imperfect Knowledge Economics: Exchange Rates and Risk*. Princeton University Press.
   2008. "Macroeconomic theory for a world of imperfect knowledge." *Capitalism and Society*, 3, Article 1.

Hellwig, M. F. 2008. "Systemic risk in the financial sector: An analysis of the subprime-mortgage financial crisis." *MPI Collective Goods Preprint*, No. 2008/43.

Hendry, D. 2009. "The methodology of empirical econometric modeling: Applied econometrics through the looking-glass." Forthcoming in *The Handbook of Empirical Econometrics*, Palgrave.

Hendry, D. F. 1995. *Dynamic Econometrics*. Oxford University Press.

Hendry, D. F. and H. M. Krolzig 2005. "The properties of automatic gets modeling." *Economic Journal*, 115, C32–C61.

Hoover, K., S. Johansen, and K. Juselius 2008. "Allowing the data to speak freely: The macroeconometrics of the cointegrated vector autoregression." *American Economic Review*, 98, 251–55.

Juselius, K. 2006. *The Cointegrated VAR Model: Econometric Methodology and Empirical Applications*. Oxford University Press.

Juselius, K. and M. Franchi 2007. "Taking a DSGE model to the data meaningfully." *Economics–The Open-Access, Open-Assessment E-Journal*, 4.

Kindleberger, C. P. 1989. *Manias, Panics, and Crashes: A History of Financial Crises*. MacMillan: London.

Krahnen, J.-P. 2005. "Der Handel von Kreditrisiken: Eine neue Dimension des Kapitalmarktes." *Perspektiven der Wirtschaftspolitik*, 6, 499–519.

Krahnen, J.-P. and C. Wilde 2006. *Risk Transfer with CDOs and Systemic Risk in Banking*. Center for Financial Studies, WP 2006–04. Frankfurt.

Leijonhufvud, A. 2000. *Macroeconomic Instability and Coordination: Selected Essays*. Edward Elgar: Cheltenham.

Lo, A., D. V. Repin and B. N. Steenbarger 2005. "Fear and greed in financial markets: A clinical study of day-traders." *American Economic Review*, 95, 352–359.

Lux, T. 2009. "Stochastic Behavioral Asset Pricing Models and the Stylized Facts." In Chapter 3 in T. Hens and K. Schenk-Hoppé, eds., *Handbook of Financial Markets: Dynamics and Evolution*. North-Holland: Amsterdam, 161–215.

Lux, T. and F. Westerhoff 2009. "Economics crisis." *Nature Physics*, 5, 2–3.

Minsky, H. P. 1986. *Stabilizing an Unstable Economy*. Yale University Press: New Haven.

Rajan, U., A. Seru and V. Vig 2008. "The failure of models that predict failure: Distance, incentives and defaults." Chicago GSB Research Paper No. 08–19.

Reinhart, C. and K. Rogoff 2008. "This Time is Different: A Panoramic View of Eight Centuries of Financial Crises." Manuscript, Harvard University and NBER.

Scheinkman, J. and M. Woodford 1994. "Self-organized criticality and economic fluctuations." *American Economic Review*, 84 (Papers and Proceedings), 417–421.

Index